Southern Counterpart to Lewis & Clark

THE AMERICAN EXPLORATION AND TRAVEL SERIES

Southern Counterpart
to
Lewis & Clark

*The Freeman & Custis
Expedition of 1806*

Edited, with Introduction and Epilogue
By Dan L. Flores

University of Oklahoma Press
Norman

Grand Ecore Bluffs, Red River

This book has been published with the aid of a grant from the Andrew W. Mellon Foundation.

This book is dedicated
to the memory of
the free-flowing Red River
of earliest recorded history.

Library of Congress Cataloging-in-Publication Data

Main entry under title:
Southern Counterpart to Lewis & Clark
    (The American exploration and travel series; v. 67)
    Bibliography: p. 345
    Includes index.
    1. Red River (Tex.-La.)—Description and travel. 2. Southwest, Old—History.
3. Louisiana Purchase. 4. Freeman, Thomas, d. 1821. 5. Custis, Peter. I. Freeman,
Thomas, d. 1821. II. Custis, Peter. III. Flores, Dan L. (Dan Louie), 1948–   .
IV. Title: Southern Counterpart to Lewis & Clark. V. Series.
F377.R3J43   1984   976.6'6   83–47833
ISBN: 0-8061-1748-6 (hardcover)
ISBN: 0-8061-1941-1 (paperback).

The paper in this book meets the guidelines for permanence and durability of the Committee on Production Guidelines for Book Longevity of the Council on Library Resources, Inc.

3   4   5   6   7   8   9   10

Contents

Preface to the Red River Books Edition   *page*   ix
Preface to the 1984 Edition   xvii
Editor's Introduction: Probing the Southwestern Wilderness   3

The Documents and Editorial Procedures   91

The Accounts
    Part One   From Fort Adams to Natchitoches   99
    Part Two   The Great Raft and the Great Swamp   123
    Part Three   Layover at the Coashatta Village   159
    Part Four   The "Wilderness" Upriver: Coashatta
                Village to Spanish Camp and Return   173
    Part Five   The Natural History Catalogues   211

Editor's Epilogue   The Last Jeffersonian Exploration   281

Appendix One   Jefferson's Letter of Exploring
                Instructions   319

Appendix Two   A List of Notable Points on the Middle
                and Upper Red River, by Peter Custis   327

Appendix Three   Meteorological Observations Made on
                Red River, 1806   335

Bibliography   345

Index   365

Illustrations

Grand Ecore Bluffs, Red River	*pages* ii–iii
Thomas Jefferson	4
Wild Mustangs, by Catlin	16
The Red River Meteorite	18
William Dunbar	41
Hunter's "Chinese" Boat	43
Natchez, Early Nineteenth Century, by Audubon	69
Dunbar's Plantation, "The Forest"	71
Page from Freeman's Letter to McKee	73
Dr. John Sibley	76
James Wilkinson	79
Bald Cypress Tree	105
Typical Vegetation on the Lower Red	*pages* 116–17
A Southeastern Indian Dwelling, ca. 1800	*page* 121
The Great Raft, 1873	*pages* 128–29
Lake Bisteneau	138–39
Red Chute Bayou	*page* 144
Scenery Typical of the Great Swamp	147
Caddo Prairie	148
Nineteenth-century Creek Indian Lodge	151
Young Warrior of the Coushatta Creeks	155
Caddo Warrior	166
Catlin's "Caddo Chasing Buffalo"	171
The Middle Red	*pages* 178–79
Red River, Coushatta-Miller's Bluffs Country	182–83

Illustrations

Topographical Profile, Red River Valley	*page* 184
"Handsome Bluff" at the Mouth of the Sulphur	185
The Caddo Medicine Mount	187
Kadohadacho Village Site	189
Caddoan Grass and Pole Lodges	197
View from Spanish Bluff	*pages* 200–201
Taovaya Village, by Catlin	*page* 202
Upper Red River Country, 1834, by Catlin	205
Carolina Parakeets, by Audubon	209
Woodpeckers, by Wilson	224
Three-toed Amphiuma	226
Louisiana Fox Squirrel	229
Black Bear	232
White-tailed Deer	233
Mississippi Kite, by Audubon	235
Louisiana Milk Snake	237
Louisiana Yucca Plant	241
Bois d'Arc Tree	243
Prairie Gentian, Collected by Custis	246
Eastern Culver's Root, Collected by Custis	247
Page from Manuscript Report by Custis	258
Wild Turkey, by Peale	269
Black-tailed Jackrabbit	270
American Bison, by Catlin	273
Antelope	275

Photographs not otherwise credited were made by Dan L. Flores.

Maps

Von Humboldt's Map Showing the "Origin" of the
    Red River   *pages* 20–21
Nicholas King's official *Map of the Red River in Louisiana*   92–93
Pedro Vial's Map of the Southwest, 1787   *page* 122
Shreve's "Rough Sketch" of the Great Raft Country   137
Northern Caddo Parish, 1839   *pages* 152–53
Detail of the Country just above the Great Raft, from the
    King-Freeman Map   *page* 156
A Portion of Nau's *The First Part of Captn. Pike's Chart of
    the Internal Part of Louisiana*   *pages* 298–99

Preface to the Red River Books Edition
A Very Different Story:
Exploring the *Southwest* from Monticello

No one has ever accused Thomas Jefferson of being uncomplicated or easy to cipher. Whether history has grappled with his political legacy, his contradictory stance on social justice, or his vision for the American West that his Louisiana Purchase folded into the country's destiny, Jefferson has remained the Great American Enigma. Part of this has to do with the pragmatism that colored most of his decisions, but there was also a certain risk-taking impulse in his personality. The man who was willing to speak in favor of the occasional revolution was the same individual who could push the envelope of possibility in areas like exploring the West, too. Sometimes, as with a Lewis and Clark expedition whose popularity in the American imagination is presently in full soar, these gambles paid off. Sometimes they didn't. When that happened Jefferson was fully capable of turning his back.

For the better part of two decades now I have been trying to untangle what Jefferson intended with his actions vis-à-vis the other—and relative to Lewis and Clark, today virtually invisible— exploration he personally launched into the West. I do not here mean either of the Zebulon Pike probes, although most people familiar with Jefferson-era exploration would assume that. Like his earlier search for the source of the Mississippi, Pike's 1806–7 overland expedition to the Southern Rockies was an exploration launched by the American military—by General James Wilkinson, in fact—and not

Thomas Jefferson. Other than being pointed in the same general direction as Lewis and Clark, it shared little in common with their probe in intent or preparation.

Nor do I mean the brief William Dunbar–George Hunter expedition to the Ouachita Mountains of present Arkansas in 1804–5, although this one preceded even Lewis and Clark as the first to report back from the Louisiana Territory and in its time made the two leaders famous enough that no less than John James Audubon would later speak reverently of Dr. George Hunter as that "renowned *Man* of Jefferson." Although that expedition did originate with Jefferson, as executed the Dunbar-Hunter probe was merely a trial balloon for the "Grand Excursion"—the southwestern counterpart to Lewis and Clark—Jefferson had in mind all along.

Two centuries later, the historical fate of this latter expedition—directed in the field by a civilian engineer/surveyor named Thomas Freeman, assisted by a celebrated American "bush fighter," Captain Richard Sparks of Virginia, along with young Peter Custis of the medical and natural history programs at the University of Pennsylvania—looks extremely intriguing. And while some hard digging and a good bit of luck enabled me to produce a first edition of this book in 1984 that adorned this "forgotten expedition" in every manner of factual dress that history hadn't known before, I still find aspects of the story puzzling, even troubling. Not, however, its invisibility in the *popular* American imagination. Unless multicultural history in the twenty-first century shapes the writing of the American past far more than at present—and the fate of Jefferson's southwestern exploration comes to be celebrated by southwestern Hispanos as one of their great early successes in *resisting* American imperialism—there should be no doubts why Lewis and Clark history is worthy of a general national celebration while not a single roadside historical marker exists to remind the American public of Freeman and Custis.

The explanation for that is simple and has to do with the truism that the winners write the version of events later generations celebrate. In the context of American continental expansion, we see Lewis and Clark's traverse of the continent as a nationalistic success, while failure (at least from the U.S. perspective) is the legacy of Jefferson's southwestern exploration. Intended originally to chart the entire lengths of both the Red and Arkansas rivers, the southwestern expedition failed even to achieve its last-minute, more limited objective of exploring the Red River only. What brought it to a halt after four months and an ascent of only half the river's length had nothing to do with daunted courage on the part of its leaders, or a disinclination to "proceed on" in the face of nature's obstacles (and there were some big ones). Jefferson's second great western exploration was intercepted, and confronted, and turned around on the Red River by a Spanish army four times its size. And the major reason it happened that way was because in the face of Spanish resolve he may have underestimated (and—perhaps—was encouraged to underestimate), Thomas Jefferson took a risk that backfired.

That a failed exploration, blocked and forced to retrograde by a foreign power, should fade in the American memory is no surprise, of course. But since the intent of Jeffersonian exploration was always at least nominally scientific discovery (and the party was to carry out the same kind of wide-ranging examination Meriwether Lewis was instructed to conduct), it has always puzzled that an exploration that did, after all, have a look at almost seven hundred miles of landscape new to Americans somehow ended up *erased* from history at every level. What is the explanation for that, and what has that meant for the process of selective historical memory? Of course, since the past is a foreign country, much history strikes us as odd, ironic, or unexpected. But given the mounting fascination with Lewis and Clark— and with the state of nature in the West as it was two hundred years ago, and as it is now—it may be worthwhile to look less myopically at Jefferson's West with a closer understanding of his southwestern exploration, whose story in American history is now attached to Lewis and Clark in the manner of a tail flapping along after a kite.

Indeed, even the genesis of U.S. southwestern exploration lay with Jefferson's goals for the Lewis and Clark expedition. While a probe to the Missouri and Columbia river systems would resolve the question of a commercial Northwest Passage, in the larger picture American exploring parties in the West could establish a presence on the continent that Jefferson hoped both competing imperial powers and indigenous peoples would acknowledge. Additionally, and famously, exploration represented an official U.S. support of Enlightenment science, aimed directly at a mysterious and wondrous part of the planet where European plant collectors and naturalists had only nibbled.

There was a whole, fascinating world out there beyond the Blue Ridge Mountains of home about which Jefferson's mind wondered restlessly.

But obviously the Lewis and Clark expedition would leave these missions unfulfilled for an enormous stretch of the Louisiana Territory, and that was hardly Jefferson's intent. Indeed, he seems from the first to have regarded an American expedition across the southern reaches of Louisiana as nearly equal in importance to his Missouri-Columbia exploration. As the president told Meriwether Lewis in November 1803 (after Lewis himself had expressed interest in exploring toward New Mexico), Congress had assented to a larger plan to examine the principal rivers of the West. "In that case I should send a party up the Red River to it's [sic] head, then cross over to the head of the Arcansa, & come down that." As the president explained to Lewis, "This will be attempted distinctly from your mission."

Once Lewis and Clark were underway in the spring of 1804, then, Jefferson began planning what he and all the principals regarded as the southwestern counterpart to the Lewis and Clark expedition. On April 14, at home at Monticello, the president composed a seven-page letter of instructions for southwestern exploration. Unpublished until it appeared as an appendix in this book in 1984, Jefferson's letter was based closely on his 1803 letter of instructions to Meriwether Lewis, a classic expression of Enlightenment science. The southwestern version differed on routes, of course, and gave southwestern explorers a greater burden in winning the Indian tribes of the Spanish border over to the Americans. It also included a line that had its origins with the Lewis and Clark letter, but that would prove far more significant in the Southwest: "If at any time a superior force authorized or not authorized by a nation should be arrayed against your further passage and inflexibly determined to arrest it, you must decline its further pursuit and return." In the Southwest, that particular line would prove critical to the history that followed.

It was not until eighteen months later that a young Irish immigrant surveyor and engineer would have the honor, at a private White House dinner, of seeing Jefferson inscribe "To Thomas Freeman Esquire" across that letter of exploring instructions. And it was not until Jefferson had asked several of America's most famous naturalists, including sixty-five-year-old William Bartram, to take "the department of Natural History in the voyage up the Red River," that the administration found its man in twenty-five-year-old Peter Custis. Jefferson personally chose Captain Richard Sparks, a good friend of Meriwether Lewis's, to lead the accompanying military contingent. (Among the changes that appear in this new edition, the most important spring directly from the work of the expedition leaders, especially Freeman's precise map work, which upon initial publication of this book enabled archaeologists to locate not only expedition campsites but some of the Indian villages described in the accounts.)

Nearly two years of detailed planning and preparation, much of it devoted to a search for personnel for the expedition, and a congressional budget of $5,000 (twice the original appropriation for Lewis and Clark) finally poised the president's "Grand Excursion" for a scientific strike at the heart of the Southwest in April of 1806. With Lewis and Clark then crossing the Bitterroot Mountains bound for Saint Louis and home, one western triumph seemed ready to proceed on the heels of the other.

Despite the Grand Excursion's outstanding personnel and minutely detailed preparations, that was not to be. In the Southwest the Americans essentially inherited the French side of a decades-old debate with Spain over whose imperialist infrastructure had controlled which parts of the region. Beginning in 1714 the French had established permanent settlements among the Caddo Indians at Natchitoches, on the Red River, and at New Orleans on the Mississippi in 1718. With century-old settlements already in New Mexico, Spain had responded with the presidio/mission of Los Adaes (present Robeline, Louisiana) in 1716, and San Antonio in Texas in 1718. Over the ensuing decades, French traders connected with the numerous and widespread Caddoan peoples had used the Red and Arkansas rivers to penetrate far into the southwestern interior. Spain had resisted those "intrusions" with its own rather less successful policy of Indian trade. Then, after the French and Indian War turned French Louisiana over to Spain in 1763, Madrid had employed its former French rivals in the trade to consolidate its hold on the Southern Plains. For their part, the native peoples—like any properly sophisticated customers—longed for the days when competing Euroamericans vied for their attentions. As far as they were concerned, let the Americans come.

In 1806 Spain was within fifteen years of the endgame of three centuries in the Southwest. Its empire was weary and stretched filament-thin, and incapable of resisting the revolutionary sentiments that had already created the United States and would soon divest the Spanish crown of the bulk of its colonies. In North America the new historical pattern was especially apparent in the Southwest, and diverse Americans (including even the vice president) awoke with dreams of revolution and conquest in their heads. Jefferson's own public pronouncements that the Rio Grande was actually the boundary of the Louisiana Purchase left Spanish officials with few doubts about the threat that an official American exploration posed. In 1804–5 they made several attempts, all unsuccessful, to intercept Lewis and Clark. The Freeman and Custis expedition was both more threatening and far more accessible. And so, in one of its last heroic acts of self-preservation in the Southwest, Spain mustered the resolve—and the military force—to resist.

If the Lewis and Clark story has functioned in American history as a kind of "tribal history for white people" (the phrase is art historian Brian Dippie's), then in our present multicultural West, how should we interpret the Freeman and Custis story? I've grappled with this personally, because I had direct ancestors on both sides of the event. My great-grandfather four times removed was Pierre Bouet Lafitte, whose French (Natchitoches) trade alliances with the Indians the Americans inherited, and whose compatriots served as guides for Freeman and Custis. Meanwhile, one of the officers who led the opposition Spanish force was another ancestor, José Flores, who undoubtedly believed his expansive Rancho Tortuga south of Nacogdoches was threatened by the American intrusion, and he was absolutely right. Whether I see the outcome of this Red River probe as regrettable failure or heroic resistance thus depends on which side of my family I identify with. The truth is, I identify with *all* the competing factions in this story, including the Indians. And I suspect that in modern America, that's how Jefferson's second great expedition to the West ought to strike us.

Two other aspects of Jefferson's southwestern expedition make it intriguing. One is that in young Peter Custis it included the first American-trained academic naturalist to explore in the West. Over the four-month duration of the exploration Custis was able to bring his skills to bear on a fascinating region, and once I found his manu-script reports in the National Archives, it became plain that Custis's natural-history work (he cataloged nearly 270 species) provides us with a marvelous time machine for understanding the ecology of the Red River as it was in 1806. And of course that gives twenty-first-century America a remarkable baseline for gauging subsequent change: what was lost, and what we might restore, in this part of the world.

The other point has to do with continental geography. Based on the best and most recent cartography he could assemble, Jefferson could only assume that the Red River, like every other sensible river, had its headwaters in mountains, in this case the Southern Rockies. Thomas Freeman had no doubts: he expected his exploration to take him somewhere near Santa Fe, New Mexico. Not even Spanish offi-cials seem to have known what a handful of traders—some Spanish, some French, evidently even an American or two—had figured out, which was that the Red River headed nowhere near the Rockies. In 1804 the Jefferson administration had gotten a glimmer of the truth. Far out on the immensity of the southern prairies, it heard, there was "a height, the top of which presents an open plain," and it was in great canyons along the east side of this "height" that the Red River headed. Then the report muddled the picture by claiming that there was another fork of the Red that "flowed thru the mountains," which must have allayed any doubts the "height" passage raised.

The truth of the matter, a truth about which neither American nor Spanish officials were cognizant in 1806, was that the river Jef-ferson called "next to the Missouri, the most interesting water of the Mississippi," would never have led his explorers where he thought he was sending them. Instead it would have pitched them atop the great, remote tableland Hispanic traders called El Llano Estacado. The Red would have taken them, in other words, not to the soaring peaks of the "Mexican Mountains," nor into the thicket of trade possibilities and revolution in New Mexico, but onto a runeless slate, the middle of nowhere.

The late exploration historian Donald Jackson once penned an essay, "What If the Spaniards Had Captured Lewis and Clark?" Jackson, who late in his career became fascinated with Freeman and Custis, used his insights to conclude that America almost certainly lost a great exploration epic when the Spanish army turned back

Jefferson's Red River party in July of 1806—regret that even led him to write a novel, *Valley Men* (1984), which sent Freeman and Custis (renamed "Dr. Raphael Bailey") up the Arkansas River to the Rocky Mountains in 1807. And more recently it tantalized me into including in my 1999 book, *Horizontal Yellow*, a novella called "The River That Flowed from Nowhere," a fictional story that imagines Freeman and Custis continuing up the Red River into a Southwest beyond all Thomas Jefferson's fantasies.

But the fact is, what actually happened to Freeman and Custis was that historical forces cut them off in mid-stride. Their fate not only ought to increase our appreciation for Lewis and Clark's success, it also throws new shadows around the Lewis and Clark story. Perhaps the best answer to Jackson's question above lies in what *did* happen with Freeman and Custis. And in Big Picture terms, what becomes clear is that America's destiny in the West didn't truly rest on Jeffersonian exploration. Despite the failure of Freeman and Custis, American traders carrying American goods (and even flags) still intruded themselves among the Indian tribes in the Southwest, and American expansionist policies still brought Texas, New Mexico, and the entire region into the United States within decades. Had Spain similarly intercepted Lewis and Clark, the American West would have lost an epic story, but western history probably wouldn't have turned out much differently. Someone else would have discovered the grizzly bear, written rhapsodically about the Great Falls of the Missouri, and crossed the Great Divide and the Bitterroots on Indian trails.

But Thomas Jefferson couldn't know that. In the context of western exploration in 1806, the reality was that his southwestern *entrada* had been turned back short of its goals, while his northwestern probe had crossed plains and mountains beyond compare all the way to the Pacific. If he concentrated on the far-happier results of Lewis and Clark, then, an exploration that had featured the grand theme of Americans confronting the wilderness rather than Americans confronting "the other," who could blame him?

The country has been emulating Jefferson in that decision ever since. Perhaps it's time to reconsider.

DAN FLORES

Bitterroot Valley, Montana
August 2001

xvi

Preface to the 1984 Edition

FOR far too long, most enthusiasts of American Western exploration history have suffered from myopia when dealing with Thomas Jefferson's exploration of the Louisiana Territory. The Lewis and Clark expedition so caught the fancy of Americans that for the most part we have forgotten the fact that Jefferson actually planned it to be only one of several scientific probes into the American West. Among the others, particularly critical was an expedition into the Southwest.

Although determined to sell Louisiana to the United States in 1803, France was unable to define the exact boundaries of the territory being relinquished. West of the Mississippi, the continent remained almost unexplored, and there were serious questions concerning the extent of Spanish holdings in that area. Already intent on securing scientific knowledge of the region by sending an expedition up the Red River, Jefferson now found it imperative to obtain more information about the Louisiana-Texas frontier in order to counter Spanish claims. For more than three y ears, Jefferson labored over the plans for a project to accomplish both objectives.

By a complicated matrix of circumstances, the end result of what Jefferson and Secretary of War Henry Dearborn referred to as their "Grand Expedition" has been virtually lost to public view for nearly two centuries. Even though Professor Joseph Ewan has called it "the forgotten expedition," it was the largest and, in terms of original appropriation, the most expensive American exploring expedition of the age. It was also the first major probe into the West to be led by civilian scientists and the first to include an academically trained naturalist.

This expedition was Jefferson's 1806 examination of the Red River of the South, led by Thomas Freeman, astronomer and civil engineer, and Peter Custis, University of Pennsylvania naturalist. In the spring and summer of that year, accompanied by a forty-five-man military escort and Indian and French guides, Freeman and Custis ascended the Red River some 615 miles, en route (they believed) to the Southern Rockies and Santa Fe. Halfway to their objective of the headwaters of the river, they were confronted by a Spanish army, and in one of the final gasps of the drowning Spanish Empire in North America, forced to abort their mission. The journals and reports they left of this incomplete exploration were later characterized by Edwin James, himself the chronicler of a government exploring foray to the West, as "extremely circumstantial," embracing "much valuable information."

Among the many reasons why the story of this Lewis and Clark expedition of the South, as exploration historian Donald Jackson has styled it, has never been fully told, one of the most important has been the apparent loss of the original journals and reports of the two scientist, Freeman and Custis. What has existed was a heretofore anonymous and obscure publication entitled *An Account Of The Red River, In Louisiana, Drawn Up From The Returns Of Messrs. Freeman & Custis, To The War Office Of The United States, Who Explored The Same, In The Year 1806.* Undated, and in the form of a third-person narrative, it is today very rare, fewer than a dozen originals surviving into our time. Even to historians who have worked on aspects of the expedition itself or on related topics, understanding has been limited and interpretation rarely attempted, in part because of what has seemed to be unusually meager documentation.

The other major reason is perhaps more unexpected. Research here presented establishes an apparent connection between the fate of the expedition and the Burr-Wilkinson Conspiracy of 1806. Although both Jefferson and Freeman evidently were unaware of this circumstance at the time, Jefferson apparently decided by late 1806 that his political enemies might indeed try to link the two in the public mind. Thus he quite deliberately sought to divert attention from the fate of the "Grand Expedition"—a fact that has misled historians in assessing its significance not only in the exploration of the West but also in terms of the near-war with Spain in 1806.

This publication of the first book-length treatment of the Freeman and Custis expedition has been made possible partially by the discovery of new documents (including Peter Custis's original manuscript reports in the unregistered letters of the War Department, the National Archives and the manuscript originals, in The Bexar Archives, of the unexamined letters between Spanish frontier officials respecting the expedition); and also by combing and interpreting the related research and documents assembled by earlier scholars like Isaac Joslin Cox, Eron Dunbar Rowland, Conrad V. Morton, John Francis McDermott, and Donald Jackson. Although some purists may object, I have used these meritorious documents collections when they were available. An unavoidable impression has been that the story was waiting for someone to tell it. The fact that I grew up in the country explored by the expedition and was trained in Western and environmental history has made assembling the documents and telling it a task I could not avoid, and indeed, never wished to.

In bringing together those documents that were recoverable in order to produce a new and more complete version of the Freeman and Custis Accounts, I have followed the lead of Herbert Eugene Bolton in his *Athanase De Mézières And The Louisiana-Texas Frontier,* in appending to the exploration accounts a somewhat lengthy introduction and epilogue. This course of action seemed necessary, since unlike that of most other American explorations, the background and aftermath of this expedition not only are little known, but until now have never been told in their entirety. This approach has enabled me to tell the story in a single volume and to interpret the expedition within the larger context of Jeffersonian borderlands diplomacy, and the early American imperial drive into the Southwest.

In assessing the importance of the Freeman and Custis story, it ought to be noted that the Accounts of the two explorers constitute the most detailed and reliable primary sources we have available on the early condition of the Red River and its valley. Despite the mediocre quality of the version assembled and published in 1807, the documents have been particularly esteemed by anthropologists and archaeologists, since they are of key ethnological importance for study of the Indian peoples of the Red River.

Of equal importance to scholars and laymen alike, the Freeman and Custis descriptions provide us with an outstanding portrayal of a major North American ecosystem still largely in its natural state. Here appear the animals, the birds, and the climax vegetation of the "natural" Red River valley. Perhaps better than most early exploration accounts, they lend themselves to a close ecological interpretation of the sort the late Professor James Malin once outlined for historians of the environment, but which has rarely been done. However, approached, the Accounts are a portal into a time much different from ours, when bison and black bears and whooping cranes frequented the river-bottom prairies, the virgin hardwood groves reverberated at the drumming of woodpeckers two feet long, and flocks of (likewise now extinct) yellow and green parrots flitted through the lofty bald cypresses and red cedars that once flanked this river. Scientifically, *this* Red River valley is our environmental control model, the gauge by which we can and must evaluate all subsequent changes. Perhaps it is ahistorical to mourn its passing, but nonetheless I do, and I think any one who reads this book and understands what has been lost will mourn it, too.

Many individuals and institutions have been interested in this project, and have given their time to it. For essential assistance in finding and procuring materials, I wish to express sincere thanks to the staffs of the Library of Congress Manuscripts Division, the Fort Worth Branch of the National Archives, the American Philosophical Society, the Smithsonian Institution, the Academy of Natural Sciences of Philadelphia, the University of Pennsylvania system, the Barker Texas History Center of the Sid Richardson Library at the University of Texas-Austin, the Peabody Museum of Natural History at Yale University, the Watson Library at Northwestern State University in Natchitoches, Louisiana, and to my "base" libraries while the book was in gestation, those at Texas A&M University and Texas Tech University.

I would also like to express my thanks to the following individuals whose expertise and aid were invaluable: Dr. Clarence Webb of Shreveport; R. King Harris of Dallas; Professor John Hall of the Geography Department, Louisiana State University in Shreveport; Professor Donald Rawson of the History Department, Northwestern Louisiana; Professors John Wunder and Benjamin Newcomb of the History Department, Texas Tech University; Professor Paul

Fryxell of the U. S. D. A. Agricultural Research Division and the Agronomy Field Laboratory at Texas A&M University; Professor Thomas R. Dale, Department of Biology, Northeast Louisiana; J. Dan Scurlock of the Texas State Archaeological Commission; Professor "Pete" Gregory of the Anthropology Department, Northwestern, Louisiana; Elizabeth John of Austin; Professor Joseph Ewan, Department of Biology, Tulane University; Professors Herbert Lang and the late Lloyd Taylor, Department of History, Texas A&M University; Ricky Adcock of Gilliam, Louisiana; and Charles Freeburg of Dallas, Texas.

I owe a special debt to these people: Haynes Dugan of Shreveport, an aficionado of Red River valley history who has provided me with countless documents over the years; Professor E. M. Parker of the Engineering Department, Centenary College of Shreveport, whose "Shreve Map" appears in this volume; Professor Jerry Stannard of Kansas University, who helped with a number of interesting botanical problems; Gabriela Vigo, for her assistance in documents translations; John Drayton and Joaquin Rogers of the University of Oklahoma Press for their interest and care with the project; my parents, W. C. and Kathryn Flores of Rodessa, Louisiana, for providing me with a "base" during field trips back to Freeman and Custis country; and to Katherine Bridges of Amarillo, Texas, former archivist in the Louisiana Room at Northwestern Louisiana, who first suggested in 1971 that the book needed to be written.

Thank you, also, Professors Donald Jackson and Savoie Lottinville.

Finally, I would like to express my gratitude to Katie Dowdy for her enthusiastic encouragement and rare understanding, and to Jerry Griffin of Austin and Benny Cash of Shreveport, who joined me in retracing part of the exploration during a memorable descent of the Red River in May of 1977.

DAN FLORES

Santa Fe, New Mexico

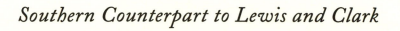

Southern Counterpart to Lewis and Clark

Editor's Introduction
Probing the Southwestern Wilderness

"FIFTEEN millions? And for what? 'Wild land'!"[1]

To the Federalist newspaper editor who penned those disparaging lines, there apparently was little that was either romantic or practical about the addition of a possible 800 million acres of North American "wilderness" to the United States. Certainly many ordinary citizens of the new republic must have agreed. Within the memories of their fathers and grandfathers, all had been "wild land," and there had been little romanticizing about it. As for practicality, there was wilderness enough to last for centuries in the Mississippi Valley.

But the American acquisition in 1803 of the Louisiana Territory—that vast, still uncharted hinterland of forest, plain, and mountain that lay shining in the sun beyond the Mississippi—produced a remarkably different effect on another type of American. Louisiana constituted a large chunk of the remaining *terra incognita* of the North American continent, a land about which there were as yet only the rumors of second-hand stories and the equally exotic guesses of armchair geographers. Imperial considerations aside, the certainty of important new geographical discoveries in Louisiana, of new additions to the natural sciences, of contact with strange and wonderful civilizations beyond the "set-

---

[1] *Columbian Centinel*, August 24, 1803

3

Thomas Jefferson, by Rembrandt Peale. Courtesy Library of Congress.

tlements," fired the imaginations of all those Americans who possessed in equal parts intellectual curiosity and a love for unraveling nature's mysteries.

Among this latter group, the leading proponent was, and had been for years, a Virginia-born philosopher-farmer named Thomas Jefferson. Since boyhood Jefferson had been delighted with, often almost consumed by, the study of nature. Few topics escaped his broad-ranging curiosity as he grew in political and scientific influence. By age forty, he was a pioneer in both meteorology and phenology (the science which correlates weather and biological phenomena), a close student of American birds and animals, a leading paleontologist with a large collection of fossils, an ethnologist who collected Indian vocabularies, and one of the country's first archaeologists. He also found time to learn to use the scientific instruments of survey and cartography, for he was keenly interested in portraying the features of the American countryside on perfectly accurate charts. As a scientist and naturalist, Jefferson found a home among peers in the American Philosophical Society, to which he was elected in 1779. From 1797 to 1814 he would serve as president of that prestigious organization.[2]

With his intense intellectual curiosity about the natural world, coupled with the scholar's yearning for new and untapped fields of study, Jefferson was inexorably drawn to the American West. He loved science, observation, and cataloging. The West of his day was little more than a shimmering, wispy mirage, and he aspired to know it more intimately, to put himself and the world in touch with its peculiarities, its inhabitants, its hills, prairies, and rivers. Eventually, as he familiarized himself with British, French, and Spanish designs on the West, his musings developed into more sagacious considerations.

It is hardly surprising that for many years before his election as president of the United States, Jefferson nurtured dreams of exploring the still unknown interior of North America. The fact that Spain controlled Louisiana did not deter him from attempt-

[2] Paul Russell Cutright, *Lewis and Clark: Pioneering Naturalists*, pp. 1–11; Dumas Malone, *Jefferson and His Time* 4:182.

ing to convert those dreams into action. As early as 1783, Jefferson wrote (without success) to George Rogers Clark in an effort to entice the hero of the western theater in the Revolution to explore the West under his sponsorship. Three years later came the Jefferson-initiated expedition by John Ledyard to cross Russia and explore North America from west to east—a wild scheme Ledyard was reckless enough to attempt alone before being apprehended by an agent of Empress Catherine. In 1792, Jefferson and several other members of the Philosophical Society attempted to raise a thousand dollars to underwrite a private botanical excursion up the Missouri by the noted Philadelphia botanist, Moses Marshall. This, too, failed of execution. A year later Jefferson and several members of the Society (including George Washington and Alexander Hamilton) contributed funds for the financing of still another western exploration. This one was to be led by François André Michaux, the noted French naturalist who had previously collected plants in the eastern states. Michaux's botanical excursion had scarcely gotten underway, however, when he was recalled on the suspicion that he was acting as a spy for an illegal western filibuster proposed by the new French minister, Citizen Edmund Genêt. Four times, then, Jefferson had attempted to have the West explored by private parties, and four times his plans had met with frustration.[3]

Two events early in the nineteenth century altered this situation dramatically. The first was Jefferson's elevation to the presidency in 1801. Now the foremost proponent of western exploration occupied the highest political office in the land, one with power and prestige he could utilize to mount *government* expeditions. The second event was the most important diplomatic development of his administration—the great Louisiana Purchase of 1803. For a multitude of reasons, Emperor Napoleon I, who had

[3] Donald Jackson, ed., *Letters of the Lewis and Clark Expedition, with Related Documents, 1783–1854*, 1st ed. Letters between Jefferson and George Rogers Clark, John Ledyard, and André Michaux are reprinted in appendix 1 of Jackson's fine documents collection. See also, Cutright, *Lewis and Clark: Pioneering Naturalists*, pp. 10–13; John W. Harshberger, *The Botanists of Philadelphia and Their Work*, p. 106.

forced Spain to retrocede Louisiana to France in the secret treaty of San Ildefonso in 1800, decided early in 1803 to sell all the Louisiana Territory to the United States. In light of this acquisition, new hinterland explorations by Americans enjoyed a color of legality and necessity never owned before.

It is clear that there would have been at least *one* government expedition to the West, purchase or no. In 1801, Jefferson had appointed twenty-six-year-old Meriwether Lewis, whom he had watched grow to manhood in Virginia, to be his personal secretary.[4] Several years earlier, at only nineteen, Lewis had entered an earnest plea through Jefferson in an attempt to obtain the appointment given Michaux. Now, in the city of Washington with Jefferson, Lewis almost seems to have been groomed to direct an exploring party. In 1803, with Jefferson's approval, Lewis asked William Clark, the thirty-year-old brother of George Rogers Clark, to be the nominal coleader of the evolving Missouri River tour. At the same time, Jefferson asked the Spanish minister, Carlos Martínez de Yrujo, whether or not Spain would object to a small scientific exploration by the Americans.[5] Already the events were unfolding that would place Louisiana firmly in American hands, and thus, after a delay of a year and a half, during which Lewis took crash courses in botany, zoology, ethnology, and astronomical observation from leading luminaries in the American academic world, the first step of Jefferson's long-cherished dream began to materialize. In May of 1804, armed with British and French passports and forty-five strong, the Lewis and Clark expedition swung into the muddy Missouri and embarked upon what was to become the epic exploration of the American frontier.[6]

It was clearly obvious that the Lewis and Clark expedition would leave an enormous chunk of Louisiana unexamined. This

[4] Jefferson to James Wilkinson, Washington, February 23, 1801. In Jackson, *Letters of the Lewis and Clark Expedition,* 1st ed., p. 1.

[5] Carlos Martinez de Yrujo to Pedro Cevallos, Washington, December 2, 1802. Ibid., pp. 4–6.

[6] British and French passports made out to Meriwether Lewis. Ibid., pp. 19–20. See also Benard De Voto, ed., *The Journals of Lewis and Clark,* pp.

was not the oversight on Jefferson's part that it would appear to be in most popular, and some scholarly, works. Actually, Jefferson very clearly intended that the Missouri-Columbia rivers tour was to be only one of several explorations to chart the West. In a letter to Lewis as early as 1803, the president had outlined his complete blueprint for the scientific examination of the Louisiana Territory:

The object of your mission is single, the direct water communication from sea to sea formed by the bed of the Missouri & perhaps the Oregon [the Columbia]. . . . I have proposed in conversation, & it seems generally to be assented to, that Congress shall appropriate 10. or 12.000 D. for exploring the principal waters of the Missisipi & Missouri. In that case I should send a party up the Red River to it's head, then cross over to the head of the Arcansa, & come down that. A 2d party for the Pani [the Platte] & Padouca [the Kansas] rivers, & a 3d perhaps for the Moingona [the Des Moines] & St. Peters [the Minnesota]. As the boundaries of interior Louisiana are the high lands inclosing all the waters which run into the Missisipi or Missouri directly or indirectly . . . it becomes interesting to fix with precision by celestial observations the longitude & latitude of the sources of those rivers, and furnishing points in the contour of our new limits. This will be attempted distinctly from your mission. . . .[7]

Of these three additional western explorations conceived by the president, only the one aimed at the Red River of the South, a stream which Jefferson regarded as "in truth, next to the Missouri, the most interesting water of the Mississippi,"[8] ever proceeded beyond plan to action. It was this exploration, since referred to

---

2-3. De Voto's introduction is the best summary of the background to the Lewis and Clark expedition that I have seen. It should be noted that fifteen men in the original Lewis and Clark party traveled only as far as the Mandan villages.

   [7]Jefferson to Lewis, Washington, November 16, 1803. In Jackson, *Letters of the Lewis and Clark Expedition,* 1st ed., pp. 136–38. For maps of the period showing contemporary river names, see Carl I. Wheat, comp., *1540–1861: Mapping the Transmississippi West.*

   [8]Jefferson to William Dunbar, Washington, May 25, 1805, in Eron Dunbar Rowland, ed., *Life, Letters and Papers of William Dunbar: Of Elgin, Morayshire, Scotland, and Natchez, Mississippi. Pioneer Scientist of the Southern United States,* p. 177; hereafter cited as Rowland, *Dunbar Letters.*

by one noted historian as "the southern counterpart to the Lewis and Clark expedition,"[9] to which Jefferson turned once the Missouri River exploration was underway. "The work we are now doing is, I trust, done for posterity. . . . We shall delineate with correctness the great arteries of this great country," Jefferson wrote.[10] Indeed, between 1804 and 1807, his energetic attempts to "delineate with correctness" the course of the Southwestern rivers became so protracted and pregnant with innuendo that none of the other expeditions he hoped for were ever planned. Ultimately, the exploration of the Southwest would assume the status of an international incident, one which came precipitously close to involving the United States in a war with Imperial Spain.

FRANCE AND SPAIN IN THE RED RIVER VALLEY

The keen interest that President Jefferson and many of his contemporaries envinced for the exploration of the Southwest via an ascent of the Red River had many origins. Evolving from its headwaters on the Llano Estacado, the Red River assumes its own identity near the one hundredth meridian and flows some 1,200 miles to its mouth on the Mississippi River. More than any other Western river, for nearly three centuries the sandy, meandering waterway with Caddoan villages strung along its lower length like beads on a string had been a major focus of imperialistic dispute in the New World. Several noted European explorers had operated in the Red River country. As the Indians did, they called the big stream Rojo or Colorado, or sometimes Vermejo in the case of the Spanish and Rivière Rouge by the French, because the red clay beds and mineral outcrops from which it derives its sources charge its waters with a distinctly rusty appearance that is evident all the way to its mouth.[11]

[9] Jackson, *Letters of the Lewis and Clark Expedition*, 1st ed., p. 270n.

[10] Jefferson to Dunbar, Washington, May 25, 1805, Rowland, *Dunbar Letters*, p. 174.

[11] Respecting the Caddo name for their river, Tonty had this to say in 1690: "*They* call this river the Red River, because, in fact, it deposits a sand which

It was largely by accident that the Red River valley was the scene of some of the very first European activities in North America. Some writers have contended, for example, that the first European to see the Red was shipwrecked Cabeza de Vaca, circa 1534. The first whites known with certainty to have visited the river, however, were the members of Francisco Vásquez de Coronado's Quivera-bound detachment in 1541. Coronado crossed the tributaries that make up the headwaters of the Red, and may also have camped in Palo Duro Canyon shortly before the Hernan De Soto expedition, hundreds of miles downstream, entered the valley of the river. Led by Luis de Moscoso after De Soto's death, these latter Spaniards crossed the middle Red (in present northwestern Louisiana) twice in 1542.[12] For the first time, Europeans had entered Cadodoquia, the ancient land of the Caddos.

The failure of these early Spanish expeditions to find gold or other easily recoverable natural resource wealth in the Southwest meant that nearly a century and a half passed before the verdant prairies and woodlands threaded by the chocolate-hued river were again visited by whites. This time, in a portent of things to come, it was the French. Following his successful descent of the Mississippi from Canada in 1682, René Robert Cavalier, Sieur de La Salle, greatest of the French New World explorers, sailed from France in 1684, determined to plant a fort at the mouth of the river whose drainage was the circulatory system of half the continent. Confused by the coastal estuaries, La Salle missed the Mississippi and struck land 300 miles to the west. An impromptu fort at Garcitas Creek, on the Texas Gulf Coast, was the result. In 1687 the remnants of La Salle's beleaguered band straggled

---

makes the water as red as blood." Henry de Tonty, "Memoir by the Sieur de La Tonty," in Isaac J. Cox, ed., *The Journeys of René Robert Cavelier Sieur de La Salle* 2:47–48.

[12] See Cleve Hallenbeck, *Álvar Núñez Cabeza de Vaca: The Journey and Route of the First European to cross the Continent of North America, 1534–1536*, p. 129; Herbert Eugene Bolton, *Coronado: Knight of Pueblos and Plains*, pp. 254, 266–67; Rex Strickland, "Moscoso's Journey Through Texas," *Southwestern Historical Quarterly* 66 (October 1962): 109–37; John R. Swanton, *The Indians of the Southeastern United States*, Bureau of American Ethnology, *Bulletin 137*, pp. 98–101.

into the Caddo villages on the Red, en route to Canada after the assassination of their leader by a disaffected element. Four years later, La Salle's crippled captain, Henri de Tonty (or Tonti) journeyed to the Caddo country in search of his leader and spent several weeks in the Red River country before abandoning his quest.

Stirred from her disinterest in the northern provinces by this French activity, in 1690 Spain charged General Alonso de León, governor of Coahuila, and Fray Damián Massanet with founding missions among the Hasinai-Caddoan groups of present East Texas. The following year Don Domingo de Terán, first governor of Tejas (corrupted from tayshas, the Caddoan word for "friend") escorted Massanet and other Franciscans to the Red River villages, where they failed in their attempt to intrude themselves among the Red River Caddos. But the stage was set for an intense rivalry between France and Spain over control of the Red River valley.[13]

Guessing at the strategic and diplomatic value of this artery into the hinterland, France quickly proved the more energetic and successful of the two. Beginning in 1700 with Jean Baptiste Le Moyne, Sieur de Bienville's expedition west from the Mississippi and overland into the Yatasi Caddo country (near present Shreveport), and culminating with Luis Juchereau de Saint Denis's founding of the post of Natchitoches near a Red River Caddo village of the same name in 1714, France had effectively secured hegemony on the lower Red and made inroads among the upriver tribes, who much preferred trade with the French to religious conversion by the Spanish.[14]

[13] Henry Reed Stiles, ed., *Joutel's Journal of La Salle's Last Voyage, 1684–7*, pp. 162–71, 202–203; for an overview, see also Robert S. Weddle, *Wilderness Manhunt: The Spanish Search for La Salle.* On Terán, see Mattie Austin Hatcher, trans., "The Expedition of Don Domingo Terán de Los Ríos into Texas," *Preliminary Studies of the Catholic Historical Society* 2 (January 1932): 1–67; Tonty, "Memoir by the Sieur de La Tonty," in Cox, ed., *The Journeys of René Robert Cavelier Sieur de La Salle* 1:47–48.

[14] Henry D. Folmer, *Franco-Spanish Rivalry in North America, 1542–1763*, pp. 212, 217–18; Robert Dabney Calhoun, "The Taensa Indians: The French

In this imperial chess game the Spaniards had countered in late 1716 or early 1717 with a mission among the Adaes Indians, who inhabited country only fifteen miles west of the French outpost, and, after the French drove the priests away (in an incident known as the "Chicken War"), by a presidio and settlement there in 1721. The village, Los Adaes, became the capital of the remote Spanish province of Tejas, and remained the locus of Spanish influence in eastern Texas until its abandonment and the subsequent founding of Bucareli, and finally Nacogdoches, by the displaced Adaeseños in the 1770s. But in this early period the Spanish had no recourse but to suffer French control of the lower Red, and after the French moved their settlement to the west bank of the river in 1735, grudgingly accepted the tiny stream called the Arroyo Hondo and a swell of high ground known as the Gran Montane as the natural features dividing the claims of these two great powers.[15]

The one avenue along which Spain seemed powerless to stop French penetration, however, was the Red River. In 1717, in the flurry of activity that had led to the founding of Los Adaes, Domingo Ramón had attempted to thwart any effort by the French to push into the interior via the river by establishing a mission called San José at the main Caddo, or Nassonite, village near present Texarkana. Again the Caddos were not receptive, and the effort appears to have been only a half-hearted one. At any rate, by 1719 the missionaries had abandoned the wilderness outpost. That cleared the way for the French explorer and representative of the reorganized Compagnie des Indes, or Mis-

---

Explorers and Catholic Missionaries in the Taensa Country," *Louisiana Historical Quarterly* 17 (October 1934), pt. 3, p. 659.

[15] Folmer, *Franco-Spanish Rivalry in North America*, pp. 232–33, 238; Charles Wilson Hackett, "Policy of the Spanish Crown Regarding French Encroachment from Louisiana, 1721–1762," in *New Spain and the Anglo-American West*, pp. 116–17. My information on Los Adaes comes from Charles Wilson Hackett, ed. and trans., *Pichardo's Treatise on the Limits of Louisiana and Texas* 4:185. The story of the Adaeseños, Bucareli, and the founding of Nacogdoches entered Texas history when Herbert Eugene Bolton assembled it from the primary documents in his *Texas in the Middle Eighteenth Century* (1914).

sissippi Company, Bénard de La Harpe, to ascend the Red and Sulphur rivers to the seat of power of Cadodoquia, near present-day Texarkana, Texas. Here, in 1719, La Harpe founded the most westerly trading and military post France was to maintain in the Southwest, La Poste des Cadodoquious. Not abandoned by French soldiers (who erected a gristmill and married Indian girls) until well after the cession of Louisiana to Spain in the Treaty of Paris, 1763, La Harpe's Post joined the Arkansas Post, founded by Tonty near the mouth of that river in 1686, as springboards from which French coureur du bois struck farther into the interior. Free of the trading restrictions Spain imposed, these Gallic plainsmen had successfully established trade with the Taovayas and other bands of the Wichitas, who were migrating from the valley of the Canadian southward to the Red and Brazos rivers. By 1746, Frenchmen, Taovaya-Wichitas, and Comanches had effected a three-way rapprochment that gave the white traders access to both Taovaya country and the Comanchería via the line of the Red. Seeking buffalo robes, pelts, and especially horses, mules, and Apache slaves to work on the plantations and farms of the settlements, the traders brought metalware, cloth, and whiskey to exchange. Most important, they armed these "Nations of the North" with guns to fight the Osages and Apaches.

But while the French traders from Natchitoches and the up-river posts stood as friends and allies, the Spanish peace in the 1750s with the retrenching Apaches adversely affected Spanish efforts to extend hegemony to the upper Red River country. It led directly to the destruction of the San Sabá mission in 1758, and the subsequent defeat of a large Spanish and Indian army, commanded by veteran Don Diego Ortiz Parilla, outside the Red River Taovaya villages the following year. So committed were these Nations of the North to the French that when Louisiana passed to Spain, appointments had to be given to Frenchmen such as Athanase ("Anastacio") de Mézières, and Pierre ("Pedro") Vial in order to at last win the northern tribes to Spain, and link Natchitoches and Santa Fe with a trail through their country.[16]

[16]Ralph Smith, ed. and trans., "Account of the Journey of Bénard de La

What they were able to find out about this earlier European activity apparently whetted the appetite of the Americans for more intimate knowledge of the Red River and of the wilderness productions over which the Europeans had struggled. From geographical and natural history perspectives, the reports of the European explorers' limited operations on the river were tantalizing, if not very helpful (La Harpe's journal, discovered in Natchitoches in 1805, reported the existence of "unicorns" in the Southwest, for example). Clearly, in the areas of botanical and zoological discovery as well as for the precise cartographic study needed to define the boundaries of Spanish lands, an American expedition into the southern reaches of the Louisiana Territory seemed practical as a companion exploration to the Lewis and Clark trek across the northern reaches of the Purchase.

When Jefferson first approached Congress with his plan to explore southern Louisiana, the suggestion was referred to the Committee on Commerce and Manufactures in the House of Representatives. Chairman of the committee at that time was the eminent scientist Dr. Samuel L. Mitchill of New York. Using the natural-history-oriented *History of Louisiana* (1758), by Antoine Simon Le Page du Pratz as its reference, Mitchill's committee reported favorably on such an exploration because of the natural curiosities of the country along the Red and Arkansas rivers. From what the committee members were able to learn, the Red seemed the more interesting of the two. It was said to have many lakes along its banks containing alligators and fish in abundance. Its shores were reputed to be inhabited by bison, tigers, wolves, deer, turkeys, and waterfowl, as well as many unknown species, and all manner of indigenous fruits were supposed to grow luxuriantly along its course. It was supposed to be navigable for 1,000

Harpe: Discovery Made by Him of Several Indian Nations Situated in the West," *Southwestern Historical Quarterly* 62 (July 1958–April 1959): 75–86, 246–59, 371–85, 524–41; see also, Folmer, *Franco-Spanish Rivalry in North America*, p. 248.

miles above Natchitoches, and was reported to run through a country abounding in rich prairie, where feral cattle and wild horses ranged in innumerable herds.[17]

In his letters and reports to Jefferson in 1804, the first on the subject written only two weeks after Lewis and Clark were underway, William Dunbar, a Natchez, Mississippi, scientist who had forsaken an earldom in Scotland and come to the New World in 1771, outlined some of the advantages of making the Red River the next target of a Jeffersonian exploration. According to the reports he had received, the river was supposed to "run a very long course thro' immense regions of the richest and most fertile lands," which "will hereafter support a prodigious population." Many medicinal plants were said to be found along its banks; salt was present in many forms, sometimes oozing from the earth in springs, and traders told him that mountains of pure or partial salt existed on the headwaters of the river. Finally, "wonderful stories of wonderful productions are said to exist."[18] Among the latter, unicorns, giant water serpents, and vague reports of masses of metal assumed to be "silver ore" seemed the most novel.[19]

---

[17] *Annals of Congress*. 8th Cong., 1st sess. (1805), pp. 1124–26. John L. Allen, in his "Geographical Knowledge and American Images of the Louisiana Territory," *Western Historical Quarterly* 1 (April 1971): 157n., 164n., documents the fact that the Red River got more discussion in the American press of the day than any other river except the Missouri. Allen speculates that this is a consequence of the wide reprinting of Natchitoches Indian agent John Sibley's letters on the Red River country.

[18] Dunbar to Jefferson, Natchez, June 9, 1804, and "Journal of A Voyage," entry for December 10, 1804, Rowland, *Dunbar Letters*, pp. 133–35, 307–308. Brought up in Elgin, Morayshire, on the northern coast of Scotland, Dunbar was educated in mathematics and astronomy in universities in Glasgow and London. A Spanish citizen after coming to the New World, Dunbar became an American citizen in 1798, after Daniel Clark had introduced him to Jefferson with these words: ". . . for Science, Probity, & general information [Dunbar] is the first Character in this part of the World." Dunbar had a plantation called "The Forest" in the hills near Natchez, where he constructed one of the outstanding early astronomical observatories in North America and lived "like a nabob." Dumas Malone, ed., *Dictionary of American Biography* 5:507–508; Rowland, *Dunbar Letters*, Introduction.

[19] In his letter of August 22, 1801, Dunbar told Jefferson that he had secured his account of the "water-serpent" (probably Avanyu, the mythic Puebloan creature) from Nolan.

The wild mustangs of the Southwest fascinated Jefferson and attracted the attention of American traders. Painting by George Catlin. Courtesy National Museum of American Art, Smithsonian Institution.

These stories must have fascinated Jefferson, particularly since they came from his friend Dunbar, whose election to the Philosophical Society he had promoted, and who was regarded as the premier scientist of the Southwest.

Dunbar's mention of "wonderful productions" raises an interesting point about the reasons for the excitement over a Red River exploration. Lewis and Clark were dispatched, we now know, in large measure to discover a trading highway to the Pacific via the Missouri and Columbia rivers. Correspondingly, a survey of the Red River could be expected to return detailed information on the most direct waterway route to that remote but fabled outpost of the Spanish Provincias Internas: Santa Fe. There were Americans who believed that, given a favorable situation, the northern cities and provinces of Mexico would find the United States their most natural trading partner. Yet it is clear to us that this particular dream was based upon a geographical mirage—a misconception about the Red River as critical as the erroneous ideas held by the administration and its Missouri River explorers respecting that "minor" mountain chain we now call the Northern Rockies. For despite the Spanish and French activity in the Red River valley over the previous three centuries, reliable information about the river's course was still unknown

---

The Thomas Jefferson Papers, 1st ser. The unicorn story (see Custis's natural-history catalogues) seems to have originated with Bienville and La Harpe, and was repeated in the Dunbar and Hunter Ouachita River account. The origin of the Southwestern "silver ore" stories, first told by the Red River traders and repeated by Sibley and Dunbar, now appear traceable to the existence of iron-nickel meteorites on the Southern Plains. Athanase de Mézières, a Natchitoches Frenchman in the Spanish service, was the first to report these "metallic masses," in 1772. He describes Po-a-cat-le-pi-le-carre, or Medicine Rock of the Taovaya-Wichitas, Tawakonis, and Comanches thus: ". . . a mass of metal which the Indians say is hard, thick heavy, and composed of iron. They venerate it as an extraordinary manifestation of nature." De Mézières to the Baron de Ripperda, San Antonio, July 4 1772, in Herbert Eugene Bolton, ed., *Athanase de Mézières and the Louisiana-Texas Frontier 1768–1780* 1:296. The largest of these meteorites was hauled back from the middle Brazos in 1810, by American traders who believed it to be platinum, and a sure indication of other rich minerals in the Red River country. The story of its retrieval from the plains is told in the Epilogue.

The Medicine Rock of the Red River tribes, a 1,635-pound meteorite, 40 inches long, 16 inches high, now called "Red River," retrieved from the plains in 1810 by American traders. The presence of meteorites on the Southern Plains is apparently the source of early stories of "silver ore" in that country. Courtesy Peabody Museum of Natural History, Yale University.

in the United States. It is true that Vial and José Mares successfully established, in the late 1780s, a direct trail between Natchitoches and Santa Fe, at least partially by way of the Red. But even if known to the Americans, their efforts were probably misunderstood.[20]

There was also strong cartographic evidence to corroborate American interest in the Red River as the best route to New Mexico. At almost precisely the same time that Jefferson began to turn his attentions to an exploration of southern Louisiana,

[20] See Noel M. Loomis and A. P. Nasatir, *Pedro Vial and the Roads to Santa Fe,* for the journals, diaries, and accounts of the Spanish expeditions of the 1780s. Although some of their routes did utilize the Prairie Dog Town Fork–Tierra Blanca Creek–Tucumcari Mesa path, there still remained a 200-mile trek through plateau country before arrival at Santa Fe.

Baron Alexander von Humboldt, the celebrated naturalist, cartographer, and tropical American explorer, visited Washington and turned over to Albert Gallatin a copy of his as-yet-unpublished "Carte Generale Du Royaume De La Nouvelle Espagne." Several copies seem to have been made, for Aaron Burr was also presented one. Von Humboldt, who had spent months in Mexico City studying the best sources available, for the section about the Provincias Internas had relied on Bernardo Miera y Pacheco, the cartographer of the Dominguez-Escalante expedition into the Southern Rockies and the plateau country of the Southwest in 1776. Miera's map of the area showed a "Río Rojo" arising in the mountains north of Taos; this area Miera had labeled "Origen del Río Rojo."[21] Apparently unaware of the Vial-Mares-Fragoso reports and of the frequent use of "Rojo" for the rivers of the Southwest, von Humboldt merged this stream—actually the Canadian drainage—with the "Río Rojo de Natchitoches," and stated on his map that this was the same river the French called "Rivière Rouge in Louisiana."[22]

Indeed, all the supportive evidence available to the Americans appeared to verify von Humboldt's conclusion that the Red River had its origins in the lofty mountains north of Santa Fe. The French and Spanish residents of Natchitoches had long believed that the river they lived on came from the mountains, not only because of an annual June rise (as if from a snowmelt) but also because the hunters, traders, and Indians who went upriver said it did. There was the testimony of Jean Brevel, for example. Brevel, a respected hunter who had been raised among the Caddos (his father was a French soldier at La Harpe's Post, his mother

---

[21] Miera's map is in Wheat, comp., *Mapping the Trans-mississippi West* 1:108.

[22] By the time the Englishman Robert Coxe was on the Mississippi in 1698, the belief that the Red headed in the New Mexico mountains was general. See B. F. French, *Historical Collections of Louisiana*, p. 227. The confused idea, held by many St. Louis merchants of the period, that the Missouri also headed near the New Mexican settlements, was based upon yet another geographical error about the West—that all of the major Western rivers came down from a "Pyramidal Height" of mountains. See Wheat's first volume for maps demonstrating the cartographic evolution of this idea, and, for a discussion, Allen's "Geographical Knowledge and American Images of the Louisiana Territory."

Von Humboldt's map confused the Red, the Pecos, and the Canadian, but seemed to provide cartographic corroboration that the Red led to Santa Fe. Courtesy Library of the University of Illinois-Urbana Champaign.

On ignore au Nouveau Mexique
sous quel nom le Rio Napestle
est connu plus à l'Est dans la
Louisiane. Seroit-il identique
avec l'Arkansas ?

Plaines immenses ou

Indiens Apaches Llaneros

de Nachitoches ou Rio de Pecos

Indiens Taos

On croit au Nouveau Mexique que la Rivière
qui nait au Nord-Est du Village de Taos et qui
reçoit le Rio Mora, est la même qui, plus à l'Est
dans la Louisiane, est connue sous le nom de la
Rivière Rouge (Red River). Cette dernière melant ses
eaux à celles de la Rivière aux Bœufs et au Black
River, se jette dans le Missisipi au dessous du Fort
Adams.

a Nasoni Caddo), maintained that in the mid-1760s he had actually followed the Red to the crest of the continental divide and visited Santa Fe. Brevel's recollection of this journey, which was almost certainly a fabrication, found its way into the John Sibley Report, forwarded to Jefferson from Natchitoches in 1805.[23] Like-

[23] The Sibley report is widely available, perhaps most accessibly in the *Annals of Congress* for 1805. I have used it here in monograph form, combined with Sibley's "Historical Sketches of the Several Tribes in Louisiana South of the Arkansas River and Between the Mississippi and the River Grand," in Thomas Jefferson, *Message from the President of the United States, Communicating Discoveries Made in Exploring the Missouri, Red River and Washita, by Captains Lewis and Clark, Doctor Sibley and Mr. Dunbar;* hereafter cited as Sibley, "Historical Sketches." The report consists mainly of second-hand information, derived from French-Caddo hunters such as Brevel and François Grappe.

Brevel's story of his journey to Santa Fe via the Red does not at first seem impossible; Athanase de Mézières is known to have dispatched him on long wilderness jaunts to the Arkansas River (see de Mézières to Unzaga y Amezaga, August 21, 1770, Bolton, *Athanase de Mézières* 1:180–81). Church records show that he was the son of Jean Baptiste Brevel, a soldier at La Harpe's Post, and "Anne of the Caddoes." His parents were married in 1736, two months after his birth. Elizabeth Shawn Mills, *Natchitoches, 1729–1803: Abstracts of the Catholic Church Registers of the French and Spanish Post of St. Jean Baptiste des Natchitoches in Louisiana* 2:4, 7. Thus Brevel was reared among the Kadohadachos. He claimed that he made his journey to the Rockies with Indian companions in 1764–65. The dates and his account of the Taovaya village are interesting. It is known from other, sketchy, sources that some time in the late 1760s and early 1770s pressure from the Osages forced the Taovayas to briefly abandon the Cross Timbers site. Brevel says they were fifty leagues higher up the river in the year of his voyage, and de Mézières's note in 1772 that they were "at the foot of a ridge which furnishes this river its chief supply of water" (de Mézières to Amezaga, San Antonio, February 25, 1772, Bolton, ed., *Athanase de Mézières* 1:294) makes me think we are dealing with the North Fork of the Red. Randolph Marcy was later convinced that this tributary had provided the principal upriver route for most of the Indians' ascents of the Red. Yet, several of Brevel's other statements are troubling. Obviously, the North Fork heads on the Llano Estacado, 300 miles from the San Juan Mountains. Even if Brevel had crossed over to the Canadian, its headwaters would not have taken him close to the continental divide. Geographically and (judging from his descriptions of flora and fauna) environmentally, Brevel's account of the Santa Fe area is clearly a fabrication. At the time the Sibley report was published, Father Pichardo doubted that Brevel made the journey upon which Sibley based his upriver account, writing that: ". . . either Doctor Sibley invented it in order to make a show of having knowledge of this river up to its source, or the Frenchman who informed him lied most excessively." I am inclined to believe

wise, the Americans assumed that the expedition of Paul and Pierre Mallet, French traders who had journeyed to Santa Fe as early as 1739 and then descended a reddish-colored river back to civilization was further proof of the Red's upper course.[24]

What Jefferson and other interested savants in the United States could not know, since Stephen Long would not make the discovery until 1820, was that the reddish river flowing east from the Southern Rockies was not the Red, but the Canadian. The main branch of the Red River—Prairie Dog Town Fork—actually takes its sources on the western edges of the Llano Estacado, in eastern New Mexico; the other major upriver tributary, the North Fork, rises in present Carson County in the Texas Panhandle and drains the northern reaches of the great Southwestern plateau. But the most reliable evidence available to Jefferson pointed to the Red's being, like the Missouri, a mountain, plain, and woodland river, a twin to the better-known Arkansas, with the economic advantage of seeming to provide a direct water route to the northern Spanish cities and the diplomatic one of being the most southerly river of the western Mississippi drainage.[25]

There were still other considerations that made the Red an attractive river for a second government exploration. Jefferson

both explanations. See Randolph B. Marcy and G. B. McClellan, *Adventure on Red River: Report on the Exploration of the Headwaters of the Red River by Captain Randolph B. Marcy and Captain G. B. McClellan,* ed. Grant Foreman, pp. xxii, 66; Hackett, ed. and trans., *Pichardo's Treatise* 2:86.

[24] Henry Folmer, "The Mallet Expedition of 1739 Through Nebraska, Kansas and Colorado to Santa Fe," *Colorado Magazine* 16 (September 1939): 161–73. For proof that the Americans thought the Red was the river the Mallets descended, see Anthony Nau's map of 1807, a portion of which is reprinted in this book. The energetic attempts by the French, from St. Denis on, to link Louisiana with New Mexico, and the Spanish attempts to block this drive, are a subject of Elizabeth A. H. John's excellent work, *Storms Brewed in Other Men's Worlds: The Confrontation of Indians, Spanish, and French in the Southwest, 1540–1795.*

[25] James Wilkinson's later report to Dearborn that it was actually the Canadian, not any tributary of the Red, that drained the New Mexico mountains seems not to have had much impact. See Wilkinson to Dearborn, St. Louis, August 25, 1805. Donald Jackson, ed., *The Journals of Zebulon Montgomery Pike: With Letters and Related Documents* 1:233. Wilkinson may have distrusted his own information, since he later told Pike to look for the Red north of Taos.

had always envisioned his explorers as American envoys to the Indian nations of the West, and a diplomatic mission to the very considerable numbers of native inhabitants of what had been Spanish Louisiana was of utmost importance to the takeover and eventual settlement of the province. This was such a vital undertaking that, Jefferson believed, nothing should be spared in carrying it out.

A Diplomatic Tangle

In one important sense, Indian diplomacy was merely a means to an ultimate end, and it provides the first glimmer of the American imperialistic drive later known as Manifest Destiny. The treaty that had turned over Louisiana to the United States had left the boundaries of the province exceedingly vague, stating only that the lines of demarcation were to be the same as they were when France had controlled Louisiana. Since French officials had never assumed the direction of Louisiana after the San Ildefonso treaty, researchers had to pore through the seventeenth- and eighteenth-century documents to determine what limits had previously been agreed upon by France and Spain. And that led to confusion, dispute, and differing interpretations that France made little attempt to resolve.[26]

Lacking any treaty-defined specifications for boundaries, Jefferson decided to create some. Shortly following the Purchase, he attempted to alleviate his ignorance of the geography and extent of Louisiana by sending a list of seventeen questions (including several on boundaries) to important figures in the Southwest.[27] From the replies he received he learned that the geog-

[26] The ambiguity of the treaty of transfer regarding boundaries sent not only Americans but also Spaniards scurrying to the archives. Texas officials voiced repeated pleas to their counterparts in the clergy for documentary enlightenment on the previous boundaries between Spain and France. Father Pichardo's *Treatise on the Limits of Louisiana and Texas* is the most important result of those studies.

[27] The seventeen questions are listed in Paul L. Ford, ed., *The Works of Thomas Jefferson*, 10:17–19.

raphy of Louisiana was almost unknown, but that none of the frontier figures he queried favored extending a claim on the southwestern border beyond the Sabine River. From his sumptuous plantation, "The Forest"—soon to be the headquarters of Southwestern exploration—William Dunbar was disposed toward establishing the boundary at the Arroyo Hondo, a less significant stream to be sure, but one which the French and the Spaniards had utilized as a boundary before, even affixing leaden plate markers to the trees there. Dunbar thought the boundary should run from there northward to the Red, and thence westward along it to the "Northern Andes."[28]

Jefferson perused these letters with interest, but their conclusions were contrary to his own convictions, arrived at through independent study in his library. In researching and accumulating material for a pamphlet he would call, "The Limits and Bounds of Louisiana," Jefferson convinced himself that the French had settled all the Gulf coast from the Perdido River to the "Bravo" (the Río Grande) during their exploration and occupation of Louisiana, and that none of the subsequent treaties had abridged that claim.[29] If Louisiana were to enjoy the same boundaries under United States dominion as had been established by the French, then Jefferson thought the Río Grande should be the western boundary, and that West Florida and a large portion of Texas should be included in the Louisiana Purchase.

The disagreements over both eastern and western boundaries of Louisiana sent James Monroe to join Charles Pinckney in Spain, in hopes of securing a convention with terms the two nations could agree upon. The Americans made their initial offer in April of 1804, expressing a willingness to erect a "district of neutral territory" between the Sabine and Colorado rivers northward to the Missouri and to "the most southwesterly source of the Red River," in exchange for Spanish recognition that West Florida

---

[28] Isaac J. Cox, "The Louisiana-Texas Frontier," *Southwestern Historical Quarterly*, 17 (October 1913), pt. 2, pp. 7–8.
[29] Thomas Jefferson, "The Limits and Bounds of Louisiana," in *Documents Relating to the Purchase and Exploration of Louisiana*, pp. 7–45.

was part of Louisiana.[30] Although the French foreign secretary let it be known that France had never so considered West Florida, in January of 1805 the American negotiators submitted to Spanish negotiator Pedro Cevallos a seven-point convention proposal that now envisioned West Florida being exchanged for a neutral territory stretching from the Colorado River north to the headwaters of the Red, and west to the Río Grande.[31] Cevallos's reply to this offer was hardly encouraging. Not only would Spain not relinquish West Florida, but the American claim that half of Texas was clearly hers, he wrote, was "absurd reasoning! which does not merit to be refuted."[32]

Jefferson's claim of Texas was ill-founded, at best; at worst it was undisguised imperialism. It exaggerated La Salle's importance in Texas (his colony, after all, had been an accidental and transient one) while ignoring the more dominant Spanish occupation. Yet, it had the virtue of placing the United States in a good compromise position vis-a-vis the boundary. The Río Grande was not a tenable boundary designation, nor was the Colorado of central Texas, but advocating them rendered the Red—where the French claim was much stronger—a palatable selection for Spain. Thus the Red River became the focal point of nationalistic interest in the Louisiana-Texas border country, ensuring that the geography of the river would be defined by diplomacy, politics, statutes, and legal decisions even into the twentieth-century border dispute between Texas and Oklahoma.

In order to overcome the handicap of unfamiliarity the United States would have in the inevitable boundary dispute with Spain, Jefferson sought to provide the American diplomats with correct geographical information through extensive scientific exploration

[30] Charles Pinckney and James Monroe to Pedro Cevallos, Aranjuez, [Spain], April 15, 1804. *Annals of Congress*, 8th Cong., 2d sess. (1805), pp. 1338-39.

[31] Maurice de Talleyrand to Pinckney and Monroe, Paris, December 21, 1804; Pinckney and Monroe to Cevallos, Aranjuez, January 5, 1805, enclosing a seven-point convention proposal, ibid., pp. 1359-60, 1364-74.

[32] Cevallos to Messrs. Pinckney and Monroe, Aranjuez, February 24, 1805. Ibid., p. 1391.

of the West.[33] If each of his exploring parties took careful astronomical observations along the major drainage systems and at their sources, it would be possible to arrive at a boundary solution logically based on hydrography and other natural features. If all the tributaries of the Mississippi were a part of Louisiana (as the Americans claimed), then a scientific survey of the Red could not fail to aid the American delegates in defining the boundary at the conference table.[34]

Simultaneously with Jefferson's activity toward setting the Southwestern exploration in motion in the spring of 1804, the Spanish government was beginning to take measures of its own concerning the Louisiana question. In April of that year the Council for the Fortification and Defense of the Indies produced as clear a definition of the Spanish interpretation of the boundary as was then possible. The international border, the Royal Council decided, was marked by a line beginning at the Gulf between the Calcasieu and "Armenta" (Attoyac) rivers, thence north to "the vicinity of Natchitoches as far as the Red River or Colorado." More specifically, it believed the western limit of Louisiana ought to be a line running through Los Adaes directly north to the Red. This was, in fact, in keeping with the line drawn by the French geographer Jean Baptiste Bourguignon d'Anville in the mid-eighteenth century. In upper Louisiana the Royal Council outdid Jefferson's claim to Texas, asserting that "without doubt" Spanish domains should extend north from the Red to the far bank of the Missouri. Until these limits were definitely set, the Council cautioned, the Americans should not be allowed on the Western rivers, whether to mark the boundaries or on any other pretext.[35] The Spanish officials distrusted the Americans on the boundary issue, for they believed that despite its libertarian principles, the young American Republic was expansionist at heart. This attitude

---

[33] Cox, "The Louisiana-Texas Frontier," pt. 2, pp. 18–21.

[34] Ibid., pt. 3, p. 140.

[35] The royal council's decision was communicated to the commandants of the Provincias Internas in a letter from Andrés Lopes Armesto, Chihuahua, April 22, 1804, The Bexar Archives, in the Barker Texas History Center of the Sid Richardson Library, The University of Texas-Austin.

would soon be exacerbated by American newspaper reports, several of them forwarded anonymously to Texas officials, that the United States was ready to go to war over the boundaries issue.[36]

SPAIN REACTS

Spain was not long in discovering the nature of America's immediate intentions in the Southwest. In the early summer of 1804, the Marqués de Caso Calvo, one-time governor of Louisiana and now Spain's commissioner to settle the boundary question, wrote Juan Bautista de Elguezabal, the governor of Texas, that secretly he had learned that Jefferson was on the verge of sending parties to the Red, Arkansas, and "San Francisco" (St. Francis) rivers for exploratory, cartographic, mineral seeking, and diplomatic purposes. "This daring undertaking" ought to be easy to frustrate, he wrote, if Spain was willing to "divert and even to destroy such expeditions." The source of Caso Calvo's information introduces into the story of the Red River exploration an element that from the beginning ties the enterprise to one of the most ambitious schemes of that revolutionary age. For in this first communication between Spanish officials concerning the exploration, Caso Calvo noted that the Spaniards were being aided

[36] On more than half a dozen occasions between 1804 and 1806, American newspaper clippings on the probable event of a war with Spain over the boundaries of Louisiana and West Florida were forwarded anonymously to Texas officials. Samuel Davenport, a Pennsylvanian who had come to the border country about 1780, was the source of at least one of these mailings (Davenport to Texas Governor Don Juan Bautista de Elguezabal, Nacogdoches, July 6, 1804, Ibid.), but there were many others. Davenport had good reason to warn the Spaniards in 1804. Since 1800, he and William Barr, another naturalized Spanish citizen from Pennsylvania, had been commissioned by the Texas government as traders to the Indian tribes of the border country. The coming of the Americans would undercut their position. Like that of most early Anglos in the Spanish provinces, Davenport's love for the crown was a fleeting thing, and mostly of a pecuniary nature. In 1812 he would join the Magee-Menchaca-Gutierrez filibuster as a captain, leading Spanish authorities to offer a reward of 250 pesos for his head. Walter P. Webb, H. Bailey Carroll, et al., *Handbook of Texas* 1:113, 467; J. Villasana Haggard, "The House of Barr and Davenport," *Southwestern Historical Quarterly* 49 (July 1945): 66–88. Sources of the other clippings and warnings are discussed below.

by an anonymous informant whose version of events New Spain officials "will believe . . . implicitly since it is true."[37] The source of this "leak" to Caso Calvo was undoubtedly Daniel Clark of New Orleans, a former clerk in the office of the Spanish governor and a long-time intermediary between Spain and American general James Wilkinson. Unknown to Spanish officials, however, Clark was also a guiding spirit in the so-called "Mexican Association," whose goal was the "liberation" of Texas and Mexico, and, as such, a principal in Wilkinson's evolving Southwestern schemes.[38]

If Caso Calvo knew at once, probably with urging from his American informants, how to deal with a Jeffersonian probe into the Southwest, most other officials on the scene were not so sure. Manuel Salcedo, the ninth and last Spanish governor of Louisiana, is a case in point. After learning of the American plan in the late summer of 1804, he wrote to his superiors in confusion:

> . . . with great activity and care [the Americans] are sending expeditions to the Upper Mississippi, Missouri, Arkansas and Red Rivers in order to reconnoitre their sources and courses, examine the lands, and attract and conciliate the Indian nations to them, which with study and with cautious skill they will separate from our friendship. . . . In this situation we find ourselves perplexed and confused without knowing what action to take. . . . [39]

Texas governor Bautista likewise seemed less than confident about

---

[37] Caso Calvo to Bautista, New Orleans, June 17, 1804, The Bexar Archives.

[38] Wilkinson apparently first learned of Jefferson's desire to explore the Red and Arkansas rivers in a letter from Dearborn posted from Washington, March 31, 1804. Clarence E. Carter, ed., *The Territory of Orleans, 1803–1812*, vol. 9 of *The Territorial Papers of the United States*, p. 217. This would have reached him in New York by mid-April.

Born in Ireland, Clark had come to New Orleans in 1786, where he became a clerk in the office of the Spanish governor. It was his actions as intermediary between Wilkinson and the Spanish government that first caused Andrew Ellicott, the American boundary commissioner in 1798, to suspect that Wilkinson was a Spanish agent. In 1805, Wilkinson wrote to Clark a letter of introduction for Aaron Burr with the lines: "To him I refer you for many things improper to a letter, and which he will not say to any other." Quoted in Thomas Perkins Abernethy, *The Burr Conspiracy*, p. 28.

[39] Manuel Salcedo to Pedro Cevallos, New Orleans, August 20, 1804. In A. P.

Spain's right to stop all American examinations of Southwestern rivers. According to his information, the sources and mouth of the Arkansas River lay within the bounds of Louisiana, and there Spain had no grounds for interference. But while the Americans now owned the Red River's mouth, Spain was in clear possession of its sources, and in his opinion "any expedition to the Colorado [Red] would be a hostile act."[40] Thus was introduced into Jefferson's southern exploration a crucial element—the disinclination (and inability) of Spanish officials to regard the Arkansas with the same paranoia they attached to the Red. This attitude could have been utilized to advantage by the Americans. For some reason it was not.

The Spaniards were sensitive about the Red, no question, and as events unfolded between 1804 and 1806, several interrelated reasons emerged. For one thing, Texas officials were convinced that when the "inevitable war" with the Americans came, the Red River would furnish one of the primary avenues of attack against the Provincias Internas.[41] But even if there was not a war, a prestigious government expedition up the Red would inevitably put the Americans in touch with two of the most populous, powerful, and difficult to control nations on the Southern Plains—the various bands of the Taovaya-Wichitas and the Comanches. Because of their martial strength and the value of their goodwill and trade, Spanish officials perceived an American exchange with those Indians as repugnant to their own interests.

Their suspicions about the Indian nations were not unfounded, of course. Early in 1804, Jefferson had appointed as "occasional"

Nasatir, ed., *Before Lewis and Clark: Documents Illustrating the History of the Missouri, 1785-1804* 2:745-50.

[40] Bautista to Caso Calvo, San Antonio, August 4, 1804, The Bexar Archives.

[41] Antonio Cordero to Nemecio Salcedo, San Antonio, October 23, 1805, ibid. In this supposition they were wrong. After arriving at St. Louis, Wilkinson wrote Henry Dearborn that the Arkansas River was the best avenue for an invasion, and that with "a Corps of 100 Artillerists, 400 Cavalry, 400 Riflemen and 1100 Musquetry" the United States could "take possession of the Northern Provinces without opposition." Wilkinson to Dearborn, St. Louis, Sept. 8, 1805, Jackson, *The Journals of Zebulon Montgomery Pike* 2:100-102.

agent to the Louisiana Indians an energetic New England physician named John Sibley. Sibley, a native of Great Barrington, Massachusetts, had started families in both Massachusetts and South Carolina before drifting to Natchitoches shortly after the cession. Introduced to Jefferson by W. C. C. Claiborne and asked to report what he knew of the Red River and the Indians of the border country, the dynamic Sibley so impressed Jefferson that the president gave him a full-time appointment in 1805, and secured an appropriation from Congress for several thousand dollars worth of trade goods for Sibley's use in winning over the tribes of the area.[42] Through the Caddo chief Dehahuit, the Americans learned that the Taovaya-Wichitas, under the leadership of their "great chief," Awahakei, were dissatisfied with Spanish trade, especially with the trading house of Barr and Davenport in Nacogdoches. They wanted contact with the Americans, and Sibley was equally determined to re-establish the old sphere of influence emanating from Natchitoches. From there, the Spaniards learned, Sibley hoped to license American traders who would not only undersell the Spaniards, but also renew the old exchange of guns for mustangs and pelts. Provincias Internas's commandant, Don Nemecio Salcedo, was adamant on the issue: the machinations of "a revolutionist, the friend of change," Doctor Sikbley, had to be stopped, for the Americans would surely win the Indians with presents and then buy their lands.[43]

[42] Biographical data on John Sibley are from G. P. Whittington, "Dr. John Sibley Of Natchitoches, 1757-1837," *Louisiana Historical Quarterly* 10 (October 1927): 467-73. Sibley was aggressive as the American Indian agent for the Southwestern border country until his removal for political reasons in 1815. Later he served in the Louisiana State Senate and as parish judge in Natchitoches. His families contained prominent sons, including George Sibley and Henry Sibley. Dr. Sibley left a voluminous and colorful correspondence, the compilations of which are utilized here.

[43] The quote is in Cox, "The Louisiana-Texas Frontier," Pt. 3, p. 161. For an additional Spanish response to Sibley, see Dionisio Valle to Juan Bautista, Nacogdoches, June 19, 1805, The Bexar Archives. The Taovaya-Wichita sent their first request for an American trader in 1804. Edward D. Turner to W. C. C. Claiborne, Natchitoches, November 21, 1804, in Carter, ed., *The Territory of Orleans, 1803-1812*, pp. 335-37.

Such concerns had worried Spanish officials ever since the Americans acquired simultaneously their independence and the east bank of the Mississippi, but shortly before the cession of Louisiana there had been an escalation of anxiety. The individual most responsible for this change was young Philip Nolan, a talented contraband trader and gunrunner who, between 1790 and 1799, had made four forays from Natchez into Spanish Texas. Nolan established contact with the Taovaya-Wichitas and Comanches, providing them with an initial, very favorable impression of Anglo-Americans, and furthermore, his expeditions carried him widely across the Southwest. Ostensibly interested only in catching or trading for mustangs—the feral descendants of the Arabian and Barb stock of the early Spaniards that had become a major component of the grasslands ecology and Indian lifeway of the Southern Plains—Nolan also made notes and maps on his journeys, and he freely talked about the Southwest to his mentor, General Wilkinson, and to other Americans like William Dunbar and Andrew Ellicott.

For Jefferson, Nolan promised to be an invaluable contact. An initial letter was sent in 1798, expressing interest in information on the Texas mustangs at "the only moment in the age of the world," as Jefferson put it, when the horse could be studied in its wild state. Jefferson's avowed interest in purchasing one of Nolan's "fine animals for the saddle, which I am told are so remarkable for the singularity & beauty of their colors & forms," finally led to a scheduled interview with "the Mexican traveller" in the summer of 1800. We now know that it was an interview that never took place. Although Nolan departed for Monticello with a fine paint stallion as a gift for the future president, he got only as far as Lexington before turning back to mount a fifth (and final) expedition into Texas. The Spaniards now suspected, probably correctly, that Nolan was gathering information for the United States, and early in March, 1801, Lieutenant Miguel Músquiz and a Spanish cavalry surrounded Nolan's camp on the Grand

Prairie, killed him, and captured more than half his party, although nearly a dozen Americans escaped.[44]

The knowledge Nolan had gathered did not die with him. His Southwestern guide and travelling companion, an expert in Indian sign language, seems to have been Joseph Lucas, later employed as a guide for Jefferson's Southwestern expedition. And Nolan's maps and discoveries would eventually find their way, via Wilkinson, into Jefferson's hands. One priceless piece of information in them, which Wilkinson placed before "the Presidential Eye" in mid-1804, was about the headwaters of the Red River:

About 20 leagues above these Tawayashos [the Taovaya-Wichita location] the Red River forks, the right descending from the Northward, and the left from the westward. . . . it appears that the right branch is appreciated to the Osage River, and takes its source west of a Ridge of mountains, in the East side of which the Arkansas and Ouichita or Black River head.

The left branch which is reputed the longest is said to have its source in the East side of a height, the top of which presents an open plain, so extensive as to require the Indians four days in crossing it, and so destitute of water, as to oblige them to transport their drink in the preserved

---

[44]"[Documents] Concerning Philip Nolan," *Quarterly of the Texas State Historical Association* 7 (April 1904): 308–17. Only twenty when he made his first Texas expedition, Nolan was described by an intelligent and perceptive contemporary as: "That extraordinary and enterprising Man . . . whom Nature seems to have formed for Enterprises of which the rest of Mankind are incapable." Daniel Clark, Jr., to Jefferson, New Orleans, June 12, 1799, in the above cited collection. In a letter of introduction, dated May 22, 1800, which Nolan was supposed to deliver to Jefferson, Wilkinson implied that "the Mexican traveller" had been reared in his household; the young mustanger thus came by his interest in the Spanish lands from an obvious source. Following the lead of Isaac J. Cox, Loomis and Nasatir assert in *Pedro Vial and the Roads to Santa Fe*, p. 215, that Nolan did meet with Jefferson. A careful examination of the documents in The Thomas Jefferson Papers, 1st ser., for May through November, 1800, induces me to a contrary opinion. Wilkinson's letter introducing Nolan to Jefferson did not arrive at Monticello until November, by which date we know that Nolan and his two dozen associates on the last expedition were already across the Mississippi, bound for Texas. I believe that while in Lexington Nolan sold the stallion he was taking as a gift to Jefferson. The best readily available treatment of Nolan's career remains chapter 9 in Loomis and Nasatir, cited above. On Nolan's last activities in Texas, see Loomis's slightly updated, "Philip Nolan's Entry in Texas in 1800," in John F. McDermott, ed., *The Spanish in the Mississippi Valley, 1762-1804*, pp. 120–33.

entrails of beasts of the Forests—west of this high plain my informants report certain waters which run to the Southward/ probably those of the Rio Bravo/ and beyond these they report a ridge of high mountains extending North and South.[45]

Despite the confusion over the mountains, this was the most precise information Jefferson was to receive respecting the sources of the Red River. Coupled with the Brevel report and other evidence, its accurate representation of the Llano Estacado, whose existence had not even been imagined by the Americans, no doubt convinced the administration that the North Fork of the Red was the correct highway to the Rockies.

Nolan was dead, but he had become what Spanish officials feared he might—an example to other would-be American traders on the frontier. The first to follow Nolan into the Southwest was a solitary hunter named Sanders. In the autumn of 1803 he ascended the Red to the Taovaya-Wichitas, spent a successful winter trading with them, but was almost caught by a patrol of 152 troops commanded by Músquiz. The Spanish officer was actually looking for a party of Americans led by Robert Ashley and John House, both of whom had escaped in the Nolan episode. Ashley was a dangerous individual, known to have been involved in plots against Spanish possessions, but he had no intention of emulating Nolan's fate. Upon learning of the Spanish reaction, the Ashley and House expedition of 1803–1804 had been called off.

A pattern was emerging, however. In May, 1804, Spanish officials learned that yet another party of American traders had departed from Natchitoches on horseback en route to the upper Red River country. José Ignacio Ybarbo was dispatched from the Nacogdoches garrison with a small detachment to stop them, but failed to do so. These Americans, led by Alexandro Dauni and John Davis, supposedly penetrated to "the mountains" (from the evidence, the Wichita Mountains), where they found what they

[45]Wilkinson to Dearborn, Washington, July 13, 1804, War Department, Letters Received, Main Series, The National Archives. Based upon his later references to New Mexico and to travelling with the Comanches on the upper Red River, Nolan must have made the journey whence this information is derived in the mid-1790s.

assumed to be silver ore, before returning to spend the winter of 1804–1805 near the Taovaya-Wichitas. Following their return, in the spring of 1805, Sibley sent what the Red River tribes called his first "messenger" to them when he licensed John House to lead a seven-man party into the hinterland. On behalf of the United States, Sibley sent presents to the Indians by House, and asked him to urge the interior tribes to visit him in Natchitoches. During these same years at least three traders setting out from American territory—Baptiste La Lande, Laurent Durocher, and James Purcell—made it all the way to Santa Fe.[46]

The American traders were actually only part of the problem for Spanish officials, although their presence was probably catalytic. The larger issue at stake was the continued allegiance of the tribes of the north. The Spaniards had cause for apprehension here, for their relations, as we have seen, had never been good with one tribe the Southwestern traders invariably were interested in: the Taovaya-Wichitas, or "Panis," as the Americans called them.

The Taovayas and their affiliated Wichita bands were actually Caddoan peoples who, like the other prairie Caddoans, the Aricaras of the Missouri and the Pawnees of the Platte and Loup

[46] This overview sketch of the pre-exploration trading frontier on the Red River comes from the introduction to my *Journal of an Indian Trader: Anthony Glass and the Texas Trading Frontier, 1790-1810* (College Station: Texas A&M University Press, 1985). Original documentation on these early American traders is principally from letters between Spanish frontier officials in The Bexar Archives, 1804–1805, and (in the case of Sanders) from Turner to Claiborne, Natchitoches, July 16, 1804, in Dunbar Rowland, ed., *Official Letter-books of W. C. C. Claiborne, 1801–1816* 2:31–33. On the New Mexico traders, see David Weber, *The Taos Trappers*, pp. 36–37.

Robert Ashley was related by marriage to William and George Rogers Clark, and had come to Natchez from South Carolina in the 1790s. Under Spanish interrogation in 1795, he had admitted that the older Clark had offered him a captaincy in the force that Citizen Edmund Genet of France tried to raise to invade Spanish possessions in the West. The interrogation is printed in J. F. H. Claiborne, *Mississippi as a Province, Territory and State, with Biographical Notices of Eminent Citizens*, pp. 152–53n. Ashley seems to have been one of Wilkinson's principals in the Southwestern conspiracy, and to have helped Aaron Burr escape from Washington, Mississippi Territory, following the collapse of the conspiracy in the winter of 1806–1807. Abernethy, *The Burr Conspiracy*, pp. 219, 223.

Fork, had taken their corn-squash culture onto the Great Plains thousands of years before. Their location, a fortified site strategically placed at the head of navigation on the Red, in a beautiful valley where the western Cross Timbers blended into the Great Plains, dated from 1757. By the first decade of the nineteenth century there were three villages of grass-covered lodges there, housing a total population of some two thousand souls. Pivotal villages in the Southwest, well-stocked with vegetables, bison meat, and rich in horses and mules, they were the final launching point for penetrations into the Comanchería, a vital link between Louisiana and New Mexico. Both Vial and Mares had made them crucial way-stations on their Natchitoches to Santa Fe trails; in 1778 de Mézières had perceptively called them the "master-key of the North."[47]

[47] De Mézières to Theodoro Croix, Taovayas Villages, April 18, 1778, in Bolton, *Athanase de Mézières* 2:201–204. The first European contact with these Indians was made by Coronado when they were living on the Great Bend of the Arkansas River, in present Kansas. It was the French, however, who established trading ties with them, following a visit to their villages on the Canadian River by La Harpe in 1719. Over the next decades, reacting to pressures on the north from the Osages, and probably to encouragement from the French traders and their Caddo allies, the Taovaya, Wichita, Tawakoni, and other prairie Caddoans migrated to the Red and Brazos rivers, displacing the Athapascan-speaking Apaches. When Parilla was defeated at their Red River village in 1759, they were flying a French flag and were assisted by a dozen or more French traders. Only through entreaty, threats, and the active support of the great cacique of the Caddos, Tinhioüen the Peacemaker, was de Mézières able to win these Norteños to Spain during the 1770s.

Modern archaeological work has fixed the location of their Red River site at the junction of 33° 59′ N. latitude and 97° 36′ W. longitude, in present Jefferson County, Oklahoma, and Montague County, Texas. Both the numbers and sizes of the villages here varied over time. In 1805–1806 there were three villages: the principal Taovaya village on the northeast bank was the home of the "great chief" of the nation, Awahakei, while the south bank harbored two adjoining villages of Wichitas and Taovayas, whose chiefs during the exploration period were Iras Coques and Kittsita Cammenuo. The best first-hand account of these villages during the first decade of the nineteenth century is Anthony Glass, "Copy of a journal of a voyage from Nackitosh into the interior of Louisiana on the waters of Red River, Trinity, Brassos, Colorado & the Sabine performed between the first of July 1808 & May 1809," Silliman Family Collection, Yale University Library, Historical Manuscripts Division. The most reliable secondary study of these Indians remains Elizabeth A. (Harper) John's

Disputes between Texas and Louisiana officials over trade jurisdiction during the 1780s had produced a ban on the traditional Taovaya-Wichita trade with Natchitoches, and Spanish trade since then had been highly unsatisfactory. The coming of American traders promised a decided upturn in Taovaya-Wichita fortunes, and at the same time paved the way for the eventual generous treatment of a party of American explorers, possibly even for an American post among them. The Jefferson administration was extremely desirous of establishing official relations with these Indians for yet another reason: their Comanche allies would have to be placated before penetration into the territory and trade with New Mexico could result, and all agreed this task could be most readily accomplished "through the Panis."[48]

It so happened that in 1804, just as the Spaniards were growing increasingly concerned over foreign traders, a Taovaya hunting party got into a scrap with a Spanish patrol and nine were killed. The Taovayas were furious over this outrage, and their increasing friendliness with the Americans, particularly coupled with Sibley's overtures from Natchitoches, seemed portentous to Spanish officials. The situation was most serious, for in the event of a war, the Taovaya-Wichitas themselves could muster more than four hundred warriors, and their defection might sway some of the bands whose good will Spain had to retain in order to hold Texas — the numerous and fearsome Comanches.

Accordingly, in the summer of 1805, Antonio Cordero y Bustamante, the new, highly popular, but impulsive fifty-year-old gov-

"The Taovayas Indians in Frontier Trade and Diplomacy, 1719–1835," in three parts: (I), *The Chronicles of Oklahoma* 31 (1952); (II), *Southwestern Historical Quarterly* 57 (1952); (III), *Panhandle-Plains Historical Review* 26 (1953). On diplomacy, however, see Ralph Smith, "The Tawehash in French, Spanish, English and American Imperial Affairs," *West Texas Historical Association Year Book* 28 (1952). Recent archaeological study of the location, known as the Longest and Upper Tucker sites, is covered in a series of papers in Robert E. Bell, Edward B. Jelks, and W. W. Newcomb, *A Pilot Study of Wichita Indian Archeology and Ethnohistory.*

[48] Louis de Blanc advised the Natchitoches traders that the Taovayas and other tribes beyond the Caddos were off-limits to them in, "Notice to the

ernor of Texas, treated with delegates of the Norteños, to hear grievances and make amends. Aricara, a subchief of the Tawakoni division, made a lyrical speech in which he admitted that traders from Natchitoches had of late ventured up the Colorado and other rivers to the north, to and beyond their villages, to trade guns, powder, and other items for horses and hides. These they had not realized were of a different nation, he said, and he promised Cordero that he would go to the villages "toward the proposed end of undeceiving their inhabitants of the error which they were in. . . ."[49] Little came of it. The Taovaya-Wichitas continued to be "faithless," as the Spaniards put it.

It was not a good time to be experiencing troubles with major Indian allies, for to the Spaniards, every sign indicated that the Americans were preparing to invade Texas. When the "inevitable war" came, it was imperative that Spain have the Taovaya-Wichitas and Comanches, if no others, at her side. Thus, in the winter of 1805–1806, Sergeant Mariano Rodriguez was dispatched to the Comanchería to affirm the continued allegiance of the Comanche bands. Rodriguez returned in March to announce that the Comanche bands were firmly behind the king.[50] But New Spain officials did not relax, and when they discovered that the American president was determined to send a large government expedition up the Red River, directly into the heart of Taovaya-Wichita and Comanche country, they were prepared to believe the worst.

Public, Natchitoches, June 24, 1788," in Lawrence Kinnaird, ed., *Spain in the Mississippi Valley, 1765–1794* 2:256. On the "Panis" as intermediaries to the Comanches, see Wilkinson to Dearborn, St. Louis, September 8, 1805. Jackson, *The Journals of Zebulon Montgomery Pike* 2:100–102.

[49] Cordero to Salcedo, San Antonio, November 24, 1805. The Bexar Archives. Zebulon Pike described Cordero in 1807 as about five feet and ten inches tall, with a fair complexion, blue eyes, and a firm physique. Widely-read, he was at ease with both Latin and French, and was "one of the select officers who had been chosen by the court of Madrid to be sent to America about 35 years since to discipline and organize the Spanish provincials." Pike asserted that he was the most beloved, respected, and popular man in the Provincias Internas. Jackson, *The Journals of Zebulon Montgomery Pike*, entry for June 13, 1807, 1: 439–40. Additional information on Cordero may be found in Félix de Almaráz, Jr., *Tragic Cavalier: Governor Manuel Salcedo of Texas, 1808–1813*, pp. 26–28.

[50] Cordero to Salcedo, San Antonio, March 12, 1806. The Bexar Archives.

DUNBAR AND A "TRIAL RUN"

While the Lewis and Clark party was engaged in its tortuous 1,600-mile ascent of the Missouri to the Mandan villages in the spring and summer of 1804, in Washington, Jefferson was making the final plans for his Southwestern expedition. Early in the spring he had approached Dunbar with a suggestion. Given his expertise and the proximity of his home to the mouth of the Red, might not the Mississippi scientist consent to taking over the direction of the tour? Dunbar expressed a ready willingness to do so, insofar as it was understood that he would only direct, as Jefferson's representative, and not be a participant.[51]

Along with Dunbar, the president had also managed to enlist a second scientist for the expedition. He was Dr. George Hunter, a forty-nine-year-old native of Edinburgh, Scotland, who was a druggist and chemist in Philadelphia. Hunter's specialties were chemistry and mineralogy, and although Jefferson was skeptical that he might want to turn the exploration into a prospecting tour for gold and silver, he himself wrote of the man that, "in the practical branch of that science [chemistry] he has probably no equal in the US."[52] With luck and shrewd maneuvering, Jefferson had also secured from Congress three thousand dollars for the expedition—not an excess of financing, to be sure, but better than the original twenty-five hundred dollars appropriated for the Lewis and Clark probe. Finally, at home in Monticello, on April 14, the president sat down and composed a seven-page letter of classic exploration instructions to the as-yet-unnamed leader of his second expedition into the West. The text of this letter is included in Appendix 1, page 319, below.

The next step was the obvious one. There was no second Meriwether Lewis, personally selected by Jefferson to conduct just the sort of survey he wanted, and from the difficulty both he and Dunbar experienced in finding an explorer, apparently there

---

[51] Dunbar frequently experienced ill health.

[52] Jefferson to Dunbar, Monticello, April 15, 1804. The Thomas Jefferson Papers, 1st ser.

existed in America few men who could combine leadership qualities, the requisite scientific education, *and* a woodsman's physique. Jefferson apparently broached the subject to several of his correspondents and friends at the Philosophical Society. Andrew Ellicott, an eccentric and argumentative surveyor and mathematician who nonetheless enjoyed a sterling professional reputation, suggested to Jefferson either Peter Walker, or a Mr. Gillespie, both of whom had worked with Ellicott on the 1798–99 boundary survey between the United States and West Florida. Dunbar regarded either as a good choice, Gillespie possessing the better mathematical education, but Walker—who was destined for a rather amazing career in the Southwest—being the better qualified by way of superior natural genius. Unfortunately, however, neither was available.[53] With a view towards the Spanish reac-

[53] Dunbar to Jefferson, Natchez, May 13, 1804, Rowland, *Dunbar Letters*, pp. 130–33. Gillespie was a native of North Carolina and, assisted by Walker and Andy Ellicott, became Andrew Ellicott's surveyor after Thomas Freeman was dismissed from the Spanish boundary survey in 1798. Andrew Ellicott, *The Journal of Andrew Ellicott*, p. 178. Walker was the son of a Scotch-Irish family that came to North Carolina before 1790. His father became a minister and the headman of a classical academy there and, by 1794, a professor at the University of North Carolina. After his son moved to the Southwest, the elder Walker studied law, and he came to the Mississippi Territory in 1800, where he secured an appointment as Adams County clerk and later a judicial post. The son, meanwhile, had secured an appointment as assistant to Territorial Secretary John Steele, where he translated Spanish documents. Walker's appointment, dated January 3, 1800, appears in Carter, ed., *The Territory of Mississippi, 1798–1817*, vols. 5 and 6 of *The Territorial Papers of the United States* 5:258–59. According to his testimony to Pike during the latter's incarceration in Chihuahua, some mistreatment of his father at Natchez had determined the younger Walker to forsake America and join the Spanish service. Whether independently or by instruction, in 1804 he was planning to ascend the Red River to Santa Fe, for Dunbar wrote him a lengthy letter of scientific questions on the region. See Dunbar to Peter Walker, Natchez, June 10, 1804, Rowland, *Dunbar Letters*, pp. 135–37; Claiborne, *Mississippi as a Province, Territory and State*, pp. 224, 231n.; Juan Ugarte to Juan Elguezabal, Nacogdoches, September 2, 1803. The Bexar Archives.

As "Don Juan Pedro" Walker, in 1805, Walker prepared two maps of the Southwest which Salcedo would eventually offer to the Americans to satisfy their curiosity about the Red. These two manuscript maps, obviously made as a consequence of his ascent of the rivers in 1804–1805, follow Vial in their general confusion of the North Fork of the Red and the Canadian, but they

William Dunbar. Courtesy Library of Congress.

tion, Dunbar suggested that Stephen Minor, an American who had worked on the boundary survey for the Spanish government, might be a "better leader."[54]

Although Jefferson would have liked for the Southwestern exploration to follow closely on the heels of the departure of Lewis and Clark, spring ran into summer, and little progress had been made toward a launch date. Hunter did not arrive in Natchez until July 24, where he discovered that Dunbar had made virtually no headway in readying the expedition. By August 25, after a trip to New Orleans to obtain supplies and have the boat he had brought from Pittsburg caulked and waterproofed, Hunter at last had the tour outfitted and ready—and on that day a letter arrived from Jefferson, postponing the "Grand Expedition" until the following spring.[55]

There had really been no other choice. Not only did the expedition still lack a leader, it had already become the subject of a ban by the Spanish government. Casa d' Yrujo, the Spanish minister in Washington, had flatly refused to issue a passport for the exploring party, and Nemecio Salcedo, the Commandant of the Internal Provinces stationed at Chihuahua, had followed up that setback with a proclamation prohibiting the Americans from launching a boundary reconnaisance. Furthermore, there was a

---

prove that Walker traversed the country. They are discussed in Wheat, *Mapping the Transmississippi West* 1:131. At the time of the Freeman and Custis expedition, Walker was a lieutenant in the Dragoons and headmaster of a military academy at Chihuahua. A friend of Melgares, he may have been on the expedition from Santa Fe to capture the Red River party. Later, he performed other survey work for the Spaniards and prepared a map showing many features of the West Coast in 1817. Most of what is known of his Spanish service is in Pike's journal entries for March and April of 1807, when he was quartered with Walker in Chihuahua. See Jackson, *The Journals of Zebulon Montgomery Pike* 1:413-24.

[54] Dunbar to Jefferson, Natchez, May 13, 1804, Rowland, *Dunbar Letters*, pp. 130-33. It is worth noting that Minor entertained Burr at his home in Natchez in 1805, and that despite his history of service to the Crown, he was denied his request to settle in Texas as a Spanish citizen.

[55] John Francis McDermott, ed., "The Western Journals of Dr. George Hunter, 1796-1805," *Transactions of the American Philosophical Society* 53 (1963): 10-11.

Dr. George Hunter's sketch of his "Chinese" boat, which failed miserably in the trial run up the Ouachita. Courtesy Library of the American Philosophical Society.

possible crisis with the Osages, whose good will any exploring party that visited the Southwest, particularly the Arkansas River, would have to have. An Osage delegation—the first Western Indians the Americans had ever seen—had appeared in Washington in July. Their great chief, White Hair I (Paw-Hiu-Skah) entreated Jefferson to suspend the expedition, warning that the disaffected Arkansas band led by Great Track (Big Track, Makes-Tracks-Going-Far-Away, or Cashesegra) would surely harass it. That became the final argument convincing Jefferson to postpone the exploration.[56]

During the month of July, Jefferson and Dunbar had exchanged views over an interesting lower tributary of the Red known as the Ouachita River. Since Dr. Hunter was already on the scene, and supplies laid in, Dunbar suggested—and Jefferson agreed—that the autumn might be used to make a trial run up this river. This journey would not require an immediate selection of a leader; since it would be a less arduous trip, Dunbar himself would accompany Hunter. A Ouachita River probe would not only avoid the Osages, it would (as Dunbar told Jefferson) prevent an international incident, for his sources indicated that the Spaniards would move to stop them if they ascended the Red. A postponement of the "Grand Expedition" would thus give Jefferson time to "remove Spanish impediments."[57]

[56] Jefferson's address to the Osage delegation on July 16, 1804, appears in Jackson, *Letters of the Lewis and Clark Expedition*, 1st ed., pp. 200-203. Four days earlier he had had Secretary of War Dearborn write Pierre Chouteau, the administration's new fur man and Indian agent, that he should take the necessary steps among the disaffected Osage bands to secure safe passage for the exploring party. Chouteau was a veteran of the trade, having been granted a six-year monopoly in the Osage country in 1794. But when Spanish officials passed him over in favor of Manuel Lisa in 1802, he persuaded the Arkansas band of some 3,000 Osages to relocate on the Verdigris River and established a trading post near the Three Forks of the Arkansas to promote the assault on the furbearers of the western Ozark and Ouachita mountains. Karen Curths, "The Routes of French and Spanish Penetration Into Oklahoma," *Red River Valley Historical Review* 6 (Summer 1981): 28-29; Wayne Morris, "Auguste Pierre Chouteau, Merchant Prince at the Three Forks of the Arkansas," *Chronicles of Oklahoma* 48 (Summer 1970): 155-63.

[57] Dunbar to Jefferson, Natchez, May 13, June 9, 1804, Rowland, *Dunbar Letters*, pp. 130-35.

In the fall and winter of 1804–1805, then, Dunbar and Hunter, with fifteen men, conducted a detailed examination of the Ouachita River as far northward as the celebrated Hot Springs, in the oak- and pine-clad Ouachita Mountains of what is now central Arkansas. It was a short and careful journey, without mishap except for an accidental gunshot wound to Hunter and the total failure of the boat he had designed—a fifty-foot vessel with sail like a "Chinese scow" that had been built in Pittsburg. It first lost its mast and ultimately had to be exchanged for another vessel at the Ouachita Post. The two men made scientific observations, regretted their lack of expertise as naturalists, and compiled the first accurate map of the Ouachita River. In just over three months they returned to Dunbar's plantation, The Forest, and became the first scientific expedition to report back from Louisiana. The official Dunbar-Hunter narrative of the Ouachita River expedition, assembled by mapmaker Nicholas King, was published not only in the congressional documents and in the compilation called *Message from the President of the United States Communicating Discoveries Made in Exploring the Missouri, Red River, and Washita* (1806), but also in serialized form in *The National Intelligencer and Washington Advertiser* in October and November, 1806. Coming ahead of the more exciting Lewis and Clark and Pike accounts, these publications made Dunbar and Hunter famous men in their time. Two decades later, John James Audubon would refer to Hunter reverently as that "renowned *Man* of Jefferson."[58]

[58] McDermott, "The Western Journals of Dr. George Hunter," pp. 5, 5n., 12–14. The official Dunbar and Hunter narrative, redacted by Nicholas King, is available in the *Annals of Congress*, 9th Cong., 2d sess. (1806), pp. 1106–46, along with Meriwether Lewis's first report, and Sibley's account of the Red River. The three were published later that year by Hopkins and Seymour Printers of New York, under the title *Message From the President of the United States Communicating Discoveries Made in Exploring the Missouri, Red River, and Washita.* Dunbar's daily journal of the Ouachita expedition has been published in this century in *Documents Relating to the Purchase and Exploration of Louisiana* (1904), and in Eron Rowland's *Dunbar Letters* (1930). It has never been edited and worked by a scholar. The principal secondary treatment of Dunbar's activities on the expedition, A. H. DeRosier, Jr.'s "William Dunbar, Explorer," *Journal*

Jefferson stayed "on top" of his Southwestern exploration during the winter of 1804-1805, and early in March he wrote Dunbar that it would be most desirable if "the Grand Expedition" could begin at once.[59] Dunbar accepted the responsibility for directing the main expedition, but he ventured serious doubts about the objective of ascending the Red, portaging to the headwaters of the Arkansas, and then descending that stream, as Jefferson had originally wished.[60] Dunbar's experiences with even short portages during the Ouachita River tour had convinced him that it would be extremely difficult to transport the party's goods and supplies between the sources of the two rivers, situated as they were believed to be in lofty, snowy mountains. These remarks, and further reflection by Jefferson on the Osage threat, were sufficient to alter the objective of the expedition, and on May 24, 1805, Secretary of War Henry Dearborn (who had been one of the main government sponsors of the expedition from the first) wrote Dunbar that Jefferson wanted the exploration confined to the Red River and some of its tributaries, completely to the source of the main river. The following day, Jefferson penned a like letter to Dunbar.[61]

It was impossible, despite the president's wishes, to accomplish a launch date in the spring or summer of 1805. For one thing, a leader was still lacking, and now the post of scientist was also open. In mid-May Dr. Hunter, who had returned to Philadelphia to visit his family before leaving on the "Grand Expedition" decided not to go. Perhaps the three dollars a day he had been paid the

---

of *Mississippi History* 25 (July 1963), pp. 165-85, is of relatively poor quality. George Hunter's journal of the Ouachita exploration, on the other hand, has received scholarly attention in a most thorough fashion by Professor McDermott on pp. 71-124 of the work cited here.

[59] Jefferson to Dunbar, Washington, March 12, 1805, Rowland, *Dunbar Letters*, pp. 146-47.

[60] Dunbar to Jefferson, Natchez, May 4, 1805, ibid., pp. 148-49.

[61] Dearborn to Dunbar, Washington, May 24, 1805 and Jefferson to Dunbar, Washington, May 25, 1805, ibid., pp. 152-53, 174-77.

year before was not enough to keep him away from his business; perhaps, since he was a mineralogist, the deletion of the rockier Arkansas River from the exploration caused him to lose interest.[62] But it seems equally likely that Hunter had some knowledge of what the Spanish reaction would be to the "Grand Excursion," and declined primarily on those grounds.

Jefferson was still no closer to the selection of a principal leader for the expedition. Dunbar, because of ill health, was not predisposed to tackle the Red, and he was, after all, in his mid-fifties (Lewis and Clark were both about thirty). Henry Dearborn at first assumed that Dr. Sibley in Natchitoches might want to accompany the expedition in some capacity, but whatever his reasons, Sibley never joined the party, although he commented in 1807 that he wanted to go on Jefferson's next exploration.[63] In mid-March, Jefferson proposed either Seth Pease, a surveyor in the Land Office, or a Mr. Wily, professor in a Washington academy, as equal to the task of astronomical observation. When neither of these men seemed disposed to go, Dunbar wrote Dearborn in exasperation that: "I am surprised that young men of talents unencumbered by family affairs are not found in numbers with you who are solicitous to go upon so inviting an expedition."[64]

Perhaps one of the reasons Jefferson did not screen more candidates early in 1805 was that he thought he had already found a

---

[62] These are the two reasons McDermott gives. Although he had "a high esteem for the Doctor," Dunbar was not surprised at Hunter's withdrawal from exploration, and not extremely disappointed. Hunter, he wrote Jefferson, was of a "very warm temper," and his chemical expertise had evidently been "applied to the object of making money." Dunbar considered him "an excellent naturalist" but not a minerologist. Dunbar to Jefferson, Natchez, March 16, 1805. Dunbar learned that Hunter had declined the "Grand Expedition" in a letter from Jefferson, Washington, May 25, 1805. Rowland, *Dunbar Letters*, pp. 147–48, 174.

[63] Dunbar to Dearborn, Natchez, May 4, 1805, and Dearborn to Dunbar, Washington, March 25, 1805, ibid., pp. 148–52. See also, Sibley to Dearborn, Natchitoches, April 20, 1807, in Julia Kathryn Garrett, ed., "Doctor John Sibley and the Louisiana-Texas Frontier, 1803–1814," *Southwestern Historical Quarterly* 45 (April 1942): 378.

[64] Jefferson to Dunbar, Washington, March 14, 1805, The Thomas Jefferson Papers, 1st ser.; Dunbar to Dearborn, Natchez, May 4, 1805, Rowland, *Dunbar Letters*, pp. 148–49.

promising prospect. Early in the search for a leader, Dunbar had made passing mention that George Davis, a young mathematician working under Isaac Briggs, government surveyor at New Orleans, had possibilities. Apparently Davis was bold enough to write to the president, recommending himself for the post. Jefferson had admired this approach, and in late May of 1805 he told Dunbar he wanted young Davis to be on the expedition. This proposal was vetoed by Dunbar, who in July informed the president that although he was sensitive to Jefferson's wish to include Davis, further acquaintance had convinced Dunbar that the young man would not do at all, that he was a very "improper person" who possessed so unhappy a disposition that no harmony would exist in any party which he accompanied, either as a subordinate or as an authority.[65]

By this time, however, Jefferson's determination to find a skilled and trained astronomer to lead the Red River expedition on a tour that almost certainly would provide information crucial to the establishment of the boundaries of the Louisiana Purchase had led the president in a new direction. Since the preliminary days of the Lewis and Clark project, Jefferson had worried lest relying on a chronometer to make longitude readings might be placing excessive trust in the wilderness reliability of what was at best a fragile instrument. In his efforts to devise a method of determining longitude without having to rely on a timepiece, Jefferson had enlisted the aid of Dunbar and of Robert Patterson, professor of mathematics at the University of Pennsylvania. He had even broached the subject, with reference to his Southwestern exploration, to von Humboldt. Now, late in the spring of 1805, Jefferson apparently sought still another opinion; the direct result of that inquiry was the selection, finally, of a leader for the "Grand Expedition" into the southern Louisiana Territory.

During the same week that Jefferson had received Dunbar's negative missive concerning George Davis, a letter had arrived

[65] Dearborn to Dunbar, Washington, May 24, 1805, Jefferson to Dunbar, Washington, May 25, 1805, and Dunbar to Jefferson, Natchez, July 6, 1805, ibid., pp. 152–56, 174–75. Isaac Briggs later described Davis as "the best mathematician of whose services I could avail the public," but also possessed of a jealous

from Philadelphia that obviously got the president's attention. From the tone it is obvious that it is a reply to an earlier inquiry concerning celestial observation without a chronometer. Both well reasoned and well written, the letter must have impressed Jefferson.

The ideas and the fine, clear style were those of a young Irish-American surveyor named Thomas Freeman. Contemporary documents do not indicate whether Patterson, who was Freeman's friend, had recommended Freeman to the president, whether someone else had, or whether Jefferson had remembered him from the days when Freeman had worked on the Washington city survey. What is evident is that Jefferson was favorably impressed enough with Freeman to ask him, sometime in August or September, 1805, to assume the leadership of the Red River exploration.[66]

The man who thus became the field leader and geographer of Jefferson's second major Louisiana probe was a civil engineer and surveyor who had emigrated to America from Ireland in 1784. Virtually nothing is known of Freeman's early life, but it is obvious that somewhere in his background there had been excellent training in the sciences. As early as 1792 he may have been employed as surveyor and inspector of the port in Plymouth, Massachusetts, and in 1794 had been commissioned by President Washington as a surveyor of the new capital city on the Potomac.[67] This position not only led to other government appointments but also probably brought him into contact with Jefferson, who was a prime mover in setting up the city of Washington, and with

temper and many "disagreeable qualities." Briggs to Albert Gallatin, Washington, Miss. Terr., Sept. 9, 1806. Carter, *The Territory of Mississippi, 1798–1817,* vol. 5 of *The Territorial Papers of the United States,* pp. 488–89.

[66]Thomas Freeman to Jefferson, Philadelphia, July 13, 1805, and Dunbar to Jefferson, Natchez, October 8, 1805. The Thomas Jefferson Papers, 1st ser. A careful scan of the correspondence between Jefferson and various influential persons—Patterson, Barton, Peale, and especially James Wilkinson—in the period before Freeman's selection failed to turn up any clues explaining why Jefferson thought of Freeman in the summer of 1805. I suspect that Patterson recommended him.

[67]Samuel Tredwell to Alexander Hamilton, Boston, Feb. 10, 1792, Harold C. Styrett, ed., *The Papers of Alexander Hamilton* 9:29.

Alexander Hamilton, whose help he occasionally solicited in later years.[68] Following the completion of the survey in 1796, Freeman had accepted a commission as an American surveyor to chart the boundary between Spanish Florida and the United States. Accordingly, in 1797 he arrived in Natchez with Andrew Ellicott, the noted mathematician who would school Meriwether Lewis in taking astronomical observations six years later. It was during this period that Freeman met Philip Nolan, William Dunbar and also the schemer of the Southwest, General James Wilkinson.

The boundary survey of 1797–98 had played a pivotal role in Freeman's life because, simply stated, he became ensnarled in what soon evolved into something of a celebrated quarrel with an important man. Andrew Ellicott was brilliant, eccentric, argumentative, and within a very short period he and Freeman were bitter enemies. Their enmity began because of Ellicott's repeated delays in starting the survey, and was accelerated with Freeman's verbalized objections to Ellicott's "Dulcinea," a woman companion the married Philadelphia luminary kept in his company and whose presence Freeman believed was the cause of the delay. Finally, in November of 1798, Ellicott dismissed Freeman from the survey camp in the Mississippi Territory, writing his wife by way of explanation that Freeman was "an idle, lying, troublesome, discontented, mischief-making man."[69] Months later, in another letter apparently designed to undermine the credibility of both Freeman and any stories he might circulate about Ellicott's morals, Ellicott told his wife: "Mr. Freeman is one of the greatest rascals and liars in existence . . . it was with difficulty that I could for some months prevent a duel between him and Andy [Ellicott's son, then twenty-two]."[70]

[68] Freeman to Alexander Hamilton, Philadelphia, Jan. 9, 1800, ibid. 24:176–77; W. B. Bryan, *A History of the National Capital, from Its Foundations Through the Period of the Adoption of the Organic Act* 1:240–41.

[69] Ellicott to Sarah Ellicott, Darling's Creek [Mississippi Territory], November 8, 1798. In Catherine Van Cortlandt Mathews, *Andrew Ellicott: His Life and Letters*, p. 160.

[70] Ellicott to Sarah Ellicott, New Orleans, January 10, 1799, ibid., p. 164. Ellicott eliminated every mention of Freeman from his journal of the boundary survey. Styrett, *The Papers of Alexander Hamilton*, p. 241n., confirms the general

One of the intriguing facets of Thomas Freeman's life, discussed at greater length in the Editor's Epilogue, was his relationship with Wilkinson, who at this stage in a bizarre career was both the ranking officer in the United States army and "Secret Agent 13" in the pay of the King of Spain. Wilkinson had rescued Freeman during the Ellicott debacle by hiring him to be the supervising civil engineer in the construction of Fort Adams, a new American outpost on the lower Mississippi. From 1798 to 1800, then, Jefferson's future explorer was at Wilkinson's headquarters, perhaps immersed in the prevailing fantasies about Texas and the Spanish Southwest. Here Freeman no doubt met most of Wilkinson's entourage, a core of people whose ideas four decades later would be universally accepted and hailed as "Manifest Destiny," but which at this time were clearly perceived as revolutionary and imperialistic. One fact that has escaped articulation by historians is crucial here: of the five major Anglo-American interventions into affairs in the Spanish Southwest between 1790 and 1820, James Wilkinson figured into every one, always through younger but talented protégés with less to sacrifice than himself.[71] By 1805, Wilkinson had wangled an influential position vis-à-vis western exploration — that of governor of the Louisiana Territory — and had established the beginnings of a grandiose scheme against the Southwest, to be carried out in collusion with the most charismatic of all his associates, Aaron Burr.

impression of all who were familiar with the incident that Freeman was right in this argument. A decade later, Freeman had his opportunity to discredit Ellicott in a critical testimony in the Wilkinson court-martial. See the Epilogue for his version of the events of 1798 and its impact.

[71] The five Wilkinson-inspired actions against the Spanish Southwest were the Philip Nolan expeditions (1790–1800), the Burr Conspiracy (1804–1807), the Pike expedition (1806–1807), the Gutierrez-Magee filibuster (1812–1813), and the James Long filibuster of 1819. Nolan was raised in Wilkinson's household; Zebulon M. Pike was a Wilkinson protégé whose expedition included Wilkinson's son (who was sent back before the party approached the Spanish settlements); Augustus Magee was another army protégé of Wilkinson; James Long married Wilkinson's niece, Jane Wilkinson, and used the Wilkinson home as his base of operations. For accounts of these connections see Gerald Ashford, *Spanish Texas: Yesterday and Today;* Julia Kathryn Garrett, *Green Flag Over Texas;* and Harris Gaylord Warren, *The Sword Was Their Passport: A History of American Filibustering in the Mexican Revolution.*

Freeman's life between his departure from Natchez in 1800 and his exchange of letters with Jefferson in the early summer of 1805 cannot be closely documented, although it is believed that he did survey work in North Carolina and Tennessee, and accompanied Indiana Territorial Governor William Henry Harrison up the Wabash River to council with the Indians of the area in 1803.[72] After Freeman's exchange with Jefferson in 1805, the president informed Dunbar, in a letter that has not survived, that he had decided to ask Freeman to lead the expedition. At first confusing Freeman with Colonel Constant Freeman of the American garrison at New Orleans (a mistake even some Burr Conspiracy researchers have made), Dunbar at length remembered him. Although Dunbar initially expressed some misgivings over Freeman's earlier lack of enthusiasm for celestial observation, in December he wrote the president that: "I am glad to learn from the Secretary at war that Mr. Freeman comes to take direction of the expedition up the red river."[73]

Early in November of 1805, Freeman was summoned to Washington to discuss the exploration with Jefferson, and spent an evening dining with the president on the sixteenth. At that time Jefferson presented him with the letter of exploring instructions he had drawn up in April, 1804, and provided him with a letter of introduction and a draft to purchase a compass, a chronometer, and other scientific instruments in the mathematics shops of Philadelphia. Any spoken instructions—directives Jefferson might not have wanted on paper—given to the president's new Louisiana explorer in this meeting have not, unfortunately, come down to us.[74]

[72] Dearborn to Freeman, Washington, June 16, 1802. War Department, Letters Sent, Main Series, National Archives. See also, Donald Jackson, *Thomas Jefferson & the Stony Mountains: Exploring the West from Monticello*, p. 238n. Jackson excepted, almost all modern historians, even careful researchers, have tried to make Freeman a military officer, most commonly a "colonel."

[73] Dunbar to Jefferson, Natchez, October 8, 1805, December 17, 1805. The Thomas Jefferson Papers, 1st ser.

[74] "Tho. Freeman will do himself the honor of dining with the President of the United States on Tuesday next, agreeably to invitation." Freeman to Jefferson,

For nearly two months (until the first week of January), Freeman conferred in Philadelphia with Patterson, who had tutored Meriwether Lewis in 1803 and who now helped Freeman purchase scientific equipment for the Red River tour. Freeman also spent time with two other men who had helped train Lewis, Benjamin Smith Barton and Charles Willson Peale, in an effort to find a naturalist who was both scientifically trained and physically able to undertake a hazardous and taxing wilderness exploration.[75]

During that stay in Philadelphia, Freeman wrote a letter to his good friend, John McKee, a surveyor, congressman, and Indian agent who was serving as the Choctaw agent in 1805. This letter, which exists as a badly-eroded and partly illegible fragment in the Library of Congress, and has heretofore never been published, is symbolic of the exuberance Thomas Freeman brought to the leadership of the Red River exploration; it may also give us some clues as to what had been said over the dinner with Jefferson on November sixteenth:

I am making arrangements to proceed from the City of Washington to Natchez, from whence I shall set out for Red River & etc. to Explore Louisiana. Fort Pitt Ohio & Mississippi was the rout contemplated from hence to Natchez, but the danger of being detained in the Ohio by Ice, at this season of the year, has changed the rout to Knoxville, Chickasaw Nation & etc. The Journey by land would at all times be tedious and Disagreeable, but peculiarly so at this time as you must well know, however, every evil has its good. I shall thereby have the pleasure of taking you by the hand, which will compensate for One thousand miles of the rout. be at home and have some of your handsome Daughters to entertain when we call. I expect to take with me a Naturalist and an assistant astronomer if such persons properly qualified can be found here willing to hazard travel in the Neighborhood of *St. Afee*—how would you like to be my Cashier in that country? [   ] probably [   ] where there are Boats and men [   ] to accompany me up, and to the Louisiana mou[ntains.] should any arrangement take place to alter that [   ] rout from hence to Natchez, I shall let you know before I proceed from Washington.

Washington, Nov. 10, 1805, and Jefferson's letter of introduction for Freeman, dated Nov. 16, 1805, ibid.

[75] Freeman to Jefferson, Philadelphia, Nov. 25, 1805, and Robert Patterson to Jefferson, Philadelphia, Dec. 16, 1805, ibid.

[A] Great many difficulties, and some personal danger will attend the expedition, but, I will—"Stick or go through" The more danger the more honor. You see how I am kept *afloat*—an expensive turn when applied to me—Afloat!, and that's all—my savings do not more than float me thro' from job to job, But I hope 'ere long to flow into a permanency.[76]

It seems obvious from this remarkable document that during their private dinner Jefferson had held out to Freeman the promise of a position in the Southwest similar to the ones Meriwether Lewis and William Clark were eventually granted.

Freeman's allusions to Santa Fe and the "Louisiana mountains" were, of course, consistent with the American interpretation of Red River geography, but since neither of these landmarks is mentioned in the official letter of instructions, it seems prudent at this juncture to critically examine those instructions (see the entire letter in Appendix 1,) since Jefferson, after all, never publicly discussed his intentions in regard to the expedition, a fact which evoked suspicion of his motives even among Americans. One newspaper editor spoke darkly of "those secret expeditions, secret orders, and secret plans," and noted accusingly that although most people assumed that the discovery of new natural wonders lay behind the Red River tour, ". . . at the same time that same philosophic mind has long wished to emancipate the people of *Old and New Mexico.*"[77]

Actually, there is little to hint of such a plan in Jefferson's handwritten letter of instructions. It is, rather, a model letter of

[76] Freeman to John McKee, Philadelphia, Nov. [?], 1805, The John McKee Papers. Library of Congress Manuscripts Division. The additional information on McKee is from Malone, *Dictionary of American Biography* 12:82-83. Curiously, at almost the same time that Freeman wrote McKee, indicating Santa Fe as an objective of the exploration, McKee also received a famous letter from a mutual friend, James Wilkinson. This letter spoke of a "distant and splendid enterprise" aimed at Mexico and based on an impending war with Spain. It concludes with Wilkinson urging McKee "to think much, and say little." See James Wilkinson, *Memoirs of My Own Times,* reprint ed., 2:300-301, appendixes 80, 81.

[77] *Louisiana Gazette,* May 16, 1811. The editor of this New Orleans newspaper was extremely suspicious of the motives for both the Pike and the Freeman and Custis expeditions, and concluded editorially that the ferment and near-war with Spain in 1806 were *not* grounded in the Burr Conspiracy, as was commonly

explicit scientific orders—the precedent (along with the similar and more famous letter to Meriwether Lewis) for all subsequent modern explorations of unknown lands. It is, likewise, an outstandingly thorough litany of instructions which reflects both Jefferson's interests and his genius, and it makes apparent as nothing else does that these early explorations of Louisiana were, in a very real sense, Mr. Jefferson's explorations.

The original letter called for an exploration of both the Red and the Arkansas rivers, although, as we have seen, this goal had been amended in 1805 to confine the exploration to the Red alone. The party was instructed to follow the Red from its mouth to the remotest source of the main branch of the river, taking astronomical observations at all remarkable points in addition to accurate measurements of distance. The members of the expedition were to observe and note: the soil and face of the country; the animals and plants endemic to it, especially those not known in the maritime states; and all mineral and volcanic appearances. A very careful meteorological chart was also to be kept.

The larger part of the letter was devoted to diplomatic instructions regarding the Indian nations which were certain to be encountered, and was introduced with the comment: "Court an intercourse with the natives as intensively as you can. . . ." Not only were the native inhabitants to be studied in detail as anthropological specimens, every effort was to be made to acquaint them with the commercial and paternal instincts of the United States. Stressing his idea of the extent of Louisiana, Jefferson instructed Freeman to advise the nations he encountered that: "their late fathers the Spaniards have agreed to withdraw all their troops . . . that they have delivered to us all their subjects . . . [and] henceforth we become their fathers and friends."

One final order, spelled out in unmistakable terms, deserves notice here. This passage provided for the discontinuation of the expedition under certain conditions. Interestingly, these com-

thought, but in the government's actions in the field of exploration. The two American activities, it is now possible to ascertain, cannot be separated this way. Yet the suspicion that Jefferson knew more than the documents tell us lingers still.

ments were lifted virtually verbatim from Jefferson's earlier letter to Lewis. For the Red River expedition this paragraph would prove to be the most important order in a very explicit letter:

. . . if at any time a superior force authorized or not authorized by a nation should be arrayed against your further progress and inflexibly determined to arrest it, you must decline its further pursuit and return. . . . to your own discretion therefore must be left the degree of danger you may risk and the point at which you should decline: only saying that we wish you to err on the side of your safety and to bring back your party safe even with less information.[78]

In a communication to Orleans Territory Governor William C. C. Claiborne in May, 1805, Jefferson had offered some additional clarification of the expedition's intent. Instructed to stress to Spanish officials in New Orleans the scientific nature of the exploration, Claiborne was also charged with the ticklish task of explaining that, although the expedition was not *really* a boundary survey, nonetheless, "as we have to settle a boundary with Spain to the westward they cannot expect that we will go blindfold into this business." Respecting any interference by Spanish troops, the Spaniards should "be made to understand that should any violence be offered the party by subjects of Spain, it will have serious consequences." Again, Santa Fe is not mentioned, nor are the Rockies, but Jefferson did add that the explorers *"are expressly instructed not to go"* beyond the sources of the Red River.[79]

In terms of personnel, there still remained the problem of securing a naturalist for the expedition. Sensitive to criticism of his failure to attach a naturalist to the Lewis and Clark expedition and to Dunbar's letters saying that he could not "sufficiently lament the absence of a good Naturalist particularly a botanist."[80] Jefferson went to considerable lengths in his effort to appoint the

[78] Jefferson to Freeman, Monticello, April 14, 1804, Freeman's personal copy (see Appendix 1) in The Peter Force Collection, Library of Congress Manuscripts Division.

[79] Jefferson to Claiborne, Washington, May 26, 1805, The Thomas Jefferson Papers, 1st ser.

[80] Dunbar to Dearborn, Natchez, June 15, 1804, Rowland, *Dunbar Letters*, p. 139.

first trained naturalist to accompany an American exploring expedition.

At the close of 1804, Jefferson had been approached by the brilliant but erratic Constantine Samuel Rafinesque-Schmaltz with the proposition that, "If it ever seems worthwhile to you, to send a Botanist in Company with the parties you propose to make visit the A[r]kansas or other Rivers, I can not forbear Mentioning that I would think myself highly honored with the choice of in [*sic*] being selected. . . ." Although only twenty-one at the time, Rafinesque was already highly regarded in natural history circles, and in December Jefferson did tentatively offer the naturalist post to him. However, the soon-to-be-famous naturalist had already returned to Europe. Too, he was already beginning to demonstrate strains of the mental fog that so beclouded his later career.[81] Fate and timing decreed that C. S. Rafinesque was not to add the position of naturalist on Jefferson's Southwestern expedition to his long string of accomplishments. Meanwhile, in his urgency to appoint a naturalist for the planned early-spring departure of the expedition, Jefferson was trying a different tack. Sometime in late 1805, in a letter which has not survived, Jefferson inquired of William Bartram, the world-famous Pennsylvania naturalist whose lyrical *Travels* (1791) was already a classic, providing a wealth of material for the emerging Romantic Movement in Europe, if the great naturalist would be interested in having "the department of Natural History in the voyage up the Red River." Because of Bartram's age (he was about to turn sixty-six), Jefferson probably did not really expect him to accept, more likely hoping he could recommend a young protégé. Bartram did decline himself, having scarcely ventured a day away from his home since 1777, but he did know someone he could recommend highly. On February 6, 1806, he forwarded to Jefferson a letter from the applicant.[82]

[81] C. S. Rafinesque to Jefferson, [?], Nov. 27, 1804, in Jackson, ed., *Letters of the Lewis and Clark Expedition*, 2d ed, 2:217–18; Jefferson to Rafinesque, Washington, Dec. 15, 1804, The Thomas Jefferson Papers, 1st ser.; Wayne Hanley, *Natural History in America: From Mark Catesby to Rachel Carson*, pp. 126–42.

[82] See Bartram to Jefferson, Philadelphia, Feb. 6, 1806, The Thomas Jefferson Papers, 1st ser. Wilson's accompanying letter of application is missing from this

The eager candidate was none other than Alexander Wilson, the Scottish-American poet-naturalist whose bird drawings and soon-to-be-published *American Ornithology* (nine volumes, 1808–14) have justifiably qualified him as the father of American bird study. Unfortunately for Wilson, who was terribly disappointed at Jefferson's failure to respond to his request, by the time Bartram's letter arrived the position had already been filled.[83]

Ultimately, it seems to have been Freeman who selected a naturalist to accompany the expedition. In Philadelphia that autumn of 1805, he was at the citadel of American natural history study. At first there was disappointment: Dr. Barton, who had already declined to accompany Lewis and Clark, demurred for what promised to be an even more dangerous mission. Barton's students would become a major pool for American nature study, but there is no hint how many of them applied for this posting. Nor do we know whether or not Barton sought out people such as William Darlington, a prize pupil of two years before, who was still in the Philadelphia area, or if he offered the position to Frederick Pursh, who conducted an exploration of the central Appalachians

---

collection, but is reprinted in Jackson, *The Journals of Zebulon Montgomery Pike* 2:389, n. 1. The pertinent section reads: ". . . hearing that your Excellency had it in contemplation to send travellers this ensuing summer up the Red River, the Arkansas, and other tributary streams of the Mississippi . . . I beg leave to offer myself for any of those expeditions; and can be ready at a short notice to attend your Excellency's orders."

[83] Until now, the entire episode respecting Wilson's application has been completely confused. George Ord, who appended a biography of Wilson to the last volume of the *American Ornithology*, is responsible, since he believed that Wilson must have applied for a position on the Pike expedition. So obscure had the details of the Red River exploration become by 1819 that neither Jefferson nor Dearborn was able to recall the true situation. Jefferson was perplexed because the Pike expedition was a secret probe authorized by General Wilkinson, and even he had not been aware of it until midsummer, 1806. How then, he wondered, could Wilson have known of it in February of that year? Bartram's letter clears the air for us, and perhaps the absence of Wilson's own missive from the Jefferson collection explains why Jefferson failed to reply to him—evidently he did not receive the letter. See also Wilson to William Duncan and Bartram later that spring, all in Clark Hunter, ed., *The Life and Letters of Alexander Wilson* (Philadelphia: American Philosophical Society, 1983), 232–49. Jackson, *The Journals of Zebulon Montgomery Pike*, 2:388–94, reprints some of the confused correspondence between Jefferson and Dearborn on this matter.

for Barton that same spring.[84] Perhaps a wish to still his critics by the appointment of a trained Philadelphia naturalist lay behind the fact that Jefferson ignored the candidacies of two men Barton could recommend—Dr. Frederick Seip and Dr. Garrett Pendergast, both prominent physicians from the Natchez area.[85] Perhaps Jefferson simply wanted Freeman to select someone he knew in advance he could get along with. In any event, during the first week of 1806, Freeman and Barton had decided that they could do no better than to offer the post to young Peter Custis, Barton's student in the medical program at Pennsylvania.

Only twenty-five, Custis was a native of Deep Creek, on the Virginia peninsula, and was from a family related by marriage to the Byrds, Randolphs, Lees, and to the late President Washington. The details of his early life are sketchy, but it is known that he asked his father to sell his share of the family estate in order that he might receive "a latin education" and "be brought up to one of the learned professions."[86] A solid secondary education had prepared him to enter the medical and natural history program at the University of Pennsylvania in 1804, where he became a student and protégé of Barton. In January, 1806, he was still a year from his doctorate, but under Barton's tutelage he had

[84] Information on Darlington, the "Nestor of American Botany" who wrote five important natural history works, may be found in American Philosophical Society *Proceedings* 9 (1863–1864): 330–43. For Pursh, author of *Flora Americae Septentrionalis*, see Malone, *Dictionary of American Biography* 15:271.

[85] Both men were interested in the exploration, and called upon Dunbar and Hunter after their return from the Ouachita, but Jefferson never seems to have considered them. Seip would later serve as surgeon of the Mississippi troops in the border country mobilization after the exploring party was stopped. Alexander Wilson met him in his quest for subscribers for his *American Ornithology*, and the two struck up a friendship, Wilson commenting that he held Seip in "very great esteem." Pendergast served as surgeon to the New Orleans military during Wilkinson's mobilization of that city against Burr in 1807. Alexander Wilson to Dunbar, New Orleans, June 24, 1810, Rowland, *Dunbar Letters*, pp. 205–206; Claiborne, *Mississippi as a Province, Territory and State* 1:266; Carter, *The Territory of Mississippi, 1798–1817* 5:263; Francis B. Heitman, *Historical Register and Dictionary of the United States Army* 1:782.

[86] General information on the Custis family and its connections, including details on Daniel Parke Custis, first husband of Martha Dandridge Washington, may be found in Douglas Southall Freeman, J. A. Carroll, et al., *George Wash-*

been educated in a diversified natural history program.[87] Although Custis clearly possessed impressive taxonomical skills as well as a command of contemporary Latin binomials, he does not appear to have had previous field experience. And since Freeman and Barton had selected him, Jefferson could only "hope we have procured a good botanist," as he told Dunbar.[88] What they actually seem to have found in Custis was a young naturalist with intelligence and a good generalist's background in natural history, but who was seriously deficient in experience. In order to join the Red River tour, Custis had to postpone completion of his degree, but he seems not to have hesitated. On January 17, just three days

---

ington: A Biography, especially volume 2, and Thomas T. Upshur, "Hill and Custis," *Virginia Magazine of History and Biography* 3 (June 1896): 319-21. On Peter Custis's early life, see Accomack County Deeds for 1804, pp. 55, 59, Ocancock Courthouse, Virginia; and Stratton Nottingham, ed. and comp., *Wills and Administrations of Accomack County, Virginia, 1663-1800*, p. 346; Alfred J. Morrison, "Two Students from Virginia at the University of Edinburgh; with a note regarding early botanical dissertations by Virginians at the University of Pennsylvania," *Virginia Magazine of History and Biography* 21 (July 1913): 322-23.

[87] In the Manuscripts Division of the Library of Congress there is still extant a student's notes on seventeen consecutive lectures delivered by Barton in 1805, while Custis was studying under him. An examination of these notes provides conclusive proof that Custis was exposed to wide training, because Barton divided natural history into zoology, botany, geology, mineralogy, hydrography, and meteorology. His lectures covered both ancient and modern work, with particular emphasis upon classification. Since Custis was a medical student, and medicine yet relied on plant *materia medica*, botany would have been a major interest. Barton's own most important work was in botany; his *Collections for an Essay Towards a Materia Medica of the United States* (2 vols.; 1798 and 1804) has earned him the title "Father of American Materia Medica." His *Elements of Botany* (1803) was the first botanical textbook. Barton is also famous for his *Fragments of the Natural History of Pennsylvania* (1799), and an early work on Indians: *New Views of the Origins of the Tribes and Nations of America* (1797). William Smallwood, *Natural History and the American Mind*, pp. 289-93; Francis W. Pennell, "Benjamin Smith Barton as Naturalist," American Philosophical Society, *Proceedings* 86 (1943): 108-22. Students of early American natural history eagerly await the publication of Professor Joseph Ewan's biography of Barton.

[88] Jefferson to Dunbar, Washington, January 12, 1806, and, for additional information on the search, Freeman to Jefferson, Philadelphia, Nov. 25, 1805, The Thomas Jefferson Papers, 1st ser. Wayne Hanley wonders at Jefferson's failure to assign a naturalist to the Lewis and Clark expedition, noting that this "never has been adequately explained. . . . Jefferson was personally interested

after receiving the confirmation of his appointment, travelling in company with Freeman, Custis left Philadelphia for Natchez.[89] Although Custis did not share leadership of the expedition, as did William Clark and Meriwether Lewis, he and Freeman jointly shared the task of scientific examination, and both kept journals of the tour. Thus, there is strong justification for referring to the Red River exploration as the Freeman and Custis expedition.

The selection of a military escort to accompany the two civilian scientists was also performed with a great deal of care, as befitting so important an expedition. Dunbar's criteria were quite specific in his letter to Colonel Constant Freeman of the New Orleans garrison:

> I cannot doubt that many young officers would be extremely ambitious of going upon this expedition, in which case it may be of infinite importance to the success of the expedition that a wise & prudent selection be made. . . . the officers (exclusive of some scientific talent) should possess a perservering disposition, an equanimity of temper & agreeable manners; those qualities are highly important upon an expedition where a few gentlemen are to be long confined to each others company.[90]

It was the president himself, however, who selected the commander of the military contingent. Captain Richard Sparks, ranking officer at Fort Adams, was a Pennsylvanian who was known to Jefferson through Meriwether Lewis. Raised for a part of his youth with the Shawnees, Sparks was regarded as "one of the best woodsmen, bush fighters, & hunters in the army. . . ." For his part, Dunbar believed Sparks's particular talents would make him a "super numerary" if the party went up the Arkansas, although

---

in natural history and was familiar with the coterie of Philadelphia naturalists. He could have tapped the wisdom of the most experienced American naturalists and had them at least recommend a promising young student who might have gained fame on the trip." Indeed. While obviously unaware of the Red River expedition, Hanley nonetheless describes exactly the procedure by which Custis was selected. Hanley, *Natural History,* p. 39.

[89] Peter Custis to Dearborn, Natchez, September 24, 1806, and Dearborn to Custis (letter of appointment), Washington, January 14, 1806, Rowland, *Dunbar Letters,* pp. 189–90.

[90] Dunbar to Constant Freeman, Natchez, June 14, 1804, ibid., p. 138.

"on the red river there may be occupation for him."[91] Dunbar favored Lieutenant Edmund Pendleton Gaines of Fort Adams, but Gaines was unable to leave his post, and Sparks, who was an ardent hunter and also due a promotion, was eager to go on the expedition.[92]

There was still an opening for a lieutenant. This post was filled at the last minute by Enoch Humphreys, a native of New York serving at Fort Adams, who was so eager to accompany the expedition that he offered to go without compensation. Dunbar was delighted with Humphreys, and described him as a "young officer of considerable talents who bears an excellent character." One of Humphreys's tasks was to take separate celestial readings to corroborate Freeman's, and this he must have done tactfully, for Freeman and his geographical assistant were soon very good friends. The remainder of the original contingent consisted of two noncommissioned officers, seventeen privates, and—in a mirror image of the Lewis and Clark expedition—a black slave, who probably arrived with Custis. The men were selected for their "general good health & . . . robust temperaments."[93] Other additions, including Indian guides and local hunter-interpreters whom Dunbar believed to be absolutely essential, were to be added to the party in Natchitoches, and will be identified in the annotation accompanying the Accounts.

Outfitting the "Grand Expedition"

From time to time Jefferson had advised Congress of the progress of his Louisiana explorations and he did so in February, 1806.

[91] Dunbar to Dearborn, Natchez, March 18 and May 6, 1806, ibid., pp. 332, 341; Jackson, *Thomas Jefferson & the Stony Mountains*, p. 240n.

[92] Dunbar to Jefferson, Natchez, December 17, 1805. Gaines would have been a superb choice. He had a distinguished career, capturing Aaron Burr in 1807, becoming a brevet major general during the War of 1812, and receiving a Congressional Medal for his victory over the British at Fort Erie. Heitman, *Historical Register and Dictionary of the United States Army* 1:442.

[93] On Humphreys, see Dunbar to Jefferson, May 6, 1806, Rowland, *Dunbar Letters*, pp. 194-95. Dunbar's general guidelines for selection of the men to go

Whetting their appetite for a comprehensive examination of the Southwest, he presented them with copies of Dunbar and Hunter's report on the Ouachita and Dr. Sibley's description of the Red River country from Natchitoches. Pointedly, he closed his remarks to the assembled senators and House members with the comment that: "The examination of the Red river itself is but now commencing."[94] Additional quiet work among the members of the House produced the desired effect, and that spring the president secured an appropriation of five thousand dollars for the Red River tour. This was less than he would have liked, but it was better than the three thousand dollars set aside in 1804, and now doubled the original Lewis and Clark budget.[95]

In actual practice, both expeditions soaked up much larger sums than the earmarked appropriations would indicate. The Red River exploration benefitted from two additional sources of money: some five thousand dollars worth of exploration and trade goods were made available to it from the leftover stores Hunter had purchased in 1804 and from Sibley's wares in Natchitoches, bringing the actual total budget up to some ten thousand dollars.[96] Out of that sum, Dunbar had to secure vessels for ascending the river, scientific instruments, supplies, and also remunerate the leaders for their services. Freeman's salary is unknown, although when George Davis was being advanced as the head of the party the offer mentioned was expenses plus $3.00 to $4.00 a day. Freeman probably got the latter figure. Custis received $3.00 a

on the expedition were not quite so exclusive as those used by Meriwether Lewis for selecting members of the "Corps of Discovery." Dunbar's criteria appear in his letter to Dearborn, Natchez, June 15, 1804, ibid., pp. 138–39.

[94] Jefferson's address to the Senate and House, February 19, 1806. In Jackson, *Letters of the Lewis and Clark Expedition*, 1st ed., pp. 298–300.

[95] The $5,000-appropriation had first been granted in 1805, but of course had not been utilized. See also, on the appropriation struggle, Jefferson to Dunbar, Washington, March 14, 1805, and Dearborn to Dunbar, Washington, March 25, 1805, Rowland, *Dunbar Letters*, pp. 150–52. Although the original appropriation for the Lewis and Clark expedition was only $2,500, that exploration eventually cost a total of $38,722.25. Bill Gilbert, *The Trail-blazers*, p. 15. See the Epilogue for additional costs information.

[96] Dearborn to Dunbar, Washington, March 25, 1805, Rowland, *Dunbar Letters*, pp. 150–52.

day, plus expenses from the day he left for Natchez.[97] Dearborn had no objection to $1.50 a day (in addition to his regular pay) as a tentative scale for Sparks, but added later that compensation for Captain Sparks and Lieutenant Humphreys would be determined not only by their respective merits and worth to the expedition, but also by the compensation allowed by Congress to Captain Lewis and Lieutenant Pike "for services of a similar nature."[98] It should also be mentioned that Jefferson held out a promise of land grants to all his explorers.[99]

Outfitting any major backcountry expedition is a cogitative process, and the vast array of stores assembled for the party in Natchez reflects that. Left over from the 1804 stock were at least half a dozen strong, tight casks of gunpowder, more than three hundred flints, fifty dollars worth of medicines, and a large variety of broaches, ear jewels, and assorted silver trinkets for Indian presents.[100] From Sibley's stock in Natchitoches would come another large supply of Indian goods. Among scientific supplies, a Nautical Almanac for 1806, to be used for mapping the river by astronomical observation, a chronometer, a portable barometer for determining elevation, a microscope, a camera obscura (an optical device used to portray topography on paper), two thermometers, and an achromatic telescope of sixty to seventy-five power (powerful enough to fix latitude by observing the eclipse of Jupiter's moons) were provided.[101] And Freeman brought his personal sextant, an instrument of very high quality, to supplement the two

[97] Dearborn to Dunbar, Washington, May 24, 1805, and Dearborn to Custis, Washington, January 14, 1806, ibid., pp. 152–53, 189–90.

[98] Dearborn to Dunbar, Washington, June 11, 1806, Rowland, *Dunbar Letters,* pp. 195–96.

[99] See Appendix 1. Of the Jeffersonian explorers, only Meriwether Lewis and William Clark were ever voted land grants. Jefferson found other ways of rewarding Freeman.

[100] Dearborn to Hunter, Washington, April 3, 1804, in McDermott, "The Western Journals of Dr. George Hunter," pp. 9–10.

[101] Dearborn to Dunbar, Washington, August 11, 1805, Dunbar to Jefferson, Natchez, May 4, 1805, and Dunbar to Jefferson, Natchez, December 17, 1805, Rowland, *Dunbar Letters,* pp. 148–49, 177, 187. Zebulon Pike was also furnished a telescope for his western exploration. His work with it was erratic, and eventually it was broken.

that were already available. The purchase of the chronometer does not appear to have relegated to backup status the method Dunbar had finally developed for operating without one. In fact, utilizing both methods to take courses, the explorers would go on to do some of the most accurate map-work performed up to that time.[102]

Additional supplies must have included a bootleg copy of von Humboldt's as-yet-unpublished map of the Provincias Internas, and almost certainly a version of Sibley's 1805 report on the Red River. Custis seems to have carried with him as his major field guides: Linnaeus's *Systema Vegetabilium,* edited by J. A. Murray (either the 1784 or the 1786 edition), a one-volume, thousand-page botanical compendium of all the known plants of the world, a condensation allowing only the most cursory of descriptions and deleting all information as to geographical distribution; and Antoine Simon Le Page DuPratz's *History of Louisiana* (probably the single-volume, 1774 English edition), wherein the natural history sections are full of errors and of limited usefulness. Custis was also clearly familiar with Humphrey Marshall's *Arbustrum Americanum Et Catalogue Alphabetique Des Arbes Et Arbrisseaux* (1785) and Thomas Walter's *Flora Caroliniana* (1778), and may have carried copies with him. Among the works he brought for

---

[102] The method for determining longitude without either a timepiece or an assistant was perfected by Dunbar in late 1805, and communicated to Jefferson in December. It was based on taking lunar meridian altitudes rather than distances, with the use of a prominent landmark as a triangulation reference, and was a method "found chiefly useful to Scientific Gentlemen traveling by land." Freeman's arrival with a high-quality chronometer delighted Dunbar, and upon calibrating it he told Jefferson that with it "the longitudes may be ascertained as frequently and as easily as the latitudes." Dunbar to Jefferson, Natchez, December 17, 1805, and March 18, 1806, ibid., pp. 185–86, 190–91. But Dunbar also instructed the party to employ the new method: "Exclusive of the usual lunar observations for the ascertainment of the longitude, the moon's meridian altitude . . . & equal altitudes of the moon may be taken in proper situations, & calculations made after the return of the party." Dunbar to Freeman Esqr. & his associates, Natchez, April 28, 1806, ibid., pp. 339–40. In 1914 the engineers in the General Land Office checked several of Freeman's readings and found them amazingly precise. By contrast, neither Lewis nor Pike ever really mastered their instruments; some of their readings are off by as much as forty miles. See Malone, *Dictionary of American Biography* 7:14.

vertebrate study, Linnaeus's four-volume *Systema Naturae* (probably the 1789 edition edited by J. F. Gmelin) was his principal source, although some of the names and classifications he used make it clear that he was also consulting Jefferson's *Notes on the State of Virginia* (1784) and Bartram's *Travels* (1791). Custis was also familiar with the most recent work reported in the three major scientific journals in America: the *Transactions of the American Philosophical Society*, Samuel L. Mitchill's the *Medical Repository*, and Barton's *Philadelphia Medical and Physical Journal*.[103] Although no information is available as to what firearms were carried by the party, probably they were a mixture of assorted Pennsylvania-Kentucky rifles and perhaps a few Model 1803 .54 caliber rifles, which would have been more suitable for the larger game expected upriver.[104]

[103] In his natural history catalogues, Custis alludes specifically to the journals and most of the texts mentioned. One strange omission was André Michaux's *Flora Boreali-Americana* (1803), which the Reverend Henry Muhlenberg later told Dunbar was the "best" work available. This small library is certainly all Custis had room for aboard the cramped boat. Given the level of knowledge about natural history in the Old Southwest at the time, these were good references, but still inadequate to the task.

[104] Carl P. Russell, *Guns on the Early Frontiers: A History of Firearms from Colonial Times Through the Years of the Western Fur Trade*, pp. 62–69. Meriwether Lewis had designed the M1803 for use on the Lewis and Clark expedition, and it is likely that at least a few of them were employed by members of the Red River military contingent.

Other stores for the original expedition, figured on the basis of seventeen members, included the following:

1 bble. Nails & spikes assorted	½ Doz Tin Cups	2 Grid Irons
1 small Grindstone	1 Tin tea pot	1 Iron Tea Kettle
2 Carpenters Hammers	1 Coffee pot	½ Doz Iron tablespoons
2 Boat Hook Irons	1 Funnel	8 pewter plates
1 Round adze	1 Hands axe	2 Tin pans
1 Iron square	1 Tinder Box	3 picks
1 Crow Bars	1 X Cut Saw	1 Hoe
1 Jack screw	3 Augers	5 ble. Junck
6 spades	3 Gouges	3 long chissels
1 Trowel	6 Axes	2 Wall Tents
48 lb. Rope	6 spades	4 Common Tents
1 piece Canvas 44 yds.	2 Caulking Mallets	½ Ream W. paper
9 lb. Twine	1 Barrel Tar	1 Ream wrapping paper
2 Brass Cocks	1 do. pitch	1 Tea Kettle
1 Frying pan	1 Fishing net	1 small Iron pot
2 Dutch Ovens	1 lb. Cotton Match	1 do. Kettle
½ Doz Knives & forks	1 Corn Mill	

All of the Louisiana explorations which Jefferson conceived and directed were, in the main, river expeditions. Transportation into the interior of the continent, therefore, was to be accomplished by flatboats as far up as the rivers were navigable. The plan for the Red River tour was to ascend the Red as far, it was hoped, as the "Panis" (Taovaya-Wichita) villages, believed to be 1,000 to 1,300 miles above the river's mouth; there to erect a post; and to continue the journey from that point on horses purchased from the Indians.[105]

Dunbar's unhappy experiences with Hunter's boat on the Ouachita had convinced him that entirely new, experimental craft would have to be built for an ascent of the rivers of the Southwestern plains. He exhorted Jefferson, and the president agreed, to make the trip with two boats rather than one so as to lessen the difficulty caused by logjams as well as boost the spirits of the men. Ever the scientist, Dunbar designed the two experimental craft to differ slightly from one another as a test in hydrodynamics. He wanted fast boats, capable of 40 miles a day ascending, so as "to leave more time for observation and research." Constructed in New Orleans, the two Red River craft measured 25 by 8 feet, were flat-bottomed, drawing only 6 to 8 inches of water when unloaded (or 16 to 20 fully provisioned for the journey), with curved gunnels at both bow and stern. Fitted out with "commodious Cabins" to house the leaders (Freeman and Humphreys's cabin housed the geographic and astronomical instruments and charts, while Custis turned the one he shared with Sparks into a natural history study), these craft would do yeoman's service on the expedition. Yet, so large did the party

From: "Memorandum of Articles Wanted for the expedition . . . distined up red river with Mr. Dunbar and Doctor Hunter," in the George Hunter Journals, Miscellaneous Manuscripts Collection, Library of the American Philosophical Society. The rather considerable number of construction implements make it seem likely that a small post was to have been built at the Taovaya-Wichita villages. The tools are used on the expedition to construct a storehouse at the Alabama-Coushatta village. An itemized cost estimate for the expedition appears in the Epilogue.

[105] See the text of the Accounts, Part 4.

eventually become, that five large river pirogues, routed from the trunks of large bald cypress trees, also had to be employed.[106]

A Passport Request and the Great Plot of 1806

All along, the American principals involved in the exploration had been well aware of the diplomatic ramifications and possible, even probable, objections of the Spanish government to such an expedition. As early as May, 1804, Dunbar had expressed the opinion that a Red River party might be interfered with by the Spanish militia at Bayou Pierre, a small settlement northwest of Natchitoches and east of the Sabine, which had been retained by Spain at the cession.[107] Even so, his scientific curiosity had originally disposed him towards an ascent of the Red, since this would allow additional time for study of "the more interesting" river. When the decision was made in 1805 to explore only one of the Southwestern rivers, the Arkansas was the obvious deletion.

[106]Dunbar to Dearborn. Natchez, Maly 4, July 13, 1805, Dunbar to Jefferson, Natchez, December 17, 1805, and Dunbar to Freeman Esqr & his associates, Natchez, April 28, 1806, Rowland, *Dunbar Letters*, pp 148–49, 157, 188, 339. One pirogue, capable of a burden of thirty barrels, will set out with the party from Fort Adams, and four others are added at Natchitoches.

[107]Dunbar to Jefferson, Natchez, May 13, 1804, and Dunbar to Dearborn, Natchez, May 4, 1805, Rowland, *Dunbar Letters*, pp. 130–32, 148–49. Bayou Pierre was one of the first permanent European settlements in northwestern Louisiana. The little hamlet, which played a surprisingly important role in teaching the art of catching wild horses and cattle to advancing Americans, was founded on rolling uplands high enough to escape the inundations of the raft-choked Red. It was located about six miles east of today's Mansfield, near the banks of the clear, running stream the French called Bayou Pierre, the Spanish knew as Las Piedras, and the American frontiersmen named Stoney Creek. In the decades after the French founding of Natchitoches, the remnants of the Natchitoches Caddos may have fled to the Bayou Pierre area. According to Major Amos Stoddard, in his *Sketches, Historical and Descriptive, of Louisiana*, during the 1730s a few French families moved to the spot, starting *vacheries* or stock ranches on the high, grassy prairies and supplying butter, cheese, and bacon hams to the inhabitants downriver (189). Spanish officials did not agree with this version of events. Father Antonio Pichardo and his researchers determined that Bayou Pierre had not been officially settled until 1783 or 1784 (while Spain held Louisiana), when

Natchez in the early nineteenth century, by John James Audubon. Courtesy Mississippi Department of Archives and History.

As events began to unfold, and information from his contacts began to filter back to Dunbar throughout 1805 and 1806, he became more and more convinced that an ascent of the Red would be an exercise in futility. At first gently, and then more urgently, he warned Jefferson that however "interesting" it was, the Red River would surely take the party into a confrontation with Spanish troops.

And yet for some reason—most likely to avoid the appearance of a concession over the boundaries—Jefferson persisted. Although he twice adopted the posture in his letters of leaving the decision about which river to explore to Dunbar, Dearborn made it clear in his letters that Jefferson was set on the Red. When Freeman and Custis arrived in Natchez in late March, Freeman left no doubt that Jefferson wanted the party on the Red, and that he had already given orders for an additional military escort to be added at Natchitoches. Faced with the knowledge that the plan he had been promoting since February—a secret ascent of the Arkansas while allowing Spain to believe that the Red was the target river—was not to be accepted, Dunbar wearily wrote Dearborn that "therefore [there is] not[h]ing to do but acquiesce."[108] But he must have been astounded at the adminis-

---

the "first" settler, Pierre Bouet Lafitte, was appointed trader to the Caddo and Kichai Indians and established a ranch in Bayou Pierre's hills with the blessing of Governor Miro in New Orleans. When he married a local Caddo woman, Lafitte became "Cadelafita," a *caddi*, or civil chief, among them. To Spanish officials, their appointment of this Frenchman was sufficient to make Bayou Pierre Spanish, and at the Louisiana Purchase they refused to relinquish it, even placing a detachment of soldiers there. Naturally this materially strengthened the Spanish claim to the west bank of the Red. See Hackett, *Pichardo's Treatise on the Limits of Louisiana and Texas* 3:434–39. According to Sibley, at the time of Jefferson's exploration, Bayou Pierre consisted of about forty families, most of them French. Sibley, "Historical Sketches," pp. 62–63. The Bayou Pierre settlement today is known by the name of Carmel, La. George M. Lawrence, "Carmel: Rock Chapel in the Wildwood," *The Shreveport Times*, March 11, 1979.

[108] Letters on the choice of rivers and Dunbar's alternate plan include the following in the Thomas Jefferson Papers, 1st ser., and Rowland, *Dunbar Letters:* Jefferson to Freeman, Monticello, April 14, 1804; Jefferson to Dunbar, Washington, May 25, 1805; Dunbar to Dearhorn, Natchez, February 25, 1806; Jefferson to Dunbar, Washington, March 28, 1806; and especially Dunbar to Dearborn, Natchez, March 18, 1806.

Dunbar's plantation, "The Forest," headquarters of Jeffersonian exploration in the Southwest. Courtesy Mississippi Department of Archives and History.

tration's stubbornness, which not only risked the destruction of a team of scientific explorers but a possible war over it. Jefferson was literally courting disaster.

In anticipation of Spanish opposition, Jefferson as early as 1804 had decided to approach the Spanish Boundary Commissioner, Caso Calvo, for a passport for the exploring party. He even offered to send along one or two Spaniards as proof of his intention to carry out a purely scientific voyage. Jefferson's appeal that the expedition would benefit Spain "as much" as the United States met with little sympathy among Spanish officials, but on July 11, 1805, the new territorial governor of the Orleans Territory (present Louisiana), William C. C. Claiborne, reiterated Jefferson's request.[109] Caso Calvo, acting on his own initiative, surprised the Americans by granting the passport, which stipulated a scientific exploration into the Southwest by Dunbar and Spaniard Thomas Power (a one-time confidential agent between Spanish officials and General Wilkinson).[110]

No one was surprised more by Caso Calvo's reversal than Nemecio Salcedo in Chihuahua. Salcedo bluntly informed Caso Calvo that he had no intention of honoring such a passport, since he suspected that the expedition, like that of "Mr. Meri [Meriwether Lewis] on the Missouri," was intended mainly to win over Indian allies. In Mexico City, Viceroy José de Yturrigaray concurred, informing Salcedo that he was wise not to honor the passport, and confirming that Salcedo's approach "on this delicate point" was most in keeping with Royal wishes.[111] Convinced that the Americans were planning to ascend the Red in the autumn of 1805, Salcedo had, in fact, already ordered that a contingent from the Nacogdoches garrison be dispatched to stop the American probe. The East Texas outpost, at this point, was hardly equipped for that sort of effort. The best it could do was to reinforce the Bayou Pierre detachment with twenty men under Dionisio Valle, and to hold fifteen cavalrymen at ready at Nacogdoches. No attempt whatsoever was made to guard the Arkansas. Optimistically ordered to make the American "in-

[109] Jefferson to Dunbar, Washington, May 25, 1805, Rowland, *Dunbar Letters,* p. 174; Claiborne to Caso Calvo, New Orleans, July 11, 1805, in Rowland, ed., *Official Letter Books of W. C. C. Claiborne, 1801–1816* 3:181.

[110] Jack D. Holmes, "The Marquis de Caso Calvo, Nicholas de Finiels, and the 1805 Spanish Expedition Through East Texas and Louisiana," *Southwestern Historical Quarterly* 69 (January 1966): 326.

[111] Salcedo to Caso Calvo, Chihuahua, October 8, 1805, and Yturrigaray to Salcedo, Mexico City, November 30, 1805, The Bexar Archives. A Royal Order in February, 1806, made it clear that Madrid would brook no passport grant for a Southwestern exploration by the Americans and berated Caso Calvo that the exploration should have been resisted from the first. Minute of a Royal Order, February 7, 1806, cited in Warren Cook, *Flood Tide of Empire: Spain and the Pacific Northwest, 1543–1819,* p. 475. Later the Spaniards used these passport requests against the Americans, citing them as proof the party was planning to enter Spanish territory.

Page from Thomas Freeman's letter to John McKee, November, 1805. Original in the Library of Congress.

vaders" fall back or to take them prisoners, Valle maintained his vigil at Bayou Pierre until December before concluding that Dunbar and the Americans were not coming.[112]

Caso Calvo's early actions had been made clearer in October, 1805, when he wrote Governor Claiborne asking for a reciprocal passport of his own. This supposedly was to enable him to journey through the frontier country to hunt, recover his health, and visit Los Adaes. The real intent of this mission, however, was to conduct his own exploration of the border country, under a commission from the King, to determine a boundary line between Louisiana and Texas—a project for which the Spanish government supposedly appropriated $100,000.[113] Claiborne signed Caso Calvo's passport on October 16. In early January, 1806, with Don Andres Armesto and Nicholas de Finiels in tow, the Marquís arrived in Nacogdoches, where he was received coolly by Sebastian Rodriguez, the commandant of that outpost. The soldier's contempt for the effete diplomat was obvious in Rodriguez's testimony to Texas governor Antonio Cordero that he would be deceived neither by Caso Calvo's "beautiful traits," nor by a belief that his reports would prove at all useful.[114]

Thus little came of this attempt by the Spaniards to mark the boundary, and in February, Caso Calvo returned to New Or-

[112] Cordero to Valle, San Antonio, October 26, 1805, Salcedo to Cordero, Chihuahua, November 2, 1805, Sebastian Rodriguez to Cordero, Nacogdoches November 4, 1805, and Cordero to Rodriguez, San Antonio, December 16, 1805, The Bexar Archives.

[113] According to Holmes, "The Marquis de Caso Calvo, Nicholas de Finiels, and the 1805 Spanish Expedition Through East Texas and Louisiana," p. 326. Claiborne advised Secretary of State James Madison of Caso Calvo's request. See, Claiborne to Madison, New Orleans, October 14, 1805, Rowland, *Official Letter Books of W. C. C. Claiborne* 3:198.

[114] Rodriguez to Cordero, Nacogdoches, December 19, 1805, and January 3, 1806. The Bexar Archives. Signed passport made out to the Marquís de Caso Calvo, dated October 16, 1805. In Rowland, *Official Letter Books of W. C. C. Claiborne* 3:202. Actually, Caso Calvo had appointed Stephen Minor of Natchez to conduct a boundary examination the preceding year, but the Spanish officials in Texas were too suspicious to allow an Anglo to perform such a survey. See also, José Joaquin Ugarte's diary for September, 1804, Bautista to Salcedo, San Antonio, December 5, 1804, Ugarte to Bautista, Nacogdoches, September 4, 1804, and February 4, 1805, The Bexar Archives.

leans to discover that, along with other Spanish officials, he had been expelled from the Crescent City. With thoughtless timing, Claiborne followed this information up with a renewed request for a passport for the upcoming exploration of the Red River by Freeman and Custis. His own mission completed, however, and mindful of the stir his earlier passport grant had caused among his superiors, Caso Calvo promptly and haughtily refused. A week later Claiborne relayed this bad news to Dunbar.[115]

At this point it is well to consider at greater length yet another aspect of Jefferson's Red River exploration, one that has heretofore entirely escaped historical examination. As previously noted, in the very first exchange between border-country Spanish officials regarding American exploration in the Southwest, there was mentioned an anonymous source of information whose reports could be trusted as "implicitly" reliable. The delicate position of their informant caused the Spaniards to protect his identity, but in several other letters between Spanish officials on the frontier from 1804 to 1807, he figures prominently as an individual connected "in a major way" with the Burr Conspiracy (which the Spaniards were led to believe was intended to separate the Mississippi valley from the United States).[116] Almost certainly there is a connection here, likewise, with the persistent and mysterious deliveries of American newspaper clippings on "the inevitable declaration of war" between Spain and the United States to the commandants at Nacogdoches during those same years.[117]

Such information became very difficult for the Spaniards to

[115] Claiborne to Dunbar, New Orleans, February 12, 1806, Rowland, *Dunbar Letters,* p. 174.

[116] Francisco Amangual to Cordero, San Antonio, March 2, 1807, The Bexar Archives.

[117] The number of Wilkinson's agents in the border country is unknown. Robert Ashley, already mentioned as one of Nolan's men who had planned (but cancelled) his own expedition onto the plains in 1803–1804, was no doubt one, but probably there were several. See Abernethy, *The Burr Conspiracy,* p. 51. The boastful nature of many of the articles and accompanying notes led Rodriguez to observe in December, 1805, that ". . . our neighbors lack the coolness with which we are watching their movements . . . it seems their arrogance is not as great as is generally assumed." Rodriguez to Cordero, Nacogdoches, December 19, 1805, The Bexar Archives.

Dr. John Sibley, Jefferson's Indian Agent for the Southwest. Courtesy Lindenwood University.

interpret. They were never really certain whether they were being befriended or manipulated. Consequently, each clandestine or anonymous warning only served to escalate their anxiety. From their informants they heard stories of an impending division of the United States, over which they gloated. But from other contacts there was more disconcerting news. In April of 1806, the same month the Red River exploration finally got under way, Governor Cordero obtained what he considered to be confirmation of a rumor that was in the air. From an "American emigrant" he heard that fifteen hundred men were preparing in Kentucky for an invasion of Texas, a testimony he considered "serious and true."[118] Three weeks later a trusted friend, Gilbert Leonard, who had served as an official for Spain in both Louisiana and Florida, wrote a statement (which was rushed from the frontier to Yturrigaray in Mexico City) that "there is a strong party in the United States to revolutionize the kingdom."[119]

What the Spaniards were finally beginning to detect wisps of, through the smokescreen that had been thrown up to disguise it, was the real intent of the fermenting "Burr Conspiracy," which its most capable historian has described as less a conspiracy than an entrenched way of thought on the American frontier.[120] Its spiritual antecedent was probably the "conspiracy" of Senator William Blount and associates to invade Spanish Louisiana in the 1790s. But now the stakes were higher, and the players more powerful and capable.

It can now be stated with certainty that James Wilkinson, the ranking American general whom contemporaries suspected and historians now know to have been Secret Agent 13 in the Spanish service, was the architect of the plan known as the "Burr Conspiracy." Wilkinson had known the talented and ambitious Aaron Burr from the time of the American Revolution, but it was not until 1804 that Wilkinson began secretly to call on the vice-president in order to lay before him his maps and evolving plans.[121] Burr's fortunes had worsened considerably by that time. Four years earlier he had alienated Jefferson and many Republican supporters in the strange tie election (both men on the same ticket) between the two. Then he had openly courted the radical New England secessionist group known as the Essex Junto, lost the gubernatorial race in New York, and shot down Alexander Hamilton in their famous duel at Weehawken Heights, all in

[118] Cordero to Viana, San Antonio, April 21, 1806, ibid.
[119] Bernardo Villamil to Yturrigaray, Pennsacola, May 12, 1806, ibid.
[120] Walter F. McCaleb, *New Light on Aaron Burr*, pp. xv–xx, 12.
[121] Documents available in the New York Historical Society's recently collected The Papers of Aaron Burr, 1st ser., Correspondence, demonstrate that

less than a year's time. By midyear, 1804, the regular avenues to power and prestige were closed to him. And yet, a man of Burr's ambition could not rest in an age of revolution and change. Like Milton's Lucifer in *Paradise Lost,* Burr was casting about for a new theater of operations. Thus he was willing to listen to a great enterprise Wilkinson had long cherished: the private conquest of Texas and Mexico and an eventual empire in the Southwest—all of which could be made to appear perfectly patriotic if the United States and Spain could only be maneuvered into a war.

Burr and "his" plot constitute what has always been considered one of the more clouded and controversial episodes in American history, not only because of the secrecy of the plotting, but also because events never progressed to the point where the objectives were clearly recognizable. The claim was made early, and has been upheld by many historians, that the intent was the separation of the West, one scholar even referring to the episode as "next to the Confederate War . . . the greatest threat of dismemberment which the American Union has ever faced."[122]

It is very likely that neither Burr nor Wilkinson ever seriously entertained any such notions. These two men, instead, were on the tip of an iceberg that, fully exposed, would one day flood Texas, New Mexico, and the Far West with Anglo-Americans.

Wilkinson began wooing Burr with his Southwestern schemes in the spring of 1804, soon after Burr lost the New York state election. That year in March (a month of great activity for Wilkinson!), he penned a letter in French to Burr, inviting him to meet some "particular" friends and to "call upon me at one o'clock and see my Maps." Two months later he sent word to Burr that he wished to stay overnight in the latter's home "if it may be done without observation. . . ." The next day the general wrote his first code letter to Burr, arguing that: "You are deceived my friend with respect to the size of the Rum Barrel of Louisiana. . . ." Wilkinson to Burr, New York, March 26, May 23, May 24, 1804. Burr's caution soon evaporated in the wake of public reaction to his duel with Hamilton.

[122] Abernethy, *The Burr Conspiracy,* p. 274. For a good example of the earlier interpretation, see Claude Bowers, *Jefferson In Power: The Death Struggle of the Fe̐ralists,* pp. 373–76. I follow the revisionist interpretation of Isaac J. Cox, "Hispanic-American Phases of the 'Burr Conspiracy,'" *The Hispanic-American Historical Review* 12 (May 1932): 145–75; and McCaleb, *New Light on Aaron Burr.*

General James Wilkinson, the master schemer of the Southwest. Courtesy Library of Congress.

Almost certainly, their immediate plan was to foster a war with Spain, and then manipulate the resulting chaos for power and economic advantage. Burr and Wilkinson were sure that the confusion of officials in New Spain over Napoleon's machinations in Iberia (he would eventually place Joseph Bonaparte on the throne in Madrid) combined with imperial neglect and incompetence, signaled the imminent collapse of Spain's North American empire. With some prior knowledge of the country, Burr and

Wilkinson reasoned, a two-pronged attack—one, with the help of the Mexican Association, launched from New Orleans against Vera Cruz, the other an overland filibuster from Natchitoches against Texas or, perhaps, Santa Fe—ought to be sufficient to undermine the Spanish hold on Mexico and the Provincias Internas.[123]

Few men in history have ever been in a better position to manipulate an incident and a military confrontation than was James Wilkinson between 1804 and 1806. For more than two years Wilkinson fed his contacts on both sides a steady diet of reports whose purpose, it is now possible to ascertain, was the creation of a confrontation. After he became governor of Louisiana Territory, Wilkinson urged on both Jefferson and Dearborn (the latter seems to have been especially susceptible to his influence) in the president's exploring efforts. There still exist in the Jefferson Papers and the files of the War Department several badly eroded and fragmentary Wilkinson letters written in 1804 and 1805, describing the upper Red River country and the Southwest, mentioning volcanoes and other enticing natural wonders, providing maps, and encouraging the president in his "proposition." Perhaps the most important of these documents is his twenty-two-page description of Texas written in July, 1804, a few weeks after he learned of Jefferson's plan of action in the Spanish borderlands. It is a detailed and rather accurate portrayal of Hispanic Texas and its productions; it also includes careful information on troop strength and on the river avenues into the interior. The land between the "west branch" of the Red and the "Río Bravo" embraced "a vast variety of surface, soil, and Natural productions," he told Dearborn and Jefferson. "Years of exploration & volumes . . . will be found necessary to the exhibition of a cor-

[123] In 1804, Burr was convinced that: "There will be no war with Spain unless we shall declare it. . . ." By 1806, as the Wilkinson plan matured, he would write that: "All reflecting men consider a war with Spain to be inevitable. . . ." Burr to Joseph Alston, Washington, November 29, 1804, Burr to William H. Harrison, Lexington, October 24, 1806, The Papers of Aaron Burr, 1st ser. Among the Burr documents assembled by the New York Historical Society are three maps (of the Louisiana-Texas border country to San

rect natural History of this Wonderful Country." Typically, the letter closes with the anticipated Wilkinsonism: "I am almost ashamed to offer to your and the Presidential Eye, these hurried desultory details, but believing it is possible, should the thread of my life be cut, that they may in the course of events, be found useful to our Country, I feel it my duty to hazard them. . . ."[124] Given his contacts and information about the frontier, no one was in a better position to warn Jefferson about the dangers of attempting to explore the Red River than Wilkinson, but his attitude stands in the starkest contrast to William Dunbar's repeated warnings.

Simultaneously with his promotion of exploration, the general attempted to sabotage these same endeavors in his capacity as Spanish spy. It is now known that in March, 1804, shortly before learning of Jefferson's full plan for examining the West, Wilkinson had written an extensive tract for the Spanish government, containing his advice on how to deal with the American problem. It is, in every way, a most remarkable document. Spain must never concede to the "territorial pretensions" of the United States, he wrote, for weakness would give the key to the New World to her "most dangerous neighbor and [to] the revolutionary spirit of the present time. . . ." If the Crown were to err through "false calculations, dilatory compacts, and lack of attention to the important crisis," he predicted Mexico and even Peru being over-

Antonio; the Gulf Coast from New Orleans to Vera Cruz; and the Mexico City area) which leave no doubt about the geographical focus of the Conspiracy. The first two of these quite possibly were acquired from Wilkinson, based on Nolan's travels and map sketches.

[124] As previously indicated, Wilkinson first learned of Jefferson's tentative plans to explore the Southwest with Dearborn's letter of March 31, 1804. His letters encouraging Jefferson's interest in the area begin on June 19, 1804, and include missives dated November 10, 1804, October 22, 1805, and November 6, 1805. The Thomas Jefferson Papers, 1st ser. The July 13, 1804 letter to Dearborn is in the files of the War Department, Letters Received, Main Series. Wilkinson was doubly busy that early summer of 1804; Caso Calvo, the first of the Spanish officials to learn of the proposed Southwestern exploration, was so informed during the same week that Wilkinson wrote the first of the letters cited here.

run by armies of "adventurous desperadoes . . . like the ancient Goths and Vandals."[125]

As for "scientific" exploration, Spain should not be deceived. Already the president had commissioned "his astronomer" to determine the mouth of the Río Grande and the source of the Missouri, to which latter end Meriwether Lewis had already been dispatched. Then Wilkinson followed with the "smoking gun" of Jeffersonian exploration history:

> An express ought immediately to be sent to the governor of Santa Fe [Alencaster], and another to the Captain-general of Chihuaga [Salcedo], in order that they may detach a sufficient body of chasseurs to intercept Captain Lewis and his party, who are on the Missouri River, and force them to retire or take them prisoners.

But Wilkinson continues. Although not yet aware of the Southwestern probe, his advice on the Louisiana-Texas frontier could have left no doubts in the minds of Spanish officials as to how they ought to react:

> The Post of Nacogdoches ought to be strongly fortified . . . [and] a fort ought to be established on the Sabine River . . . in order to locate there an army of observation. That army should consist of one thousand five hundred men . . . and by its position would hold in check every movement of the United States toward Mexico . . . Spain will show evident proofs to the United States of its determination to . . . drive back every illegal usurpation toward the region of Texas.

And finally, there was the matter of the gem city of the Southwest. Here Wilkinson urged that particular resistance be offered to Americans on the western rivers, for if "allowed to advance,

[125] The following quotes are from this document, which under the title "Reflections on Louisiana" is found in the Archivo de Indias, Papeles procedentes de la Isla de Cuba, Estados del Misisipi, and is reproduced in James Robertson, ed., *Louisiana Under the Rule of Spain, France, and The United States, 1785–1807* 2:325–47. Robertson credited Vicente Folch, governor of West Florida, as its author. Not until Cox examined the original in Cuba was it discovered that Folch was only the translator, and that Wilkinson was the author. See Isaac J. Cox, "General James Wilkinson And His Later Intrigues With The Spaniards," *American Historical Review* 19 (July 1914): 798n. Lewis and Clark scholars have seized upon the specific paragraph referring to that party without dovetailing the other instructions with subsequent history (i.e., the stopping of

they will very quickly explore the right path which will lead them to the capital of Santa Fe."[126]

Just who was privy to this letter, which was forwarded to Havana, cannot now be determined, but Salcedo and Alencaster both reacted. Not even the vastness of the Western wilderness prevented the latter from dispatching trailblazer Pedro Vial in August of 1804, to observe the movements of the Missouri exploration. Only an Indian attack kept the Frenchman from completing a second such mission, begun in October of 1805, to persuade the Pawnees to attack the Americans on their return trip.[127] Similarly, once informed of Jefferson's intent to explore the Southwest, Salcedo reacted with anger and dismay at Caso Calvo's handling of the passport request and emerged quickly as the driving spirit behind opposition to the Red River exploration. For his part, once Wilkinson had confirmed and relayed the news that Jefferson was targeting an expedition at a quarter of the West more accessible to Spanish troops, where penetration was, if anything, even more threatening than Lewis and Clark on the Missouri, the wheels really must have labored. And from this point the general and his cohorts seem to have concentrated their efforts on the local officials who would directly confront an "illegal usurpation toward the region of Texas." The "anonymous source" whom the Spanish frontier officials describe as a principal in the Burr Conspiracy could have been no other.

Given the controversy over the boundaries of Louisiana, coupled with their precarious position with the Indian Nations of the

---

Freeman and Custis). I use the Robertson reproduction here, pp. 334, 337–42, 347.

[126] Ibid., p. 343. Astoundingly, one section of the document even encourages an annual appropriation to allow the boundary commissioner (Caso Calvo) and Folch to procure "secret services," else Spain is in danger of "losing in the cause which we are discussing, a man of great talent and national influence." That Wilkinson was a pensioner of the Spanish government in 1806 is proved in Carlos Martinez Yrujo to Cevallos [Washington], Jan. 28, 1807 (quoted in Abernethy, *The Burr Conspiracy*, p. 198), which closes with Cevallos being thus assured: "Wilkinson is entirely devoted to us. He enjoys a considerable pension from the King." In fact, Wilkinson received $10,000 for "Reflections on Louisiana."

[127] Abraham P. Nasatir, "More on Pedro Vial in Upper Louisiana," in Mc-

North, Spanish officials probably needed little urging from any quarter to recognize the threat posed by this American probe into the heart of the Provincias Internas. The danger was very real. Thus the chilling pronouncements that their frontier officials began to hear with alarming frequency during the months before the embarkment of the American party must have seemed to validate the testimony of an intriguing figure who had appeared in Texas during early August, 1805, with "important matters" about which the Crown should be immediately advised. The man was Felipe Enrique Neri, or the Baron de Bastrop, the self-styled title he preferred. Bastrop was nearing fifty, a European soldier of fortune with Teutonic features (he claimed to be Dutch), a French title, a Spanish first name, an Italian surname, and a somewhat suspect reputation.

In 1796, Bastrop had managed to obtain a huge grant of land in present northern Louisiana and southern Arkansas for the purpose of bringing in settlers for the Spanish Empire. Now, two years after the cession, he appeared in Texas, expressing a desire to plant new colonies and full of warnings about the imperialistic Americans. It is not especially likely that Bastrop was an agent of Burr and Wilkinson, but he may as well have been, for he added cogent testimony which could have come from the mouth of Caso Calvo's secret informer. Regarding the Americans, he said that all indications were "announcing an immediate movement of their forces to invade the dominions of [H]is M[ajesty] *merely awaiting the movement for running the boundary . . . before this work is undertaken.*"[128] Now the Spaniards had yet another reason to oppose Jefferson's exploration. The Americans were known to be carrying instruments of celestial observation and map-making on the expedition; obviously, the Spaniards reasoned, "scientific exploration" was just a euphemism for surveying a

---

Dermott, *The Spanish in the Mississippi Valley*, pp. 100–19. This article reproduces the documents and journal of the first of these Vial expeditions.

[128] Bastrop's warning is in Cordero to Salcedo, San Antonio, September 25, 1805. See also, Valle to Bautista, Nacogdoches, August 28, 1805. The Bexar Archives.

boundary which they would then attempt to hold by reason of the survey itself. The Spanish officials distrusted Bastrop anyway. Had they known that the final transfer of title to much of the baron's Ouachita Valley Grant was to Aaron Burr—who, along with Bastrop's former partner, Abraham Morhouse, was planning to use the grant as headquarters and training ground for their secret and private move against Mexico—they might have refused Bastrop's entry into Texas.[129] Intended or no, the baron had played a card directly from the hand of Wilkinson and Burr.

THE STRUGGLE FOR THE PINEY WOODS

At first the frontier commanders who were on the scene in the northern provinces experienced great difficulty convincing their superiors in Mexico City that there was a gestating crisis. Both Cordero and Salcedo were deadly serious. While Salcedo packed in preparation for transferring his headquarters to San Antonio, where he could personally supervise the resistance, he had Cordero draw up a plan of defense from the point of view that the war "is already fact."[130] After repeated pleas for dramatically increased garrisons from Cordero, Viceroy Yturrigaray replied that because of short supplies, including a complete dearth of cannon, provisioning Texas to such an extent was impossible. Salcedo then added his voice to Cordero's, calling upon Yturrigaray to recognize that the danger was real and of "the greatest urgency." Only seven hundred troops were stationed in Texas, he told the viceroy, fewer than half the number required to even make a show of resistance. Unless Cordero were supplied, Salcedo warned,

---

[129] For general information on Bastrop, including the transfer of part of his grant to Burr, I have relied upon Webb and Carroll, *Handbook of Texas* 2:120; R. Woods Moore, "The Role of The Baron de Bastrop in the Anglo-American Settlement of the Spanish Southwest," *Louisiana Historical Quarterly* 31 (July 1948): 615; and, especially, Jennie O'Kelly Mitchell and Robert Dabney Calhoun, "The Marquis de Maison Rouge, The Baron De Bastrop, and Colonel Abraham Morhouse. Three Ouachita Valley Soldiers of Fortune: The Maison Rouge and Bastrop Spanish Land 'Grants,'" *Louisiana Historical Quarterly* 20 (April 1937): 405–13.

[130] Cordero to Salcedo, San Antonio, October 23, 1805. The Bexar Archives.

he was washing his hands of the matter.[131] So pitifully ill-manned were the Texas garrisons that when the threat of a possible fili-buster naval attack was raised in mid-January, 1806, only twenty-five troops could be spared to reinforce the coastline.[132]

On February 5, whatever complacency still existed among Spanish officials evaporated with the news that 150 Americans under Captain Edward D. Turner of Fort Claiborne in Natchi-toches had fallen on José Maria Gonzalez and his eighteen men at Los Adaes, forcing the Spaniards to abandon their former capital and withdraw to the Sabine. Turner claimed that the bloodless attack was in keeping with the spirit of President Jef-ferson's declarations about the boundaries of Louisiana, but Texas officials were enraged. None seethed more than the hot-blooded governor in San Antonio. Within a week Cordero issued top secret instructions to Rodriguez at Nacogdoches, ordering a sud-den surprise attack against all American strongholds west of the Arroyo Hondo. At the same time he drew up a burning procla-mation calling upon all Texas commanders to "blindly obey" these orders, and to "resolve to attack and destroy every Anglo-American party."[133]

[131] Yturrigaray to Salcedo, Mexico City, November 30, 1805; Salcedo to Ytur-rigaray, Chihuahua, December 3 and 23, 1805, ibid. These exchanges clearly refute Abernethy's contention that the Louisiana-Texas crisis was initiated in October, 1805, when "a Spanish force of 1300 men crossed the Sabine." Aber-nethy, *The Burr Conspiracy*, p. 47. Nothing like that number of troops was in Texas in 1805. It now becomes apparent that it was, instead, a combination of Turner's raid on Los Adaes and concern—both contrived and real—over Jeffer-son's exploration that led to mobilization. Spain was again doing what she always did so well: reacting rather than initiating.

[132] Cordero to Salcedo, San Antonio, January 14, 1806, ibid. This alarm was probably a response to the so-called Miranda Expedition, which increased the mutual hostility between Spain and the United States. Early in January, Fran-cisco de Miranda, a Venezuelan radical who hoped to revolutionize Spain's Latin American colonies with the help of the American Republic, set sail from New York with an American-equipped vessel called *The Leander.* The Spanish government, forewarned, captured *The Leander* at sea, and Miranda was hustled off to a Spanish dungeon. It was speculated during the trials that Miranda was to have rendezvoused at some point with Burr's force. Ibid., pp. 123, 270.

[133] José Maria Gonzalez to Rodriguez, Los Adaes, February 13, 1806, ibid. The proclamation of the existence of hostilities by Governor Cordero (February

Cordero had obviously declared war. It must have shocked him to discover that Nacogdoches officials had no intention of carrying out his orders. At first Rodriguez put on a show of martial bluster, advocating an attack on Fort Claiborne in conjunction with a proclamation promising freedom to any slaves who would aid the Spanish cause. Then quite suddenly, on February 13, Rodriguez announced his decision to resign as Nacogdoches commandant.[134]

Cordero refused to honor that request, but Rodriguez did not last long at any rate. Furious that the East Texas commander had not only ignored the direct order to attack, but also suppressed the distribution of Cordero's proclamation, Salcedo finally relieved Rodriguez in early March, upon learning that the Nacogdoches commander had visited Turner at Fort Claiborne in late February. For "errors" and consorting with the enemy, Rodriguez was replaced, but he was not silenced. He had resisted Cordero's orders, he bluntly told Salcedo, because he knew that if he attacked the Americans there would be a war, and if there was a frontier war now, Spanish arms would be disgraced.[135]

That meant that a new commander—a hard-liner much more sympathetic to Salcedo's and Cordero's approach—must be appointed to the Nacogdoches garrison to head off whatever moves the Americans might try next. The new East Texas commander must be aggressive, inflexible, and ramrod-straight in military discipline. And Salcedo knew just such a man.

He was Don Francisco Viana, the adjutant inspector of the troops in the Provincias Internas of New Spain. A year after his appointment, Zebulon Pike described Viana as a veteran soldier with a frank mind who expressed his opinions perhaps too freely, highly respected and regarded as a model of military conduct by his superiors, but with insufficient flexibility to allow him to

13, 1806) is in The Nacogdoches Archives, Blake's transcripts, Supplement 5.

[134] Rodriguez to Cordero, Nacogdoches, February 13, 1806, ibid. Rodriguez attempted to turn the command over to Dionisio Valle, "another officer of more talent and experience," but Cordero angrily returned the resignation letter.

[135] Rodriguez to Salcedo, Nacogdoches, March 12, 1806, and Salcedo to Cordero, Chihuahua, March 25, 1806, The Bexar Archives.

rise in the administration of the colonies.[136] In short, Viana was every inch the soldier. He had been ill during the winter, but by mid-April Viana had made the journey from La Bahia to Nacogdoches, and there he quickly whipped the garrison into shape. And while Salcedo and Cordero urged him repeatedly to watch for American activity, reinforcements at last began arriving in Texas. Late in April Viana dispatched from the Nacogdoches garrison 134 troops, 400 horses, and 63 beeves under the command of Lieutenant Juan Ignacio Ramón, who had instructions to move to the Neches River for training exercises at a camp called San Miguel del Salto (probably somewhere in the present Davy Crockett National Forest). In May, the Nacogdoches commander wrote Governor Cordero that since he had learned that the expedition of Anglo-Americans was to consist of only fifty men, he was preparing to send a hundred Spanish regulars against them. At the same time, however, he ordered José Maria Guadiana to visit the Alabama-Coushatta villages on the Attoyac and Sabine rivers in an attempt to raise a hundred Indians to ride against the Americans. Guadiana was then to move discreetly to Bayou Pierre, from which point he was to send out spies to reconnoiter the river. As reinforcements continued to arrive (543 troops were on the march to Nacogdoches from various frontier garrisons by early June), Viana found supply his only problem. Except for a dearth "of cartridges, paper, and lead," the move to intercept the American expedition, he informed his superiors, was proceeding according to plan.[137] The Spaniards were girding their loins for battle.

Indeed, by early 1806 that sentiment existed not only in the piney woods of East Texas, but on every level of American-

[136] Pike's entry for June 27, 1807, in Jackson, *The Journals of Zebulon Montgomery Pike* 1:446.

[137] Announcing Viana's appointment (which Cordero opposed), Salcedo to Cordero, Chihuahua, March 25, 1806, The Bexar Archives. Rámon to Viana, Neches River, April 26, 1806, Viana to Cordero, Nacogdoches, May 29, 1806, Guadiana to Viana, near the Alabama-Coushatta village [Sabine River], May 31, 1806, ibid. See also, Statement, June 12, 1806, Nacogdoches Garrison, The Nacogdoches Archives, Supplement 5.

Spanish relations. Diplomatically, each new announcement of Jeffersonian policy seemed to worsen the already shakey status quo. Initial negotiations, in fact, had already collapsed. In May, 1805, Monroe had packed his bags in disgust and departed for London, leaving it to a new team of negotiators to resolve what he referred to as "this interesting crisis."[138] Monroe's disillusionment was not made any more palatable by the news that France publicly expressed the intention to side with Spain in the event of a war over the Louisiana boundary. Jefferson responded by securing a two-million-dollar appropriation promise from Congress in order to obtain a peaceful (and pro-American) boundary settlement. Even as his expedition for examining the border country was in its final preparation, he sent John Armstrong to Paris in an effort to patch things up with the Spaniards at a joint meeting to be held under the watchful eyes of Emperor Napoleon and Foreign Secretary Maurice de Talleyrand. Late in the spring of 1806, James Bowdoin and Wilson C. Nicholas joined Armstrong in this endeavor, and, of course, Robert Livingston was already on hand. Jefferson took the trouble, however, to draw up a tentative treaty with England, which would have committed the British to fight for the American version of the Louisiana boundary—in return for American aid against Napoleon. Indeed, it appeared for several months as if things might come to that, for in what one historian has called "one of the most dishonorable diplomatic entanglements of our history," the American negotiators eventually could recommend to the home government nothing beyond the outright seizure of both East Texas and West Florida.[139]

This was the complicated and volatile stage of affairs in which President Thomas Jefferson's second major Louisiana probe— "The Exploring Expedition of Red River" as the leaders styled

[138] Monroe and Pinckney to James Madison, Aranjuez, May 23, 1805. *Annals of Congress*, 8th Cong., 2d sess. (1805), pp. 1459–62.
[139] Cox, "The Louisiana-Texas Frontier," 3, p. 187. Nathan Schachner, *Thomas Jefferson: A Biography*, pp. 798–812, treats American diplomatic efforts harshly. The *American State Papers, Foreign Relations* 2, provides an overview on pp. 634–69.

it—finished final preparations during late March and early April. A quick trip to New Orleans for supplies was necessary, and there Governor Claiborne told Freeman that the "jealous" Spaniards were moving to stop the exploration.[140] But back at "The Forest" spirits were high, and Dunbar was "fully persuaded that the most perfect harmony" would prevail among the party.[141]

Nevertheless, on the very day that Dunbar wrote Jefferson with understandable exultation that the exploring party, "very commodiously fitted out," had at long last departed for the Red River, Secretary of War Dearborn was writing to James Wilkinson in St. Louis, ordering him to proceed at once to the Louisiana-Texas frontier to confront the "hostile views of the Officers of his Catholic Majesty in that quarter."[142]

Rumors and threats, plots and counterplots, legitimate fears and diplomatic bluster: to the principals of the Red River exploration, to Dunbar particularly, the situation must have portended failure, perhaps even disaster. In any case, Mr. Jefferson's expedition into the Southwest was one exploration that clearly was destined to have as many implications for empire as for science.

[140] Claiborne to Jefferson, New Orleans, March 26, 1806. The Thomas Jefferson Papers, 1st ser. Freeman had already drawn a draft on the War Department for $820 for supplying the expedition when Claiborne told him of the Spanish activity. Freeman to the War Department, New Orleans, March 20, 1806. War Department, Letters Received, Main Series, The National Archives. The level of excitement on the Southwestern frontier was publicly evident during the explorers' New Orleans visit. The *Louisiana Gazette* of that city was that week (issue of March 21, 1806) editorializing: "It appears to be a demonstrable fact that . . . the Spaniards must be dispossessed of some of the provinces which border on, and lie contiguous to, our own territory. . . . Hundreds of thousands of hardy, resolute, enterprising republicans would penetrate into all the rich and secret recesses of those regions. . . ."

[141] Dunbar to Freeman Esqr. & his associates, Natchez, May 6, 1806. Rowland, *Dunbar Letters*, pp. 339-40.

[142] Dunbar to Jefferson, Natchez, May 6, 1806; Dearborn to Wilkinson, Washington, May 6, 1806, The Thomas Jefferson Papers, 1st ser.

The Documents and Editorial Procedures

BOTH Jefferson and Dunbar instructed the leaders of the Red River party to keep journals and scientific charts during the exploration. Freeman complied fully, assembling a detailed daily journal, which Dunbar forwarded to Washington in two parts in August and October of 1806. Custis's daily journal was written up, and has survived, in the form of four lengthy narrative reports to Secretary of War Dearborn and Professor Barton during and after completion of the exploration. Along with his natural history catalogues, meteorological tables, and a chart of Red River landmarks, Custis's four reports and Freeman's extensive tables of geographical courses for producing a map complete the documentary materials from the actual exploration.

Sometime in the late autumn of 1806, following his own careful perusal of them, Jefferson passed the documents along to Nicholas King, who, it now emerges, was a central figure in the preparation of the returns of Jefferson's western explorations for publication. King, the city surveyor in the capital and a talented architect, artist, and mapmaker, who also wrote remarkably clear longhand, was the forerunner of Nicholas Biddle in the field of western exploration. Already he had redacted the Dunbar and Hunter journals of the Ouachita River exploration for presentation to Congress, and late in 1806 was similarly at work on Zebulon Pike's journal of the 1805 Mississippi River exploration. King did particularly

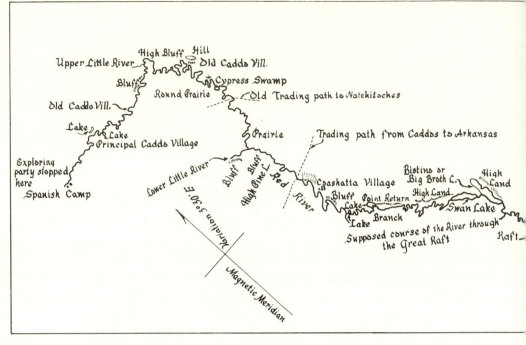

Nicholas King's Map of the Red River in Louisiana, *drawn up from the survey notes of the party, definitively mapped the lower 615 miles of the Red and was widely adopted. It appears here redrawn from the original.*

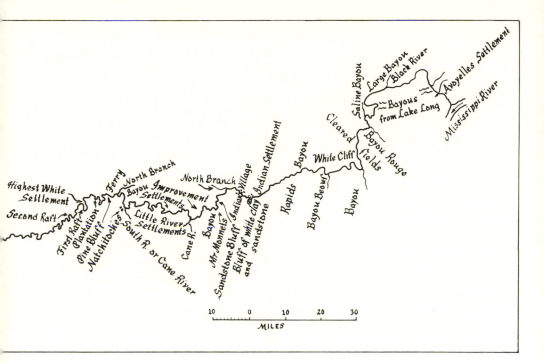

Highest White
Settlement

Second Raft

First Raft

Plantation

Pine Bluff

Natchitoches

Ferry

North Branch

Bayou Improvement
Settlements

Little River
Settlements

South R. or Cane River

Cane R.

North Branch

Bayou

Mr Monnet's

Sandstone Bluff Indian Village

Bluff of white clay
and sandstone

Indian Settlement

Rapids

Bayou

Bayou Beouf

Bayou

White Cliff

Cleared
fields

Bayou Rouge

Saline Bayou

Large Bayou
Black River

Bayous
from Lake Long

Avoyelles Settlement

Mississippi River

10   0   10   20   30

MILES

accurate and beautiful maps. He provided a map "blank" for Lewis and Clark, produced maps from both the Lewis and Clark and the Pike expeditions, and drew a map of the Ouachita River that Dunbar called a "mirror-image" of his own. King's "Map of the Red River in Louisiana," from Freeman's field courses, was completed before the year was out. Redrawn and reproduced in this volume, it can be considered the most accurate map produced by any of the early American explorations.

King's subsequent redaction of the Freeman and Custis accounts into a single longhand narrative of 142 pages, the original of which is now in the Peter Force Collection of the Library of Congress, was skillfully done, albeit with some errors and mysterious omissions. King's weakness in handling exploration documents was his lack of familiarity with natural history nomenclature in Latin. The errors in King's version, published with the map in a run of no more than two hundred copies in March, 1807, under the title *An Account Of The Red River In Louisiana, Drawn Up From The Returns Of Messrs. Freeman & Custis, To The War Office Of The United States, Who Explored The Same, In The Year 1806*, are confined to garbled Latin binomials and his failure to insert longitude figures computed from the field courses. More troubling is the omission of material from the original documents, particularly the elimination of all references to the objectives of the exploration, to military additions at Natchitoches, and to the substance of Freeman's address to the Indians. Finally, King altered the narrators' relationship to the journals, converting them into a third-person discourse, which diluted the impact they had as first-person accounts.

The Accounts as presented here represent an improvement over King's redaction in many substantial ways. The discovery and utilization of Custis's original (and previously unpublished) manuscripts, still on file in the records of the War Department in the National Archives and in the Benjamin Smith Barton Papers at the Library of the American Philosophical Society, make it possible for the first time to properly credit the two chroniclers of the exploration with the passages they wrote. In addition, where they have been preserved by Edwin James, entries from Freeman's original journal are here reproduced. James, who wrote on the "Freeman & Sparks" expedition in 1821, was given Freeman's journal by General Daniel Parker of the War Department. He never returned it, and its subsequent loss to history apparently can be traced to orders James gave his housekeeper to burn all his papers at his death.[1] Thus, for the bulk of Freeman's journal we must depend upon King's version, the only one extant. As with Custis's material, I have here reproduced Freeman's journal (via King) from the manuscript copy in the Library of Congress, faithfully retaining all punctuation and spelling as they appear in the original. The only editorial change I have made to any of these documents is to restore—with a view towards consistency and originality—the Freeman-King sections to Freeman's original first-person account. The result is a more complete, original, and precise version of the Red River exploration than has ever been available before.

The key to the documents as they appear in the Accounts, properly credited to their authors, is found on page 98.

The style of both the Accounts is in the tradition of eighteenth-century nature reporting: spare and straightforward, with a clear concern for utility. The adjective "beautiful" as Custis uses it, for example, connotes not just a pleasing visual impression, but also potential agricultural fertility. Freeman's own focus, moreover, is that of an engineer, with the expected commitment to measurement and precision. Both men, in fact, incline towards leaner and more professional nature reporting than their less-educated counterparts on the Missouri River expedition, an effect enhanced by the narrative nature of the documents.

Including Custis's natural history catalogues, the Accounts break naturally into five parts, for which I have provided titles. The meteorological tables and the Red River landmark chart (which was not included in the published King version) are included here as appendices. My annotation is both explanatory and interpretive of the documents, but readers ought to note that, in an

---

[1] Item on James's death in the Louis H. Pammel Papers, University Archives, Iowa State University Library.

effort to avoid duplication, the majority of Custis's botanical references are fully worked out only in the annotation to Part V. Finally, the desirability of following the Spanish response, among other reasons, has necessitated the use of editorial headnotes to introduce the five parts of the Accounts.

The Accounts

Accept Gentlemen my fervent wishes for your individual health & satisfaction being fully persuaded that the most perfect harmony will reign among you, upon which will greatly depend the valuables & discoveries & information expected by the Genl. Govt. & by our Country from your successful labors.

William Dunbar, *Dunbar Letters.*

KEY TO THE DOCUMENTS AS THEY APPEAR IN THE ACCOUNTS

Freeman 1. Freeman's journal as redacted in the King manuscript copy.

Freeman 2. Freeman's journal, original entries as preserved by Edwin James in *Account Of An Expedition From Pittsburgh To The Rocky Mountains Performed In The Years 1819, 1820.*

Custis 1. Custis's manuscript report to Dearborn, Natchitoches, June 1, 1806.

Custis 2. Custis's manuscript report to Dearborn, Coashatta Village, July 1, 1806.

Custis 3. Custis's manuscript report to Dearborn, Natchez, October 1, 1806.

Custis 4. Custis's manuscript report to Barton, Natchitoches, June 1, 1806.

PART ONE

﹃ *Fort Adams to Natchitoches* ﹄

﹃ *April and May 1806* ﹄

EDITOR'S NOTE: Only one muster roll has survived for the Freeman and Custis expedition, Captain Richard Sparks's April 30 to June 30 muster for the 2nd Regiment. It lists only seven members of the party—Joseph Parsons, Samuel Reed, Eliphalet Kelsey, John Martin, Edward Mooney, Nimrod Fletcher, and Doughty Nicholson. The men were carefully selected from the companies that composed the American garrisons at Fort Adams and New Orleans in April of 1806. Constructed between 1798 and 1800, on the site of a seventeenth-century French mission on the east bank of the Mississippi some 60 miles downriver from Natchez, Fort Adams was the logical departure point for an exploration into the American Southwest. Designed and built under the supervision of Freeman, whom Wilkinson had hired for the task after the Ellicott debacle, it was strategically located on the frontier, commanding the Mississippi River with cannon and howitzers from a 100-foot overhanging bluff called Loftus Heights. Surrounding the fort was the modest village of Wilkinsonburg, long a center of intrigue against Spanish Texas. Wilkinson had used the fort for secret meetings with both Spanish officials and members of the Mexican Association; Abernethy believes it was to have served as one of the bases for the Burr Conspiracy.[1]

[1]Muster Roll of a Company of Infantry under the Command of Captain Richard Sparks, Records of the Adjutant General's Office, 1780–1917, Record Group 94, National Archives. On Fort Adams: John Campbell to Thomas Cushing, Fort Adams, Mississippi Territory, April 4, 1806, War Department, Letters Received, Unregistered Series; and Fortescue Cuming, *Sketches of a Tour in 1807*, in *Early Western Travels, 1748–1846*, ed. Reuben Gold Thwaites, 4:328–29. See also, Abernethy, *The Burr Conspiracy*, p. 30; and Dunbar Rowland, ed.,

As Custis's initial entry in the Accounts makes clear, the expedition seems to have been beset by a series of delays which, with the water ever dropping in the Red, will throw them seriously behind schedule for a successful ascent of the upper river during the dry summer months. The trip to New Orleans in late March uses up nearly three weeks. And although Freeman cites April 19 as the launch date from Fort Adams, we know that the explorers first journeyed upriver, for a final round of preparation under Dunbar's supervision at The Forest, before finally disembarking for the mouth of the Red on April 28.

One interesting omission from the King transcription of Freeman's opening entry ought to be noted. Based on his own examination of Freeman's original journal, Edwin James leaves no doubt that Freeman included here a sentence respecting the objectives of the expedition: it was to ascend the Red to the "Pani" villages and, using them as a base and for a supply of horses, "proceed to the top of the mountains."[2] King may have been instructed to strike out this phrase, as he appears to have done with others, in order to save the administration embarrassment over the fate of the expedition.

Custis 4.

The boats not being in readiness on our arrival at Natchez, we had to proceed to New-Orleans, for the purpose of fitting them out, and from thence to return to Natchez, for the final equipment of all which, much time was necessarily required.

Freeman 1.

The party employed to explore the Red River, at leaving Fort Adams, consisted of [myself], Thomas Freeman, Surveyor, who was furnished with the requisite instruments, for determining Geographical positions, by Astronomical Observations; Dr. Peter Custis whose attention was directed to Botany, and Natural History;[3] Captain Sparks, and Lieut. Humphreys, two noncommissioned officers, seventeen private soldiers, and a Black servant.

Mississippi: Comprising Sketches of Counties, Towns, Events, Institutions, and Persons, Arranged in Cyclopedic Form 1:728.

[2] James, *Account of an Expedition from Pittsburgh to the Rocky Mountains Performed in the Years 1819, 1820,* Thwaites, *Early Western Travels* 4:67.

[3] The use of Custis's title is apparently in anticipation of his being awarded his M.D. degree in 1807.

We left Fort Adams, on the Mississippi, on the afternoon of the 19th of April, in two flat bottomed Barges and a Periogue, taking with us such stores and other articles, as it was probable we might want, in the course of the expedition, calculating, however, on the receiving of a supply at Natchitoches, for the prosecution of the survey, beyond that port.

The only mode of travelling, which the nature of the country admits of, while it furnishes the means of making the survey of the river sufficiently accurate for geographical purposes, precludes attention to topography, and the general face of the country, which is important, and furnishes the widest field for observation.

In ascending a navigable river, whose banks are generally elevated considerably above the surface of the water, the remarks of the survey will be confined to the width, depth, and course it pursues; and its rise during periods of inundation; the quality of the water, the vegetation on the banks in the immediate vicinity of the river; as well as the animals and fish which art or accident may bring within his reach; together with the mineralogical and geological facts, which the abrasion of the waters furnish, confine the naturalist and chemist within very narrow bounds.

On entering the Red River, it was the wish of the party to have ascertained the Longitude and Latitude of its mouth, by celestial observation, but the spot where we encamped, and the unfavorable weather, prevented this circumstance from taking place; other observers had determined it to be in 31 deg. 1 min. 15 sec. N. L. and 91 deg. 47 min. 45 sec. west from Greenwhich.[4]

---

[4] These were the figures provided by Dunbar and Hunter during the Ouachita expedition, but actually fixed by the Spanish geographer Jóse Joaquin de Ferrer. See his "Astronomical Observations made by Jóse Joaquin de Ferrer, chiefly for the Purpose of determining the Geographical Position of various Places in the United States, and other Parts of North America," *Transactions of the American Philosophical Society* 6 (1809): 158-64, first read before the society in 1803. See also, Dunbar's "Journal of a Voyage," entry for October 17, Rowland, *Dunbar Letters*, pp. 216-17. The mouth of the Red River has shifted many times since 1806, and modern United States Geological Survey (USGS) Natchez Quadrangle, indicates that today it is at about 30° 59' N, 91° 39' W.

Since Dunbar and Hunter had already mentioned it in their Ouachita River journals, Freeman and Custis apparently do not consider it necessary to discuss a theory about the mouth of the Red that Ellicott had advanced in 1803: the

On the 3rd of May, we had ascended Red River as far as the mouth of Black River, a distance of 26 miles;[5] Red River is nearly half a mile wide at its mouth, which width it preserves for about a mile, when it contracts to about one fourth of a mile; the depth of the river at its confluence with the Mississippi is 84 feet; and where it receives the water of Black river, 42 feet. A mile from the mouth of the river, its banks were 14 feet above the surface of the water, at the time the party passed up; in ascending the river, these were observed to rise, and when they had reached the mouth of Black river, they were found to be 25 feet above the surface of the water. The face of the land is nearly level to the distance of a mile from the banks of the river, where the ground becomes swampy. At a small distance from the margin of

---

hypothesis that the Red's junction with the Mississippi was a recent one, and that the original lower end of the Red River had become the Atchafalaya River. Amos Stoddard, in his *Sketches, Historical and Descriptive, Of Louisiana,* pp. 380–81, did the most to popularize the idea that the Mississippi had cut off the bottom end of the Red, but twentieth-century geologists have refuted this once widely-held opinion. The modern concept is that the Atchafalaya is a separate river, but one utilized by the Red and Mississippi for floodwater release. H. N. Fisk, *Geology of Avoyelles and Rapides Parishes,* Louisiana Geological *Bulletin No. 18,* pp. 29–34; "Red River, La., Ark., Okla., and Tex.," *House Doc. 378,* 74th Cong., 2d sess. (1936), p. 1.

[5] Several methods were utilized by early rivermen to determine speed and distance travelled. For a scientific expedition intended to procure exact data, Freeman and his assistant, Enoch Humphreys, employed the most accurate: the log line. The log line was reliable and simple to use, although annoying because the experiment had to be repeated at regular intervals. It consisted of a rope line divided into known lengths (usually perches or rods — 16.5 feet — although Dunbar advised Freeman that a half-perch division was sufficient), which was then attached to a buoy and tossed into the river beside the boat. With the assistance of a chronometer, or sometimes a special instrument known as an accrometer, the time interval required to play out the line could be arrived at. Of course the current in a river complicated the figuring, but that, too, could be computed with the log line from a stationary point, and then plugged into the equation. Actually, in a large river the current can often be avoided and the ascent made over slack water on the insides of the bends. Dunbar to Freeman Esqr. & his Associates, Natchez, April 28, 1806, Rowland, *Dunbar Letters,* p. 339.

Dunbar and Hunter had turned up the Black River in the autumn of 1804, since the Black represents the united waters of the Ouachita, Tensas, and Catahoula rivers. Theirs is the most useful account of the nineteenth-century Black

the river, there is a second bank or rise in the land, elevating the surface nearly as high as the water rises in the periodical floods, which the marks left on the trees denote to be from 25 to 28 feet higher than at this time:[6] the soil on each side of the river has the appearance of being rich, and seems to have been formed by the deposition of the soil, and earthy particles brought by the water in the periodical inundations, to which this river is subject.

Custis 1.

On the first of the present instant [May] we left Fort Adams & arrived here [Natchitoches] on the nineteenth. Owing to Mr. Freemans great anxiety to proceed to this place as quickly as possible I have not had so compleat an opportunity of examining the country and its productions as I could have wished. I shall therefore be able to give you only a rapid & imperfect sketch.

The Red River is at its mouth about a half mile wide and preserves that width for one mile and contracts to about a fourth of a mile and continues of that width as far as the mouth of Black River, a distance of 30 miles from the Mississippi.—The water of

—actually a clear stream, but called "Riviere Noire" by the French because of the marked contrast between it and the ruddy Red.

[6] One of the unique aspects of the natural environment in the Red River valley was the complete inundation of almost all the country along the lower 150 miles of the river from February through April, and sometimes (but apparently not in 1806) until June. When the floodwaters of the Red and Mississippi rivers united—as they usually did—boats were able to pass across an enormous extent of east-central Louisiana in every direction. Stoddard, who found the upland country farther up the river delightful, was depressed by the lower Red: "The country for this distance exhibits a gloomy prospect; it presents to the eye a world of waters." Stoddard, *Sketches, Historical And Descriptive, Of Louisiana*, p. 134. The recession of the high water was not always an improvement. Years later Freeman described the overflow lands thusly: ". . . few men can be found hardy enough to stand the poisonous effects of Half dried mud, putrid fish & Vegetable matter—almost impenetrable cane brakes, and swarms of mosketos—with which these low lands abound after the waters are withdrawn." Freeman to Albert Gallatin, Washington, Mississippi Territory, July 15, 1811. Carter, *The Territory of Mississippi, 1809–1817*, vol. 6 of *The Territorial Papers of the United States*, pp. 210–11.

Red River is of a reddish brown colour caused by the suspension of an argillaceous marle of which the banks, in many places after passing Black River, seem to be almost entirely composed.[7] From the colour is derived its name. For two or three miles this River is beautifully bordered with willow trees[8] which extend back for half a mile where there is a second bank about 6 feet above the first.[9] The first bank is 8 ft. above the present level of the River. — Upon this second bank we find a variety of trees. The pecan is the most abundant. — This is a species of *Juglans* which bears a fruit known by the name of Illinois nut, which is so universally admired. The pecan though it is so very different in its habits from that of the *Juglans alba*[10] as not to be mistaken for it by the most common observer: yet the only difference which can be pointed out consists in the leaf—Both have pinnate leaves, the *Alba* has an odd leaflet sepista [?], the Pecan the odd one petiolate.

[7] This marle has its origins in the Permian Redbeds formation of present West Texas, between the 99th and 100th meridians. Prairie Dog Town Fork of the Red River and its southern affluents, the Little Red, the Pease and the Little Wichita, drain the exposed buttes and mesas of this formation. The waters of the Red are given a further rusty tinge from iron and other mineral residues brought from the Wichita Mountains by Otter Creek, an affluent of the North Fork. Erwin Raisz, "Landforms of The United States," in Wallace W. Atwood, *The Physiographic Provinces of North America* (Boston: Ginn and Co., 1940); "Red River, La., Ark., Okla., and Tex.," *House Doc. 785*, 74th Cong., 2d sess., pp. 1-4. Carl N. Tyson, in his recent *The Red River in Southwestern History*, p. 7, cites Marcy's report of 1852 crediting the North Fork with giving the river its color, but ignores the effect of marle in coloring the Red.

[8] As indicated in the Editorial Procedures, only those rare natural history entries which do not appear in Custis's catalogues are treated with full annotation here. On the lower Red, Custis is observing willow stands composed of black willow (*Salix nigra* Marsh.) and sandbar willow (*S. interior* Rowlee). Above the Great Raft, in the vicinity of the Alabama-Coushatta village, he will be within the range of the coastal plain willow (*S. caroliniana* Michx.), although the other two species will remain prevalent. Robert Vines, *Trees of East Texas*, pp. 29-35.

[9] The second rise marked the extent of the high-water sediment deposits in the river, and was the natural flood-level "cutbank" against the slightly higher ground of the older Prairie Terrace alluvial deposits, laid down in the Pleistocene Age.

[10] If he is following Bartram, probably the white-heart hickory (*Carya tomentosa* Nutt. in present classification), but perhaps the shagbark hickory (*C. ovata* [Mill.] K. Koch).

A virgin bald cypress (Taxodium distichum) *from the original forest towers over newer tree growth.*

Why not call the Pecan *Juglans petiolata?*[11] Here too we see the cotton tree which of late has excited much attention. It is said to be a species of *populus* and by some considered as the Lombardy poplar. — I can draw no resemblance except in the leaf which is very like that of the Lombardy.[12] — The other trees are oaks (*Quercus rubra,*[13] *alba*[14] and *phellos*)[15] Persimmon *(Diospyros virginiana)* Hagberry *(Prunus padus)*[16] Honey Locust *(Gleditsia tricanthos)*[17] which is every where abundant on this River, Sycamore or American Plane tree *(Platanus occidentalis)* and *Crataegus aria.*[18] After passing 3 miles up there are no other trees to be seen from the River except Willow & Pecan until we come within 4 or 5 miles of Black River, where we meet with Cypress *(Cupressus disticha).*[19] — The pecans are covered with misleto *(Viscum album).*[20] The bank at Black River on the right side is about 30 ft. high and runs off pretty pretty [*sic*] level for one mile and becomes swampy. — The land is of a very rich, black light soil. — It is said by a man resid-

---

[11]*Juglans petiolata* will be properly described and entered as a name for the pecan with the publication of Custis's letter to Barton on June 1, under the title: "Observations relative to the Geography, Natural History, & etc., of the Country along the Red River, in Louisiana," *The Philadelphia Medical and Physical Journal* 2, Pt. 2 (1806), p. 45, and also in the official account of the exploration, published in 1807. The pecan is now *Carya illinoinensis* (Wangh.) K. Koch, but *Juglans petiolata* Custis ought now finally to go into synonymy in the botanical literature.

[12]The eastern cottonwood (*Populus deltoides* Marsh.), and perhaps the swamp cottonwood (*P. heterophylla* [L.]).

[13]He could be referring to any number of American red oaks but most likely this is the southern red oak (*Quercus falcata* Michx.).

[14]The common white oak.

[15]The willow oak.

[16]Probably instead the black cherry (*Prunus serotina* Ehrh.).

[17]King fails to include this species in the published account.

[18]Evidently instead, the red chokeberry (*Pyrus arbutifolia* [L.] L. F.).

[19]Now reclassified as a member of the redwood family, the bald cypress (*Taxodium distichum* [L.] Richard).

[20]It is thus left to botanists from Europe to recognize that this semi-parasitic shrub is distinct from the Old World types. This undoubtedly was the Christmas American mistletoe, either *Phoradendron flavescens* [Pursh] Nutt.) or *P. seriotinum* (Raf.) M. C. Johnston, found in several varieties on deciduous trees from New Mexico east to Florida, north to Ontario and Kansas. Robert Vines, *Trees, Shrubs, and Woody Vines of the Southwest,* p. 222.

ing at this place[21] to be sometimes overflowed. Here we see the Sweet Gum *(Liquidambar styraciflua)* of a very large size, and the Iron wood *(Sideroxylon mite)*[22] the others are the same with those mentioned, except the *Platanus occidentalis* & cotton trees which disappeared immediately after entering the river. The River which is 350 yards wide at the mouth of Black River contracts pretty suddenly to about 250 yds. and becomes narrower as we approach the Avoyelles settlement,[23] a distance of 35 miles from B. River. — Here the River is 115 yards wide. The whole country to this place is subject to overflow and is covered with an argillaceous marl which I have before mentioned as giving colour to the water. In some places this marl extends to the depth of 4 or 5 ft.[24] At the Avoyelles the *Platanus occidentalis* and cotton trees begin to make their appearance again. We likewise see the *cornus sericea*[25] and

[21] At least three American pioneers are squatting near the mouth of the Black in 1806. Joseph Thomas and Joseph Harris are located a bit upriver; this resident is probably Alexander Mahon, who had settled in the area in 1802. "Land Claims In The Eastern District, And In The District North Of Red River, In The State of Louisiana," *American State Papers, Public Lands* 3:528, claims 76, 77, 78.

[22] He refers to an African genus not found in Louisiana. This is evidently a buckthorn, probably either the woollybucket bumelia (*Bumelia lanuginosa* [Michx.] Pers.) or the Carolina buckthorn (*Rhamnus caroliniana* Walt.).

[23] The Avoyelles settlement, also called "Baker's Landing" after a Virginian who had settled there, is located on Marksville Prairie (present Avoyelles Parish, La.), one of the few spots on the lower Red not subject to inundation in the natural ecology. Other early observers' remarks fill in some of the details. They describe a settlement based on a prairie knoll some 40 miles in circumference, over which 600 or so inhabitants (150 slaves, the rest French, Irish, and American frontiersmen) plant corn, tobacco, and cotton, and graze considerable herds of stock. Sibley, "Historical Sketches," pp. 56–57; Stoddard, *Sketches, Historical and Descriptive, of Louisiana,* p. 185.
"Avoyelles" is a Muskhogean term meaning "people of the rocks," and refers to a small tribe that had once dwelt on the prairie and exploited a famous flint quarry in the region.

[24] The Red River marle deposits also attracted Dunbar's attention in 1804, and he wrote that: ". . . the last single inundation of the red river appears to have deposited on the high bank a stratum of red marl above ½ inch thick now dry." Dunbar, "Journal of a Voyage," entry for October 20, 1804, Rowland, *Dunbar Letters,* p. 218.

[25] Instead, the roughleaf dogwood (*C. drummondii* C. A. Meyer), a new species in 1806.

some cypress. The pecan *Juglans petiolata* & Persimmon *(Diospyros virginiana)* are the most abundant. — The Persimmon frequently grows to the height of 100 feet. — From thence the bank becomes more elevated, but still appears subject to overflow in many places. — Nine miles above is a beautiful bluff of about one mile in length and 50 ft. in height formed of a reddish yellow sandy clay.[26] — At this place is first seen the *Quercus nigra* or black oak,[27] the *Myrica cerifera* or Candle berry bush[28] and Maple *(Acer pennsyl- vanicum).*[29] — Six miles above this I saw a stratum of large trees 30 feet below the surface [of the riverbank]. — The pine *(Pinus syl- vestris)*[30] Dogwood *(Cornus florida)*[31] Sassafras *(Laurus sassafras)*[32] Chestnut oak *(Quercus esculus)*[33] Holly *(Ilex aquafolium)* —[34] Hick- ory *(Juglans alba)* Spice wood *(Laurus Benzoin)*[35] and Buck eye *(Esculus parviflora* of Walter)[36] make their appearance at this place.

[26] U.S.G.S. Alexandria, (La.) Quadrangle shows this bluff to be a short dis- tance upstream from present Moncla, Avoyelles Parish, La. As this is written, Lock and Dam No. 1 of the Red River Navigation Project is being completed in this stretch of the lower Red.

[27] Commonly known as the water oak today.

[28] Now known as the southern wax-myrtle.

[29] Instead, a Southern species, either the Florida sugar maple (*A. barbatum* Michx.) or, more likely, Drummond's red maple (*A. rubrum* var. *drummondii* [Hook. & Arn.] Sarg.).

[30] Rather than the European species he lists, this is the longleaf pine (*P. palustris* Mill.). Dunbar characterized these Red River pinelands as elevated 100 to 200 feet, and wrote that: ". . . those high lands from report are poor & badly watered, being chiefly what is termed a pine-barren." Dunbar, "Journal of a Voyage," entry for Oct. 31, 1804, Rowland, *Dunbar Letters,* p. 230.

[31] The common flowering dogwood.

[32] Subsequently renamed *Sassafras albidum* (Nutt.) Nees.

[33] Instead, a new species, the swamp chestnut oak (*Q. michauxii* Nutt.).

[34] In this stretch, probably, instead of the European type, the American holly (*I. opaca* Ait.).

[35] Subsequently reclassified *Lindera benzoin* (L.) Blume, this plant seems to have been the only undergrowth of the great pine barrens of the lower Red, a cir- cumstance pointing to a fire ecology that preserved the subclimax and parklike nature of the Red River pine barrens.

[36] This is probably a correct identification, since the red buckeye is found here, but it might be the scarlet woolly buckeye (*Aesculus discolor* var. *mollis* Sarg.), an East Texas and Louisiana buckeye. Vines, *Trees, Shrubs, and Woody Vines,* pp. 679–82. The buckeye is one of the plants used by the Indians of this area to stun fish.

The *Benzoin* is almost the only undergrowth which is found on this river for a pretty considerable extent. The black [manuscript mutilated] *nigra*) are occasionally met with. — There is a shrub growing in great abundance every where along this River and as I have not seen the flowers am unable to ascertain what it is. It grows to the height of from ten to twenty ft. and bears a drupe which resembles the Olive, but is not so large. When ripe it is of a reddish-purple colour. The putamen is of a woody fibrous structure and may be easily separated by the fingers. The same peduncle supports from ten to twenty drupes. The peduncles are rameous and subopposite. — Its leaves are elliptic. — Possibly it may be the *Elaeagus* of Linn.[37] —

Freeman 1.

Almost immediately after passing Black river, which enters at right angles, and is here the most beautiful of the two, the width of the Red river is contracted to about 120 yards, which breadth it preserves, with little variation, for about 72 miles, to the rapids. Its depth at this season varies from 18 to 20 feet; and it flows generally at the rate of from two to three miles an hour. The banks, on either one side or the other, and sometimes on both, are bold and steep; the land level, very rich and subject to be overflowed during the annual inundation. The banks of the river are from 8 to 25 feet higher than the water at this season, and the land generally declines from them, for about one fourth of a mile to Cypress

[37] No species of *Eleagnaceae* occurs on the Red River, but the Oleaceae family is represented by other genera. This is almost certainly a new genus later named *Forestiera*, the plant a species now called the swamp privet (*F. acuminata* [Michx.] Poir), found from East Texas to Florida, and northward up the Mississippi Valley into Illinois and Indiana. Ibid., pp. 848–50. Although Custis would write up this description in his "Observations relative to the Geography, Natural History, &c.," p. 46, the sexual taxonomical system in use at the time required him to have observed the flowers before proffering a name for the plant. He does not list this tree in his catalogues, and the absence of a binomial caused him to lose credit for it. My thanks to Professor R. Dale Thomas of the Biology Department, Northeast Louisiana University, who is an expert on Red River valley flora, for assistance in identifying this entry. Thomas to Flores, Monroe, La., April 3, 1981, in possession of the editor.

swamps. The few bluffs, or spots of ground higher than the waters flow in the season of inundation, which approach the river, are cultivated.

The Great Rapide, or the falls, are in Lat. 31 deg. 20 min. 19 sec. N. and Longitude _____ deg. _____ min. _____ sec.—West from Greenwich.[38] The rapids, or falls, are occasioned by a stratum of indurated clay, which crosses the river in two places, about three fourths of a mile apart. The river is here about 300 yards wide. At the lower fall the current is very rapid, for about 100 yards, in 50 of which there is a fall of 10 feet, when the river is low: at the time the exploring party passed it, the fall was five feet, four feet of which was a perpendicular pitch. The second fall is in every respect similar to the first; with a very swift water for 100 rods above the fall.

Freeman 2.

This stone, when exposed to the air, becomes as hard as freestone; but under water it is found as soft as chalk. A channel could, with very little labour or expense, be cut through any part of the bed of the river, and need not be extended more than two hundred yards. It appears to me that twenty men, in ten days, with mattocks only, could at low water open a channel sufficiently wide and deep for all the barges that trade in this river to pass with safety and ease.[39]

[38] According to U.S.G.S. Topographical maps for the Alexandria (La.) area, Freeman's latitude reading is almost letter-perfect. The longitude figures were mathematical equations that had to be worked up after the exploration, but though King computed all of the courses in order to render his map of the exploration, he neglected to enter the longitude figures throughout his redaction of Freeman's account. Modern topo maps represent the longitude of this place at about 92° 26′ W.

[39] Clearly the perspective of an engineer! Sibley was no less optimistic about removal of the famed Red River rapids. He noted that from July to December, low water exposed the two rock shelves, interfering with navigation to the point of making unloading or portaging a necessity. In his opinion, "Nothing but the nature of the government we have lately emerged from, can be assigned as a reason for its [removal] not having been effected long ago." Sibley, "Historical Sketches," pp. 58–59. The rapids, and the impediment to river shipping, proved

Custis 1.

At the passage of the falls on the left bank is rapide Court-house.[40] — When we passed there was a fall of about four feet perpendicular & in the course of fifty yards the extent of the falls there was probably a fall of two feet more. The water was so shallow immediately above, that our boats which were very small & flat bottomed had to be unloaded & drawn over. The bed of the River at this place is formed of an indurated clay which when exposed to the Sun approaches the appearance of stone. — Proceeding back from the River on the right side[41] we find besides

more enduring than Sibley did. In fact, the "Great Rapids" were much more difficult of removal than these early observers suspected, thwarting even the Union Army during the Civil War. When General Banks's vessels were trapped above them by low water, he was forced to dam the river, for: "It was found . . . upon survey of the river, that the channel was narrow and crooked, formed of solid rock and that it would be impossible to deepen its bed." In G. P. Whittington, "Rapids Parish, Louisiana: A History," *Louisiana Historical Quarterly* 28 (January 1935): 16. The rapids were not "fixed" until dredging was initiated under government contract in 1883 — and completed fourteen years later! "Red River, La., Ark., Okla., and Tex.," p. 45.

[40] The area around the Great Rapids was settled early in Louisiana history. Legend has it that Spanish Franciscans set up a mission there in 1690. Certainly by 1718 (the year New Orleans was founded) French settlers began arriving, under grants issued by the Mississippi Company, to live the life of graziers in the lush river bottoms. In 1723 or 1724, a small fort called Poste du Rapide, was established to protect them. Before mid-century, men from the British Isles also began to come. Edward Murphey, an Irish merchant who set up on Bayou Rapide (a stream used to detour around the rapids during favorable water) is supposed to have been the first to turn one of the Red's navigational hazards into a profit-making enterprise. This is the same Edward Murphey who, under the Spanish, joined Barr and Davenport in consolidating control of Indian trade in the Red River country during the pre-Sibley, pre-American period. The "Rapide Settlement" (present Alexandria) grew rapidly between 1770 and 1790, laying the foundations for the great cotton plantations that eventually extended far up the Red. By the time of the American exploration in 1806, the population of the widely spread settlement was probably in excess of 750 persons. Stoddard, *Sketches, Historical and Descriptive, of Louisiana*, p. 186; Whittington, "Rapides Parish, Louisiana," 25:573–80; Alcee Fortier, ed., *Louisiana: Comprising Sketches of Parishes, Towns, Events, Institutions, and Persons, Arranged in Cyclopedic Form* 1:29; 2:346.

[41] This excursion, and at least one other made during the delay caused by the necessity of portaging the rapids, allowed Custis to perform some of the most extensive botanizing he was able to find time for on the exploration. Two forays,

the trees before mentioned the Chinquapin *(Fagus pumila)* which grows to a very great size. I have seen them 30 ft. high and 7 feet in circumference. I was told there were some much larger.[42] The *Myrica cerifera* is very abundant. The surface of the land is somewhat broken and unequal of a very light soil between the sandy and clayey and is well adapted to the growth of cotton. Most of the Red River lands are either of a clayey or marlaceous soil and appear to be not worth cultivating, but far from it they are found to be more productive than the best Mississippi lands and the cotton always commands a higher price than that of the Mississippi.

Freeman 1.

Twenty-three miles higher up the river than the falls, on a bluff about 50 feet higher than the surface of the water, is an Indian Village, called the Appalaches, on the right side of the river as you ascend. These Indians appear to be rapidly advancing towards civilization; they possess horses, cattle and hogs; dress better than Indians generally do, and seem to derive a considerable portion of their support from the cultivation of the earth. They migrated from the Appalaches river, on the frontiers of Georgia, when the white settler approached their towns.[43]

---

on May 9 and 11, in the vicinity of present Alexandria, would net him twenty-six herbaceous species, several of them exotics. See Part 5.

[42] The only chinquapin of this size here is the Alleghany chinquapin (now rendered *Castanea pumila* Mill.). Custis is near the southern extent of the range of this chestnut in the Red River valley. "Natchitoches" is a Caddoan word meaning "Chinquapin-Eaters."

[43] The Appalaches were Muskhogean speakers, native to Florida. During the decades after the transfer of Louisiana from France to Spain, Spain had endeavored to establish an Indian barrier between her trans-Mississippi settlements and the relentless westward drive of first the English, then the Americans. The drastic decline in the Caddoan population made lands near the Red River desirable for relocation of the Southeastern peoples. Most of the Indians Freeman and Custis encounter are immigrant Creeks moving west ahead of the Americans.

About 1764 these Appalaches, along with the Taensa and the Pakana Creeks, had settled on the lower Red between Bayou d'Arro and Bayou Jean de Jean. That the Appalaches were still on the banks of the Red in 1806 is a testimony to their tenacity, and to their attachment to their lands. Only four years before,

Custis 1.

Six miles above [the village] on the left side is a rock of sandstone projecting into the River, but on account of its slight cohe-
sion is unfit for building. — Two miles above this are the Pasque-
goulas Indians inhabiting both banks. — They appear to be a peaceable friendly & industrious people.[44] — Here we first find the Tooth-

they had nearly been the victims of a swindle involving a pair of American specu-
lators and traders named William Miller and Alexander Fulton, to whom the
Taensas and Pakanas had become indebted. These had agreed to sell their own
lands, some 46,000 arpents of prime river bottom and hill country, obtaining
only 3¢ an acre. Although the Appalaches were not involved in the transaction,
Miller and Fulton insisted that they had also bought title to the Appalache lands.
As Freeman here indicates, they steadfastly refused to abandon their site, located
about where Louisiana Highway 8 now crosses the river in Grant Parish, across
the river from present Boyce, La. Sibley says there were only fourteen warriors
among the Appalaches; this village could not then have numbered many more
than sixty people. Most of the Appalache people eventually united with other
tribes or went to Oklahoma with the Creeks, but a small number are believed
to have lived out their lives here on the Red. Sibley, "Historical Sketches," p. 50;
Whittington, "Rapides Parish, Louisiana," 17:36; John R. Swanton, *The Indians
of the Southeastern United States,* Bureau of American Ethnology, *Bulletin* 137
(Washington: Government Printing Office, 1946):89–91; U.S.G.S. Alexandria,
(La.) Quadrangle.

[44] There is some confusion among the contemporaries concerning the makeup
of this village. Sibley says that the village just below the fork in the river was
a "Boluxa" (Biloxi) settlement, making a distinction between these and the "Pas-
cagolas," whose village, he says, was twenty miles lower down the river. Custis's
account represents a different situation; the Biloxi are not mentioned, and the
Pasacagoulas seem to be in their location. In 1805, Sibley gave a population for
the Red River Pasacagoulas as twenty–five men (about a hundred persons total),
but by 1809 this village is completely broken up, the majority of the remaining
Pasacagoulas having gone to live with the Natchitoches Caddos, and the "Bo-
luxas" having been entirely removed by the "land company." Sibley, "Historical Sketches," pp. 50, 52; Sibley to Eustis, Natchitoches, May 8, 1809, in Garrett,
"Doctor John Sibley and The Louisiana-Texas Frontier," 47:319–20. When
visited by Freeman and Custis, this village site was located near present Colfax,
in today's Grant and Natchitoches parishes. See, for the archaeology of the site,
Hiram Gregory and Clarence Webb, "European Trade Beads from Six Sites in
Natchitoches Parish, Louisiana," *Florida Anthropologist* 18 (1965): 24–40.

The Pasacagoulas had moved to the Red River some time before 1791, where
they grew corn and vegetables and raised stock and poultry in much the same
lifestyle as the Euro-American pioneers. They had a distinctive language of their
own in the Muskhogean family, but also spoke Mobilian, the *lingua franca*
of the Southeastern tribes. Frederick Webb Hodge, ed., *Handbook of American
Indians North of Mexico,* Bureau of American Ethnology, *Bulletin 30,* 2:205.

ache tree *(Zanthoxylon Clava Herculis)*[45] & a little higher up is seen the Prickly ash *(Zanthoxylon fraxinifolium)*.[46] Seven miles above the Pasquegoula village the River divides into two branches; that to the right is very narrow and rendered impassable by Rafts and retains the name of Red River, but is better known to the inhabitants by the name of *Rivière de Petit Bon Dieu,* from the circumstance of a Priest who, in ascending the River, was upset and lost his images at this place; that to the right [he means the left] is about 80 yds. wide and is called Cane River, because of the cane *(arundo donax)*[47] being more abundant [manuscript mutilated]— The banks at the mouth of Cane River are about 40 feet high and diminish gradually to little river.—There is an abundance of excellent sand stone, for building, on the Cane River.—Ash *(Fraxinus americana)* and elm *(Ulmus americana)* are plenty here.—I have seen a few of the Sugar Maple *(Acer Saccharinum).*—The Cane River after running twenty miles divides that branch to the right is called little River and is about 50 yds. wide at its mouth; the other is broader, retains the name of Cane River & is the most direct way to Natchitoches; but like the *Bon Dieu* is impassable.— The banks of little River are in most places very low, not more than eight feet but are not overflown.—On this river is first seen the pawpaw *(Annona Glabra).*[48] The other trees are the same with

[45] Custis has fixed here the southeastern range of the hercules-club in the Red River valley.

[46] Humphrey Marshall's plant (his name is a synonym with *Z. americanum* Mill.) is out of range here. Perhaps this is the Texas hercules-club (*Z. hirsutum* Buckl.), a new plant in 1806.

[47] Custis is instead seeing a new species of cane, soon to be called giant cane (*Arundinaria gigantea* [Bartr.] Muhl.), found in low grounds and along rivers and swamps from Texas to Florida, north to New Jersey and Missouri. Vines, *Trees, Shrubs and Woody Vines,* p. 44. Although mentioned by Bartram and Walter, the full classification of this giant grass was a product of Jefferson's Southwestern explorations. In 1808 Dunbar sent twenty or more specimens from the Ouachita River voyage to the Reverend Henry Muhlenberg of Lancaster, Pa., in the process mentioning the bois d'arc tree and the great canes he and Custis had observed. Muhlenberg excitedly requested specimens, and in 1814 wrote up a complete description of the cane which now bears his name. See Henry Muhlenberg to Dunbar, Lancaster, July 5, 1808, Rowland, *Dunbar Letters,* pp. 198–204.

[48] Probably the *Asimina triloba* (L.) Dunal, whose range in the Red River val-

those already named.—The Ash *(Fraxinus americana)* and Elm *(Ulmus americana)* are the most abundant.—The Pecan continues plenty.—I saw one near the mouth of L. River which measured 19 feet in circumference five feet above the ground.

Freeman 1.

Almost immediately above these Indian villages [those of the Pascacagoulas], Red River divides into two branches; that to the right is about one third of the whole width of the river, retains the name of Red River, but is impassable, on account of the rafts of timber which are lodged in it. It separates from the other branch of the river, called Old river or Cane river, four or five miles above Natchitoches, forming an Island nearly sixty miles in length, and not more than five miles wide. The banks of these rivers are high and bold, presenting settlements occasionally on both sides. Twenty-four miles above the junction of the *Petits Bon Dieux* [*sic*] with the Old river, or as it is sometimes called, Cane river another branch falls in from the left hand or south side, which left the principal stream immediately below Natchitoches; it forms an island 32 miles long, and 4 miles wide.[49] The branch which here falls in on the left hand, takes, or rather continues the name of Cane river, and is the largest of the two, being 100 yards wide; but in consequence of the rafts and impediments which it contains, the other is used in navigation. It is the middle branch of the three,[50] and is generally known by the name of Little River. The banks of the river are here 25 feet above the present surface of the water. At their junction there is a depth of 36 feet; a small distance above this, Little river is 70 yards wide, and 24 feet deep, and continues thence, from 40 to 50 yards wide, and 18 feet deep up to Natchitoches. From the confluence of little river with cane river, to Natchitoches, the land on both banks is gen-

ley does indeed begin here, rather than the tropical species he identifies.

[49] Isle Brevel, named after the famous Southwestern frontiersman, Jean Brevel.

[50] The "three" being Cane River (the most westerly), Little River (the middle branch), and the main fork of Red River, or *"La Rivière de Petit Bon Dieu"* (the most easterly). Today "Cane" is the name given the middle branch.

*Typical vegetation tiers of willows (*Salix *spp.) and eastern cottonwoods*

(Populus deltoides) *along a braided channel of the lower Red.*

erally cultivated, particularly the left bank, which presents a series of small plantations, each having one field in front, and extending back from 80 to 100 perches to the Cypress Swamps. The inhabitants are a mixture of French, Spanish, Indian, and Negro blood, the latter often predominating, and live in small cottages on the banks and near the river.[51]

Custis 4.

The trees of this country are nearly the same which are found on the Mississippi.—The *Lyriodendron tulipfera, Magnolia Grandiflora* & *Tilia Americana* which are abundant on the other side of the Mississippi, in the Mississippi Territory & West Florida, I have never seen on this side.[52]—The Pecan (*Juglans petiolata* as I have called it) is every where on this river abundant.—The cotton tree is plenty.—The banks of this River are in most places covered

[51] Freeman's ethnic characterization of these Cane River settlers is omitted from the King version, but is quoted in James, and so has been restored to his entry here. John Maley, an adventurer visiting Natchitoches in 1810, will claim that the women from this interesting ethnic mix were "captivating figures" who were much in demand as mistresses among both Latins and Americans, despite the more fastidious "official" attitude of the latter towards miscegenation. See Dan Flores, ed., "The John Maley Journal: Travels and Adventures in the American Southwest, 1810–1813" (master's thesis, Northwestern State University, Natchitoches, La., 1972), p. 17. A number of Southern writers and novelists, among them Kate (O'Flaherty) Chopin (*Bayou Folk*, 1894) and Lyle Saxon *(Children of Strangers*, 1937) have found these Cane River people compelling literary subjects. They are also the subject of a fine new socio-historical study by Gary Mills, in *The Forgotten People: Cane River's Creoles of Color* (1977).

[52] These are interesting and valuable observations. The yellow-poplar, or tulip-tree (*Liriodendron tulipfera* L.), one of the tallest and most beautiful of the native trees of the American forest, *is* confined principally to regions east of the Mississippi; three scattered stands do exist in Louisiana, but none in the Red River valley. The range of the southern magnolia does today include northwestern Louisiana and East Texas, but Custis's comments here and later (he does encounter the umbrella magnolia, *M. tripetala* L., upriver, but not *grandiflora*) is possible evidence that the tree's range was later extended westward through transplanting by Southern pioneers. The *Tilia* species Custis saw in the Mississippi Territory was not *T. americana* L., but one of the Southern species of this genus. These, along with *americana*, will appear farther upriver, and Custis will go on to list linden trees in his natural history catalogues. Vines, *Trees, Shrubs, and Woody Vines of the Southwest*, pp. 279–81, 732–34.

from low to high water mark with the *mimosa punctata*.[53] — At Rapide I saw the *Erythrina herbacea* in flower.[54]

Freeman 1.

On the left hand or south bank of the river, 32 miles above the junction of Little and Cane rivers, stands the town and fort of Natchitoches.[55] It is on a handsome plain 16 feet higher than the present surface of the water; distant 184 miles and 266 perches from the Mississippi, by the meanders of red river, as measured in boats, by time, and the rate of ascending. Its latitude is 31 deg. 45 min. 45 sec North, and Longitude _____ deg. _____ min. _____ sec. West of the meridian of Greenwhich.[56]

[53] This mimosa was a new species, the powderpuff (*Mimosa strigillosa* Torr. & Gray).

[54] The cardinal spear, or coral bean, which seems to interest him because of its medicinal and utilitarian properties. The hard, bright red seeds were sometimes used as beads, and as a poison for vermin in Mexico. Southeastern Indians made a decoction from the roots to reduce fevers. George Usher, *A Dictionary of plants used by man*, p. 235.

[55] Founded in 1714 by St. Denis, Natchitoches was the oldest continually occupied European site in the Louisiana Purchase. It had been garrisoned by the United States in 1804. John Sibley provides some of the less scientific particulars of the town as it was shortly after the transfer. He describes it, with a strong trace of Yankee disdain, as a small, irregular, and "meanly-built" village of about forty families, strung along the west side of Cane River. The tendency of the Latin inhabitants to abandon the town for plantation sites along the river had reduced its size from that of forty years before, and allowed newly arrived Americans to man most of the technical and professional jobs. Enterprising immigrants from the States seem to have been a bit disgusted with Natchitoches's easy pace. Maley accused the inhabitants of being addicted to ". . . the vices that this town is given to, which is gambling and night strolling," which made them "unfit for the business of the day." Sibley charged that there was neither plow nor ferry until an Irish Pennsylvanian introduced them ". . . under similar opposition to the Copernican system." Sibley, "Historical Sketches," pp. 60–61; Flores, "The John Maley Journal," p. 17.

In 1806, Natchitoches had a population of five or six hundred. See Robertson, *Louisiana under the Rule of Spain, France, and the United States* 1:125; William Darby, *The Emigrant's Guide to the Western and Southwestern States and Territories*, p. 102.

[56] Again, the latitude figures are nearly perfect, but the longitude not computed from Freeman's course-notes. Modern topo maps represent Natchitoches's longitude at 93° 6' W. Freeman's log line figure is also quite accurate, and re-

Custis 1.

About half a mile below Natchitoches the cane and little River unite. — The town of Nachitoches is situated on the left bank of the River 47 miles above the mouth of little River and 220 above the mouth of Red River. — The banks here are 18 ft. high. — The town is almost surrounded by hills which are composed of clay sand and lime intermixed. — The lime prevails. — In some of these hills the lime extends to the depth of 30 ft. — Four or five feet under ground we find some masses of the Carbonate with pieces of shells inherring.[57] — Doctor Sibley of this place put into my hands an ore which he says is found in the greatest abundance on some of the branches of this river. — It turned out, upon examination, to be Iron Pyrites.[58] It was chrystallized in small cubes. — The party are all in the enjoyment of health and unanimity, pleased with the prospect, & resolved on the prosecution of the expedition, let what will oppose.

---

duces Sibley's 1805 figure of 266 miles (arrived at with a chronometer) to a wild inaccuracy, a third too far. Sibley's Red River mileage chart is in "Historical Sketches," pp. 72–73. Custis's mileage figures are estimates, evidently obtained from river traders. See Appendix 2.

In this first test of Dunbar's boats, the party has ascended only 184 miles in eighteen days, far short of Dunbar's hopes of 40 miles a day. Soldiers were notoriously poor at the oars, but the necessity of taking sextant readings at every bend for the purpose of making an accurate map no doubt slowed progress considerably.

[57] Custis's observations here provide us with some very early geologic references, perhaps the first, on the Natchitoches area. The light yellow, calcerous concretions referred to as comprising the Natchitoches hills were later regularly burned for their lime content. The "masses of the Carbonate with pieces of shells inherring" undoubtedly is an early reference to the extensive Natchitoches lignitic deposits containing marine fossils of the Eocene Age. See G. D. Harris, "Natchitoches Area," Special Report No. 1, and, by the same author, "The Cretaceous And Lower Eocene Faunas Of Louisiana," Special Report No. 6, in Gilbert D. Harris and A. C. Veatch, *A Preliminary Report on the Geology of Louisiana,* pp. 144–45; 299–310, plates 49–55. Custis's geological knowledge seems to have been rudimentary; certainly his comments do not compare to the geological discourses on the Red River valley by Dunbar and William Darby.

[58] This is the earliest record in the literature pertaining to the vast iron-ore beds stretching from East Texas across northern Louisiana into southern Arkansas. In the Red River country, these deposits (which would not be "officially" dis-

Sketch of a Southeastern Indian dwelling, circa 1800, by Basil Hill. Courtesy National Anthropological Archives, Smithsonian Institution.

Although Freeman & Custis probably did not see it, this Pedro Vial map of 1787 summarizes Spanish knowledge of the Southwest, confusing the Red's North Fork with the Canadian. From Loomis and Nasatir, Pedro Vial and the Roads to Santa Fe.

covered until 1885) occupy a belt twenty miles wide in the hill country between the middle Ouachita River on the east and Bayou Dorcheat on the west. See Clarence O. Durham, *Iron Ore of Central North Louisiana*, Louisiana Geological Survey *Bulletin* No. 41, pp. 3–6

PART TWO

The Great Raft and the Great Swamp

June, 1806

EDITOR'S NOTE: The layover in Natchitoches, which lasts from May 19 to June 2, is a time of great activity that results in the party's evolution into a much larger and better-outfitted expedition. Natchitoches is, in 1806, the last outpost of supply and American presence on the Red River. Accordingly, Freeman first will arrange with Sibley and Thomas Linnard, government trader at the Natchitoches Indian Factory, to procure guides and translators for their penetration of the wilder land upriver. He will then lay in a supply of flour sufficient for nine months (about two dozen barrels) and appropriate from Sibley's and Linnard's stores an unspecified quantity of trade goods and presents (which he will later believe to be insufficient). Among the stores assembled for Indian diplomacy were at least three United States flags, which the explorers planned to distribute among the tribes upriver.

Following Dearborn's orders to Colonel T. H. Cushing, who had replaced Captain Turner as commanding officer at Fort Claiborne, the expedition was augmented by an additional detachment of twenty soldiers under the command of Lieutenant John Joseph DuForest, a Louisiana native who had served in several previous instances as a Spanish interpreter for the Americans. This force had been ordered to join the expedition "for the purpose of assisting the exploring party to ascend the river to the upper end of the Great Raft, and to continue as far afterwards as might appear necessary to repel by force any opposition they might meet with."[1] If we can take this at face value, it means that the

---

[1] Quoted in James, *Account of an Expedition from Pittsburgh to the Rocky Mountains* 17, pt. 4, p. 67. Most of the details provided here come from James's examination of Freeman's manuscript journal. Since King's incorporation of

administration was apparently willing at this point to engage in an armed confrontation with the Spaniards in the wilds of the Southwest in order to pursue the exploration—was, in fact, preparing for it.

Spanish agents and officials on both sides of the Sabine are equally active during this period. On June 2, the day the party casts off, an anonymous dispatch posted from Natchitoches to Spanish authorities in Nacogdoches reports that two barges are in the river, provisioned to ascend the Red as high as possible, and there to "plant the American flag." "From the way they boast," the informant wrote, "I believe they intend to go higher than the place where Don Felipe Nolan was killed, with the object of acquiring land and mines." As a final prick at Latin pride, the letter closes thusly: "Do not let them brag about making this expedition as they bragged about having forced the four men stationed at Los Adaes to retreat. . . ."[2]

Viana will react immediately. The day following he will write to Governor Cordero, assuring him that he knows "the irremediable damage that would result to this Province if the union is accomplished of the Expedition of the United States with the faithless Taboayases Indians, and the Comanches, who are already joined with these," and further telling the Texas governor that Sibley had "gone out to join with the Caudadachos for the same expedition, since to him has been confided the project of buying their lands." He would, therefore, give Ramón orders to march northward on an intercept course to the *old* Caddo village "which is located where the territory of the Taboayaces begins," since "this territory is ours."[3] Although this assertion was not true (Cadodoquia actually extended across the Blackland Prairie buffalo grounds to the Cross Timbers), Viana's plan did have merits.

Distressed at the reluctance of the Texas Indians to join the campaign

---

other material from the Freeman manuscript appears to be quite complete, I suspect that these deletions were ordered by Jefferson.

[2] Anonymous to Viana, Natchitoches, June 2, 1806, The Bexar Archives. The original is in Spanish, and subsequent developments render it quite certain that the author was Indian trader Juan Cortes. Cortes has an interesting career on the border. He will continue as the principal Spanish informant in Natchitoches, particularly providing information on American trading expeditions, until his request to establish a trading post at Bayou Pierre is denied. By 1810 he will join the Americans, becoming an employee of Thomas Linnard at the Natchitoches Indian Factory, his previous role as informant evidently unsuspected. See Simon de Herrera to Cordero, enclosing a copy of a letter from Juan Cortes, San Antonio, August 14, 1808; Salcedo to Cordero, Chihuahua, June 14, 1808, ibid.; and Thomas M. Linnard, ledger entry for March 31, 1810, Natchitoches/Sulphur Fork Agency Ledgers, 1809–1821, the National Archives.

[3] Viana to Cordero, Nacogdoches, June 3, 1806, The Bexar Archives.

against the American expedition and worried that the exploring party might elude the Nacogdoches force, in Chihuahua, Nemecio Salcedo had already arranged with Don Real Alencaster, governor of New Mexico, to launch yet another Spanish expedition, this one to go east from Santa Fe. This expedition, referred to by Zebulon Montgomery Pike as "the most important ever carried on from the province of New Mexico,"[4] was charged with the twin objectives of capturing the "Dunbar expedition" should the Americans elude the East Texas forces and placating the tribes of the Red and Arkansas rivers. It was to be commanded by Lieutenant Don Fecundo Melgares, a stellar Spanish soldier and a man of wealth and education (he later became the last Spanish governor of New Mexico). The very day the Freeman and Custis party left the docks at Natchitoches and swung once more into the current of the Red, preparations for this foray were already commencing, nearly 800 miles away in Santa Fe.[5]

Custis 4.

To morrow morning we leave this [Natchitoches], with 7 boats, 40 men, three commissioned & four non-commissioned officers. — It is expected that the Spaniards will endeavor to stop us. — They are reinforcing at Nachidoches [*sic*], 150 miles from this, for what purpose it is not known.[6]

[4]Jackson, *The Journals of Zebulon Montgomery Pike* 1, entry for September 25, 1806, p. 323.

[5]The documents are the following: Salcedo to Alencaster, Chihuahua, April 12, 1806, in Herbert Eugene Bolton, *Guide to Materials for the History of the United States in the Principal Archives of Mexico*, p. 309; Salcedo to Cordero, Chihuahua, July 13, 1806, The Bexar Archives; and Fecundo Melgares to Alencaster, Santa Fe, June 2, 1806, The Spanish Archives of New Mexico. Until now, the intentions of the Melgares expedition have entirely confused historians. Pike stated, and most historians have repeated him, that Melgares was searching for *him*. These documents destroy that contention, since Pike will not receive orders from Wilkinson relative to his expedition until June 28, 1806, many weeks after the Melgares expedition was set in motion. Apparently the obscurity of the Freeman and Custis expedition has caused historians to simply ignore the objectives, clearly stated for Melgares, in these documents. Warren L. Cook, in *Flood Tide of Empire*, correctly cites the Bolton summary of Salcedo's April 12 letter (p. 477), which clearly reveals Melgares was "to watch the Dunbar expedition, drive it back, or capture it and take it to Santa Fe," yet then goes on for several pages attempting to prove that the Melgares expedition was actually intended to capture Lewis and Clark.

[6]The third commissioned officer is John Joseph DuForest, who at this time

Freeman 1.

The party left Natchitoches on the second of June, having made all the necessary arrangements for the prosecution of our voyage.

From the town of Natchitoches to where the Northern Branch of *La Rivière de petits bon Dieux* [*sic*] runs out, the Red River varies in width from 150 to 200 yards, and is from 30 to 40 feet deep; the banks were about 15 feet higher than the water. Plantations occur on both sides of the river. About nine and an half miles from Natchitoches, the Bayou runs out from the south [west] side of the river, which enters it again at the bluff above the town. Above this Bayou, and where a bluff seventy feet in height approaches from the south, there is a ferry across Red River.[7] The river above this bluff is contracted to 70 yards in width; passing through first rate land, elevated from 15 to 20 feet, above the surface of the water at the time the exploring party passed up. The timber is White Gum, Cotton Wood, very large Pecan, Ash, Hickory, Mulberry, and Locust.[8] About three miles from the ferry, a large bayou (150 yards wide) runs in from the South West, and forms the principal communication with the Bayous, branches,

---

held the rank of ensign in the Second Infantry at Natchitoches, and who had given a good account of himself in the attack on Los Adaes in February. DuForest would be promoted to Second Lieutenant after the exploring party returned. He died in 1810. Heitman, *Historical Register and Dictionary of the United States Army* 1:386.

[7] The ferry and bluffs had been purchased by Sibley soon after his arrival in Natchitoches. The bluffs, which were (and are, today) known as "Grand Ecore," have inspired observers for centuries, from St. Denis to Caroline Dorman and Lyle Saxon. I have not seen a better description of these bluffs, however, than the one Sibley wrote in 1805: "Grand Ecore is near one hundred feet high. The face next to the river, almost perpindicular, of a soft, white rock; the top, a gravel loam, of considerable extent, on which grow large oaks, hickory, black cherry, and grape vines. At the bottom of these bluffs, for there are two near each other, is a large quantity of stone-coal, and near them several springs of the best water in this part of the country; and a lake of clear water within two hundred yards, bounded by a gravelly margin." Sibley, "Historical Sketches," pp. 62–63.

[8] These are the first botanical notices Freeman has made. Custis already has mentioned six of them. But Freeman is the first to enter the native red mulberry (*Morus rubra* [L.]). See, however, Custis's identification of this tree in his natural history catalogues.

lakes and ponds, which lie on the south side of Red river, and pass the settlement of Bayou Pierre.[9] The depth of the water in the River here, varies from 25 to 30 feet. The annual inundations rise nearly to the top of the bank, and in some places pass nearly a foot over it. Five miles below the first raft, there is a bluff on the north bank of the river, 30 feet high. Above this bluff, high cane appears on the south bank, and frequently on both banks of the river. The first raft is not more than 40 yards through. It consists of the trunks of large trees, lying in all directions, and damming up the river for its whole width, from the bottom, to about three feet higher than the surface of the water. The wood lies so compact that, that [*sic*] large bushes, weeds and grass cover the surface of the raft.[10] The party encamped on the evening of

[9] This is Bayou Pierre ("Rock River" because of its stony bed), occupying a former channel of the Red. It is the small but pretty stream that follows the line of the hills behind Shreveport today, branching out from the Red near downtown. Until just before the turn of the nineteenth century it had been navigable up to the Bayou Pierre settlements and through them back to the main river above the Raft. This was the preferred and traditional route of detour around the Raft, and its logjams probably could have been removed by a party this size.

The problem is that Spain claims the Bayou Pierre settlements, and is, in fact, using the location as a close-quarters spying headquarters against the expedition. Consequently, the Americans will be forced to avoid the Great Raft by using a far more complicated and difficult route. This is the eastern route, through countless bayous, swamps, and inter-connecting lakes, which will require two weeks (several days of that spent lost) to traverse. It was, in fact, a waterland wilderness even the Indians knew as "The Great Swamp." The citizens of Natchitoches had scoffed at any talk of taking barges through this route; traders commonly detoured the entire region, depending upon horses rather than boats to penetrate to the "great prairies." A century earlier Bénard de La Harpe had gone by way of Bayou Pierre.

[10] The Great Raft was one of the amazing phenomena of natural North America. In terms of size and age, the gigantic logjam had no parallel on the rest of the continent's rivers. Just when or where the Great Raft first formed has never been satisfactorily determined. Early Louisiana geologist A. C. Veatch thought it must have formed about A.D. 1100 to 1200, but all we really know is that it was in existence long before the coming of the Europeans. Indian legends place its formation downward towards the mouth of the river, but geologic evidence as far north as present Alexandria does not support this. Fisk, in *Geology of Avoyelles and Rapids Parishes*, pp. 40–42, discusses both early and modern theories. One hypothesis is that the Raft was created when a flood on the Mississippi river backed up the waters of the Red, producing a reverse flow that

The Great Raft, photographed in 1873 by R. B. Talfor.

Courtesy Library of Louisiana State University, Shreveport.

the seventh at the highest white settlement, which is a small plantation on the North side of the river, 45 miles above Natchitoches.[11] Two miles below the settlement, and on the same side, there is a bluff, 40 feet high, and 100 yards in length. The Cotton Wood Tree grows to a great size in this neighborhood; one standing in a Cornfield, was found to be five feet in diameter and 141 and a half feet high.[12]

---

caused an accumulation of driftwood the Red could not wash out. It seems quite likely, however, that the Red River has always been inclined to block itself with drift debris. It is a shallow river, with many sandbars and sharp bends. It flows through an alluvial, loamy country, much of it almost entirely free of rock, with banks that are friable and cave readily. The minimal slope of its valley causes the river to braid and meander widely and to eternally eat away at the edges of the thick woodlands through which it threads for half its length. Freshets thus toppled into the stream great numbers of living trees, with their root systems. Durable timber, such as red cedar and bald cypress from the middle Red, lodged together to compose the basic skeleton of the Great Raft.

This enormous logjam exerted a tremendous influence on the environment and history of the Red River valley. Over the centuries it had inched upriver like a gigantic snake, adding about four-fifths mile of timber to its upper end every spring, while its lower edge rotted away at two-thirds that rate. By 1806 it was a tangle of drifted timber almost 100 miles long, its segmented lower end—according to Freeman here—somewhere near present Campti, Natchitoches Parish, La. As it moved steadily upriver, it blocked the mouths of tributaries, annually creating new lakes and swamps, and killing the ancient climax hardwood forests abutting its floodplain. By, in effect, damming the river and causing it to drop its sediment load prematurely, the Raft contributed to the rapid development of floodplain prairies above it, as well. J. E. Guardia, "Some Results of Log Jams in the Red River," Geographical Society of Philadelphia *Bulletin* 31 (July 1933): 106–13; "Red River, La., Ark., Okla., and Tex.," p. 45; Dr. Joseph Paxton to A. H. Sevier, Mount Prairie, Arkansas Territory, August 1, 1828. *House Doc. 78,* 20th Cong., 2d sess. (1830), pp. 1–5; Dr. Clarence Webb to the editor, Shreveport, April 26, 1979.

[11] The scattered settlements and plantations made up the village of Campti, one of the oldest white occupations in the Red River valley, and one with a colorful history. The Campti area was recommended for settlement by Bienville and St. Denis, but it was not until the middle of the eighteenth century that Frenchmen occupied the spot. The majority of these were the remnants of the French soldiers and settlers who abandoned La Harpe's Post and moved downriver following the transfer of Louisiana to Spain. Sibley says the first raft began at the upper house, which belonged to Hypolte Bordelin. Beyond Bordelin's house, the Red River valley in 1806 was wilderness. Sibley, "Historical Sketches," pp. 40, 64; Fortier, *Louisiana: Cyclopedic* 1:153.

[12] The bluff is undoubtedly the one now known as Grappe's Bluff, Natchi-

Next morning we came to the second raft, which crosses the river here 100 feet in width, and extends for 200 yards along its course. This raft rises nearly three feet above the water, and is covered with bushes and weeds: the trees of which it is composed are Cotton Wood, Cypress, Red Cedar, &c. and they lie so close that the men could walk over it in any direction.[13] With great exertions we opened a passage for the boats, through this raft on one side, by floating the large trees down the river.

Here we were overtaken by Talapoon, a guide and interpreter, hired at Natchitoches,[14] to go as far as the Panis nation; he had

toches Parish, La. See U.S.G.S. Natchitoches (La.) Quadrangle. This gigantic cottonwood, whose height was obviously triangulated with a sextant, is fully half again taller than the normal maximum for this tree.

[13] Freeman's eyewitness description here contradicts the popular story, much repeated on the frontier and even appearing in *The Medical Repository* in 1806, (vol. 3, p. 308), that the Great Raft was covered with fully-grown trees of the surrounding forest, and except for the gurgle of water underfoot might be passed over without detection.

[14] Lucas Talapoon, Lucas el Talapuz, or Joseph Lucas, is a tantalizingly obscure figure on the early Southwestern frontier. Freeman seems to regard him as an Indian; he probably was a *métis*, although we have no hard clues about his ethnic background. His engagement in the service of the exploration can be traced to Dunbar's insistence to Jefferson and Dearborn that it was of "the utmost importance to the Success of the Expedition" that he employ a person "in the triple capacity of Interpreter, hunter, and guide," else the party "might find themselves in the situation of a Ship at Sea without Compass or rudder." Evidently living for at least part of his life among the Indians of the region, Talapoon's expertise with the Caddoan dialects spoken on the Red River and his mastery of Plains sign language, was ably demonstrated on several occasions during these same years: when the exploration is aborted he will join the 1806-1807 Lewis and Alexander trading expedition as interpreter-guide to the Taovaya-Wichita villages and will return in the same capacity with Anthony Glass in the latter's travels with the Penateka Comanches in 1808-1809 (see the Epilogue). See also, Ramon to Viana, Arroyo de Nasada, June 20, 1806, The Bexar Archives; Dunbar to Dearborn, Natchez, June 15, 1804, Rowland *Dunbar Letters*, pp. 138-39.

The circumstantial evidence is quite strong that this is the same man who befriended and guided Philip Nolan during the expeditions Nolan made in the 1790s, and who was the source of American excitement over Plains Indian sign language in 1800-1801. Daniel Clark, Jr., told Jefferson this of him: "In company with [Nolan] is a Person a perfect master of the Language of signs. . . . I have proposed to Nolan to send him on to the U-S. that you might have an opportunity of learning from him many curious particulars respecting his Country. . . ." Clark offered to pay him expenses and a salary if he would journey to Monticello

a mule and a package of goods, for the purchase of horses at the Panis nation, to prosecute the expedition upon, when the river ceased to be navigable.

Intelligence which he brought of the marching of Spanish Troops from Nacogdoches, determined the Party to halt at a small Indian Village, a few miles higher up the river,[15] and there wait for the arrival of the U. S. Agent, who was expected. Dr. Sibley and the gentleman from Nacogdoches, who had witnessed the marching of the Spanish Troops,[16] reached the party about noon: after having communicated this information, which was the occasion of their visit, we parted again about 2 o'clock P. M. the exploring party up the river, and Dr. Sibley on his return to Natchitoches.

---

so that Jefferson might "know the Man." Clark to Jefferson, New Orleans, November 12, 1799, "[Documents] Concerning Philip Nolan," p. 312.

[15] According to James, in his original journal Freeman names the inhabitants of this village as Pasacagoulas and Natchitoches Caddos (*Account of an Expedition from Pittsburgh to the Rocky Mountains* 17, Pt. 4, p. 68). In the Meteorological Charts (Appendix 3) the latitude of this village is fixed at $31°56'27''$N, in the vicinity of modern Coushatta, Red River Parish, La., a town whose name is derived from an early bayou much used by the Indians, and known as "Coshada Chute." John Maley will stop at this Indian village in March, 1812, and describe it as: ". . . very good log houses with good clap board roofs and hung doors. . . . peach trees in great abundance, [and] no fencing, all laid in common." Flores, "The John Maley Journal," pp. 62–66.

[16] At this point in the exploration, Spanish and American spies must have been passing one another in the woods en route between Nacogdoches and Natchitoches. The marching of troops that Sibley's informant has observed was the departure of a reinforcement detachment sent out on June 3 to bring Ramón's total in the drill camp on the Neches River up to about 230 troops, the largest army ever assembled by Spain in East Texas up until this time. After hearing the disappointing news from Guadiana, manning the spy post at Bayou Pierre, that only seven Alabama-Coushatta warriors from the Sabine village have shown up for the expedition against the Americans, Viana on this day (June 8) will send Ramón his marching orders, instructing him to move north on an intercept course toward the vicinity of the old Caddo villages. Ramón should move slowly, Viana cautions, and should join with Guadiana, who will send spies through the woods along the river to report when the expedition makes a landing "in order that we may take the proper steps, as soon as they reach our territory." Viana says nothing at this time about coming himself to direct the interception. Viana to Cordero, Nacogdoches, June 3, 1806; Guadiana to Viana, Bayou Pierre, June 5, 1806; Viana to Ramón, Nacogdoches, June 8, 1806, The Bexar Archives.

The river here seldom exceeds 70 yards in width, is 32 feet deep, and in time of flood rises from 15 to 20 feet above the present surface, flowing over the banks, which are only from 4 to 12 feet above it. The Timber constitutes the same as below, with Cane on one, or both banks all the way. The rough rust of the Mississippi is also frequently met with.[17] The trees are so covered with vines and creeping plants, as to present an impermeable mass of vegetation, while the low banks of the river are edged with willows.[18]

In this flat country Bayous are met with communicating with the river, almost as frequently conducting the waters out of, as bringing an accession to the principal stream.[19]

On the evening of the ninth we arrived at the third raft, like the two former, composed of the trunks of trees, brought down by the floods, and lodged on sand bars; forming an almost impenetrable mass, which extends from the bottom of the river, to two or three feet above the surface of the water, a thickness of 30 or 40 feet. This raft extends up the river nearly 300 yards. Many of these logs were of Red Cedar, from 1 to 3 feet in diameter, and 60 feet in length. With much difficulty a passage was effected through this; as the vacancy, occasioned by the removal of any part of the logs, was soon filled by others. The labor incident to the formation of a passage, through these small rafts, is so

[17] The reference is to one of the rust fungi of the order Uredinales. Joseph C. Arthur, *Manual of the Rusts in the United States and Canada.*

[18] Stoddard's 1812 observations complement Freeman's in rounding out the picture of the natural ecosystem of the lower Red River valley. Below Natchitoches, he writes, 70 percent of Louisiana stayed under water five months out of the year. Above, the country changed. Near the river there were canes and willows and the "impermeable mass of vegetation" Freeman describes. Beyond this lay tall grass prairies in the floodplain flanking the river, at the outer margins of which were cypress swamps and lakes of clear, black water. Beyond these were rolling upland hills, forested with lofty trees and virtually free of underbrush. Stoddard, *Sketches, Historical and Descriptive, of Louisiana*, pp. 187, 380–81.

[19] Without realizing it, Freeman has hit upon the key which later Raft engineers will employ to prevent the Great Raft from re-forming. The Red's many braided channels, remnants of former river beds, ultimately had to be closed off before the main river would maintain a water level sufficient to ride floating timber over its sandbars.

great, that the navigation of this part of the river is never attempted; for it would require to be repeated every time a passage was attempted.

The country is intersected with swamps, lakes, and bayous, communicating with and running into each other, for perhaps 6 or
8 miles on each side of the river. The current of the river is
very gentle, seldom exceeding the rate of three fourths of a mile
in the hour.

On the morning of the 11th we reached a place, where a branch
of the river, or a Bayou ran rapidly in from the north. Being
informed by M. Touline (a French gentleman born in the Caddo
Nation, and who now accompanied the party to that nation, to
render his good offices[20]) that it was absolutely impracticable to
pass the great raft in boats of any kind; as neither Red nor White
men had attempted it for 50 years before, and, that this was the
only communication, through which the passage could be effected;
we here left the river, and entered the Bayou. This Bayou is by
the Indians called *Datche*, (which in their language, signifies a gap
eaten by a Bear in a log, from the circumstance of the first Indian
who passed this way, seeing a bear gnawing at a log at this
place.)[21] The current in the Bayou is very rapid, it being the dis-

---

[20]"Touline," or "Tulin," was the name by which François Louise Grappe was
known to most Indians and whites in the border country. He was unquestionably the best guide into the Cadodoquia to be found in Natchitoches—and
yet he was also still in the pay of Spain in 1806. Grappe's father, Alexis Grappe,
had settled at La Harpe's Post in 1748, where he acted as superintendent of
Indians for French Louisiana. Young Touline had grown up with the Caddos
until the age of thirty, had hunted with them throughout the Red River valley
before moving to Lake Bisteneau about 1780. Since the cession of 1803, Grappe
had augmented his Spanish salary by becoming Sibley's assistant and providing
the Indian agent with a description of the middle Red. Salcedo to Cordero,
Chihuahua, August 13, 1805, The Bexar Archives; Sibley, "Historical Sketches,"
p. 54; *Biographical and Historical Memoirs of Northwest Louisiana*, p. 296.

Grappe's family later settled at Campti, and at his death in August, 1825,
he would leave about eighty descendants in central and northern Louisiana.
Courrier des Natchitoches, August 2, 1825.

[21]There are several bayous through which the exploring party can detour
eastward around the Great Raft, but "Datche" is not one of them. Datche,
Daichet, and Dacheet, are all early names for modern Bayou Dorcheat, a stream
which heads in present Arkansas and flows into the northern extremity of Lake

charge for the water which runs out above the great raft: indeed, appearances seem to promise, that this will in time be the principal channel of the river, as no hope can be entertained of the great raft being ever removed.[22]

Bisteneau. Judging by what he says here, Freeman seems to be under the impression that Bayou Dorcheat flows all the way through the lake to join the river below the main Raft. Reality will prove to be much more complicated.

Unfortunately for historians attempting to reconstruct the expedition's exact route, none of the contemporary maps agree on water courses and distances in the area under question. The most useful is Henry Miller Shreve's *Rough Sketch of that part of Red Rivir* [sic] *in which the Great Raft is situated and* [of] *the bayous, lakes, swamps, &c. belonging to or in its vicinity. 31.50' to 32.20'; 93.10' to 93.40', 1833.* The original is Louisiana *House Doc. 98,* ser. 256, p. [14]. A copy appears in this work. Another helpful contemporary map is P. H. Marcotte's *Map of the Parishes of Caddo, Claiborne, Natchitoches with Part of Rapides Louisiana.* This was distributed by the Land Office in Natchitoches, ca. 1840, showing both land claims and natural features. The copy I examined is in the Louisiana archives, Watson Memorial Library, Northwestern State University in Natchitoches. These maps show the following routes from the river to Lake Bisteneau, some of which intersected: starting with the most southerly, Coshada Chute, Bisteneau Chute, Loggy Bayou, and Bayou Pasacagoula. By forcing their way past the smaller, detached rafts lower down, the exploring party is able to utilize one of the more northerly communications. Loggy Bayou seems the obvious choice, but the abbreviated length of the watercourse they ascend causes me to suspect Bayou Pasacagoula.

[22] Like Zebulon M. Pike, who later this same year (1806) will proclaim the mountain now named for him unclimbable, Freeman underestimates the resolve of later generations. Removing the Great Raft was a herculean task, however, and one that required half a century and the use of technology which did not exist in Freeman's day. Removal of the Great Raft was one of the early, federally funded "internal improvements" in the Trans-Mississippi country. John Quincy Adams's administration first appropriated money for it in 1828, but it was not until 1832 that Captain Henry Miller Shreve, superintendent of the Army Corps of Engineers' Western Waters Department, confronted the logjam with his steam-powered "snagboats" and a technique little different from the one the exploring party is using in 1806. From 1832 through 1839, the federal government spent nearly a quarter of a million dollars on Shreve's project, only to witness the reformation of the Raft every spring. The historic ties between the Freeman and Custis exploration and the Long expedition of 1819–20 were strengthened when Colonel Stephen H. Long, in 1841, assumed direction of the removal project. But Long's efforts to employ private contractors in the task were all dismal failures.

Another $100,000-appropriation was placed at the disposal of Colonel Joe E. Johnston, of later Civil War fame, in the early 1850s, but again nature prevailed. It took the invention of nitroglycerine by Alfred Nobel to enable engineers

After passing up this Bayou, about five miles against a current, running at the rapid rate of three miles an hour, we entered a lake.

Freeman 2.

This beautiful sheet of water extends, from the place we first entered it, seventy miles in a northwesterly direction; and, as far as we saw it, is beautifully variegated with handsome clumps of cypress trees thinly scattered in it; on the right-hand side it is bounded by high land, which ascends from the surface of the water, and at the distance of one hundred yards is elevated about forty feet, and covered with forests of black oak, hickory, dogwood, &c.; soil good second-rate. It is bounded on the left by a low plain covered with cypress trees and bushes. The depth of water is from two to six feet. High-water mark ten feet above the present surface. It is called by the Indians *Big Broth*, from the vast quantities of froth seen floating on its surface at high water.[23]

Freeman 1.

A few miles above the entrance into the lake, we stopped in a beautiful cove, where M. Touline has numerous herds, kept by

---

to finally blast apart the densely packed underwater sections, but by 1873, Lieutenant E. A. Woodruff had finally effected a complete removal. The total cost since 1828: $633,000. Even then much rechanneling and elimination of braided channels was necessary before the river would remain raft-free. "Red River, La., Ark., Okla., and Tex.," p. 45; Webb to the editor, Shreveport, April 26, 1979; Guardia, "Some Results of Log Jams in the Red River," 106–13. Tyson, *The Red River in Southwestern History*, pp. 94–101, 150–53, provides a fairly detailed summary based on the engineering reports of Shreve, Long, Johnston, and Woodruff.

[23] Custis calls the lake by its white name—"Bistino." It was, of course, Lake Bisteneau, of present Bossier, Bienville, and Webster parishes, La. Bisteneau in 1806 is a cypress rim swamp for much of the year, but accretions to the Raft are beginning to divert much of the river's water through it during spring, making it a shallow natural lake. Within thirty years these inundations will kill many of the groves of trees Freeman describes. Shreve, *Rough Sketch of that part of Red Rivir in which the Great Raft is situated.* The froth which gave

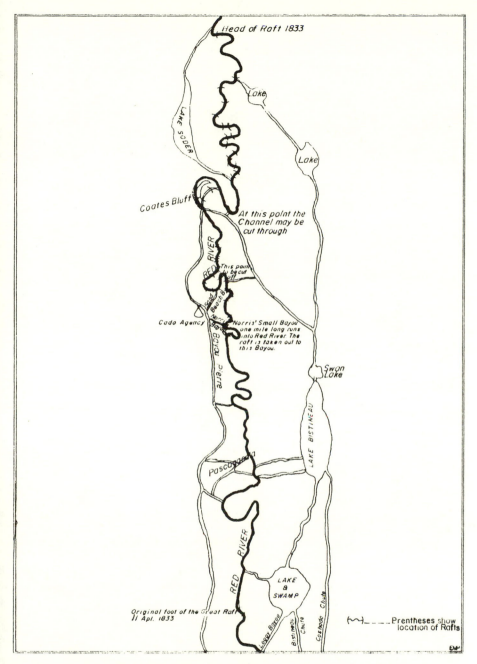

Henry Miller Shreve's "Rough Sketch" of the Great Raft country, 1833. Rendered by E. M. Parker, Centenary College.

"This beautiful sheet of water . . . called by

the Indians 'Big Broth' " *(Lake Bisteneau).*

herdsmen.[24] There we waited a day or two, for a rise in the water, which we observed was taking place, that we might the more easily make our way through the Bayous and Swamps above. M. Touline procured us an Indian as a guide[25] through the intricacies of the lakes and bayous, by which the water forces its passagees, from where it leaves the Red River above the great raft.

Freeman 2.

The passage out of this lake is by a very difficult communication, through bayous, into another very handsome lake of about one mile wide called Swan Lake,[26] and so on, through long crooked bayous, lakes, and swamps, full of dead standing timber.

---

the lake its Indian name is evidently a natural occurrence on the Red. In the spring months it may readily be observed floating on the surface of the river even today; to my knowledge it has not been chemically analyzed.

[24] Touline had bought his "vacherie," or ranch, from a Caddo Indian named Cajahdet in 1787. A well-known frontier landmark on Lake Bisteneau, it was located in Township 16 N., Range 10 W., in present Bienville Parish, La., near the tributary of Loggy Bayou. See *Biographical and Historical Memoirs of Northwest Louisiana,* p. 296. Grappe offers an outstanding example of the second wave of European frontiersmen—the graziers. In 1812 Maley would visit Grappe's ranch during the course of a trading foray up the Red. According to his account, Grappe had two Indians for companions and herdsmen, who helped him keep some 1,500 head of "the most elegantest" cattle in separate droves in the woods, and constructed "licks" for them from hollowed-out trees. "When we came to the licking logs," Maley relates in his colorful style, "their were but few cattle their, but he [Grappe] blew his horn which they are trained to. They came in from every direction, runing and skipping enough to break their legs." Grappe, says Maley, made no attempt to raise crops, living solely on meat, and he existed "worse than any Indian I have yet seen as to dirt and nastiness." But the wily Frenchman made yearly cattle drives, moving 500 or so head down the Red, and even to the Mississippi, where he took payment only in specie. Flores, "The John Maley Journal," pp. 76–78.

[25] This Indian seems to have been an Alabama-Coushatta (contemporary spelling: Alabami, Conchetta, Coashatta, Kashotoo) from the village above the head of the Raft. Linguistically the Alabama-Coushattas were of the Muskhogean family. See note 40.

[26] Detouring through the Great Swamp in March, 1812, Maley will remark on the large numbers of white swans inhabiting one of the lakes in "this watery world." He particularly will note the abundant alligators that "roared like great bulls." Ibid., p. 75.

Freeman 1.

From the west side of the Big Broth Lake, we passed through a very rapid bayou of 100 yards wide, and one mile long, with large timber on its banks, into Swan Lake, which at its entrance is 500 yards wide, [and] to the Eastern shore of which the upland approaches as you ascend. At the upper end of this lake, we had to enter and pursue our course through several small Bayous, in which it was necessary to make use of the trees and bushes growing on their margins, to aid the progress of the Boats. When the boats descend[27] through these short, crooked and rapid passages, we are obliged to stay their motion by means of ropes. The bed of the River at the great raft, was supposed to be seven miles from hence, in a southerly direction. Our course now lay through Bayous of various widths, in which the water was from 4 to 12 feet deep; and at this time 10 feet lower than in the season of the great inundation.

Pursuing our course through a bayou, on the evening of the 16th we arrived at a point where it touched the high land. Here we stopped for the purpose of making Astronomical observations, particularly of the Solar Eclipse, which took place the morning after. The observations then taken determined our position to be in Lat. 32 deg. 26 min. 53 sec. N. and Long. _____ deg. _____ min. _____ sec. W. from the Meridian of Greenwich.[28]

The passage up the Bayou had been dangerous, from the frequency of dead trees, ready to fall on receiving the least shock. The high land, which occasionally approached the Bayou on the Eastern side, was elevated 40 or 50 feet above the surface of the water; it had a wavy surface, of good soil, covered with Black Oak and Hickory. We stopped on the evening of the 17th, at a

---

[27] He means ascend.

[28] The explorers are at this point a small distance southeast of present Bossier City, traveling up a rapid little stream now called Red Chute Bayou — according to N. Philip Norman's fine navigational history of the Red, a vital link in the eastern route around the Raft. See "The Red River Of The South," *Louisiana Historical Quarterly* 25 (April 1942): 400. The point of land from which the solar eclipse of 1806 is observed appears on U.S.G.S. Caspiana (La.) Quadrangle just north of present Sligo, La.

point of the high land, which approaches the Bayou, where it leaves the lake. This high land we named Point Return, from the circumstance of our having been obliged to come [to] it again, after our first unsuccessful attempt to discover a passage, out of the lake of which it forms the Eastern margin.[29] This lake is full of dead trees, very rotten and standing close together. Discovering no passage from it, we sent our Indian guide forward by land, to the Coashutta Village, not more than 20 miles, for a better pilot, and awaited his arrival at Point Return. The Indian came again on the 21st, and said he had seen the Chief at the Village, who had given him some directions, and would be with us himself on the day following. We did not wait but pushed on, through bushes in a kind of Bayou within the Lake, and at last got through the lake, and entered a Bayou, by which we entered a handsome Prairie; the surface of the land was four feet higher than the water in the Bayou; the soil rich; the grass high and luxuriant.[30] There was a border near the Bayou of trees, thinly scattered, consisting of oaks, some of which were very large.

On leaving this Prairie, we passed through a Bayou, varying in width from 50 to 100 yards, with rotten Cypress and Ash trees standing in it so thick, as to very much impede the progress of the boats; whilst the falling trees rendered it dangerous to run against any of them. The underwood, which grew in this water course, was so large and thick as to prevent the view from extending much beyond the length of the boats in advance.[31]

[29] The party establishes a campsite in the vicinity of the high land they have named Point Return from June 17 through June 21, allowing Custis an opportunity to do some botanizing in the area. On June 19 the clouds part long enough for Freeman to take an astronomical reading, and he determines their position to be 32° 34' N. (see Appendix 3). This would put their Point Return camp very near the town of Red Chute, Bossier Parish, La.

[30] Some of Custis's botanical specimens, which he will begin to collect in this area, seem to have been native grasses, but since the collection has been lost, they cannot now be identified.

[31] Custis elsewhere calls this bayou "Badtka," so we know this was modern Bayou Bodcau. In its unspoiled state, Bodcau was described by Sibley (from Grappe's account to him) as a very handsome stream of clear, wholesome water. Sibley, "Historical Sketches," p. 65. See also, U.S.G.S. Bossier City (La.) Quadrangle.

On the morning of the 24th, we entered a beautiful lake, near a mile in length, and about 500 yards wide, margined by beautiful willows, over the tops of which appeared lofty trees in every direction. The ease with which the boats glided over the smooth surface of the water, was a pleasing contrast to the laborious passages we had previously made through the Bayous. Out of this lake we passed into a Cypress swamp, over which the water was from 3 to 5 feet in depth; the trees were large and stood very close. This was followed by a swamp covered with Willow bushes growing very close, and through which it was almost impossible to propel the boats. The certainty of being within a very small distance of the river, gave a vigor to our exertions which carried us through the swamps by evening, when we reached the entrance of a small bayou. Here we had the first certainty of effecting our passage to the river above the great raft, without having to abandon our boats, or else be obliged to haul them over the land. After removing such impediments as existed in this bayou, consisting of small rafts of trees, we by a passage of about half a mile through it, reached the river above the raft, to the great joy of the party.[32]

Freeman 2.

Thus after fourteen days of incessant fatigue, toil and danger, doubt and uncertainty, we at length gained the river above the Great Raft, contrary to the decided opinion of every person who had any knowledge of the difficulties we had to encounter.

[32] From Bayou Bodcau the party seems to have passed into a lake (the one over which their boats "glided") called Swan Lake on modern topographical maps. At least one of the swamps they traversed here was probably Bodcau Swamp, while the smaller bodies of water they describe now bear names such as Clear Lake, Round Lake, and Green Lake, present Bossier Parish, La. The small passage that reunited them with the river (very near present Benton, La.) will later be called Willow Chute. The best raft era map for this section is T. S. Hardee, *Hardee's Geographical, Historical and Statistical Map of Louisiana Embracing Portions of Arkansas, Alabama, Mississippi and Texas from Recent Surveys and Investigations and Officially Compiled under Authority from the* [Louisiana] *State Legislature* (1871). I examined the photocopy in the Louisiana Archives, Watson Memorial Library, NSU, Natchitoches. But see also, U.S.G.S. Bossier City (La.) Quadrangle.

Red Chute Bayou, part of the party's route through what they called "The Great Swamp."

Freeman 1.

On entering the River, we found a beautiful stream of 230 yards wide, 34 feet deep, and running with a gentle current; its banks are from 10 to 12 feet high, bordered by lofty trees, of the Cotton Wood, Oak and Red Cedar.[33] On the right of the river, ascending, at the distance of from 50 to 100 yards, the land rises to the height of 50 feet above the banks, and is covered with Oaks, Hickory, Ash, and some Pine. On the left it is level and very rich; a large Prairie extending for several miles below the place where the party entered the River, and as far above.[34] Beyond this Prairie there is a large lake,[35] on the west of which, and nearly 30 miles from Red River, lies the principal Village of the Caddos.[36] When ascending the river to the Coashutta Village, which is upwards of 19 miles from where we entered it, we met a canoe with two men in it approaching us: one of them proved

[33] The eastern red cedar (*Juniperus virginiana* [L.]). See Custis's natural history catalogues for complete annotation on this species, and Part 4, note 7.

[34] This prairie early became known to the frontiersmen as "Caddo Prairie." It lies in present Caddo Parish, La., stretching 40 miles along the western bank of the Red from present Shreveport to the Arkansas line.

[35] Although during times of high water, large natural lakes must have existed continuously for centuries in the region of present Northwest Louisiana and East Texas, the approach of the Great Raft into this country would be responsible for many changes, some already evident in 1806. As the Raft climbed and continued to block the river, waters from the Red inundated the countryside above, dumping enormous sediment deposits into the tributary bayous and streams, thereby converting those in the prairies into shallow lakes. One was the lake here mentioned, a body of water known to the Indians as Tso'to (literally translated from the Caddoan: "water thrown up into the drift along the shore by a wind"), located in the open country of Caddo Prairie in present Caddo Parish. The etymology of the name is briefly this: Sibley will call it "Sodo," and Shreve, in the 1830s, "Soder"; modern useage and maps render the name "Soda." Once the Raft was finally removed, the process which created Tso'to Lake reversed itself. The bayou began to cut a channel through the sediments that had converted it into a lake, eventually draining itself and restoring pre-Raft conditions by the early twentieth century. See John R. Swanton, *Source Material on the History and Ethnology of the Caddo Indians*, Bureau of American Ethnology *Bulletin 132*, pp. 12, 24; "Report Of Survey Of Cypress Bayou And Channels Connecting Shreveport, La., With Jefferson, Tex.," *House Doc. 785*, 59th Cong., 2d sess. (1906).

[36] The Caddo Indians and their village locations will be discussed fully in the annotation to Parts 3 and 4 of the Account. Although Freeman and Custis

to be Talapoon, the interpreter and guide, who had been sent round from Natchitoches, with a message to the Caddoo Chief, requesting him to meet the party at the Coashutta Village; the other was an Indian, whom the Chief had sent to deliver a message from him to M. Touline. This message was to inform him, that about 300 Spanish Dragoons, with 4 or 500 Horses and Mules were encamped a few miles back of the Caddo Village.[37] He did not know from the officers, what their intentions were; but believed it was to meet the American Party on the river. The officer, who commanded the Spanish troops, had given the Chief his hand, and asked if he loved the Americans. His answer was evasive—"he loved all men; if the Spaniards came to fight, they must not spill blood on his land, as it was the command of his forefathers, that white blood should not be spilled on their land." The officer left him without giving any answer, and did not return.

After delivering this message, the Indian said the Caddo Chief requested Mr. Touline to go to him immediately on our arrival at the Coashutta Village, as he wished very much to see him; but if M. Touline could not go to the Caddo Village, the Chief would meet him at the Coashutta's, and expected the Spanish officer would wish to accompany him.

The man was dispatched immediately, with a request that the Caddo Chief should meet M. Touline alone, at the Coashutta Village.

Custis 2.

About eighteen miles below the [Coashutta] Village we were met by an express from the Caddo Chief to a Mons. Touline, a

---

will not visit this village, the Spanish opposition force has already arrived there. Because of an incident with an American flag that will shortly transpire, as well as the roles played by Caddos on both sides of the dispute, these Indians and their village location will be of central importance to the clash between Spain and the United States in this summer, 1806.

[37] Ramón's force, about 230 strong, had marched from Camp Miguel del Salto on the Neches on about June 10 and, after 100 or more miles of forest trails, had arrived in the vicinity of the Caddo village, quite by mistake, around June 20. Ramón to Viana, Arroyo de Nasada, June 20, 1806, The Bexar Archives.

Much of the Great Swamp would have resembled this Lake Bisteneau backcountry.

". . . you are more than compensated by the beauty of the country." But in contrast to this modern scene, Caddo Prairie in 1806 featured Alabama-Coushatta gardens and extensive brakes of giant cane.

worthy and respectable old French gentleman, whose friendship for the Americans induced him to accompany us this far, informing him that three hundred Spanish Troops were then encamped near their village, waiting for us with a determination to stop the expedition and requesting that he would go to the Village as the Spaniards were desirous to hold a parley with them and that he could not speak to them on business of such importance without the advice of Mons. Touline. Mons. Touline sent the express back to inform the Chief that he could not go to the Village, but would wait here for him.

Freeman 1.

We Visited the Chief of the Coashutta Village, who resides a few miles below it, and has a large corn field. He appears comfortably fixed.[38] About sun-set on the 26th of June, we arrived at the Village. It stands on the North side, on a handsome bluff, about 30 feet high, composed of sand stone rock, and washed by the river.[39] This little Village has been built within two or three years,

[38] The chief, whose residence seems to be in the vicinity of present Carolina Bluffs, Bossier Parish, is named Echean He is described by Sibley in 1807 as: "Sensible, quiet, & not addicted to drunkeness, [Echean] made great efforts to oblige Major Freemas [sic] exploring party, & is well thought of by the Caddo Chief, on whose land they live." John Sibley, *A Report from Natchitoches in 1807*, Annie Heloise Abel, ed., entry for November 10, 1807, pp. 83–84.

[39] Freeman's astronomical reading for June 26 puts the party at N. latitude 32° 47', a reading repeated by Custis in his letter heading of July 17 and again given when the explorers return to this village in August (see Appendix 3). The location of the village is further confirmed by King's map of the expedition, clearly showing six lodges located atop a bluff at the third of four distinctive loops occurring in the river above Willow Chute. The location of the original Alabama-Coushatta settlement in the Caddo country and of the Freeman and Custis encampment of 1806 thus was on Cedar Bluffs, almost directly across the river from present Gilliam, La. Scholars have always assumed that the next bluff upriver, at 32° 51' and very early named "Coushatta Bluffs," was the site of Alabama-Coushatta occupation in this region, but this view must now be modified. The Coushatta Bluffs-Silver Lake Creek region was obviously a later occupation, perhaps selected as a result of the rapid growth of the Creek populatiun here. Sibley tells us late in 1809, in fact, that "The Alibamus and Coushittes are collecting together and setting themselves on the no East side of red River nearly at no. latitude 32.50." Quoted in Daniel Jacobson, Howard N. Martin, and Henry Marsh *(Creek) Indians: Alabama-Coushatta. American Indian Ethnohistory, Southern and Southeastern Indians*, p. 30. See also, Clarence H. Webb, *The Belcher Mound: A Stratified Caddoan Site in Caddo Parish, Louisiana*, map on pp. 5–6. Shreveport archaeologist Claude McCrocklin used this book's first edition to excavate eight Indian (and possible expedition) sites from the Alabama-Coushatta village of 1806. What may have been Echean's home downriver showed wealth, with much English china. Likely Freeman-Custis artifacts include several 1802–1810 military buttons. Claude McCrocklin, "The Red River Coushatta Indian Villages of Northwest Louisiana, 1790–1835," *Louisiana Archaeology*, Louisiana Archaeological Society Bulletin 12 (1985).

The visual appearance of this village is easily imagined. Although Jacobson has opined that the Creek public square plan was not used by the Alabama-Coushattas after they left Alabama, Freeman's account here indicates otherwise for this village. Around the square on the high bluff were grouped the individual lodges, rectangular structures in the fashion of log houses with cypress (or cedar) frames, perhaps with a circular, clay-insulated "hot house" nearby for winter use. Swanton, *The Indians of the Southeastern United States*, pp. 391–94.

and consists of 6 or 8 families of stragglers from the lower Creek Nation, near the Mobile.[40]

Custis 2.

On the second of June we left Nachitoches and after many difficulties arrived here on the 26 instant. — The country is settled for about 35 miles above the Post and is perfectly similar to that of which we have before given an account, that I deem it un-necessary to say anything respecting it more, especially as you will receive it from another source.

---

[40]The village is actually peopled by both Alabamas and Koasatis (now, Cou-shattas). These two groups always had been closely associated with one another, the Coushattas being merely a somewhat independent division of the Alabamas. Linguistically, ethnically, and culturally they were members of the Upper Creek Confederacy and originally had lived in several large villages in present northern Mississippi and Alabama. The Alabama-Coushattas who are settled on the east bank of the Red were a part of the large migration of Indian bands into Louisi-ana after the Treaty of Paris, 1763. Most of the Alabama-Coushattas had settled in the Opelousas district before moving, with Spanish encouragement, into East Texas, particularly to the Sabine River. It was the East Texas Alabama-Cou-shattas, under chiefs Red Shoes and Pia Mingo, whom Viana has tried (in vain, as we have seen) to enlist in the move to stop the American exploration. The origin of the Red River group was distinct from the East Texas villages, how-ever. The latter had first settled on the lower Red, above the rapids near present Pineville, Louisiana. Following a red ant epidemic, early in 1804 sev-eral of these families secured permission from the Caddos to re-locate their village some 200 miles upriver. In 1805, Sibley says, there are thirty men in the Red River village, indicating a total population of around 120 people. In time it became one of the largest Indian villages in northern Louisiana, with a population of well over 350 souls. These Indians remained close allies of the Caddos and the Americans, occupying their river bluff villages until the early 1830s, when the advance of the Great Raft and the Caddo treaty of 1835 prompted their removal. After three decades on the Red, they finally joined their kinsmen in Kinder, La., and in the Texas Big Thicket, where their de-scendants still occupy the only Indian reservation in Texas. Their occupation of the Red River country led them, in the early 1970s, to intervene in the Caddo case before the Indian Claims Commission, asserting ownership of ten parishes in western Louisiana. Helen Hornbeck-Tanner, "Rebuttal Statement To Direct Evidence Of Alabama-Coushatta Indians Of Texas And Coushatta Indians Of Louisiana," in Helen Hornbeck-Tanner, *Caddoan Indians* 4:149–54. See also, Sibley, "Historical Sketches," pp. 50–51; and for a history of these people, Dan Flores, "The Red River Branch Of The Alabama-Coushatta In-dians: An Ethnohistory," *Southern Studies* 16 (Spring 1977): 55–72.

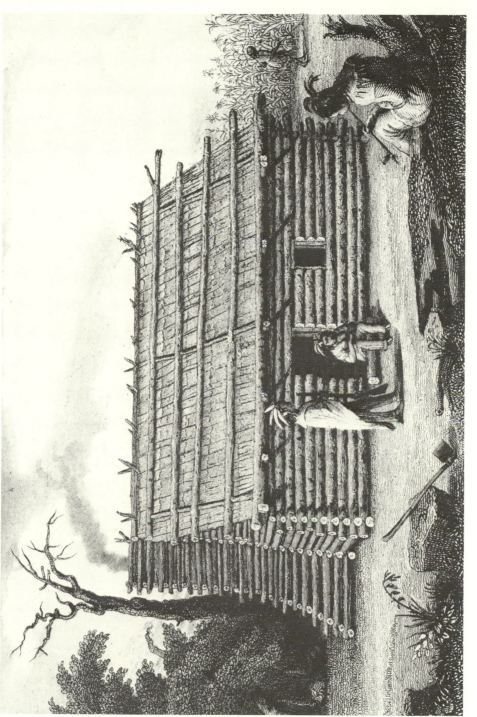

A Creek Indian lodge of the early nineteenth-century type built by the Alabama-Coushattas. Drawing by J. C. Tidball. Courtesy National Anthropological Archives, Smithsonian Institution.

PLATE 16

GEOLOGICAL SURVEY OF LOUISIANA, REPORT, 1899

ARKANSAS

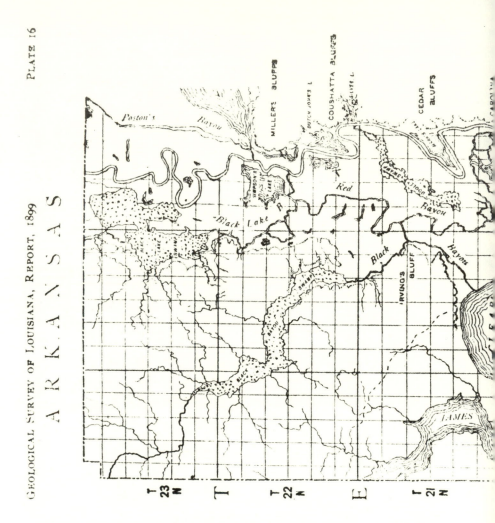

Map of northern Caddo Parish, Louisiana, done from surveys of 1839. From

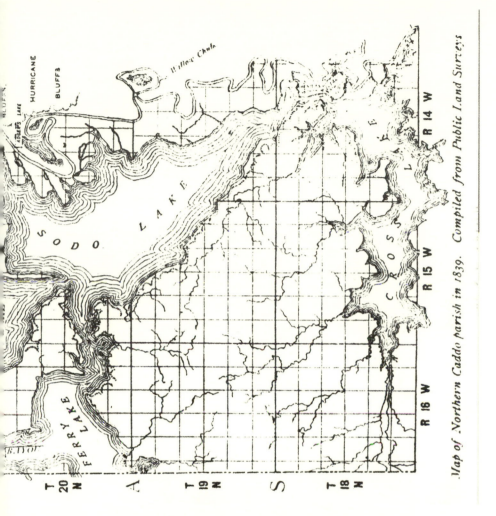

Map of Northern Caddo parish in 1839. Compiled from Public Land Surveys

A. C. Veatch, A Preliminary Report On The Geology Of Louisiana.

After leaving the settlement we meet with almost impenetrable Swamps & Lakes for more than 100 miles. — One who has not passed through them cannot form an Idea of the great difficulty attending it, but when effected you are more than compensated by the beauty of the country. The river which below the Raft was narrow, rapid, and meandering in every direction, above is broad & placid, with high banks covered with lofty Cotton trees. — Were the Rafts removed so as to admit of navigation this country in a very short time would become the Paradise of America. — It stretches forth independence to every person who may please to settle in it. — The soil is generally clayey & clayey strongly tending to the sandy and judging from a field of corn which the Coashattas have under cultivation I suppose it will produce from 50 to 60 bushels to the acre. — Cotton might be cultivated here to as great advantage as any part of the world. — In addition to the trees which I have already given you an account of we meet with Sour Gum (*Nissa integrifolia*)[41] Lime tree (*Tilia americana*)[42] Locust (*Robinia Pseud-acacia*)[43] this I have only seen on Bayou Badtka. *Cephalanthus occidentalis* or button wood, which is abundant all along the River, Haw (*Viburnum Prunifolium*)[44] Red Cedar (*Juniperus Virginia*) this first makes its [appearance] about 20 miles below the Coashutta Village, Wild Cherry (*Prunus virginiana*),[45] two kinds of Plum, both of which are small, round & red, the one ripens about the middle of June, the other in August & is too sour to be eaten.[46] There are an abundance of grapes, the Fox grape, the wine & a small blue one that ripens about the first

[41] A synonym for *Nissa sylvatica* Marsh., now accepted. This tree is commonly called the black tupelo.

[42] Probably instead either the Carolina linden (*T. caroliniana* Mill.) or the Florida linden (*T. floridana* Small). Vines, *Trees of East Texas*, pp. 390–95.

[43] Rather than this tree, Custis has become the first naturalist to see the rare and new Texas honey-locust (× *Gleditsia triacanthos* var. *texana* Sarg.).

[44] Instead the closely-related new species, *V. rufidulum* Raf.

[45] Rather than the northern species he indicates, this is the wild cherry (*P. serotina* Ehrh.).

[46] The first is probably the Chickasaw plum (*Prunus angustifolia* Marsh.); the other either the wildgoose plum (*P. munsoniana* Wight & Hedr.) or the Mexican plum (*P. mexicanus* Wats.).

A young warrior of the Coushatta Creeks. Drawing by John Trumball. Courtesy National Anthropological Archives, Smithsonian Institution.

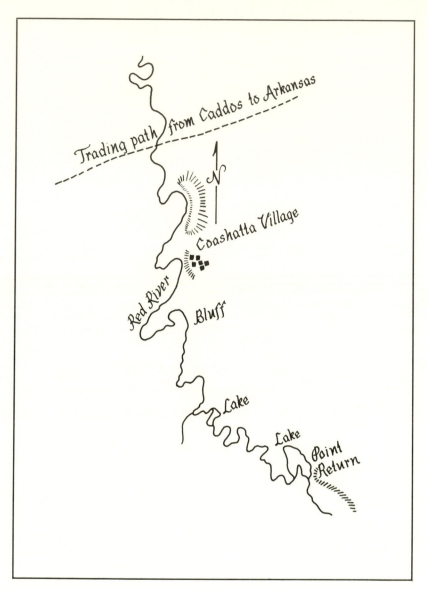

Detail of the country just above the Great Raft, from King's official map of the exploration, showing the accuracy of Freeman's geographic work when compared with Veatch.

of June.[47]—Oaks (*Quercus rubra, alba, & nigra*) & the Hickory (*Juglans alba*) are the most abundant [trees], except on the River where the Cotton tree & *Platanus occidentalis* abound.—

Freeman 1.

Cat Fish were taken at the camp near the village, of from 15 to 70 pounds weight, equal in taste and flavor to any caught within the U. States.[48]

On the 29th, the Chief of this little Village visited the American camp, and went up to his Village; from whence he was going to send home for a flag, which had been presented to them by the Spaniards, to hoist previous to the arrival of the Caddo Chief. The interpreter who brought this intelligence from the Village was requested to inform the Chief, that if he would hoist the American instead of the Spanish flag, I would furnish him with one. To this he acceded, and the flag of the U. S. was hoisted on a pole in the middle of the square in the village, where it was kept constantly flying.[49]

[47] These grape species are not ennumerated in the natural history catalogues of the expedition. The fox grape, *Vitus lambrusca* L., is out of range in north-western Louisiana; possibly this was instead the riverside grape (*V. riparia* Michx.), found along streams from East Texas across the Southeast. The small, blue grape was probably a muscadine, evidently *Muscadinia rotundifolia* (Michx.). Small, endemic to high bottomlands from East Texas to Florida and north to Maryland and Kansas. The "wine grape" mentioned could be one of any number of native grapevines of the region that are popularly known as "wine" grapes. See Wilbur H. Duncan, *Woody Vines of the Southeastern United States*, pp. 28–32, for choices.

[48] There are several possibilities concerning species. See Part 5.

[49] Indian trader Anthony Glass, whose party passed through this village two years later, described the location as "a rich beautiful place," and noted that upon their arrival Echean proudly hoisted this American flag presented to him by Freeman. Glass, "Copy of a Journal of a Voyage from Nackitosh into the interior of Louisiana," entries for July 15 and 16, 1808.

PART THREE

Layover at the Coashatta Village
June and July, 1806

EDITOR'S NOTE: Having overcome severe obstacles in detouring around the Great Raft by way of the "Great Swamp," by late June the reinforced Freeman and Custis expedition has found itself once again on the river, now in the ancient homeland owned by the Caddo Indians. At the Alabama-Coushatta village the leaders elect to rest the men from their exertions, treat with the tribes of the area, and prepare to pursue their probe into the Southwest.

At this point fewer than 25 miles separate the American explorers from the Spanish force dispatched to oppose them. Going overland, guided by a Caddo, Ramón's force has been pacing the Americans. Ramón personally is completely unfamiliar with the country and immediately botches the original plan conceived by Viana. This plan, which was at least diplomatically sound, had called for Ramón to march to "the old Caddo village" (above La Harpe's Post) and there to prepare to intercept the American party. The degree of sympathy with which Viana's superiors will view this plan is indicated by the fact that Cordero will shortly ask General Simón de Herrera, Governor of Nuevo León now on assignment in Texas, to take over the resistance, informing Salcedo in Chihuahua that Viana is "permitting the introduction of the foreign expedition."[1]

Ramón had been expressly ordered *not* to approach the inhabited Caddo village, for Viana at first had believed those Indians to reside in Louisiana at that time. Predictably, Ramón's guide took him directly to the inhabited village west of Lake Tso'to. This error at first distressed the Spaniards, but eventually reflection and a bit of archival work by

[1]Cordero to Salcedo, San Antonio, June 14, 1806, The Bexar Archives.

their priests would convince them that Ramón's blunder could be used to advantage. Indeed, the Texas officials eventually will convince themselves that the new Caddo village is west, not *east*, of the d'Anville line of the previous century, and thus the Caddos are on Spanish soil.

Expecting to be reprimanded, Ramón united with Guadiana's small spy force at the Caddo village on or near June 20. From Guadiana he learned that the American expedition, in two barges and several canoes, was detouring by way of the lakes to the east, but on June 20 is still far downriver. From the Indians, Ramón discovers that there are several old village sites upstream, including one which "has an old French fort." Ramón will decide to stay put and await a guide and further instructions from his superiors. In fact, the Spanish army will remain encamped near the Caddo village for more than a month—during which time an event will take place between Spaniards and Indians that will prompt discussion as far away as Paris and Madrid—before finally moving to confront the American expedition.[2]

Freeman 1.

The Caddo Chief[3] not arriving on the 30th as was expected, Mr. Touline dispatched a favorite Indian, the same one who had piloted the party through the swamp, to the Caddo Nation to learn the cause of his delay; with instructions to return almost immediately. The next morning a runner arrived at the camp, with intelligence, that the Chief and 40 of his young men and warriors

[2]Ramon to Viana, Arroyo de Nasada, June 20, 1806; Guadiana to Viana, Nachadaes Arroyo, June 20, 1806; Ramon to Viana, Caddo village, June 29, 1806; Fray Bernardino Vallejo to Cordero, San Antonio, July 11, 1806. Ibid.

[3]The Caddo Chief is Dehahuit. Described by Sibley (who will study him closely over the next decade) as a fine-looking man possessing "a strong mind," he was the Kadohadacho leader under whom the remnant Kadohadachos and perhaps some of the other Red River Caddo bands had assembled when they relocated west of Lake Tso'to. Dehahuit, by his own testimony (recorded in the *Mississippi Messenger*, Sept. 30, 1806), seems to have been the son of the great "Peacemaker," Tinhioüen—undoubtedly the young son who had accompanied Tinhioüen to meet the Spanish governor, Galvez, in 1779. Dehahuit probably was no more than forty in 1806, yet he was an Indian leader who, despite the reduced condition of his own people, commanded great influence and respect from all the tribes of the area. Governor Claiborne later told Andrew Jackson of him: "The chief of the Caddoes, is a man of great merit, he is brave, sensible and . . . is the most influential Indian on this side of the River Grande, and his friendship, sir, will give much security to the western frontier of Louisiana." Claiborne to Jackson, New Orleans, October 28, 1814, in Row-

were on their way from the Caddo Village,[4] and would arrive about noon. At the time expected, they made their appearance on the south side of the river, about a quarter of a mile above the camp, and opposite to the Coashutta Village. On arriving at the bank of the river, they saluted the Village, by an irregular firing, for a few minutes, which was returned. The U. States party were drawn up in single file to receive them with marked attention; while all the canoes of the Village were employed in transporting the Caddo Chief and his party across the river. When they had all got over with their horses, which they swam, they sent to enquire where the Exploring Party wished them to encamp. A pleasantly situated cleared spot at the upper end of the Village was recommended, at which they left their horses and marched down to the camp. A salute was fired as the Chief entered the camp, with which he seemed well pleased; observing to the Coashutta Chief that he never had been so respectfully received by any people before.

The Chief and the United States party being seated under the shade, with the young men and warriors of the Caddo Nation in a semicircle behind them, the Chief after a short pause observed, that we must have suffered a great deal of hardship in passing the great swamp, with our boats, and expressed his wonder at our success.

land, *Official Letter Books of W. C. C. Claiborne* 6:293–94; Sibley to Secretary of War John Armstrong, Natchitoches, October 6, 1813, in Garrett, "Doctor John Sibley and The Louisiana-Texas Frontier," 49:602; exchange between Mézières and Louisiana governor Bernardo de Galvez, Natchitoches and New Orleans, May and June, 1779, in Bolton, *Athanase de Mézières* 2:248–52.

[4] Riding their horses along the woodland trails and across Caddo Prairie, the Caddos were only three hours away—perhaps 20 miles—from the Alabama-Coushatta village (references to 30 or 50 miles must mean by the water route). The Caddos call their village here Sha'-childni'ni ("Timber Hill"). Swanton, *Source Material on the History and Ethnology of the Caddo Indians*, p. 27. Custis will shortly tell us that they had moved to this location in 1795, and we know that they continued to reside there until the 1840s. But exactly where Sha'-childni'ni was located has long been the subject of dispute. The Spaniards insist that when the Caddos moved to this location they had crossed d'Anville's obscure line of division between Louisiana and Texas and had settled on Texas soil. William Darby, in running the boundaries for the Louisiana state survey in 1811, was concerned (so Sibley says) because the Caddos were, in fact, just

He was informed that we had suffered much,[5] but were not to be deterred by obstacles of that nature, from paying a visit to him, and the other Chiefs and Nations on this River. I then explained to them the wishes of the President of the U. S. and the American People, respecting the Indians of that Country, as also the route we proposed, and the distance we expected to go.

Custis 2.

The object of our mission was explained to them by Mons. Touline.—He told them that France for certain consideration had sold to the United States the whole country of Louisiana together with its inhabitants, French, Spanish, and Indian and that hence-

---

inside Texas. Darby's testimony is in Sibley to Eustis, Natchitoches, November 28, 1812. Garrett, "Doctor John Sibley and The Louisiana-Texas Frontier," 49:417–18. Period events made some case for a Louisiana location, however. In 1838, three years after the Caddo Cession, troops from the Republic of Texas invaded Louisiana to attack Caddos still living here. Louisiana's 1839 survey map of Township 21 N, Range 16 W, shows the site of an "old" but large Indian settle-ment west of Jeems (formerly "Coushatta Jim's") Bayou, but in Texas. In 1998 archaeologist Clarence McCrocklin and the Texas Historical Commission—again relying in large part on Freeman and Custis materials—discovered and com-menced excavation work on this important Indian village, whose name they have now refined to Sha'chahdinnih ("Timber Hill") in eastern Marion County, Texas. The best guess is that Sha'chahdinnih draped across several miles of ridges and will take years of work to understand. Mark Parsons, Jim Bruseth, Jacques Bagur, and Claude McCrocklin, "Finding Sha'chahdinnih (Timber Hill): The Last Vil-lage of the Caddo of the Kadohadacho in the Caddo Homeland," *Plains Anthro-pologist* (paper under review, used here with permission of the authors); Clarence Webb to the editor, Shreveport, April 26, 1979; William B. Glover, "A History of the Caddo Indians," *Louisiana Historical Quarterly* 18 (October 1935): 935–37; J. Dan Scurlock, "The Kadohadacho Indians: A Correlation of Archeological and Documentary Data," M.A. thesis, University of Texas at Austin, 1965, map 1.

[5] Through Grappe, who acted as interpreter (see Custis's next entry). Custis will provide us with some of the particulars, though not many, of Freeman's address. The basic format had been outlined in Jefferson's letter of exploring instructions (see Appendix 1), which Freeman seems to follow fairly closely. This is the same address which Meriwether Lewis has been giving to the tribes of the Missouri and Pacific Northwest during the northern exploration. Along with Custis's com-ments, published here for the first time, King's redaction of the accounts for offi-cial publication also omitted the notes Freeman must have made on his address.

forward the People of the United States would be their fathers & friends and would protect them & supply their wants.—His answer I am very sorry it is not in my power to give verbatim, but the substance was this. "That being well treated by the French while under their Government he loved them, that under the Spanish Government he was well treated and he loved them, that now it had pleased the French (for what reason he knew not) to give them up to the Americans, he loves them and hopes they will love and treat him as well as the French & Spanish did and that he doubts not that will be the case as two years have now elapsed since he came under their Government & has not yet had any cause for complaints.[6] He added that he was sensible the Supreme Being had made a difference between us and his people, that he had been pleased to endow us with more sense and that he had also seen proper to grant us means which they were entirely destitute of; he therefore would look to them for protection and comfort, to be his fathers, brothers & friends.—He expressed great satisfaction that we had been pleased to inform him of our intentions, saying he placed the utmost confidence in what was said & that it shewed a frankness which the Spaniards did not evince; instead of Communicating to him their views they incamped near his Village & the first question put to him by the Commandant was 'Do you love the Americans' his reply was 'I do', but [I wonder] whether or not I think it improper for you to ask a question of the kind

[6] It is obvious from Dehahuit's comments that the Caddos have regarded themselves as aligned with the Americans since they first accepted presents in 1804. By the summer of 1806, Sibley has been courting them for more than a year. It is essential, however, that the exploring party have their good will, for upon it may depend the treatment they will receive from the interior tribes, and possibly from the Spanish army. As will presently emerge, the Caddos are now being caught up in an artificial division of their country. Their new location in the hills west of Lake Tso'to, the Spanish officials in Texas will claim, lies outside Louisiana and within Texas. Their country thus partitioned, the Caddos will find themselves in the impossible situation of having their ground claimed by one white nation, themselves and their allegiance by another. "The other day," Dehahuit will tell Claiborne in September, "when I saw the Spaniards on one side of me, and your people on the other, I was embarrassed—I did not know on which foot to tread." Quoted in the *Mississippi Messenger*, September 30, 1806.

and begged that he [Ramon] would say no more and was not then prepared to answer any question however trivial. — He said he was extremely afraid they intended to spill our blood & that it had created in his breast much uneasiness, that it had been a law among his Ancestors not to suffer the blood of whites ever to be spilt on their ground,[7] and he was determined while he lived not to admit of it, on his grounds, rivers, lakes, or Bayeaux; that if the Spaniards were desirous to fight he had not the least objection, provided they would go on their own ground. — He said, he was glad we had undertaken to explore the River & again repeated that in making him acquainted with the object of the expedition we had given him much pleasure and wished us all possible success, that we were going where we might possibly be harassed by the Osage Indians who had always been the inveterate enemies of the Caddoes, that if we should kill any of them he & his people would dance for a month, but on the contrary if they should kill us he would, although his warriors are few, make it a common cause & avenge the deaths.[8] —

[7] Except for the initial clash between the Cahinnios and DeSoto's Spanish exploring force at Caddo Gap (present southwestern Arkansas) in 1541, the Caddo peoples had good reason to make such a claim, for they had been consistently peaceful towards all Europeans for 250 years. Indeed, Dehahuit told his people that: "If they met [white people] in the Woods, or in the Prairies to divide what they had with them, to be their Pilots & guides. If they were unable to help themselves to bring them home and feed them. — " Sibley to John Armstrong, Natchitoches, October 6, 1813, Garrett, "Doctor John Sibley and The Louisiana–Texas Frontier," 49:602–603. Swanton describes the initial hostilities of 1541 in *Indian Tribes of the Southeastern United States*, p. 98.

[8] Perhaps no feud between nations was more malevolent than the enmity between the Caddos and the Osages. The Osages constituted, in 1806, one of the most important divisions of the Siouan linguistic stock. The name is probably a corruption of their name for themselves: Wazhazhe — a synonym for "enemy" to most of the tribes of the southern plains and woodlands. Osage domains joined those of the Caddos on the north. Historically, the principal Osage villages were in present southwestern Missouri. But the reader will recall that in 1802 the Arkansas Band had moved into the country just north of the Ouachita Mountains, and their hunting and war parties are now on many of the northern tributaries of the Red. Osage warriors are among the largest Indians in the West, with many six-footers and some seven-footers among them. Their own numbers reduced by smallpox, the Caddos had been unable to put up much resistance against Osage raids over the previous thirty years. One famed Osage

He said he was sorry his village was so far or he would invite us to see him & though he could not take us to large, elegant & well furnished houses and treat us as well as we did him yet he could take us to a cool shade & make us welcome to such as he had. — He hoped we would excuse him for taking with him so many men to trouble us, as most of them were young men who had never been so far as the Post and had a great curiosity to see their new friends. — "

Freeman 2.

[Dehahuit's reply was]: "You have far to go, and will meet with many difficulties, but I wish you to go on. My friends, the Panis, will be glad to see you, and will take you by the hand. If you meet with any of the Huzaa's (Osages),[9] and kill them, I will dance for a month. If they kill any of your party, I will go with my young men and warriors, and we will be avenged for you."

Freeman 1.

After this communication, provision was given to the Visitors; and some liquor was furnished, that the soldiers of the Party and the young Indians might drink together.

The soldiers were then drawn up in a single file in open order. The Caddos marched along shaking hands with them from right to left; after which they formed a line in front of the soldiers, about three paces distant, with their faces towards the soldiers. On their principal warrior coming opposite to the U. S. serjeant, he stepped forward, and addressing him men, observed — "that he was glad to see his new brothers had the faces of *men*, and looked

---

chief even acquired the name Hi-Sha-Ki-Hi-Ri, "Caddo Killer." John Joseph Mathews, *The Osages: Children of the Middle Waters*, p. 509; Hodge, *Handbook of Indians North of Mexico* 2:156; Swanton, *Source Material on the History and Ethnology of the Caddo Indians*, p. 85; John R. Swanton, *The Indian Tribes of North America*, Bureau of American Ethnology, *Bulletin 145*, pp. 271–73.

[9] Among other interesting particulars appearing in this preserved Dehahuit speech is the Caddoan name for their archenemies, the Osages.

A Caddo warrior and his horse. Photograph by James Mooney. Courtesy National Anthropological Archives, Smithsonian Institution.

like men and warriors;" then addressing the serjeant by the interpreter, he said—"Here we are, all men and warriors, shaking hands together, let us hold fast, and be friends for ever."

The Caddo Chief dined and spent the 2nd of July at the American Camp. He informed the party that he should return to his Village on the next day early, with his people; he had already kept them several days from hunting: not knowing with what intentions the Spaniards came so near: and hearing of the U. S. party, he thought it best to keep all his people together, that they might prevent hostilities in his land.

He had now seen the U. S. party, knew our business, and had been well treated by us. He believed what we had told him, and would hold us fast by the hand as fathers and friends.

He said that the day before he left his village, three Spanish soldiers came to it from their camp, and informed him, that their Commander had sent an express to Nacogdoches, and as soon as it returned, with dispatches and orders from Government, they should go to the Americans on Red River, stop them, and drive them back or take them prisoners. The Chief supposed the express from Nacogdoches would arrive at his village, as early as his party could effect their return; and might be waiting for him. He would endeavor to find what their object was, would return with the Spanish officer to the American camp, if he wished to visit it, when he should hear the talks of both parties. When he arrived at his village, if the express had not returned, and he could not learn that their intention was to interrupt the party, he would send three of his best warriors to the camp, with whatever information he could obtain.

Custis 2.

On the morning of the second he [Dehahuit] called to inform us that he should set out the next morning for his Village and said immediately on his arrival how (if the Spaniards had not left) he should entreat them in the most suppliant manner possible not to spill blood on his ground, that it was not fear which would make him this humble, because he did not fear man, that although his men are small and may appear to us like nothing, they are unacquainted with fear.[10] if the Spaniards had a desire to speak to us

[10] These Caddo warriors were, evidently, largely Kadohadachos, although they may have represented other remnant Red River tribes (Nassonites, Natchitoches, Yatasis, Adaes, and Nanatsohos) of the Great Caddo Confederacy. These people are virtually all that is left, in 1806, of a great mound-building culture that had probably dominated the midsouth for more than 4,000 years. The Spanish explorers compared them to the Aztecs. As late as 1710, according to La Harpe, there had been at least 2,500 Kadohadachos, but, in 1805, Sibley reported the whole number of warriors of the "Great Caddo" amounted to only about 100. This group, which composed the *amaxoya*, the Caddoan honored caste of warriors, was regarded by other tribes as somewhat like a "Knights of Malta or some distinguished military order," according to Sibley. The Caddo village contains forty or fifty more women than men, and perhaps 100 "old men and strangers," for a total adult population of about 350 souls. Their enemies, the Choctaws, Chickasaws, and Osages were partially responsible for this reduction, but the greatest calamity to befall them in the eighteenth century was their contraction of alien diseases such as cholera and smallpox. Against these unseen enemies the Caddos were unable to raise a defense, and the frontier documents are full of tragic stories relating their reactions. One epidemic in

in a friendly manner he himself would accompany them to our
Camp, but if they wish to be hostile he will order them quit his
ground instantly and will not suffer them to interfere with us at
least 50 leagues above the old Caddo Village which is about 450
miles above this.[11] He repeats that there was a great probability
that we should be attacked by the Osages, if so he should then
have an opportunity to convince the American Government of his
friendship, no matter what their numbers may be he will show us
what his men are capable of doing, that he will send everyone
capable of bearing arms. The Caddoes reside about 50 miles from
this according to some accounts & not so far according to others /
on a small Creek emptying into a lake which communicates with
the River a little above the Raft.[12] It has been 11 years since
they came to that place. — They formerly lived on the River in a

---

1778 killed more than 300 in the Kadohadacho village alone. It is reported
that in their horror they ran into the Mother Red for salvation, but even the
river could not wash away their spots, and they must have died bewildered that
after so many centuries of peaceful coexistence with their country, the world
could have suddenly gone mad. The ancient sites of the Kadohadacho villages
(several of which will be fixed by this exploring expedition) were situated east
and west of present Texarkana, all of them on the banks of the Red. William
B. Glover, "A History of the Caddo Indians," *Louisiana Historical Quarterly*
18 (October 1935): 876–79; Sibley, "Historical Sketches," pp. 40–41; Swanton,
Source Material on the History and Ethnology of the Caddo Indians, pp. 5, 12, 24.
The map on page 8-A of Swanton's excellent work shows the probable locations
of the tribes and villages of the Great Caddo and Hasinai confederacies.

[11] Probably the original Upper Nassonite village, where La Harpe's Post had
been located. Seventy-five or more miles upriver from this village was the site
of the most westerly Caddo confederacy village, at Pecan Point, long since
abandoned by the Nanatsoho division. But the Spaniards undoubtedly regard
the more recently occupied site as the perimeter of the Caddo country, and
Ramón may have already told Dehahuit (as this suggests) that the Americans
were to be stopped there, asserting that Taovaya–Wichita domains began at this
point, and that "this territory is ours." Ramón to Viana, Arroyo de Nasada,
June 20, 1806, The Bexar Archives. Modern Indian Claims Commission testimony, in fact, convincingly demonstrates that in terms of land use, the Caddo
perimeter on the Red actually extended to the western edge of the Blackland
Prairie (about 96° W. longitude), the historic buffalo grounds of the Caddo
peoples. See, in particular, the testimony of Helen Hornbeck-Tanner, in *Caddoan Indians* 4.

[12] The original chain of communications westward from the river was from
Twelve-Mile Bayou into and through Lake Tso'to, thence along Little Willow

large Prairie said to be 150 leagues above this.[13]—They were dri-
ven from thence by the Osage Indians who have always been at
war with them. The Caddoes are a very small race of men without the least appearance of savage ferocity. They have some
firearms among them, but their principal weapon is the Bow &
Arrow which they wield with astonishing dexterity & force.—It
is said they can with great ease throw the Arrow entirely through

Pass into Jeems Bayou, which Custis leaves unnamed but Sibley calls after the
lake: "Sodo." It was here that the Caddos had sought refuge from the Osages and
from diseases of the white man that their woodlands had not shaped them to
resist.

Custis is providing crucial testimony here, for he is saying that Twelve-Mile
Bayou is still "a little above" the Raft in 1806. Today it is commonly believed in
Louisiana and Texas that Caddo Lake, the "only natural lake" in the near Southwest, was created in 1811 when the New Madrid earthquake induced geologic
upheaval on such a vast scale that a number of new lakes (such as Reelfoot, in
Tennessee) were created in the lower Mississippi drainage. Caddo Indian legend
also holds that Caddo Lake was created suddenly, when the "earth had a chill and
began to tremble . . . [and] the ground sank, and floods poured over the land
where the tribe had lived." Quoted in Mildred Mays McClung, *Caddo Lake: Mysterious Swampland*, p. 9. Geologic evidence does not support this interpretation,
and neither do the historical documents. Custis locates the Great Raft just below
the mouth of Twelve-Mile Bayou in 1806, and tells us that Jeems Bayou is yet a
"small creek"; by 1811 William Darby will find most of the northwestern corner of
the proposed state of Louisiana flooded by a lake 60 to 70 miles long, and about 8
miles wide. At some time during the interval since 1806, the mouth of Twelve-
Mile Bayou obviously had been blocked by the Raft. Sibley, in fact, says in 1812
that the lake "has been [formed] within about Twelve Years." Sibley to Eustis,
Natchitoches, November 28, 1812, in Garrett, "Doctor John Sibley and The
Louisiana-Texas Frontier," 49:417–18.

This circumstance, rather than seismic activity, "naturally" created Caddo Lake
in the hills west of Caddo Prairie. When the Great Raft was removed in the 1870s,
the lake was restored to bayou-swamp status until navigation interests promoted
Corp of Engineers' construction of a dam (1910–14). Arthur C. Veatch, "The
Shreveport Area," Special Report No. 2, in Harris and Veatch, *A Preliminary Report
On The Geology Of Louisiana* pp. 185–88; "Report Of Surveys Of Cypress Bayou
And Channels Connecting Shreveport, La., With Jefferson, Tex." The early work
done by Veatch proves the fallacy of the earthquake theory, but Veatch, unaware of
these historical documents, placed the formation of Caddo Lake in 1777.

[13] The Lower Kadohadacho village, which had suffered a bloody massacre at the
hands of the Osages a decade or more before and subsequently had been abandoned. The exploring party will visit and examine the remains of this village, the
last of the historic Red River sites to be occupied by a major Caddoan village.

a Buffaloe. It would be worth a journey of two or three thousand miles to see them use it, particularly to the admirers of Homer, as they would be enabled to relish beauties in the Iliad that must be in a great measure lost to those who have never seen the Bow used by the Indian.[14]

There is a custom among the Caddoes which deserves mention, it is that of the Parents selling their Daughters in marriage. — The daughter has no right to choose for herself a husband, but is obliged to be the wife & servant to the purchaser. — The price is generally a horse and a man is permitted to have as many wives as he is able to purchase. — If one man should take the wife of another, which sometimes happens, the man aggrieved is entitled to the best horse which the other possesses & can go and take possession without application.[15]

There is a tradition among them which on account of its great similarity to the account given by Moses deserves some attention. — They say that a long time since a civil war broke out among them at which *Enicco* or the Supreme Being was so displeased as to send a great flood which destroyed all but one Family, consisting of fourteen, the Father, Mother & Children. — That this family were saved by flying to a knoll at the upper end of the Prairie, which was the only spot left uncovered; that in this knoll was a cave in which was preserved a male & female of all

[14] The Caddos were legendary wielders and craftsmen of the bow. Their bows made from the wood of the bois d'arc, or Osage-orange (regarded on the Southwestern frontier as "the most elastic of long woods known"), were highly prized and were major items of trade in this part of the world. Custis is witnessing the use of this tool in the hands of masters, an experience that seems to call for a classical allusion.

[15] This is a bit of ethnological information not provided by other observers of the Caddos, virtually all of whom were more impressed by the looseness of the marriage tie, the high incidence of "divorce," and the casual attitude toward sexual relations among these people. Custis seems certain that his understanding is correct here, and he may, indeed, be documenting a late cultural practice induced by the Indian acquisition of horse culture. I think it more likely that he is mistaking a traditional gift exchange for "purchase." The Caddoan peoples always struck early observers as more egalitarian towards women than was usual in Indian societies, and Anthony Glass will notice a similar practice among the Taovayas two summers later. Glass, "Copy of a Journal of a Voyage from Nackitosh into the interior of Louisiana," entry for September 9,

George Catlin's "Caddo Chasing Buffalo," painted in the Blackland Prairie, 1834. Courtesy National Museum of American Art, Smithsonian Institution.

kinds of animals; that after the flood had continued for one moon they set at liberty a bird which they called *O-Wah* which returned in a short time with a straw. — They then set out on a Raft in search of that place from whence the straw was brought, that going a west course for two leagues they came to land; that they there saw a fish which they called *Toesha* and being very much frightened at its enormous size, they all shed tears, from which circumstance they ever after called the place *Chacanenah*, signifying the ground upon which tears have been shed; that this fish remained there for many years after and was large enough for 30 men to encamp under. — All the Mexican & Louisiana Indians they say are offspring of that family. I am told that some of the other Nations have a similar tradition.[16] — That many of the tribes

---

1808. See Swanton, *Source Material on the History and Ethnology of the Caddo Indians*, pp. 160-62 for other observations on Caddo marriage practices.

[16] Custis has done here, via the standard methodology of modern cultural

used to meet on a certain day every year at the knoll upon which this family was saved and there offer up prayers and sacrifices to the Supreme Being[17] for his singular favor of not destroying the whole race.

---

anthropology, the most careful ethnological work among the Caddos since Fray Francisco Casañas, missionary to the Hasinais, described Caddo culture as it was from 1691 through 1722. Custis's literal transcription of this interview with one of the Caddos is a major document on the religious traditions of these people, important enough that Swanton's study of the Caddos quotes all of it from the published version, although Swanton mistakenly believes Freeman was its author.

The flood tradition does appear widely among North American Indians, perhaps most prominently in the mythological destruction of Kuskurza, the Third World of the Hopis, and in the Popul Vuh of the Quiché Maya. See Frank Waters, *Book of the Hopi*, p. 18n. Certainly environmental conditions in the natural Red River valley would have encouraged the development of a flood mythology, and the continuing references to varying forms of this tradition, although later Caddos will refer to the hill cave itself as Cha'kani'na (Mooney, 1896, as cited in Swanton), and call it the origin point for ther people, leaves little doubt that the basic story is culturally authentic. Custis's version, however, demonstrates graphically the effect of missionary work among the Caddos, for the references to paired animals and the straw symbol undoubtedly represent a grafting of Judeo-Christian tradition onto the original native tradition. Both Swanton, *Source Material on the History and Ethnology of the Caddo Indians*, pp. 26–28, and George A. Dorsey, *Traditions Of The Caddo*, pp. 18–19, report Caddo flood traditions gathered from their informants and by scholars such as James Mooney. Dorsey, in *The Mythology of the Wichita*, pp. 290–97, confirms Custis's report of a similar tradition among neighboring peoples.

To contemporaries, the questions were different. Given the interest of both Jefferson and Barton in Indian origins, the amount of space Custis devotes to this tradition is not surprising. In fact, it is evidence contrary to Barton's own hypothesis, in *New Views of the Origins of the Tribes and Nations of America*, that linguistic evidence pointed towards an Asian origin for American Indians. John Adair, in *History of the American Indians* (London: 1755), had earlier postulated a Middle Eastern origin, in a work Barton singled out for "much ingenious extravagance." There is today a resurgence of interest in the topic of Indian origins, a debate handled and argued well by the noted geographer George Carter in *Earlier Than You Think*.

[17] "Enicco" is Custis's mishearing (or someone's mispronouncing) of *Caddi Ayo*. Sibley-Grappe briefly allude to this flood tradition and indicate that the famous ceremonial knoll behind the Nassonite-La Harpe's Post village, near present Wamba, Texas, is the hallowed ground of Caddoan mythology. See Sibley, "Historical Sketches," pp. 66–67. The Grappe-Brevel testimony is frequently unreliable, however, and in this instance is contradicted by the Caddo guides who will now join the Freeman and Custis expedition and pinpoint for us the "Medicine Mount" of Caddoan religious mythology. See Part 4.

Part Four

The "Wilderness" Upriver: Coashatta Village to Spanish Camp and Return

July and August, 1806

EDITOR'S NOTE: "This expedition seems to have thrown their whole Country into commotion," reads Custis's last entry at the Alabama Coushatta village, and we know now that he was not exaggerating. Cordero, in San Antonio, had been suspicious of Viana from the first, convinced that he was "permitting the introduction" of the American party. In June he had taken upon himself the responsibility for calling to the frontier Lieutenant Colonel Don Simon de Herrera, governor of the state of Nuevo León and Cordero's personal friend, a man considered a first-rate military figure in New Spain. In Chihuahua, Salcedo agreed to this move, and assigned 1,007 men to protect the Texas border under Herrera's direction. On or about July 15, Herrera, the Baron de Bastrop, and at least part of this large force would arrive in Nacogdoches. With Viana in tow, Herrera would rapidly move this force along the piney woods trails of East Texas to rendezvous with Ramon's force at the Caddo village, while Bastrop would sound out Colonel Cushing in Natchitoches. Meanwhile, Cordero likewise would make plans to go to the scene of confrontation on the Louisiana border, while in Santa Fe, Melgares, with a reported one hundred dragoons and five hundred mounted militia, would be departing for a 233-league descent of the Red.[1]

---

[1] Cordero to Salcedo, San Antonio, June 14, 1806; Salcedo to Cordero, Chihuahua, July 14, 1806; Salcedo to Cordero, Chihuahua, August 14, 1806. The Bexar Archives. Herrera, whom Pike (and many historians) credited with preventing an outbreak of war in the summer of 1806, was originally from the Canary Islands. He spoke both English and French (he was married to an English woman), and was a close friend of Cordero's. Pike described him, following their meeting in June, 1807, thus: "Don Simon Herrara is about five feet eleven inches high, has a sparkling black eye, dark complexion and hair. . . . He is

Two related developments, far to the north, are not uninteresting. On July 15, Zebulon Montgomery Pike, with orders from General Wilkinson to strike overland across the plains to the headwaters of the Red River, would set out from St. Louis with twenty-three men. Six days later, Secretary of War Dearborn, in Washington, would communicate the annual copies of "The Rules and Articles of War" to American military commanders in Louisiana and Orleans territories.[2]

Freeman 1.

It was found adviseable to engage three Caddo Indians, to proceed up the river with the party; to act as guides, spies, or on express, as circumstances might require.[3] One Indian will not go with a party of strangers; two are company for each other; and by engaging the third, he could be dispatched on express, to the Caddo Nation, or to Natchitoches in case of necessity.

Custis 2.

The Caddoes who are to be our guides have just arrived at Camp, they tell us that the Spanish forces have retired to the Sabine; but it is generally believed to be a sham and that they intend to meet us on the River a little above this. This expedition seems to have thrown their whole Country into commotion.—

engaging in his conversation . . . and in all his actions one of the most gallant and accomplished men I ever knew." Jackson, *The Journals of Zebulon Montgomery Pike,* Pike's entry for June 13, 1809, 1:440–41.

Since Melgares's journal has been lost, Pike tells us probably all we can know about his route in pursuit of the American explorers. After his descent of "the Red River" and councils with the Comanches during July and August, he would strike off to the northwest to the Kiowa and Pawnee country, then follow the Arkansas back to the mountains, where he would precede Pike by about six weeks. Ibid. Pike's entry for September 25, 1806, 1:323–24.

[2] Dearborn to Louisiana and Orleans Military Commanders, Washington, July 21, 1806. War Department, Letters Sent, Main Series. The role of the Pike expedition is treated in the Epilogue.

[3] Two of the Caddo guides can be definitely identified. One is Cut Finger, favorite of the Caddo chief. The other is a leading warriur whose name, Grand Ozages, attests to his war prowess and standing. He is described in an Indian agent report as having accompanied Freeman "from the Caddo [Alabama-Coushatta] Village as far up the River as he went and back again to Natchitoches,

Freeman 1.

The Party left the camp near the Coashutta Village on the 11th of July. Opposite to the village, on the south side of the river, there is an extensive Corn Field.

Eight miles above the village, a high bank of Pine Land comes in from the right, the opposite side is level. In this bank there is a bituminous shale, interspersed with small particles of mica.[4] The water is 20 feet deep, but gradually decreases as you ascend the river, and above this place, it overflows its banks but in a very few places.

From the Coashutta Village to where the upper little river[5] enters the red river, a distance of 162 miles, the Valley of the Red river is one of the richest and most beautiful imaginable. It is from

and was Particularly Servisable in hunting, as a Guide & keeping the Other Indians together, and is in Major Freemans Opinion one of the Best Indians he ever saw." John Sibley, *A Report from Natchitoches in 1807*, Annie Louise Abel, ed., entries for February 21 and April 14, 1807, pp. 13–14, 21. If the third "Indian" guide is not Lucas Talapoon, I do not know who he is.

[4] The party, in the original (unstraightened) bed of the river which carries them in a series of loops hard against the highlands on the east bank, is observing modern Coushatta and Miller's Bluffs, composed principally of Tertiary carbonaceous shales, a specimen of which Custis will collect here. The expedition is at this point passing one of the highest points in the Orleans Territory (present Louisiana). A short distance back of the river the "high bank of Pine Land" (the Sabine Uplift) forms a high ridge, 482 feet in elevation, now known as Delaney Mountain. It is visible for a considerable distance across the Caddo Prairie bottomlands, and was a landmark for the Indians. King's map from Freeman's field courses shows a trading path from Texas to the Arkansas country crossing the Red at its base. Somewhere just south of here, Bénard de La Harpe, late in March, 1719, had gone ashore to kill a bison. He planted a cross and had the Coat of Arms of the Bourbons carved on a tree, thereby claiming the region above the Raft for France. The chronicle of his expedition noted this ridge as high land, covered with pines. Smith, "Account of the Journey of Bénard de La Harpe," entries for March 23 and 26, 1719, pp. 248–49. See also, Otto Lerch, *A Preliminary Report upon the Hills of Louisiana, North of the Vicksburg, Shreveport and Pacific Railroad*, pp. 8–9; Douglas Epps Jones, "Geology of Bossier Parish," Ph.D. diss., Louisiana State University, plate 1; USGS, Gilliam (La.) Quadrangle. Delaney Mountain, and the highlands described here, can be seen to good advantage from the Louisiana Highway 2 bridge, which crosses the Red between Hosston and Plain Dealing.

[5] The Little River, which drains the southern slopes of the Ouachita Mountains and empties into the Red near present Fulton, Hempstead County, Arkansas.

6 to 10 miles in width, and except for a few days in the year, it is all elevated above the rise of the water in the river. It cannot be exceeded either in fertility or beauty, by any part of America, or perhaps of the world.[6] Through this valley, the Red River pursues a very winding course, in a bed varying from 200 to 250 yards in width, and between banks of from 15 to 20 feet high.

In the summer season, when the water in the river is low, the stream seeks its passage between banks of sand and gravel which project from the alternate shores, as the river changes its direction. Extensive prairies and small lakes occur in this valley; the former frequently approaching the margin of the river are elevated at least forty feet above the low water. The Timber of this Valley is Cotton Wood, Sycamore, Cypress, Black Gum, White and Black Oak, Hickory, Black Walnut, Pecan, Ash, Locust, and Red Cedar: handsome groves of this latter are frequently observed in the vicinity of the river.[7] In some places the growth of timber is observed to

[6] This section of bottomland prairie came to be regarded as the garden spot of the entire Red River valley, and for years frontier farmers' mouths watered over these lush prairies. But while two dozen or more white squatters, who hunted and traded with the Indians, did settle in this stretch by 1825, it was not until Shreve's early successes with the Raft and the Caddo Cession of July 1, 1835, that Caddo Prairie and other bottomlands above Natchitoches became the scene of legal pioneer operations, developing almost overnight into the richest cotton-producing region of the Old South. By 1838 Shreve's Landing (Shreveport), founded on land sold to Shreve by a pioneer, was a bustling pioneer settlement. Fortier, *Louisiana Cyclopedic* 1:143–44; Charles H. Lange, "A Report on Data Pertaining To The Caddo Treaty of July 1, 1835: The Historical and Anthropological Background and Aftermath," in Robert W. Neuman and Charles H. Lange, *Caddoan Indians II*, pp. 159–61; J. Fair Hardin, "An Outline Of Shreveport And Caddo Parish History," *The Louisiana Historical Quarterly* 8 (October 1935): 773.

[7] By the 1890s the Texarkana & Shreveport Railroad, a logging line, had cut nearly every vestige of these extensive cedar groves. Modern residents have no inkling that such stands once existed in the valley, but in the nineteenth century they attracted much attention. Doctor Joseph Paxton, of Mount Prairie, Ark. Terr., noted that they seemed to grow in the same soils that bald cypress did farther downriver, and described them in these words: "It would be difficult for a person acquainted only with upland cedars, to form a correct idea of the beauty, size, and symmetry of those that grow in the bottoms of Red River. I have seen, with wonder and never-ceasing astonisment, those vast, lofty cedar groves. . . . They had frequently been described to me, but I had formed no adequate idea of them; nor do I believe it is in the power of language to give a representation

be of one particular kind, whilst in others, there is an admixture of almost all the species here enumerated, and all of large dimensions. The undergrowth is almost universally of cane, so close and strong, as seldom to allow the party to penetrate far from the margin of the River.[8]

This valley is bounded by high land, with an undulating and varied surface, generally 100 feet higher than the plains below. The soil on this upland is said to be rich, and very productive, when in cultivation.[9] It is cloathed with White and black Oak, Hickory, and Pine, without much undergrowth.[10]

of their imposing grandeur, that would not fall short of reality upon seeing them." The eradication of these cedars—critical to the elimination of the Great Raft— stymied Paxton's prediction that the day would come "when the cedars of Red River will become as celebrated in these United States, as those of Lebanon were once in Palestine." Dr. Joseph Paxton to A. H. Sevier, Mount Prairie, Ark. Terr., August 1, 1828. *House Doc. 78*, 20th Cong., 2d sess., p. 13.

[8] Anthony Glass, who would traverse Caddo Prairie two summers after Freeman and Custis, also noted that the river-bottom prairies were "generally Covered with strong cane." Glass, entry for July 16, 1808, in Flores, *Journal of an Indian Trader*, 39–40. Reporting the fate of the Red River exploration, the *Richmond Enquirer*, October 10, 1806, interpreted the observance of extensive stands of this giant grass as an indication that the country was extremely rich, and informed its readers that cane would be "no more difficult to clear than a cornfield."

[9] "Undulating" is rather an appropriate adjective for the hill country bordering the Red here, an uplift raised by see-saw action from the weight of sediments in lower Louisiana. Topographical relief in these hills is relatively gentle, the result of stream dessication, folding, and some faulting, all produced by water erosion on at least three layers of sediment beds laid down millions of years ago, when the waters of the Gulf of Mexico lapped over this country as far north as Missouri and Illinois. The soils of the Sandy Hills (west hills) and the Sulphur Wold (east hills) in this section of the river valley are principally gray and red clays and loamy sands, primarily of the Woodtell, Bowie, Nacogdoches, and Tonkawa types. Farmers early developed a preference for the red sandy loams, but all these upland soils really lack nitrogen and are quickly exhausted. Like the Creek immigrants, early white settlers favored these hills for their homes, not because of the soil—they still preferred the river prairies for planting but because the uplands are cooler and healthier. The hill breezes tended to carry away the mosquitoes, the source (unknown at that time) of the malaria that was the scourge of the river bottoms. Lerch, *A Preliminary Report upon the Hills of Louisiana*, pp. 8–40; *1982–1983 Texas Almanac*, Dallas: Dallas Morning News, 1982, p. 97.

[10] Coupled with Custis's botanical remarks at the Alabama-Coushatta village (Part 2), Freeman establishes here the ecologically mature tree growth of the mid-

177

The Middle Red.

At the mouth of the lower little river,[11] which enters the Red
River about 40 miles higher than the Cooshatta village, there is
a beautiful bluff, elevated nearly 100 feet higher than the surface
of the water, and extending about a quarter of a mile down the
river. At 70 feet below the surface, on the side next the river, is a
stratum of stone coal, eighteen inches in thickness, which runs
horizontally into the bank: it presents a face of more than 200
yards along the bluff. The clay over the whole side of this bluff
is incrusted with allum. This bluff rises as it recedes from the
river, about 200 yards, where it exhibits a beautiful wavy surface,
thinly covered with Oak and Hickory.[12] The Latitude at the con-

---

dle Red. Bald cypress and red cedar were the most common species of the
floodplain, while lofty deciduous species of 80 to 100 feet were the dominants
in the hills—although pines were obviously common, including a new one,
Pinus echinata Mill., the shortleaf pine. Tornadoes, lightning, and insects were
the only disruptors of the mature forest, but the Indians shaped and greatly
influenced its appearance. Freeman provides, for example, conclusive testimony
that the upland forests were far more park-like in 1806 than today's second-
and third-growth woods would ever indicate. The interlocking of the lofty upper
story into a shading canopy was partially responsible, but ecologists are now
convinced that Indian-set ground fires, to facilitate hunting and travel, were the
most important factor in curtailing undergrowth in the Eastern Forest before
the coming of whites. See R. H. Whittaker, "Recent Evolution of Ecological
Concepts In Relation To The Eastern Forests Of North America," in Frank
Egerton, comp., *History of American Ecology*, pp. 343–52; and Stephen J. Pyne's
new *Fire in America: A Cultural History of Wildland and Rural Fire*, chapters
2 and 3.

[11] Reference is to the Sulphur River of present northeast Texas and Miller
County, Ark. The Sulphur heads in the Blackland Prairie, and served as an
avenue of travel to the nearest year-round bison grounds for the Indians farther
east. It is today a green, languid river, although it probably ran more rapidly
before it was impounded to form Wright Patman Reservoir. In March, 1719,
La Harpe became its first European explorer when he followed it for five
leagues before heading overland for the Upper Nassonite village. He called the
river, Rivière de L'Ours (or Bear River), because of the astonishing number of
black bears along it. Smith, "Account of the Journey of Bénard de La Harpe,"
entry for April 6, 1719, p. 249. The American party has now crossed the 33d
parallel, into present Arkansas. Dunbar and Hunter had reported that when
they passed this line the landscape began to change; Spanish moss vanished from
the trees and the country began to assume a hillier, rockier aspect. Dunbar,
"Journal of a Voyage," entry for Nov. 17, 1804, *Dunbar Letters*, p. 243.

[12] The bluff, located two miles east of present Doddridge, Ark., in Miller
County, is now known as Spring Bank, and is far and away the handsomest

fluence of the Rivers here is 33 deg. 05 min. 37 sec. North.[13] Above this Little River, the beaches of Red River are composed of white sand, slope down from one or other side alternately, to near the opposite bank, confining the stream to one third of the width between the banks. The Water is here very clear, and so shallow, that the men passed over from the termination of a sand beach on one side, to the commencement of one on the other side, as occasion suited in towing the boats along:[14] the boats frequently rubbing on the bottom as they proceeded.

On the evening of the 17th of July, the party stopped for the night, in a handsome Prairie, on the left, or west side of the river, elevated 40 feet above the water. The surface was level and interspersed with clumps of trees, which added much to the beauty of its appearance. It was expected that the Spaniards would here have interrupted us.[15] The Indians in the company refused to

and most imposing bluff on the lower half of the Red River. It is today almost precisely as Freeman described it in 1806. It rises 50 to 100 feet above the surface of the water at a perpendicular angle, and stretches for nearly half a mile along the western banks of the Red and Sulphur. Stratified layers of various clays appear in the face of the bluff, as well as the seam of coal, which is still visible. Spring Bank is now beautifully vegetated with loblolly and shortleaf pines. The commanding aspect of this bluff would lead to the establishment, twelve years later, of a United States Indian factory (trading post) here—the exact location is now unknown, since there has never been an excavation. Directed by John Fowler, this factory was in existence until 1822. In 1825 the two-story pine structure was dismantled and the lumber used to erect a new Red River Indian agency on Caddo Prairie. Ora Brooks Peake, *A History of the United States Indian Factory System, 1795–1822,* pp. 17–18, 31. A ferry, operated on the Red River at this place continuously since 1821, today is well worth taking for the splendid ride and view. It is to be replaced by a bridge in 1992.

[13] According to U.S.G.S. Doddridge (Ark.) Quadrangle, the latitude of the confluence is about 33° 06 ' North.

[14] Before this, the party had enjoyed the options of rowing, poling, or tracking. This condition is a serious development that will limit the options essentially to tracking, a tedious process in a river where the bottoms of the barges scrape the riverbed. Stated simply, the party had delayed getting underway in the spring, and now has been caught by low water.

[15] The Sibley-Grappe account calls this Little Prairie, but the King map represents it as Round Prairie and indicates that an Indian Trace from the old Caddo villages to Natchitoches crossed the river at this place. A latitude reading of 33° 12' N. had been taken two days before, but both the seventeenth and eighteenth are cloudy, and the party is unable to take a reading here. Modern

"Eight miles above the village, a high bank of Pine Land comes in from the

right"—the Coushatta-Miller's Bluffs and Delaney Mountain country.

Approximate profile of Red River Valley

1. Red sandy clay   2. Tertiary   3. Upland flats   4. Grayish loam with mamillae

Topographical profile of the Red River Valley. Adapted from Harris and Veatch, A Preliminary Report On The Geology Of Louisiana.

come upon this Prairie, but slept upon the sand beach on the opposite side of the river.

Shortly after leaving this prairie, we picked up pieces of stone coal on the beach, weighing from three to four pounds each: they had the appearance of having been brought from a considerable distance by the water. Fine white salt was met with about 15 miles above the prairie, and often afterwards on the beaches; and the hunters frequently killed deer, while licking it.

On the evening of the 19th we passed a beautiful prairie, on the North-East side of the River, 125 miles from the Cooshutta Village. This prairie was the scite of an old Caddo village, deserted by that nation in consequence of a surprize, and the massacre of the greatest part of the inhabitants, by the Osage Indians. The Caddos with the exploring party, expressed a wish to visit this place when they were approaching it: and shewed a remarkable hill in its rear, on which their Old Chiefs used frequently to meet in Council. They proposed to visit it with a bottle of liquor, that they might take a drink and talk to the great spirit!

This remarkable mount or hill stands on a level plain about two miles from the river, having the Prairie on which the Caddo Village stood in front, or between it and the river. It is about two

topo maps indicate that the large prairie just south of present Garland City, Ark., is the likely location for this campsite. See Sibley, "Historical Sketches," p. 66.

The "handsome bluff" at the mouth of the Sulphur. Spring Bank was later the site of an Indian trading factory, 1817–1822.

miles in length, 250 or 300 feet in elevation, very narrow at the top, in many places not exceeding two or three paces, and so steep, that it is with difficulty that it can be ascended. The angle formed with the plane on which it stands, is from 45 to 50 degrees: in some places almost perpindicular.

This hill is an irregular mass of iron colored porous rock, in which there is a great number of small round pebbles. It has the appearance of having been in fusion at some former period.[16] There is very little clay or soil on the surface, but a red colored

---

[16] Cut Finger and Grand Ozages have led Freeman, and now modern readers, to the mythical Medicine Mount of the Caddo Indians. It is almost certainly the hill of the Caddo flood tradition, and to some Caddo groups, their people's mythic point of emergence into this world. Although Custis's informant does not so label it, later Caddos will preserve its memory with the name Cha'kani'na —"place of crying." For moderns, the location of this hill not only pinpoints an important Indian shrine, but also serves as a ready clue to the location of one of the main Caddo villages of antiquity. Seen from the air, the mount is actually a narrow ridge 2 miles long, with a rather abrupt northern termination. Today it is known as Boyd Hill, and is located about 6 miles northwest of Lewisville, in Lafayette County, Ark. Rising strikingly out of the table-flat river-bottom prairie to an elevation of about 390 feet (perhaps 175 to 200 feet higher than the prairie below — high enough to escape any Red River flood) it can be seen from the south and west for a distance of several miles and is particularly noticeable from the river itself. In May, 1977, Jerry Griffin and I hiked from our camp on the river across to the mount. Our examination of it leads me to believe that the explorers and their Indian guides ascended the northern end of the ridge (at about 33° 20' N.). Here the climb is almost straight up, and the crest of the hill extremely narrow, almost a shelf. From the summit a fine panorama of the Arkansas Red River prairies can be had, including a distant view of the hills on the opposite side of the valley. See U.S.G.S. Boyd Hill (Ark.) Quadrangle; and for my account of it in 1977, Dan Flores, "A Final Journey Down The Wild Red," the *Shreveport Times Sunday Magazine*, August 14, 1977, entry for May 24, 1977.

Freeman's geologic particulars on this hill are accurate. The Caddo Medicine Mount is a cretaceous ridge, uplifted in late Pliocene and Tertiary times, so that its crest remained uncovered by the sea of younger, Quaternary deposits blanketing the surrounding country. At some point, its western flank was eroded to a perpendicular angle of 45° to 80° by the rush of floodwaters from the Red, exposing boulder-sized calcareous concretions of clay, ferruginous sand, iron ore, and gravel, the "irregular mass of iron colored porous rock" containing "small round pebbles," which Freeman describes in 1806. These had indeed been "in fusion," but by the pressure of great weight rather than heat. Carl H. Dane, "Upper Cretaceous Formations Of Southwestern Arkansas," *Bulletin of the Arkansas Geological Survey*, pp. xiii–xiv, and plate 1; David D. Owen, et

The Caddo Medicine Mount, or Cha'Kani'Na.

gravel; it produces small scrubby Oaks and Pines only. In front of this mount lies a beautiful and rich meadow, extending from its base to the river, and downwards for about two miles. It is interspersed with small clumps of trees, and has a small lake or pond in its centre.[17] Around and near to this pond, are to be seen the vestiges of the Caddo habitations; it was the largest of their villages, and their cultivated fields extended for five or six miles from it in every direction.[18]

From the summit of this hill, the high ground, which bounds the valley on both sides, is distinctly seen; the distance to the opposite side appeared to be about ten miles. In the rear of the

al., *Second Report of a Geological Reconnoissance of the Middle and Southern Counties of Arkansas*, p. 134.

[17] This is probably the lake shown on USGS Boyd Hill (Ark.) Quadrangle as Clear Lake, a handsome body of water fringed with trees today.

[18] Because of the accuracy of its topographical descriptions and the incorporation of bracketing astronomical observation, Freeman's account is the most important of all the early documents for fixing the sites of the historic Caddo villages. This village was the Lower (or Petit) Kadohadacho village, to which most of the Caddos upriver had fled in April, 1790, only to be itself abandoned in 1795 following the Osage attack. This was apparently a very old Caddo site, and interestingly, it answers to the description of the mythical location referred to by Dorsey's Caddo informant in 1903, who told the anthropologist that upon emergence from "Old-Home-in-the-Darkness" to the present world, the Caddos had erected their first village, called "Tall-Timber-on-Top-of-the-Hill" near a high hill covered with blackjack oak timber. "This was the beginning of the real people," Dorsey was told. It is believed that early Caddoan speakers separated from the Iroquoian family about 4,000 B.C., and began moving up the Red toward the plains about 2,000 B.C. A few miles to the south of the medicine Mount, in fact, there still exists one of the largest ceremonial mounds in the entire river valley, a multi-tiered structure some 300 feet long, with a faint causeway still visible. Dorsey, *Traditions of the Caddo*, pp. 8–9; Jack Thomas Hughes, "Prehistory of The Caddoan-Speaking Tribes," *Caddoan Indians III*, pp. 320–31.

Freeman reports this to have been the largest of the Caddoan towns, but for most of the historic period that distinction probably belonged to the village originally occupied by the Upper Nassonites. The only population figure we have on the Lower Kadohadacho village, provided by Gaignard in 1773, was sixty warriors (total population about 250), but this was before the upriver groups assembled here, and certainly must reflect a great decline from earlier days. Gaignard, "Journal Of An Expedition Up The Red River," entry for October 9, 1773, in Bolton, *Athanase de Mézières* 2:83.

This area has never been confirmed archaeologically as the site of the Kadohadacho village. Shortly after the turn of the twentieth century, the Smithsonian

View of an ancient Kadohadacho village site, from the crest of the Caddo Medicine Mount.

hill the land was nearly level, and the ascent from the base very gentle. The soil good, covered with White and Black Oak and Hickory.

About twenty miles higher than the scite of the old Caddo Village, a small bluff reaches the river on the south west side.

Institution sent distinguished archaeologist Clarence B. Moore to explore the Red River as far north as the Great Bend. In addition to measuring the mound just described, Moore examined three sites (Friday, Moore, and Foster) in the area, but though many Caddoan artifacts were found, no historic-focus materials were among them. Moore summarized: ". . . not in a single site in this section was any object found indicating contact with white people." Clarence B. Moore, "Some Aboriginal Sites on Red River," *Journal of the Academy of Natural Sciences of Philadelphia* 14 (1912): 487, 584–619. Modern scholars believe that floodwash and extensive cultivation over the intervening years are likely to make the discovery of this village site very difficult. Hiram Gregory to the editor, Natchitoches, April 14, 1975. In the absence of an excavation, then, Freeman's topographical description and map work, matched with on-site investigation, remains the only way to fix the location of this major Indian village of the near Southwest.

It ascends from the river to the height of 100 feet, to a very narrow ridge, falling with a gradual slope on the opposite side.[19] At the foot of this bluff, on the beach, is a quantity of dark colored stone, which when broken exhibits the appearance of Grey Lime stone or Gypsum; as also some specimens of petrified wood.[20] This ridge extends about half a mile along the river; Buffaloe tracks were first seen by the hunters of the party in the Vicinity of this Hill.[21]

On the morning of the 22nd of July we reached the mouth of the upper Little River, which enters from the West. The width of this river at its mouth is 100 yards, contracting to about 20 yards at a small distance above. It preserves this breadth between banks 15 or 25 feet high, for a considerable distance. The land is high, rich, and very level, producing White and Black Oak, Hickory, Pecan and Ash, with very little undergrowth. The confluence of these rivers is in Latitude 33° . . 36' . . 59'' N.[22]

Red River here retains its general width of 200 yards, having banks about 30 feet higher than the water at this season, to near

[19] This was Buzzard Bluff, located in present Miller county, Ark., about seven miles below Fulton. According to USGS topo maps, it is 50 feet high and is located at 33° 31' 30'' N. A centuries-old game trail, later used by Texas cattlemen, crossed the Red here.

[20] Custis collected a piece of this gypsum, undoubtedly washed down from the great gypsum belt that crosses the Red far upriver. See his mineralogy collection, Part 5, for additional details.

[21] This is the only mention of Bison (*Bison bison bison* [L.]) in the exploring accounts of either leader, but Custis in his natural history catalogues (Part 5) states that bison "are first met with about the second little River." Whether this statement is based upon an actual sighting of the animal cannot now be determined, although I think it likely. A fuller treatment is found in Part 5, but it ought to be noted here that not only human pressure, but also the inundation of the Red River prairies by the advancing Great Raft, was contributing to the contraction of the bison range in the early Red River valley. According to Joseph Paxton, as late as the 1790s, Caddo and Bodcau prairies were the resort of large herds of bison. Once these pastures were flooded by the backup of waters, the herds rarely visited them. Paxton to Sevier, Mount Prairie, Ark. Terr., August 1, 1828, p. 10.

[22] U.S.G.S. Fulton (Ark.) Quadrangle represents the latitude of the confluence of the two rivers at about 33° 36' 30 '' N. The party has now passed the Great Bend of the Red, and from this point the river flows from the west. The Little River does enter from the west, as Freeman states, but on the north bank of the

the top of which it rises in high freshe[t]s. The land is very rich: a thin cane brake, with Oak, Hickory and Pecan timber.

From the lower little river to this place, the precise width of the River cannot be defined: for, whilst one bank is almost perpendicular, the other side is a gently sloping beach, thickly covered with Cotton Wood bushes, which at this season occupy two-thirds of the distance across.

A little above where the upper Little river enters, Red River is much obstructed by logs and trunks of trees, which are fixed in the bed of the river: the water too, is so shoal, that in the summer season, the boats get aground at almost every turn, in a very rapid current.

On the 25th,[23] at about 20 miles above the Little river, on the right hand side, ascending, is a prairie, considerably above the water, of a rich soil, and now overgrown with high grass, bushes

Red. The Sibley-Grappe account of Little River reads thus: "You now arrive at the mouth of the Little River of the right; this river is about 150 yards wide; the water is clear as crystal; the bottom is stony, and is boatable, at high water, up to the great prairies. . . ." Sibley, "Historical Sketches," p. 66. The Little River actually drains the southern slopes of Kiamichi Mountain, in the Oklahoma end of the Ouachita range.

[23] On this date, Viana, now commanding Ramón's force, is setting up camp on a carefully-selected bluff four days upriver; here they will await the Americans. The route of their march from the Caddo village across northeast Texas appears on Fray José Maria de Jesús Puelles' *Mapa Geographica de la Provincias Septentrionales de esta Nueva España* (1807), in the Map Collection of the Barker Center at the University of Texas, Austin. From the village, Viana seems to have swung out to the west to the Post Oak Savannah, where grass was more plentiful and travelling easier, passing through the vicinity of present Linden, Cass County. Two years later, Anthony Glass's party will find lingering evidence of the passage of the Spanish army in the vicinity of present Naples and Douglassville, and Glass will note in his journal: "Crossed the Road made by the Spaniards in 1807 [*sic*] under the command of Captain Vianne who was in pursuit of Freeman and Sparks who were ascending Red River on an exploring expedition by order of Mr. Jefferson the Hon. president of the United States." Glass, entry for July 24, 1808, in Flores, *Journal of an Indian Trader*, 41, 41n.22.

At the general Spanish camp near the Caddo village, Bastrop has returned with word that Cushing regards both the act of stopping Freeman and the Spanish advance across the Sabine as hostilities. With a force of some four hundred poorly-equipped men, Herrera will now begin preparations to march to Bayou Pierre. Viana to the Acting Commandant at Nacogdoches, at the Caddo village, August 4, 1806, The Bexar Archives. Abernethy, *The Burr Conspiracy*, p. 51,

and briars. This prairie extends back from the river about half a mile, and is bounded by open woods of Oak and Hickory.

Here was formerly a considerable Caddo Village:[24] many of the Cedar Posts of their huts yet remain, and several Plum Trees, the fruit of which is red and not good. A bunch of Hemp,[25] of several stems, nearly an Inch in diameter, and Ten feet high, was found on the left bank of the River opposite this Village. From Red River across to little river, is about eight miles, over a level and rich plain, and open woods.

A quantity of clay, of a high blue color, and so hard as to resist the current of the water, appeared in the bank of the river at this Prairie, projecting some yards beyond the general line of the bank.

---

provides the figures for Herrera's army, but is much confused about the reasons for all these Spanish troop movements.

[24] This was the ghost town of the Upper Kadohadacho village, a very old Caddo location. Joutel and the remnants of La Salle's last expedition passed through it in July, 1687, as did Tonty three years later, the Frenchmen finding it a considerable settlement, led by a woman. See Stiles, *Joutel's Journal of La Salle's Last Voyage*, pp. 165–69. The Europeans carried with them the seeds of the town's destruction, for in 1690–91 a smallpox epidemic left three thousand Caddos dead, many hundreds in this village. The north bank location also seems to have been particularly vulnerable to Osage attacks, and within a century after Joutel, the Kadohadachos had largely abandoned it in favor of the Nassonite location with its small, protective post of Frenchmen. When Gaignard went upriver in 1773, he found only ten Caddos still living at this village, and called the prairie, descriptively, "Preiry dest Enemy." Gaignard, "Journal Of An Expedition Up The Red River," entry for October 14, 1773. In Bolton, *Athanase de Mézières*, 2:83.

In 1916, the Museum of the American Indian, Heye Foundation, sponsored an archaeological expedition, led by M. R. Harrington, to begin excavation on the Red where Moore's earlier survey had left off. This village was the first location on their agenda, but when the team arrived the Red was at flood stage, and none of the work here was attempted. See M. R. Harrington, *Certain Caddo Sites in Arkansas*, pp. 14–15. Relying upon Freeman's mapwork, ethnologists such as Swanton have placed the probable location near Ogden, in Little River County, Ark., but the Burrows Site excavation in this area did not yield historic-focus pottery or European trade goods. Scurlock, "The Kadohadacho Indians: A Correlation of Archeological and Documentary Data" (master's thesis), pp. 48–49, 76–79. Based upon the location of the gravel bar that Freeman describes, the area just west of Index seems the more likely area.

[25] The Indian hemp (*Apocynum cannibinum* [L.]). Custis misidentifies it, but his name is close enough to allow it to be correctly identified. See his "Vegetables" list for this day.

At the head of this prairie, a bar of stones and coarse gravel, crosses the bed of the river, on which was found not more than 14 inches of water.[26]

On the 26th, the Indians discovered three of their Nation ahead, on the bank of the river, which appeared to give them much pleasure. They were runners sent from the Caddo nation by the Chief, agreeably to the arrangement made before the exploring party left the Cooshutta Village. The information which these Indians brought was, that the day before they left their Village, the Spanish troops upwards of 1000 in number entered it, and cut down the staff on which the American Flag was flying, and carried off the Flag with them.[27] They insulted the Chief, said they were going after the Americans on Red river, whom they would serve in the same manner, and, if resistance was made, either kill them, or carry them off prisoners, in irons. They had taken with them

[26] This clay and gravel bar is the first place from its mouth where the Red may be forded year around, and was utilized over centuries by both Indians and whites travelling overland from present Illinois to the Texas country. Quite likely this ford was one of the environmental features that attracted the Caddos to the Great Bend region. Early white squatters, such as Ben Milam, who would move into this area in 1816, would call this ford "White Oak Shoals." Barbara O. Chandler and J. Ed Howe, *History of Texarkana and Bowie and Miller Counties, Texas-Arkansas*, p. 16. A sure clue to the location of the Upper Kadohadacho village, this clay-gravel bar today appears in the river about a quarter-mile upstream of the bridge crossing at Index on U.S. highways 59 and 71, north of Texarkana.

[27] John Sibley had presented Dehahuit and the Caddos this flag back in 1805 (Sibley to William Eustis, Natchitoches, January 30, 1810, Garrett, "Doctor John Sibley and The Louisiana-Texas Frontier," 47:388). Apparently Ramón had seen the American flag flying over Sha'–childni'ni for some two weeks before the arrival of Viana and Herrera. Since Tripoli had, during Jefferson's first administration, declared war on the United States via a similar action, this "flag incident" would lead to anger and dismay in the states. A number of newspapers carried the story under titles such as "A hostile demonstration of war" (*Orleans Gazette*, August 25, 1806), and the incident would figure prominently in the sharp diplomatic exchange soon to ensue. According to Pichardo, who gives the Spanish version, the flag had been flying over a "deserted" Caddo lodge, and was partially hidden by a Spanish flag attached just below it. Viana, who had just arrived at the Caddo village from Nacogdoches, ordered the staff cut down, since there was no cord to lower the flag, and positioned an officer (so the Spaniards claimed) beneath the flags to catch them before they could hit the ground. According to the Spanish version, Dehahuit was *not* there, but they admitted that the other Caddos were angered to the point of taking up arms. Hackett, *Pichardo's*

two young Caddos as guides to a handsome bluff on the River, a few miles above the old Caddo Village,[28] and 230 miles (by water) higher than the Cooshutta Village. The Chief directed these Indians farther to say, that the Commanding officer of the Spanish Party was a Cross and bad man, who would do all the mischief he could to the party, and in his name to advise their return; should the determination, however, be to proceed, he advised the killing of the Spanish Commander first; and for that purpose, sent a particular description of him.[29] The runners were to accompany the party, and see the result, that they might carry the news to their Chief.

On receiving this intelligence, the Indians were very much distressed and wished the party to return without seeing the Spaniards. On my declaring that my instructions were to proceed until stopped by a superior force, but, that they were perfectly at liberty to return, if they had any wish so to do, they said they would proceed with the party, but were certain none would ever go back.

On the Interpreter making a particular enquiry as to the number of Spaniards who had passed through the Caddo Village, for the purpose of interrupting the progress of the party, it was asserted to be 1050 or 1060.[30] On enquiring the distance of the bluff, where we were expected to be met with, the Indian said the party would sleep twice, and meet them on the morning of the third day.

Treatise on the Limits of Louisiana and Texas 3:422–29; Richmond *Enquirer,* September 19, 1806.

[28] The original Upper Nassonite location, which the party will visit later this day.

[29] It is unclear whether Dehahuit's description is of Herrera or Viana, but probably the latter, who now may be compensating for having been thought "soft" before.

[30] The Indians' estimate of Spanish troop strength may be an exaggeration, but perhaps not by much. Abernethy says the Herrera-Bastrop army numbered about 400; Ramón's we know was about 225. The *Mississippi Messenger,* September 30, 1806, sets the Spanish force at some 1,500, but Herrera later insisted he commanded no more than 700 troops in Texas during the crisis of 1806. See Isaac J. Cox, "The Louisiana-Texas Frontier During the Burr Conspiracy," *Mississippi Valley Historical Review* 10 (December 1923): 281.

Towards evening we were opposite to a lake on the south of the River,[31] round which the Caddos had Cornfields, when they occupied their principal village, which was situate[d] in the prairie just above it.[32] This lake is about two miles in length, and parallel to the river. Astronomical observations taken this evening, determined our latitude to be 33° . . 34' . . 42'' North. The next morning we selected a spot on the north side of the river, where we deposited part of our provisions, ammunition, and Astronomical Instruments; near which, and in a more secret place, we left

[31] Although a team of Dallas archeologists (see note 34) has designated modern Roseborough Lake as the lake Freeman mentions here, Morris L. Britton, a Sherman, Texas, physician, has done some fine mapwork study founded upon the King-Freeman map which convinces me that modern Roseborough is a later horse-shoe cutoff that did not exist in 1806 (it was, in fact, the channel of the river then). Britton believes, and I concur, that two remnant lakes, both now called "Clear Lake" on modern topos and located about 2 miles due north of Wamba, Bowie County, Texas, joined in 1806 to create the lake around which the Caddos had once planted their cornfields—a very important reference for site locations here. This lake is described attractively in the Sibley-Grappe account as ". . . about 5 miles in circumference, in an oval form, neither tree nor shrub near it, nor stream of water running in or out of it; it is very deep, and the water so limpid that a fish may be seen 15 feet from the surface." Sibley, "Historical Sketches," pp. 66–67. See also, Morris L. Britton, "The Location of Le Poste des Cadodaquious" (unpublished paper, copy in possession of the editor); U.S.G.S. Barkman (Texas) Quadrangle. The Caddo guides, it ought to be noted, make no mention of a sacred hill in this vicinity.

[32] This was originally the Upper Nassonite village, a site that the Caddos had occupied for untold hundreds of years before the exodus to Jeems Bayou and, during historic times, the center of Caddoan power and population. Describing their approach to this town on June 23, 1687, the French diarist, Joutel, writes that: ". . . we cross'd most lovely Plains and Meadows, border'd with fine Groves of beautiful Trees, where the Grass was so high, that it hinder'd our Horses going, and [we] were oblig'd to clear the Passage for them." Stiles, *Joutel's Journal of La Salle's Last Voyage,* pp. 167–68. Three years later Tonty noted of these "Cadadoquis" that they tattoed their faces and bodies, possessed about thirty horses (a considerable number that early), and that although they fished and hunted, "their fields are beautiful." Tonty, "Memoir By The Sieur De La Tonty" 1:47–48. Thirty years later, another French explorer, La Harpe, spoke thus of the country of the Nassonites: "The terrain of the Nassonites is a little elevated, the soil sandy, but at half a quarter of a league from the river, the country is fine, the earth black, and the prairies most beautiful and most fertile. Near the place that I have chosen for my establishment, there is an expanse [probably the lake shown on early survey maps as Hawkins Lake] two leagues long covered with ducks, swans, and bustards." Nuts, plums, and grapes were plentiful, bison were killed within twenty leagues of the village, and bears, deer, rabbits, and wild

a trunk of stationery, with the field notes of our survey to this part of the river. Round the place of deposit we made a small enclosure of Saplings. The bank where this was done, was about 40 feet higher than the water in the river, and formed a barrier or mound between the river and a lake of considerable extent.[33] A thick growth of Oak, Ash, Hickory and Walnut timber, made a complete cover, and rendered it capable of defence, to a small and active party, should we, as was expected, have had to retreat to it.

On the side opposite to this deposit, the Indians said *the French once had a small military post;* and there also, was one of the principal villages of the Caddos. The Prairie in which they were is very extensive, and now grown up with bushes. The growth of Briars and Bushes was so rank as to prevent us from ascertaining exactly where the French post was, unless some Cedar posts which were found standing denoted the place.[34]

---

turkeys were abundant. Smith, "Account of the Journey of Bénard de La Harpe," entry for April 25, 1719, 253–55. The location of the French fort here seems to have induced many changes in the Caddo world, among them a consolidation of surrounding bands to this location for defensive purposes, and, with Tinhioüen's removal here, a domination of this site by Kadohadachos. (The fate of the Nassonites is unknown; de Mézières speaks of them as living "remotely" from the Kadohadacho as early as 1778, but many must have been consolidated.) In 1773, Gaignard found 90 warriors at this "Great Cado" village, indicating a total population of more than 350. But an attack by the Osages in 1777, the epidemic later that year, and the removal of the French finally led to its abandonment, in 1788, and an exodus to the Medicine Mount village in 1790. Luis de Blanc to Estevan Miró, Natchitoches, March 27, 1790, in Kinnaird, *Spain in the Mississippi Valley* 3:316; De Mézières to Unzaga y Amezaga, Natchitoches, May 2, 1777, and to Croix, Natchitoches, Nov. 15, 1778; Gaignard, "Journal Of An Expedition Up The Red River," entry for October 23, 1773, all in Bolton, *Athanase de Mézières* 2: 130–31, 231–32, 83. See also Sibley, "Historical Sketches," p. 67.

[33] The lake near where the party hid its instruments and reports and threw up this hasty breastworks is clearly portrayed on the official (King) map of the exploration. No lake exists in this vicinity today, but early Republic of Texas survey maps for this area show a body of water called Hempshill Lake near the spot in 1840, and a stream called Hemphill Creek still drains the hills here today. The location for this little stockade, then, would be about 4 miles south of the hamlet of Richmond, in Township 13 S., Range 30 W., Little River County, Ark., according to modern topo maps.

[34] The italicized phrase appears in King's redaction of the Freeman journal

The characteristic Caddoan grass and pole lodges. This Caddo village scene was photographed in the 1860s by William S. Soule. Courtesy National Anthropological Archives, Smithsonian Institution.

On the morning of the 28th, two Indians were sent up the river to reconnitre the positions of the Spaniards. After dark, the firing of several guns was heard further up the river, which led them to suppose themselves in the vicinity of the Spaniards. At 8 o'clock on the morning of the 29th, the two spies were met returning: they said the firing was on a sand beach nearly opposite to where they slept, and as they believed, by a party of Spaniards. They would have continued on and viewed the Spanish Camp, had not one of them lost his bullets in crossing the river. Captain Sparks

---

(per administration instructions?). Freeman's account offers the only concrete evidence we have of the location of La Harpe's Post, since it is the only first-hand description incorporating accurate celestial observation. La Harpe's own readings are worthless, leading Smith into major errors in retracing his travels. La Harpe, a former captain general in the French Coast Guard, had been granted a concession of land in Louisiana during the initial wave of French colonization. Arriving with Bienville and the contingent that founded New Orleans, he was sent up the Red with 40 men to exploit his claim. On April 25, 1719, after examining a likely spot higher upriver, he returned to the Nassonite village and began construction of his post on land "within a musket-shot" of the chief's lodge, and only an eighth of a league from the river. As fort and trading post, La Poste des Cadodoquious marked the upper limit of official French establishments on the Red River, but from it, French traders completely dominated the upper river as well. The post was abandoned in 1778, when the fifteen or so Frenchmen, with their families, collected the mill irons and millstones they had used in wheat cultivation and flour making and retreated to the civilization line. Smith, "Account of the Journey of Bénard de La Harpe," pp. 75–77, entry for April 25, 1719, pp. 253–55; Sibley, "Historical Sketches," pp. 40, 54, 64. Sibley had found a version of the La Harpe chronicle in a trunk in a Natchitoches home in 1805.

During the early 1970s, using Freeman's account and celestial readings as their key documents, a team of Dallas archaeologists led by R. King Harris excavated a site just east of Roseborough Lake that is evidently within the La Harpe's Post–Nassonite village location. The evidence presented in their paper makes a convincing case. Historic focus pottery and numerous artifacts of European trade were unearthed, including axes, iron tomahawks, bottle fragments, mirrors, buttons, knives, scissors, trade beads, and an assortment of dateable gun parts. At least one researcher, M. L. Britton, argues for a location in the hills to the south, but the documentary testimony seems to confirm the archaeological evidence in placing both village and French post in Hickman's Prairie. Unless further archaeological work indicates otherwise, the Roseborough Lake Site will probably stand as the location of this important fort and village of a bygone time. See, M. P. Miroir, R. King Harris, et al., "Bénard de La Harpe And The Nassonite Post," *Bulletin of the Texas Archeological Society*, 44 (1973): 113–67; Britton, "The Location of Le Poste des Cadodaquious."

and myself with one of the Indians, walked on the beach before the boats. The former shot a deer, and turned out to secure it, while [we] two latter crossed the river to the opposite sand beach. The Indian was very watchful, he discovered some track, ran up the banks, and immediately returned, beckoning me to go back. He made signs that the Spaniards were there. We recrossed the river, were joined by captain Sparks, and caused the boats to halt, until the arms were taken out, examined, and laid ready for use at a moment's notice. We all embarked and pushed on. This was a Spanish Piquet guard, consisting of 22 men, about a mile and a half in advance of the main body. When they perceived the Americans approaching, they fled into the woods and hid themselves, leaving part of their cloathing and provision behind.

On passing the next projecting point, a fine reach of upwards of a mile in length appeared; where the river was confined between banks 200 yards apart, and nearly 30 feet high, in which the shallow stream, occupying not more than one third of the space, pursued a serpentine direction between level sand beaches. Heavy Timber and thick Cane brake was on the margin on both sides.

A sentinel and horse was discovered about a mile before us on the beach, and the Bluff on which the Spaniards were encamped was in view.[35] The party continued to advance, until the usual time of dining, when the boats stopped, and the men were directed to make their fires, and prepare for dinner as soon as possible. The Spanish guard was distinctly seen from hence, about half

[35] The bluff that marks the westernmost penetration into the Southwest by Jefferson's Red River expedition is situated on the south bank of the Red, in present Bowie County, Texas. It has come down in local folklore as "Spanish Bluff," and is located a short distance from the present Oklahoma state line, a few miles north of New Boston, Texas. Today, Texas Highway 8 crosses the Red a bit more than a mile northwest of the bluff. U.S.G.S. Daniels Chapel (Texas) Quadrangle shows it at 94° 23' 30" W. longitude.

In the eighteenth and nineteenth centuries, this bank was a well-known landmark on the river; on or very near it, the Nanatsohos and Upper Natchitoches had a village in pre-European days. It is a handsome and imposing bluff that rises nearly 100 feet above the river and commands it for a mile in either direction. It was a sound choice militarily, and selection of it shows a shrewd diplomatic calculation by Viana. Had his force moved to stop the Americans farther downriver, a case might be made that Spanish troops had used force to repel

View from Spanish Bluff of the beach where the fate

of Jefferson's Red River exploration was decided.

Taovaya village on the North Fork of the Red River. Painted by George Catlin. Courtesy Gilcrease Institute of American History and Art.

a mile further up. A party of horse was observed to gallop up to the next bend of the river, through the Cotton Wood bushes, and return with the same speed to the sentinel. They were observed at short intervals passing from the Sentinel to the Camp.

About half an hour after the party landed, a large detachment of Horse, with four officers in front, advanced in a full gallop from the Spanish Camp along the beach towards us. As soon as they reached the water, and were about crossing to the side on which

an American scientific party on United States soil. But the bluff selected was some distance beyond the former locations of both the historic Caddo villages and the most westerly recognized French outpost on the river, and since the Americans had been ceded a Louisiana based upon French boundaries, these could now be considered the uppermost limits of American influence.

the Americans were,[36] the men were ordered to ascend the bank and range themselves along it in the cane brake and bushes, and be ready to fire at the same time with the sentinels below, and to keep up their fire in the most effectual manner possible.

The men being thus concealed from sight, with rests for their pieces, in a position inaccessible to horse, could, with perfect safety to themselves, have given the enemy a severe reception. A non-commissioned officer and six privates were pushed along the bank so far as to be in the rear of the Spaniards, when their attack should be made. The Spanish Column passed on at full speed through the water, and came on towards the party. The Sentinels, placed about 100 yards in advance of the barges, hailed them according to orders, and bid them halt. They continued to advance with the apparent determination to charge. The sentinels a second time bid them halt, cocked their pieces, and were in the act of presenting to fire, when the Spanish Squadron halted, and displayed on the beach, at about 150 yards from the sentinels.[37] The officers slowly advanced, and were met about 50 yards in front of the centinels by Capt. Sparks, who was soon joined by myself, when a parley of nearly three-quarters of an hour long ensued, in the presence of both parties.

The Spanish Party consisted of 150 horse on the beach, 37 foot on the opposite side of the river, and the 22 foot about half a mile below, who had deserted their post on the approach of the ascending party.

The American party in view were the four sentinels, a serjeant Capt. Sparks, Lieut. Humphry, Dr Custis, myself, and a black

---

[36] The north side.

[37] Captain Richard Sparks ("Espargues" the Spanish letters call him) is responsible for the defensive measures employed in the confrontation with the Spaniards, and it ought to be recalled that Dunbar had called him one of the best "bush fighters" in the American army and that Jefferson had personally recommended his appointment. In its article titled "Storm To The West," the *Richmond Enquirer* (October 10, 1806) would find solace in Sparks's testimony that "The Spanish commander appears to have perceived our advantage, and the awkward situation in which he had placed himself and brought his troops to a halt immediately." Many readers may have been unable to find consolation in that, but the fact remains that Sparks's actions perhaps did prevent a military exchange and an inevitable triggering of the war. For his performance, Sparks would be promoted

servant, eleven in number;[38] the remainder of the people, 32, were completely secure on the bank, had rests for their pieces, and aim taken, ready to make an effectual fire if it should be necessary.

The Spanish officers seemed to respect and fear, the decision and arrangement made for their reception. And during the conference, watched with anxiety the bank where the men were posted. Their principal cause of alarm however seemed to arise from some cotton bushes, stuck on the beach near the boats, which they supposed to be a musket Battery, as they believed the party had Artillery with them.

The Spanish officers were Capt. Don Francisco Viana, Adjutant and Inspector of the Troops, &c. &c. Don De Ortoland, a Capt. or Lieut.; Juan Ignatio Ramon de Burga, Lieut.; and another officer of the same grade.[39]

In this conference the Spanish Commanding officer stated that his orders were not to suffer any body of armed troops to march through the territory of the Spanish Government; to stop the exploring party by force, and to fire on them if they persisted in ascending the river, before the limits of the territory were defined.

I stated that the object of my expedition was, to explore the river to its source, under the instructions of the President of the U. S. and I requested the Spanish commander to state in writing his objections to the progress of the party, and the au-

---

a full rank, to major, the promotion being drawn up to date from July 29, 1806. Dearborn to Sparks, Washington, October 13, 1806, War Department, Letters Sent, Main Series.

[38] Freeman mentions only ten. The eleventh is the interpreter, Ensign John DuForest. DuForest is well known to the Spaniards, having participated in Captain Turner's attack on Los Adaes earlier in the year. Following the return of the exploring party he will act as an envoy in the diplomatic exchange between Herrera and Claiborne. *Louisiana Gazette*, February 28, 1806; *American State Papers, Foreign Relations* 2:803.

[39] "Don de Ortoland" is Captain Bernard d'Ortolan, a Frenchman, the brother-in-law of François Grappe, who had moved to Nacogdoches about ten years before. D'Ortolan seems to have been in charge of the advance guard that had fled at the approach of the American party. The fourth Spanish officer present is probably Lieutenant Don José Flores, a member of d'Ortolan's staff. See The Bexar Archives, Nacogdoches garrison militia muster, 1805–1806.

George Catlin's landscape of the upper Red River country in 1834. This setting is now inundated by Lake Texoma. Courtesy National Museum of American Art, Smithsonian Institution.

thority upon which it was made. This was refused by the Spaniard, but he pledged his honor for the truth of his assertion, that he was acting under the orders of his government, who would be answerable for his conduct in the affair.

He then asked if the American party would return, and when?

The great superiority of the Spanish force, and the difficulty the party had already experienced in ascending the river, from the shallowness of the water rendering a further progress impracticable, I replied that I should remain in my present position that day, and would return the day following.

On the Captain of the Spanish Troops saying to his interpreter something respecting sending a detachment of foot below the American party; I became apprehensive they wanted to place sentinels round my party and perhaps surround us; I therefore directed Lieut. Duforest to inform him, that none of the Americans should cross the river until the next day; and that if a Spanish guard was placed near us they should be fired upon. The intention was politely disavowed; he [Viana] only wanted permission for an officer and party to pass the centinels and fetch up the Spanish detachment from below, least any accident should happen from their not knowing the result of the conference which had taken place.

This request was acceded to; the party passed the sentinels, and soon returned with the troops that had been posted below.

Fortunately, the party were not stopped before we had made almost the greatest progress the state of the water would admit of; we were then nearly 200 miles from the Panis Nation,[40] where only the necessary supply of pack horses could be obtained for the prosecution of our route, and we had not with us a sufficiency of Indian Goods for their purchase. The practicability of exploring this river completely, was established, and sufficient information collected, to enable a party to execute it in future, more advantageously, than it could have been done at this time, and against any opposition the Spaniards can make.

On the 30th of July, the party began to descend the river, and proceeded to the place where we had deposited part of our baggage and provisions, which were found safe and undisturbed.

---

[40] Overland, 200 miles is a good estimate, but by water it was considerably farther (Custis says 454 miles in his landmark chart, Appendix 2, but that is too far by 20 percent). According to Freeman's own (very precise) estimate, appearing in the newspapers, the expedition ascended the Red 615 miles—about half its actual length. Since leaving the Alabama-Coushatta village they have averaged about 16 miles a day. That rate puts them three weeks away from the Taovaya-Wichita villages. But Freeman quite likely is not merely saving face when he says that the river has nearly become unnavigable for their boats. Before the Red was dammed, the river commonly carried no more than $2^1/2$ feet of water in August in the stretches above the mouth of the Kiamichi, with at least three rock shoals between there and the Taovaya-Wichita villages. Since 1806 seems to have been a dry year, it is quite likely their boats would have become stranded. In the fall of 1910, Corps of Engineers workers under William T. Rosell were unable to navigate this stretch in a bateau drawing but $5^1/2$ inches of water. "Report Of Preliminary Examination Of Red River, Tex. And Okla., From Mouth Of The Washita To Mouth Of The Big Wichita River," *House Doc.* 193, 63rd Cong., 1st sses., 1913. David Stahle and Malcolm Cleaveland, "Texas Drought History Reconstructed and Analyzed from 1698 to 1980," *Journal of Climate* 1 (January 1988): 59–74.

On the 8th of August,[41] we arrived at the Cooshatta Village, where we spent two days in erecting a small house, in which to deposit our provisions and such Baggage as could not be conveniently transported on Pack horses.[42] On the 23rd I reached Natchitoches, and the remainder of the party a few days afterwards.

Custis 3.

With respect to the Country it will be unnecessary to say anything as it it [*sic*] is similar to that of which you have before had accounts.[43] I will however repeat what I mentioned in my last that in point of beauty & fertility & Salubrity there is not its equal in

[41] By this time the Herrera-Bastrop force has arrived at Bayou Pierre, where they will bivouc for more than a month. Viana, who had returned to the Caddo village on August 4, temporarily loses track of them and will await developments, his men weary from forced marches and suffering from want of food. By August 10, he will rendezvous with Herrera, and from Bayou Pierre the Spanish army will survey the ferment and await a counter-move by the mobilizing American forces. They are officially congratulated by Salcedo on August 24. Viana to the Acting Commandant at Nacogdoches, at the Caddo village, August 4, 1806; Salcedo to Cordero, Chihuahua, August 24, 1806, The Bexar Archives.

[42] Unwilling to again detour through the Great Swamp, now at low water, the expedition elects to leave its boats at the village and effect an overland return by way of the "Quechata Path," looping east of the swamp through the pine uplands of present Bossier, Webster, Bienville, and Natchitoches parishes. Darby shows this Indian trail on his *Map of Louisiana* (1812) accompanying his guidebook for emigrants; Glass travels it in 1808, estimating the distance between the village and Natchitoches to be about 120 miles. Glass, "Copy of a Journal of a Voyage from Nackitosh into the interior of Louisiana," entry for July 15, 1808.

Along with the boats, the party leaves twenty-three barrels of flour and four soldiers under command of a Corporal Reid to guard the shelter constructed to protect this equipment. Over the next months Reid would distribute some of the expedition's provisions illegally, apparently in return for favors from the Indians, and rather than waiting to be called to account, would defect across the Neutral Ground to Nacogdoches. Reid was back in Natchitoches in 1807, but another soldier who is supposed to have "deserted" from the exploring expedition, Private Nimrod Fletcher of Virginia, remained in Texas. Sibley reported five years later that Fletcher had become a lieutenant colonel in the revolutionary army of Hidalgo, but had been killed while en route with Hidalgo and other rebel chieftains to secure assistance from the United States. Sibley to Dearborn, Natchitoches, January 10, April 3, April 20, 1807; Sibley to Eustis, Natchitoches, December 31, 1811. All in Garrett, "Doctor John Sibley and The Louisiana-Texas Frontier," 45:295, 378; 49:414–15.

[43] Vegetation maps and the reports of other travelers indicate, however, that

America, nay in the world. — The water of Red River above the Coashatta Village is so strongly impregnated with salt as to render it unfit to drink. When the water is low we find the Sand beaches rendered white with salt.[44]

Freeman 1.

Above the mouth of the upper Little river, Red river is said to preserve nearly the same width for three or four hundred miles. The Valley opens into level, rich, and almost continued prairies, where range immense herds of Buffaloe, upon which the Indians almost entirely subsist, moving their camps, as these animals migrate with the season, from North to South and back again. Mounted on horseback, and armed with the Bow & Arrow, they kill any number they please. The Panis Nation are possessed of fire arms, having smoothbored guns and ammunition, which they reserve for war, but never use them in hunting.[45] They have the character of a peaceable and friendly people.

The extensive prairies which are found in this rich and level

---

during the last three days of the exploration the party did penetrate into the Post Oak Savannah ecoregion, the transition oak and prairie province between the Eastern Forest and the Great Plains. Some of Custis's final natural history entries confirm this (see Part 5). He can probably be excused for his failure to note the change, since fear of Spanish patrols no doubt confined him to the river here, and along it the slow disappearance of pine and the transition to upland oak and bluestem flats is not readily distinguishable in this stretch. Anthony Glass, who two years later would follow an Indian trace across this country about 25 miles south of Spanish Bluff, observed the change, writing in his journal that: "The country all allong here pretty much timbered with Ash Oak Hickory and . . . here and there interspersed with Rich Handsome Prararies containing from 50 to 2 or 300 acres affording beautiful situations." Glass, "Copy of a Journal of a Voyage from Nackitosh into the interior of Louisiana," entry for July 24, 1808. See also, "Vegetational Areas," Texas A&M Experiment Station Leaflet 492, in *1982-1983 Texas Almanac*, p. 100; and Terry Jordan, "Between the Forest and the Prairie," *Agricultural History* 38 (October 1964):205-216.

[44]While affirming that the Red is salty, Custis neither confirms nor denies Jefferson's theory that the river drained a "salt mountain." Actually, the saline character of almost all of the rivers of the Southern Plains comes from the presence of the great Permian salt bed, which underlies a vast portion of the southern Great Plains.

[45]This reflects the cutoff of the traditional firearms trade from Natchitoches, and is one of the reasons why the plains tribes are in this period so anxious to establish trade relations with the Americans.

Carolina parakeets (Conuropsis carolinensis ludovicianus), *once exceedingly numerous on the Red River, are now extinct. Painting by John James Audubon, Courtesy Library of Congress.*

country, appear to be owing to the custom which these nations of hunters have, of burning the grass at certain seasons. It destroys the bushes and underwood, and in some instances the timber, preventing the future growth where once the timber is destroyed. The small spots of wood with which these prairies are interspersed, are found in the poorest spots, and on the margin of the water courses, where the under growth is less luxuriant, or the water stops the progress of the flames. It is observed, that where these prairies are enclosed, or otherwise protected from fire, they soon become covered with bushes and timber trees, a circumstance which proves, that neither the nature of the soil, nor any other natural cause, gives rise to these extensive and rich pastures, with which Western America abounds.[46]

[46] There are several important insights here into the environmental perceptions of early nineteenth-century Americans confronting for the first time the unfamiliar Great Plains region. On the face of it, Freeman evidently intends to anticipate any preconceptions that the Southern Plains are a desert by discrediting the pioneer tactic (and often an ecologically sound one) of judging soil fertility by vegetational growth. In the eastern woodlands, pioneers usually were suspicious of prairies. Historically more important, however, this is the earliest published explanation ventured by an American explorer of the factors that caused the Great Plains. (William Dunbar also endorsed the fire ecology explanation in his unpublished daily journal of the Ouachita trip.) It may be, then, that Jefferson's later-expressed opinion to John Adams that fire hunting was "the most probable cause of the origin and extension of the vast prairies in the western country," originated with the opinions of his Southwestern explorers. Jefferson to Adams, Monticello, May 27, 1813, The Thomas Jefferson Papers, 1st ser.

In assigning to the fire ecology of the Indians the sole responsibility for causing the prairies, Freeman is ignoring (perhaps because he did not explore far enough to see it) the salient climatic fact of increasing aridity westward towards the mountains. At that he is more accurate than Caleb Atwater, whose "On The Prairies and Barrens of the West," *American Journal of Science and Arts* 1 (1818): 116–25, heretofore considered the earliest plains-causation theory ventured by an American, argued that the plains were remnant lake beds. The controversy over the role of fire in creating and maintaining the grasslands, particularly in the fluctuating prairie border where woods and tall grasses shaded into one another, continues to attract debate. Carl Sauer credits fire as the principal influent and plays down climate in his "Grassland Climax," *Agricultural Origins and Dispersals*, pp. 15–18, while Waldo Wedel argues that Indian fires did not extend the prairies in "The Central North American Grassland: Man–made or Natural?" in *Studies in Human Ecology*, pp. 36–69. Stephen Pyne, in chapters 2 and 3 of *Fire In America*, discusses the theories and the considerable body of evidence that without regular burning, former grasslands often have given way to a climax vegetation of brush — exactly the pattern Freeman cites in his account.

PART FIVE

--*{ *The Natural History Catalogues* }*--

EDITOR'S NOTE: The section of the Account that follows consists of Peter Custis's official catalogues of natural history observations made during the exploration. Transcribed from the manuscript originals in the files of the National Archives, the catalogues published here were submitted by Custis to the War Department in three sections in June, July, and October, 1806. Slightly more extensive than the error-filled version redacted by King and published in 1807, the catalogues are here presented just as Custis prepared them, in the form of three separate reports. Thus it is now possible to determine approximately where on the river Custis first observed Carolina parakeets, black bears, and so forth.

Geographically, the examination was largely confined to the immediate valley of the river, with occasional forays into the adjacent swamps, lakes, bayous, and hill country of the present states of Louisiana, Arkansas, and Texas, and nearly to the southeastern corner of Oklahoma. The period of observation, May 2 to September 1, was favorable for botanical study, and it is in this field that Custis does his most extensive work. However, Jefferson clearly intended him to do a general survey, and some of Custis's most important work on the expedition is in the various fields of zoology. Even mineral specimens were collected.

Although heretofore Custis has been virtually an unknown, interest in him is now mounting.[1] As a young doctoral student studying under

---

[1] In 1967, Conrad Morton, whose attention had been drawn to Custis by John R. Swanton of the Bureau of Ethnology, wrote a study analyzing the published botanical sections of Custis's catalogues, entitled, "Freeman And Custis' Account Of The Red River Expedition Of 1806, An Overlooked Publica-

the leading American academic in natural history at the time, Custis was not only the first professionally-trained naturalist to work from the Mississippi River westward, he was also the first scientist with American training to accompany a government exploration into the West. Awareness of his Red River examination thus puts into clearer context the subsequent work done in the American Southwest by Thomas Nuttall, Jean Louis Berlandier, and Edwin James and Thomas Say of the Long expedition. Further, it serves to push back, in several fields by a decade or more, the beginnings of scientific examination of interior western America. Susan McKelvey's statements in her massive opus, *Botanical Exploration of the Trans-Mississippi West, 1790–1850*, that: "Lewis and Clark and [Georg Heinrich] von Langsdorff were the only men to collect plants in the trans-Mississippi west during this decade [1800–1810]" and that "John Bradbury [in 1809] must therefore have been the first trained botanist to work from the Mississippi River westward,"[2] must be revised. Similarly, Custis's record of sighting peregrine falcons on the border of today's Bowie County, Texas, on July 24, 1806, clearly negates the claim of Harry Oberholser in the definitive, two-volume *The Bird Life of Texas* that scientific ornithology in that state dates from observations made when the Long expedition crossed the Panhandle in 1820.[3]

tion Of Botanical Interest," in the *Journal of the Arnold Arboretum* 47 (1967): 431–59. More recently, Donald Jackson—apparently unaware of Morton's earlier effort—has offered a brief, tentative analysis of Custis's work in exploration natural history, arrived at in consultation with Paul R. Cutright, their source the misleading published version. See Jackson, *Thomas Jefferson & the Stony Mountains*, pp. 233–38. Interest in Custis has finally led to the appearance of a biographical sketch of him; see Dan Flores, "Peter Custis," in Keir B. Sterling, ed., *Biographical Dictionary of North American Environmentalists.*

[2] Susan D. McKelvey, *Botanical Exploration of the Trans-Mississippi West, 1790–1850*, pp. 64, 164. McKelvey also errs (page 246) when she writes that Edwin James of the Long expedition was "the first botanist to penetrate any distance south of the Arkansas River." Samuel Geiser concurs in *Naturalists of the Frontier*, pp. 11–21, when he writes (p. 17) that: "Scientific exploration in Texas seems actually to have begun with the work of Dr. Edwin James . . . in 1820." Geiser later offered credit to Nuttall for this distinction with his "Thomas Nuttall's Botanical Collecting Trip to the Red River, 1819," *Field and Laboratory* 24 (1956): 43–60. Berlandier collected with the Mexican Boundary Commission in 1828 (see Geiser, *Naturalists of the Frontier*) while Nuttall made excursions in several directions through present Arkansas and Oklahoma from 1818 to 1820. See, on the latter, Thomas Nuttall, *A Journal of Travels into the Arkansas Territory During the Year 1819*, Savoie Lottinville, ed.; Thomas Nuttall, "Collections towards a flora of the territory of Arkansas," *Transactions of the American Philosophical Society* 5, new series (1835–36).

[3] Harry C. Oberholser, *The Bird Life of Texas*, Edgar B. Kincaid, ed., 1:3.

Although Custis managed, in fewer than four months, to observe and catalogue 22 mammals, 36 birds, 17 reptiles, fishes, and amphibians, 4 insects, 58 trees, and more than 130 vegetable species, his lists appear today to be somewhat cursory. Very disappointing, for example, was his inability to do much botanizing in the wilderness upriver from the Alabama-Coushatta village. In two and a half weeks of exploration in this area, he added only eleven additional plant species to his lists. Fear of Spanish patrols no doubt restricted his movements, but a consistently pressing problem seems to have been Dunbar's insistence that he participate in the surveying, so that a perfectly accurate map could be made.[4] Since he was also responsible for ethnological observations and the compilation of a meteorological chart necessitating several entries a day, Custis clearly had little time left for tramping and botanizing. His own testimony confirms this. "Owing to Mr. Freemans great anxiety to proceed . . . as quickly as possible," he told Dearborn in his first communication, "I am able to give you only a rapid and imperfect sketch." At the same time he informed Barton: "I have very little respite from business." Finally, he summed up his anxieties about his exploration duties this way: "I have to lament that a more complete opportunity had not occurred, that I might have been enabled the better to perform the duties allotted me, but it is a thing well known that a person subject to the movements of another has little, or, I might add, no time to make botanical excursions."[5]

Custis did assemble a botanical collection of twenty-six plants during the layover at the Alabama-Coushatta village, harvesting them from the prairies and woodlands of present Caddo and Bossier parishes, Louisiana. This small collection, one of the first ever made in the trans-Mississippi country,[6] became a part of the Barton Herbarium of the American

[4] Dunbar to Jefferson, Natchez, May 6, 1806; Dunbar to Dearborn, Natchez, May 6, 1806, Rowland, *Dunbar Letters*, pp. 195, 341. Dunbar appended a third sextant to the expedition's stores so that "Mr. Custis will be able to take celestial altitudes so as to form a complete set of observers with Mr. Freeman."

[5] Custis to Dearborn, Natchitoches, June 1, 1806; Custis to Dearborn, Natchez, October 1, 1806, War Department, Letters Received, Unregistered Series; Custis to Barton, Natchitoches, June 1, 1806, The Benjamin Smith Barton Collection.

[6] Du Pratz, in the 1720s, was probably the first to make a collection of plants from Louisiana when he "put into cane baskets, above three hundred simples, with their numbers, and a memorial, which gave a detail of the virtues. . . ." Most were from the Natchez area, although a few appear to have come from west of the Mississippi. Before Custis's collection, some sixty advance specimens had been sent back from the Missouri by Lewis in 1805. Hunter had also collected plants on the Ouachita trip, although his brief botanical catalogues were not published in the official report of that expedition. His specimens were forwarded by Dunbar to Jefferson, and on to Barton, in

Philosophical Society, now housed at the Academy of Natural Sciences of Philadelphia. Its probable fate is discussed in the Epilogue, but it should be noted here that only two of the specimens from it are still listed as Custis Red River specimens. Probably several were new species, but though the annotation remains (and is included here), lacking the accompanying specimens, very few can now be identified with certainty.

As my annotation, here and earlier, attests, Custis's work suffers in one other respect. Because of his own inexperience and the inadequacy of the texts he used to make difficult literary identifications of the specimens he examined, he missed literally dozens of opportunities to add new species to science. In contrast to that of the European naturalists who collected in America, Custis's training seems not to have prepared him to recognize that virtually every ecoregion produces its own peculiar species and subspecies, and since the Linnaean botanical text upon which he relied did not list geographic ranges, a large number of European, Asian, and African plants appear in his lists.[7] A dozen or more, mostly medicinal herbs, are correctly-identified exotics, already invading the "virgin" Red River valley in 1806. Most, however, are misidentifications of native species. Thus, out of some 267 total species identified, Custis recognized only twenty-two as new (not counting his botanical collection), while proposing only seven new scientific names.

Nevertheless, Custis's zoological catalogues are quite solid, and his botanical lists — even when he misses the exact species — do seem generically precise. Their significance, therefore, is great, for they are one of the earliest scientifically-accurate lists of plants and animals endemic to a major river system of North America. Analyzed and interpreted, they enable us to ascertain to an exciting degree what the environment of

---

the spring of 1805. In 1808, Dunbar sent a second Ouachita River collection to the Reverend Henry Muhlenberg. M. Le Page Du Pratz, *The History of Louisiana, or of the Western Parts of Virginia and Carolina,* p. 45; Cutright, *Lewis and Clark: Pioneering Naturalists,* pp. 357–58; Dunbar to Jefferson, Natchez, March 16, 1805; Dunbar to Muhlenberg, Natchez, May 12, 1808; Muhlenberg to Dunbar, Lancaster, July 5, 1808, Rowland, *Dunbar Letters,* pp. 147–48, 198–204, 363.

[7] Since the principles of evolution and natural selection were unknown, the geographic distribution of species was poorly understood in Custis's day, with Americans evidently somewhat less sensitive to its concepts than Europeans. Custis's mentor, Barton, thus believed that many of the new species whose descriptions Meriwether Lewis was sending back from the West were identical to Old World species. See his "Miscellaneous Facts and Observations," *Philadelphia Medical and Physical Journal* 2 (1806):159–60; and also, Joseph Ewan, "Early History," in Joseph Ewan, ed., *A Short History of Botany in the United States,* pp. 27–48.

the Red River valley was like in the natural setting. Immediately apparent is the fact that the river valley Custis describes bears little relationship to what now obtains. Many of the more dramatic species are now extinct on the Red; some are lost to us entirely. My interpretation of Custis's data re-creates not a vacant wilderness or "virgin" river valley, but instead an organic, evolving environment, one much shaped by its human inhabitants.

The annotation to this section is an attempt to assess Custis's catalogues from both contemporary and modern perspectives. It ought to be noted that a general debt is owed to the research by Conrad Morton of the United States National Herbarium, who worked on the published botanical sections of the catalogues for his article in Harvard's *Journal of the Arnold Arboretum* in 1967. Since my identifications were done independently from his, and in some instances differ, any errors in the following annotation are exclusively my responsibility.

--✠ *The Report of June 1: Mouth of the River to Natchitoches* ✠--

A Catalogue of Vegetables seen on Red River with their time of flowering.—When I do not mention where they are found, it is to be understood that they are confined to no particular situation.—

May 2nd *Amorpha fructicosa* in flower[8]

    3rd *Oxalis acetosella* out of flower[9]
        Aquilicia sambucina in flower[10]

---

[8] A shrubby species of false indigo found from New Mexico across Texas to Indiana, and northwest to Saskatchewan. Harold Rickett, *Wild Flowers of the United States* 3:256. Hereinafter cited as Rickett, with the indication of appropriate volumes.

[9] The common wood-sorrel (*O. montana* Raf.) is the American counterpart of the European species Custis lists here, but it is out of range on the lower Mississippi. Custis was observing a different wood-sorrel than either—probably the yellow wood-sorrel (*O. stricta* [L.]), an abundant and variable species found from Texas across to Georgia, north to Quebec and North Dakota. Ibid., 2:272.

[10] Custis is designating an Asiatic species of the grape family. Morton believes he must have seen instead the species *Ampelopsis arborea* [L.] Koehne, which possesses bipinnate leaves and bushy characteristics. Morton, "An Overlooked Publication Of Botanical Interest," 449.

5th *Atropa physaloides* in flower[11]
　　Clematis cirrbosa — Do.[12]
　　Convolvulus Arvensis — Do.[13]
　　———— *repens* — Do.[14]
　　Ranunculus bulbosa out of flower[15]

[11] Now re-classified *Nicandra physaloides* Gaertn., the plant listed here is a South American indigen called the apple-of-Peru, escaped from the early settlers and growing wild from Louisiana to Florida, north to Nova Scotia and Missouri *Ibid.*, 2:438; B. Daydon Jackson, comp., *Index Kewensis: An Enumeration Of The Genera And Species Of Flowering Plants.* Hereinafter cited as *Index Kewensis.* This entry is the first definite record in Custis's catalogues of the presence of non-native species, introduced into the New World environmental setting by Europeans over the preceding century, in the Red River valley. (Du Pratz mentions such an ecological transfer in this region, already in process in the 1720s, in *History Of Louisiana*, p. 208). During the course of the exploration he will describe fifteen additional ones — most on the outskirts of the settlements of Avoyelles, Rapide, and Natchitoches. This remarkable discovery is the earliest documentation for the widespread ecological transfer of plants from Europe to western North America. Peter Kalm, an associate of Linnaeus who spent nearly four years in North America (1748–51) collecting plants, was the first to comment on this phenomenon on the Atlantic Seaboard when he found many common European plants growing as weeds in New Jersey. See Adolph Benson, ed. and trans., *Peter Kalm's Travels in North America.* Rev. Henry Muhlenberg, in his "Index Florae Lancastriensis," *Transactions of the American Philosophical Society*, 3 (1793), also referenced, with some confusion, exotic plants he found growing wild in Pennsylvania. Rafinesque finally confronted the issue with his "An Essay on the Exotic Plants, Mostly European, which have been naturalized and now grow spontaneously in the Middle States of North America," *The Medical Repository* 8 (1811): 330–45.
[12] Instead this must have been a native leather flower, probably the new species, *C. glaucophylla* Small., found in rich woods along streams from East Texas and Oklahoma to Florida, north to Virginia. Rickett, 2:172.
[13] The field bindweed is undoubtedly correctly identified, and is a European transplant to North America, now found as a troublesome weed in fields and poor lands over much of the continent. Ibid., 2:428.
[14] Now *Calystegia sepium* var. *repens* (L.) Gray, the hedge-bindweed, found on the Gulf and Atlantic coasts, although rarely much distance inland. Donovan Stewart Correll and Marshall Conring Johnston, *Manual of Vascular Plants of Texas*, vol. 6 of *Contributions from Texas Research Foundation*, p. 1247.
[15] The entry refers to another European immigrant, the bulbous buttercup, now naturalized from Louisiana to Georgia, north to Newfoundland and Ontario. It could have been here in 1806, but there are many similar native species of the genus. See Rickett, 2:166.

6th *Rhus Toxicodendron* in flower[16]

Mimosa Punctata in flower.—This plant is first seen a mile above the mouth of the river & from thence to Nachitoches is found in great abundance. In many places it completely covers the banks from the low to high water mark. Like other species of the same genus it moves from the touch.—[17]

7th *Arum triphillum* out of flower[18]

Echinops Sphaerocephilus in flower[19]

Hypericum quadrangulare in flower[20]

—— *kalmianum*—Do.—[21]

Orobus tuberosus—Do.—[22]

[16] Poison oak, now rendered *Toxicodendron quercifolia* (Michx.) Greene, and found in mixed forests and pinelands from Texas to Florida, north to New Jersey. Cyrus Longworth Lundell, comp., *Flora of Texas* 3:106.

[17] This entry is actually of a new species. Custis must have seen here the touch-sensitive powderpuff (*Mimosa strigillosa* Torr. & Gray), an inhabitant of grassy prairies and the banks of streams and rivers from Texas to Georgia, and inland along the rivers to Arkansas. Rickett, 2:318; Correll and Johnston, *Vascular Plants of Texas*, p. 778.

[18] Perhaps this was the arrow arum, or tuckahoe (*Peltandra virginica* [L.] Kunth.), found in swamps and near streams from Texas to Florida, north to Maine and Michigan, but instead it may have been the white arum (*P. sagittaefolia* Raf.), a new species not described by Rafinesque until 1819. It is found in swamps from Mississippi (?) to Georgia, and flowers in July and August, so would have been out of flower, as the entry indicates. Rickett, 2:133–34.

[19] Another European weed brought by the French to Louisiana, and now scattered locally throughout North America. Ibid., 6:708.

[20] Morton indicates that, in this range, the species of *Hypericum* with the most noticeably quadrangular stems is *H. drummondii* (Grev. & Hook) Torr. & Gray, a new type. It is a resident of oak flats from East Texas to Florida, north to Maryland and Kansas. Morton, "An Overlooked Publication Of Botanical Interest," 450; Correll and Johnston, *Vascular Plants of Texas*, p. 1065.

[21] The plant identified is out of range on the lower Red. This was a new plant, although two species in this range are similar in certain appearances to *kalmianum*. Thus, this one must have been either *H. densiflorum* Pursh, or *H. buckleyi* Curtis, both found on pinewood slopes and at the edges of wooded streams and swamps from Texas to Florida and north to New York and Missouri. Rickett, 1:150, 2:208–13; *Index Kewensis*, 1:1192; Correll and Johnston, *Vascular Plants of Texas*, p. 1772.

[22] *Lathyrus tuberosus* [L.], which is out of range here. He may have seen *L. venosus* var. *intonaesus* Butt. & St. John, found in open woods from northeast

9th *Mimosa tenuifolia* beginning to drop its flower[23]
    Hydrocotyle Vulgaris in flower — [24]
    Malva caroliniana in seed. — [25]
    Alcea rosea in flower[26]
    Rudbeckia hirta in flower[27]
    Erythrina herbacea seen at Rapide only and in flower[28]
    Spigelia marylandica in flower[29]
    Indigofera hirsuta in flower[30]
    Symphitum officinale.[31] — *Solanum paniculatum* in flower[32]

Texas to Georgia, and north to eastern Canada. Rickett, 1:258–59; Correll and Johnston, *Vascular Plants of Texas*, p. 877.

[23] In all probability this was a new species, the shame vine (*Schrankia hystricina* Britt. & Rose), a plant in the mimosa family, found in sandy, forested areas only in southern Louisiana and southeastern Texas. Rickett, 3:206; Correll and Johnston, *Vascular Plants of Texas*, p. 778.

[24] Probably *not* the European *vulgaria* in this case, but an American species of pennywort, *H. umbellata* Michx., is much like it and is found in the Red River valley. Rickett, 2:282.

[25] This species of *Malvaceae* is now classified as *Modiola caroliniana* (L.) G. Don, and is found from Texas to Florida and north to Virginia and Georgia. Ibid., 2:200–205; Correll and Johnston, *Vascular Plants of Texas*, p. 1034.

[26] Custis was examining on this day the country back of the French settlements in present Rapide Parish, Louisiana. Thus several European cultivars will appear, including this one, the common hollyhock, now rendered *Althaea rosea* (L.) Cav. Correll and Johnston, p. 1037.

[27] The black-eyed Susan (*Rudbeckia hirta* L.) is what the entry refers to, but I am inclined to believe that Custis actually saw the more southerly species, a new plant now called the brown-eyed Susan (*R. serotina* Nutt.). Officially credited to Nuttall from his collections in the Arkansas Territory more than a decade later, it is found in dry soil from Texas to Alabama and northward to the Northeast. Rickett, 2:577–78; Correll and Johnston, *Vascular Plants of Texas*, p. 1642.

[28] The cardinal spear, or coral bean, found in pinelands from Texas to Florida, and north to North Carolina. Rickett, 2:346.

[29] The Indian pink, or worm grass, endemic to moist woods from Texas to Florida, north to Maryland and Indiana. Ibid., 2:389.

[30] Custis's use of *hirsuta*, misspelled in the published version, causes Morton to believe this was "a wild determination" of the native plant, *Tephrosia virginiana* (L.) Pers., the devil's shoestring, Texas to Florida, to Wisconsin. Morton, "An Overlooked Publication of Botanical Interest," p. 451.

[31] Another European species, a coarse exotic known as the comfrey, which colonizes disturbed grounds and is now found from Louisiana to Georgia and north to Newfoundland and Ontario. Rickett, 2:421.

[32] The plant he identifies is a native of Brazil and belongs to the genus of

Aristolochia serpentaria.[33]

Rosa eglanteria[34]

Rubus fruticosus and *Caesius,* fruit ripe.[35]

11th *Phytolacca decandra* in flower[36]

Sambucus nigra in flower[37]

Oenothera longiflora in flower. This is a solar plant. It folds up its flower as soon as the Sun rises, & expands at Sunset.[38]

Portulaca oleracca in seed. — [39]

Oxalis purpurea in seed[40]

potatoes, tomatoes, and eggplants. This was probably the native horse-nettle (*Solanum carolinense* L.). Correll and Johnston, *Vascular Plants of Texas,* p. 1396.

[33] An inconspicuous little plant, often overlooked even where it is common, this was the Virginia snakeroot, so called because it was used medicinally for treatment of snakebite. It is found from Texas to Florida and north to Connecticut and Kansas. Rickett, 2:139.

[34] A cultivated exotic which he probably identifies correctly, this was the eglantine, or sweet-brier rose, a European rose escaped to the wild in North America and now found from Texas to Georgia, to Nova Scotia and British Columbia. Vines, *Trees, Shrubs and Woody Vines,* pp. 436–37.

[35] These determinations are of European blackberries and dewberries, but he no doubt was seeing instead some native species of *Rubiaceae.* The choices are too numerous to make a positive determination. See Rickett, 1:142, 5:147–48.

[36] Later rendered, *P. americana* (L.), this was the common pokeweed. Poke salad is the name given the young shoots when cooked as greens. The species is found from Texas to Florida and north to Maine and Minnesota. Rickett, 2:148.

[37] The *nigra* species is a plant of the Middle and Far East. What Custis was seeing here was the American elder, *S. canadensis* (L.). It is found across most of eastern North America. George Usher, *A Dictionary of plants used by man,* p. 521; J. C. Willis, *A Dictionary Of The Flowering Plants and Ferns,* rev. by H. K. Airy Shaw, p. 1023.

[38] One of the several evening primroses, probably either the common evening primrose (*O. grandiflora* [Britt.] Smyth.), found from Texas to Alabama and Tennessee, or a new species, *O. heterophylla* Spach., a species of Louisiana and East Texas. See Rickett, 2:306; and Correll and Johnston, *Vascular Plants of Texas,* pp. 1130–31.

[39] The Purslane, or "pussley," another Eurasian plant introduced across environments to North America by European colonists. Rickett, 2:296.

[40] Undoubtedly the violet wood sorrel (*O. violacea* [L.]), found in open woods and prairies from Texas to Florida, north to Massachusetts and Minnesota. Ibid., 2:270.

Passiflora every where in the greatest abundance &
in flower[41]

Verbascum thapsus in flower.[42]

Rhus coppallinum[43] & *Cotinus* in flower[44]

Physalis pubescens in flower. — [45]

Viola palmata out of flower. — [46]

Allium odorium in flower. — [47]

16th *Leontodora taraxacum* in flower. — [48]

Physalis angulata in flower. — [49]

17th *Datura stramonium* in flower. This plant is very abundant at Nachitoches. — [50]

---

[41] Either the maypops, or apricot-vine (*P. incarnata* [L.]), or the yellow passion flower (*P. lutea* [L.]), both found from Texas to Florida, north to Pennsylvania and Kansas. Ibid., 2:268.

[42] Yet another species introduced from the Old World, this was the common
mullein, now found from Arizona to New England. Ibid., 2:495.

[43] *R. copallina* L., the flame-leaf sumac, found from Texas to Georgia, north
to New Hampshire and Michigan. Vines, *Trees, Shrubs and Woody Vines*, p. 633;
Lundell, *Flora of Texas*, 3:95–96.

[44] This was a new species, in fact, the only species of this genus in North
America: *Cotinus obvatus* Raf., the American smoke tree. It is found from Texas
to Tennessee and north to Missouri. Correll and Johnston, *Vascular Plants of
Texas*, p. 988.

[45] The downy groundcherry, found from Texas to Florida, north to Virginia
and Iowa. Rickett, 2:436.

[46] The wood violet is what this entry refers to, but it is slightly out of range
here, extending westwardly (according to contemporary botany) only to Mississippi. This entry more probably refers to *V. triloba* (L.), found from Texas to
Florida, north to Vermont and Missouri. Ibid., 2:368.

[47] Several species of wild garlics are possible in this range; probably this was a
variety of *A. canadense* (L.). This species is found on prairies from Texas to
Florida and north to Maine and South Dakota. See Correll and Johnston, *Vascular Plants of Texas*, pp. 386–91 for possible choices.

[48] Probably *Taraxacum officinale* Weber, the common dandelion, an Old World
weed transplanted to virtually all of North America by Europeans. Rickett,
2:640.

[49] A groundcherry species found from Texas eastward to the Atlantic in bottomlands and on prairies. Ibid., 2:436.

[50] The next eight entries were made at Natchitoches during the expedition's
two-week layover in that village. At least three times during this layover, Custis
made brief natural history forays. This, the first of the eight, refers to the poisonous jimsonweed, a species found from Texas eastward. It was widely used in

Marrubium vulgare[51] & *mentha sativa.* — [52]

19th *Cactus opuntia* very plenty at Nachitoches & in flower[53]
Tillandsia usneoides I found on almost all the trees in
the country, in flower. — [54]

27th *Spigelia Anthelmia* near Nachitoches in flower[55]
Lonicera sempervirens—Do.[56]
Podophyllum peltatum—Do. — [57]

Birds.

Paroquets *(Psittacus carolinensis)* very numerous. They are always

---

Indian religion as an hallucinogen and also as a curative, hence its noticeable abundance in the Natchitoches area in 1806 may indicate a previous promotion of this plant by tribes who once lived here. Ibid., 2:440; and Virgil J. Vogel, *American Indian Medicine* pp. 326–28, provide information on *Datura.*

[51] The horehound (*Marrubium vulgare* [L.], a European immigrant widely-cultivated as *materia medica* for the treatment of colds and sore throats and now found throughout the United States. Rickett, 2:490.

[52] *M. sativa* is a synonym for *M. aquatica* L., found along streams and wet swamps throughout the Eastern United States. *Index Kewensis* 2:207; Rickett, 2:476.

[53] Almost certainly this prickley pear species was new. Probably he saw either *Opuntia allairei* Griff. or *O. nemoralis* Griff. Both are found locally in western Louisiana and East Texas. Vines, *Trees, Shrubs and Woody Vines*, pp. 779–80.

[54] Spanish moss, not a true moss, of course, but a relative of the pineapple, of the family Bromeliaceae. It is an epiphyte which does appear throughout the forest in the latitude of Natchitoches, but upriver its appearance will gradually be confined to watercourses. Rickett, 2:86. Custis offers an interesting note on its northern range on the Red in the Report, October 1.

[55] Custis refers to a species of worm grass confined to Florida and out of range here. He probably saw specimens of *Spigelia marylandica* (L.), perhaps a local variant. See note 167.

[56] *Lonicera sempervirens* (which King transcribes as "Sonicera Sempervivum" in the published account) is the trumpet honeysuckle, found from Texas to Florida, and north to Maine and Nebraska. Vines, *Trees, Shrubs and Woody Vines*, p. 956.

[57] The May-apple, or American mandrake, found in open woods and meadows from Texas to Florida, north to Quebec and Minnesota. Rickett, 2:220. The May-apple is an herb once widely-used as a cathartic in folk medicine. According to Professor Stannard, it is one of only two native American plants still listed in recent editions of the U. S. *Pharmacopoeia.* Jerry Stannard, "Medical Botany," in Ewan, *A Short History of Botany in the United States*, p. 149.

seen in large flocks. — [58]

Herons *(Ardea Ludoviciana*[59] & *Alba)*[60]

Swallow-tailed Falcon *(Falco furcatus)*[61]

Goatsuckers *(Caprimulgus virginianus*[62] & *Carolinensis)*[63]

White-billed Woodpecker *(Picus principalis)*[64]

[58] The western Carolina parakeet (now *Conuropsis carolinensis ludovicianus* Gmelin), and now extinct. The lower Red, particularly the rim swamps of bald cypress along its floodplain, was in its natural state the center of a very heavy Carolina parakeet population. As late as the 1880s flocks were still frequenting the Red in northeast Texas. The large, bright green and yellow parrots were so gregarious and bold that slaughtering them as agricultural pests and for the millinery trade was easy. The last bird in captivity died in the Cincinnati Zoological Garden in 1914. A wild flock of the Eastern subspecies may have survived in the Santee Swamp of South Carolina into the 1930s, but the possibility of saving the species was lost when that swampland disappeared beneath the Santee-Cooper hydroelectric project. Oberholser, *The Bird Life of Texas* 1:430-33; George H. Lowery, *Louisiana Birds*, pp. 364-65; Doreen Buscemi, "The Last American Parakeet," *Natural History* 87 (April 1978): 10-12.

[59] The Louisiana heron (now *Hydranassa tricolor* Muller.) a coastal nester which wanders widely over Louisiana after June. Lowery, *Louisiana Birds*, pp. 148-49.

[60] Probably the great white heron (now *Ardea occidentalis* Audubon), since Barton so uses the name in his works. This might be the American egret (*Casmerodius albus egretta* Gmelin), however, since Custis does seem to have used Bartram's *Travels*, and Bartram uses *Ardea alba* to designate the egret. Benjamin Smith Barton, *Fragments of the Natural History of Pennsylvania*, reprinted in Keir B. Sterling, ed., *Selected Works by Eighteenth-Century Naturalists and Travellers*, p. 5; Francis Harper, ed., *The Travels of William Bartram*, p. 442.

[61] Custis must have seen specimens of the swallow-tailed kite (*Elanoides forficatus* [L.]). This beautiful bird is actually a hawk, with many external characteristics of the falcons. Perfectly suited to the Red River prairies, where it hunted frogs, snakes, and dragonflies, and nested in the towering virgin bald cypress, it has become rare on the river since the virgin timber has been cut and much of the prairie converted to agriculture. Oberholser, *Bird Life of Texas*, 1:208-209; Lowery, *Louisiana Birds*, pp. 219-21.

[62] This is evidently the Florida common nighthawk (*Chordeiles minor chapmani* Coues), a new subspecies in 1806. However, it could have been the eastern whip-poor-will (*Setochalcis vocifera vocifera* Wilson), a transient in this range during the spring and, like many species of common eastern birds, not yet scientifically described. Unlike the nighthawk, it is a true goatsucker. Oberholser, *Bird Life of Texas*, 1:462-65; Lowery, *Louisiana Birds*, pp. 386-91.

[63] The chuck-will's-widow, the common breeding goatsucker of the wooded uplands adjacent to the Lower Red. Oberholser, *Bird Life of Texas*, 1:462-65; Lowery, *Louisiana Birds*, pp. 386-91.

[64] The ivory-billed woodpecker (now *Campephilus principalis* [L.]) was the largest of all woodpeckers native to the United States, at a total length of 21 inches. It evolved as a specialized species of the virgin forests, and was always associated

Pileated W.[oodpecker] *(Picus pileatus)*[65]
Red-headed W. *(—— Erythrocephalus)*[66]
Carrion Vulture *(Vultur Aura)*[67]
Carrion Crow *(Corvus corone)*[68]
Mexican Crow *(Corvus mexicanus)*[69]
Blue Jay *(Corvus cristatus)*[70]
Mocking-bird *(Turdus polyglottus)*[71]
Virginian Quails *(Tetrao virginianus)*[72]

with oft-flooded wooded bottomlands near rivers. When lumbermen and other developers destroyed the grub-infested virgin timber this bird depended upon it ceased to be a viable wild species, and was declared extinct in 1932. Although it is sometimes called "endangered" today, a series of much-publicized ivory-bill searches in Louisiana and Texas in the 1960s provided no solid evidence that the bird was not already extinct. Oberholser, *Bird Life of Texas*, 1:527–29; Lowery, *Louisiana Birds*, pp. 415–19.

[65] Either the pileated woodpecker (*Hylatomas pileatus* [L.]) or the single subspecies, the southern pileated woodpecker (*H. p. pileatus* [L.]). A crow-sized woodpecker sometimes confused with the ivory-bill, pileated woodpeckers are denizens of rivers, streams, and bayous lined with cypress and cottonwood stands. Oberholser, *Bird Life of Texas*, 1:509–11.

[66] In this range, the subspecies, eastern redheaded woodpecker (*Melanerpes erythrocephalus erythrocephalus* [L.]). Ibid., pp. 514–15.

[67] Either the subspecies, the western turkey vulture (*Cathartes aura teter* Friedmann) or the black vulture (*Coragypes atratus* Bechstein). Probably both. The subspecies of the turkey vulture would have been new. Oberholser, *Bird Life of Texas*, 1:201–203; Lowery, *Louisiana Birds*, pp. 213–16.

[68] Probably the southern subspecies (*Corvus brachyrhynchos paulus* Brehm) of the common crow. Oberholser, *Bird Life of Texas*, 2:596–97; Lowery, *Louisiana Birds*, pp. 450–53.

[69] Most likely the fish crow *(Corvus ossifragus)*, a new species later credited to Alexander Wilson. It is slightly smaller than the common crow, and is the only other species to inhabit the Lower Red River. Lowery refers to it as being primarily a Gulf crow that "is present at least as far north as Shreveport on the Red River. . . ." Its range is the Atlantic seaboard and its larger river systems, from Texas to Rhode Island. Lowery, *Louisiana Birds*, p. 54; Oberholser, *Bird Life of Texas*, 2:597–98.

[70] The southern blue jay (*Cyanocitta cristata cristata* [L.]) here. Oberholser, *Bird Life of Texas*, 2:585; Lowery, *Louisiana Birds*, pp. 449–50.

[71] In this range, the eastern mockingbird (*Mimus polyglottos polyglottos* [L.]). Oberholser, *Bird Life of Texas*, 2:646; Lowery, *Louisiana Birds*, pp. 466–69.

[72] In this range, the subspecies known as the interior bobwhite (*Colinus virginianus mexicanus* [L.]. Oberholser, *Bird Life of Texas*, 1:270–71; Lowery, *Louisiana Birds*, pp. 249–51.

Custis saw all three species of these woodpeckers, here drawn by Alexander Wilson, on the lower Red. The ivory-bill (Campephilus principalis) *is now extinct. Courtesy Library of Congress.*

Wild Turkeys. — *(Malaegris Gallipavo)*[73]
Loxia cardinalis. — [74]

The fish of Red River are the following

Catfish *(Silurus catus)* very abundant and of a very large size. —
   The largest I have seen was one caught at Nachitoches. It mea-
   sured 3¼ ft. in length & Seven inches between the eyes. — [75]
Garfish *(Esox osseus)* very abundant. — [76]
Alligator fish very plenty. — [77]
Herring *(Clupea thrissa).* — I have not seen these above the Rapide. — [78]
Perch *(Perca ocullata).* — [79]

[73] All of the wild turkeys seen during the exploration would have been eastern wild turkeys, correctly, *Meleagris gallopavo* Vieillot. Oberholser, 1:282–85;
Lowery, pp. 253–55.

[74] Loxia is the genus name of the crossbills. Custis must have observed specimens of a new subspecies, the Louisiana cardinal (now *Richmondena cardinalis
magnirostris* Bangs). See Oberholser, 2:853–54. Barton calls "Loxia cardinales"
the "Cardinal Grosbeak" in his *Fragments of the Natural History of Pennsylvania,* p. 12. Either this, or Jefferson's *Notes on the State of Virginia,* William
Pedin, ed., p. 68, must have been Custis's source for this binomial.

[75] The Red River is home to a large number of catfish. Among those Custis
could be describing here are the great forked-tail, or blue, cat (*Ictalurus furcatus*
Cuvier & Valen.); the channel cat (*I. punctatus* Raf.); the white cat (*Villarius
catus* [L.]); and the mud, or Opelousas, cat (*Opladelus olivaris* Raf.). Most of these
genera and species would not be recognized until more than a decade later.
Henry Sherring Pratt, *A Manual of Land and Fresh Water Vertebrate Animals
of the United States,* pp. 85–89.

[76] If a true garfish, either the eastern long-nosed gar (*Lepisosteus osseus osseus*
[L.]) or the eastern short-nosed gar (*Cylindrosteus platostomus platyrhincus* De Kay).
More likely it was the common eastern pickerel, or jackfish (*Esox reticulatus* Le
Sueur), found from Louisiana to Florida and north to Maine. Ibid., pp. 98–99.

[77] This would have been the alligator gar (*Atractosteus tristaechus* Block &
Schneid.), found from the southern states north to Ohio and Illinois. Ibid., pp.
32, 102; David Starr Jordan and Barton W. Evermann, *American Food and Game
Fishes,* p. 235. In his June 1 letter to Barton (The Benjamin Smith Barton Collection), Custis mentioned that the alligator fish had "been seen, in this river,
15 feet long."

[78] Undoubtedly the freshwater herring known as the blue herring (*Pomolobus
chrysochloris* Raf.), and a new genus, rather than the common herring of Linnaeus.
The range of the blue herring is the larger streams of the Mississippi River
system. Jordan and Evermann, *American Food and Game Fishes,* p. 101.

[79] Much re-classification of fishes was about to be done in the first decades of

"Syren quadrupeda Custis" *was actually a member of a new family. His animal is now the three-toed amphiuma* (Amphiuma tridactylum). *Photograph by Tom R. Johnson.*

Amphibia.

Alligator *(Lacerta alligator)* in the greatest abundance. There are some of a very large size, but the largest which I have had the opportunity of measuring was only 12 ft. in length. — [80]

---

the nineteenth century by Cuvier, Rafinesque, and others. Rather than a member of the genus *Perca* of Linnaeus, probably what Custis encountered was the largemouth bass (*Micropterus salmoides* Lacépède), common in sluggish waters from Mexico to Canada. Ibid., pp. 357, 364–65.

[80] Now *Alligator mississippiensis* Cuvier. Range: South Texas to Florida and north on the coastal plain to Cape Hatteras, N.C. The alligator has been known to reach 19 feet in length, but 12 feet is a large adult. Actually, the alligator was not recognized as a species different from the Old World crocodile until Cuvier, noting the difference in head shape, did so in 1807. Cuvier, however, did not believe the Red River lay within the alligator's original range. Custis's entry here obviously modifies that early assumption, for he found them abundant as high as Spanish Bluff. Doris M. Cochran and Coleman J. Goin, *The New Field Book of Reptiles and Amphibians*, p. 125; Hanley, *Natural History in America*, pp. 222–23.

Cameleon (*Lacerta cameleon*) very plenty.—[81]

Twenty one miles below Nachitoches I saw an animal which had
been caught in a pond near the River, that resembled in every
respect, except the number of its legs, thc *Syren lacertina* of
Linn.—The Lacertina has two legs, it has four, the two hind-
most of which are about 6 inches from the end of its tail. It measured 3 feet in length & 6 inches in circumference. I have called
it *Syren quadrupeda.*—Had it not been in a very advanced state
of putrifaction I should have preserved & sent it on.—[82]

[81] There is only one species of chameleon in the United States, the *Anolis carolinensis* Voigt, which ranges throughout the coastal regions of the southern states
from North Carolina into Mexico. Henry Sherring Pratt, *A Manual of Land and
Fresh Water Vertebrate Animals of the United States*, p. 183.

[82] Custis was not hallucinating. He probably had examined a living *Siren lacertina* during visits with Barton's classes to Charles Willson Peale's museum in
1805. The creature he had found almost exactly matched the descriptions of *Siren
lacertina* (L.), the largest of the "mud eels," except for the number of legs (Custis's
animal also lacked the external gills of the *Siren*, which ought to have alerted him
that the two were not closely related). A similar description to this one, including
his suggestion for a new "species" name, was forwarded to Barton, no doubt astonishing Custis's mentor, for Barton had disagreed with naturalists who believed that
Siren lacertina was a "mere larva." Custis's creature gave him pause, and when he
published Custis's letter that fall of 1806 he omitted all mention of this new discovery. But following Custis's return and their discussion of it, Barton finally mentioned the animal in an address before the Philadelphia Linnaean Society,
remarking that: "My pupil Dr. Peter Custis, of Virginia, has observed near the
Red-River, a new and singular species of Proteus, which resembles the Protinus
anguinus, and some other European species in being furnished with *four* legs." B.
S. Barton, "A Discourse on Some of the Principal Desiderata in Natural History,
and on the Best Means of Promoting the Study of this Science in the United
States," in Keir B. Sterling, *Contributions to the History of American Natural
History*, p. 23. Both this creature and the Mississippi kite he would collect later
were major discoveries. That Custis never seems to have pressed on with published
descriptions and proffered names for either following the exploration argues for
something beyond mere neglect. It makes me think that the Jefferson administration's shoddy handling of his work left him disillusioned.

Custis had actually discovered not merely a new species but an entirely new
family, designated by Garden in 1821 as Amphiumidae. Six years later Baron
Georges Cuvier, examining a specimen collected near New Orleans, named Custis's specific animal *Amphiuma tridactylum*, the three-toed amphiuma, a bi-
colored eel-like amphibian reaching 40 inches in length and found from East
Texas to Alabama and north to Tennessee and Missouri. See Richard G. Zweifel,

There is a species of tortoise very abundant in this River called the soft shell tortoise which is esteemed by connoisseurs as a very great delicacy. I have not seen it. Probably it is the *Testudo cartilaginea* of Linn. [Later Custis appended:] I have since seen the soft shell Tortoise. It is the *Testudo Ferox.* — The one which I saw measured eighteen inches in length and fifteen in breadth. — [83]

The Scorpion *(Scorpio Hottentotta)* is found here. — [84]

Quadrupeds. Of these I have seen very few.

I have seen three species of Squirrel, *Sciurus cinerius*[85] & *niger*;[86] the other is not described by Linnaeus. — Its body is of a dark

---

ed., *Catalogue of American Amphibians and Reptiles,* pp. 147.1-152.1; Sherman Bishop, *Handbook of Salamanders,* pp. 49-57; Francis W. Pennell, "Benjamin Smith Barton As Naturalist," *Proceedings of the American Philosophical Society* 86 (1943):113.

The emergence now of Custis's published description and name ought to win him at least partial credit for the three-toed amphiuma, within the context of the species' subsequent reclassification. Thus it is proposed that the name be changed to *Amphiuma quadrupeda* (Custis), citing the publication [King], *An Account of the Red River, in Louisiana* (1807), pp. 62-63.

[83] In this range, the only softshell to reach such a size was a new species, the Texas softshell (*Trionyx spiniferus emoryi* Agassiz), a southwestern turtle whose main range begins in western Louisiana and extends into New Mexico. It is primarily a riverine turtle. Smaller softshells, including the Mississippi smooth softshell (*T. muticus muticus* LeSueur) are also found on the Red. Cochran and Goin, *Reptiles and Amphibians,* pp. 164-66.

[84] Custis would have seen a member of the scorpion family *Vejovidae,* which includes all of the North American scorpions. The principal genus in the Red River country is *Vejovis.* Cecil Warburton, "Arachnida Embolobranchiata (Scorpions, Spiders, Mites, etc.)," in S. F. Harmer and A. E. Shipley, eds., *The Cambridge Natural History* 5:308.

[85] Rather than *S. cinereus,* Custis must have seen a new subspecies of fox squirrel not separately classified until 1942. This was *S. niger bachmani* Lowery and Davis, the fox squirrel of Mississippi, Alabama, and the Florida parishes of Louisiana. Custis would have been at the western edge of its range on the Red. E. Raymond Hall and Keith R. Kelson, *The Mammals of North America* 1:387-88; George H. Lowery, *The Mammals of Louisiana and Its Adjacent Waters,* p. 187.

[86] This was not the type fox squirrel of Linnaeus, but instead must have been the subspecies, *S. n. subauratus* Bachman, a subspecies whose range is restricted to the lower 400 miles of the Mississippi valley. It was new in 1806, not classified until 1839. Hall and Kelson, *The Mammals of North America* 1:387-88; Lowery, *The Mammals of Louisiana,* p. 187.

Sciurus niger ludovicianus *Custis, the Louisiana fox squirrel, is the only animal from the exploration now credited to Custis.*

grey; belly, inside of the legs & thighs reddish brown; ears not bearded; tail longer than the body & very broad, above the colour of the body, below the colour of the belly; about the size of the Cat squirrel. [Appended to the end of this description, in Custis' hand, is the following:] I have called it *Sciurus Ludovicianus.* — [87]

Ursus lotor or Racoon. — [88]

[87] Custis concludes his treatment of the trio of native Louisiana fox squirrels— a division not made by other naturalists until the middle of the twentieth century—with an accurate description of the distinctive fox squirrel of East Texas, North Louisiana, and southwestern Arkansas. *Sciurus niger ludovicianus* Custis is at this writing the only animal discovered on the Red River exploration credited to Custis by naturalists. Significantly, it is not the published exploring account to which naturalists trace the published description, but instead to Custis's article, "Observations relative to the Geography, Natural History, & etc., of the Country along the Red-River in Louisiana," *Philadelphia Medical and Physical Journal* 2, Pt. 2 (1806), p. 47. See Hall and Kelson, *The Mammals of North America* 1:387–88; Lowery, *The Mammals of Louisiana*, p. 187.

[88] From the mouth of the river to the upper end of the Great Raft (the present

-⊷ The Report of July 1:
Natchitoches to the Alabama–Coushatta Village ⊷-

A List of Animals. —

Quadrupeds. —

Ursus Americana very numerous[89]
Cervus Virginianus plenty[90]
Didelphis Opossum[91]

Shreveport area) the party was within the range of the subspecies of raccoon now called *Procyon lotor varius* Nelson & Goldman, not differentiated from neighboring subspecies until the 1930s. Upriver they would encounter two more subspecies, *P. l. fuscipes* Mearns from the head of the Raft to the Great Bend, and north of about 33°40' the subspecies *P. l. hirtus* Nelson & Goldman of the Ouachita uplands. Hall and Kelson, 2:885–87.

[89] The American black bears the exploring party observed in the Great Swamp region of northwestern Louisiana were of a new subspecies, *U. a. luteolus* Griffith, published as a new type in 1821. It is confined to East Texas, Louisiana, and southern Mississippi. Above 33° they will be within the range of the black bear typical of the eastern United States, *U. a. americanus* Pallas. Ibid., 2:865–68; Lowery, p. 411. Bears must have been plentiful in the country explored by Freeman and Custis. La Harpe, as has already been noted, in 1719 named the Sulphur River the "River of Bears." Sibley also tells us that in 1805 a party of Alabama-Coushattas "consisting of 15 persons, men, women, and children, who were on their return from a bear hunt . . . had killed 118." Sibley, "Historical Sketches," p. 51.

[90] The whitetailed deer, and a new subspecies, *Dama virginiana macroura* (Raf.), occupying the central prairies in the first tier of states west of the Mississippi, from Louisiana north to Minnesota. Rafinesque added this subspecies to science in 1817. Virtually eradicated in the region covered by this exploration, it has since been replaced by stocked whitetails from the midwest. Hall and Kelson, 2:1007–10; Lowery, p. 498. An idea of the relative abundance of deer in the early-day Red River valley may be inferred from de Mézières, who wrote that in 1775 Natchitoches had exported 36,000 deerskins. Sibley relates that in 1804 a single Indian, hunting for the market, had taken 400 deer during the summer and fall. Victor Shelford has estimated that the virgin Eastern forest supported between 100 and 800 whitetails per 10 square miles, with 400 the optimum number. De Mézières to Unzaga y Amezaga, Natchitoches, February 16, 1776, in Bolton, *Athanase De Mézières* 2:120–21; Sibley, "Historical Sketches," p. 51; Victor E. Shelford, *The Ecology of North America*, pp. 28–29.

[91] This would have been the opossum of the Eastern timber, now *D. marsupialis*

Viverra mephitis or skunk, very abundant about Lakes[92]

Talpa longicaudata caught at Coashatta Village. — [93]

A species of *Mus* which I believe to be the same with that which is called in Georgia Salamander a description of which Dr. Barton has before this favored the world with; lest however this may be somewhat different from that I will describe it. — — Body reddish ash; belly rather lighter cast; foreteeth wedged, upper grooved; Cheeks pouched; feet 5-toed; inner toe of fore-feet very short, the second much longer, the two next much longer than the second, fifth rather shorter than the second, formed for digging; toes of the hind feet all small; ears small, naked tubular; eyes very small, black; body 5 inches long; tail 2⅛, naked, somewhat quadrangular, tapering. Burrows in the ground; is said to feed on acorns which it lays up in September. — [94]

virginiana Kerr. Hall and Kelson, *Mammals of North America*, 1:5-8; Lowery, *Mammals of Louisiana*, p. 66.

[92] Probably a composite entry including the eastern spotted skunk (*Spilogale putorius indianola* Merriam south of the Shreveport area; *S. p. interrupta* [Raf.] above) and the striped skunk (the Midsouth subspecies *Mephitis mephitis mesomelas* Licht.). All of these were new and undescribed in 1806. Hall and Kelson, *Mammals of North America* 2:929-36; Lowery, *Mammals of Louisiana*, pp. 438-45.

[93] The eastern mole, and certainly the new subspecies *Scalopus aquaticus aereus* Bangs, described in 1896, found throughout the uplands of Louisiana and southern Arkansas, as well as eastern Oklahoma and Texas. Hall and Kelson, *Mammals of North America* 1:72-73; Lowery, *Mammals of Louisiana*, pp. 86-87.

[94] Barton's *Mus tuza* is of uncertain application, but apparently referred to a subspecies of southeastern pocket gopher. His description was published in early 1806 in J. H. Voigt, ed., *Magazen für den neuestren Zustand der Naturkunde* 12 (6):488. Cited in Hall and Kelson, *Mammals of North America*, 1:448. But it also appeared in partial form even earlier, in a "Miscellaneous Facts and Observations" column in the *Philadelphia Medical and Physical Journal, Supplement 1* (1805):66-67, where Barton adds that there was a larger, undescribed form west of the Mississippi. In 1817 Rafinesque superseded Barton's hazy classification when he created the genus *Geomys* for the pocket gophers. His type, *Geomys pinetis*, is a Georgia subspecies, evidently the same animal Barton called *Mus tuza*. But Custis's animal is indeed different. He describes, and very precisely, the plains pocket gopher, the subspecies *Geomys bursarius dutcheri* Davis, whose range begins in central Louisiana and covers southwest Arkansas, northeast Texas, and eastern Oklahoma. His failure to assign his animal a Latin name is the only thing that prevents him from being awarded credit for its discovery now that his work has come to light. See Hall and Kelson, *Mammals of North America*, 1:448-50; Lowery, *Mammals of Louisiana*, pp. 205-12.

The exploring party first encountered the native black bears (Ursus americanus luteolus) *and white tailed deer* (Dama virginiana macroura) *during the detour through the Great Swamp.*

Anas Carolinensis. — [95]

Strix aluco. — This is rather larger than the European species. — [96]

Ibis (*Tantalus Albus*, 2nd variety) found very numerous. — It is probably the Bec-croche of Du Pratts; if so he has not given a good description of it. — [97]

Falco communis. — [98]

A species of *Falco* which I have not seen described. — Cere, lores and bill black; legs yellow; head and neck blueish white; body and wing coverts lead colour; quill and tail feathers black-brown, — each tail feather with white stripes extending half way across; claws black; belly blueish; wings below with white & ferruginous spots; inside fulvous. 14 inches long. — [99]

[95] Apparently a slip of the pen (or the eye): the green-winged teal is what his name designates, but its summer breeding range is thousands of miles from North Louisiana. Custis must have seen instead the blue-winged teal, whose breeding range does extend into the region covered by this report. This duck, *Anas discors* L., is the only duck catalogued in the lists. Lowery, *Louisiana Birds*, p. 185.

[96] The barred owl, a species that hunts during daytime, and probably the Florida barred owl (*Strix varia georgica* Latham), a subspecies not yet differentiated in 1806. Oberholser, *Bird Life of Texas*, 1:455–57; Lowery, *Louisiana Birds*, pp. 381–82.

[97] Du Pratz, who included a drawing of the "Crook-bill," said the bird had a crooked bill, red flesh, and whitish-gray plummage. Du Pratz, *The History of Louisiana*, p. 261. The description is evidently of the white ibis (now *Eudocimus albus* [L.]). Although other ibises are found in Louisiana, this is the only bird whose summer range extends as far north as the Red River valley. The only conclusion I can come to is that Custis examined an immature bird, with its different plummage pattern. It is not an unusual mistake with the white ibis. See Lowery, pp. 157–60.

[98] The merlin, or pigeon hawk. It is listed as *Falco columbarius* in Lowery and in the *A. O. U. Check-List of North American Birds*, but as *Aesalon columbarius* in Oberholser. This would have been the subspecies *F. c. columbarius* (L.), the eastern pigeon hawk.

[99] Only Custis's strange oversight in failing to provide a Latin name for it prevents him from a clear claim to the discovery and addition to science of this bird. His description is an exacting one of the strikingly beautiful Mississippi kite (*Ictinia mississippiensis* Wilson), probably (since it has a banded tail) of an immature bird. The omission of a binomial left the way open for Custis's rival for the Red River naturalist post, Alexander Wilson, to "discover" this falcon-like hawk during a visit to Dunbar's plantation in 1810. The episode is a famous one: Wilson wounded the bird, and when he reached to secure it a talon pierced

"A species of Falco *which I have not seen described. . . ."* *John James Audubon's paint-ing of the Mississippi kite* (Ictinia mississippiensis). *Courtesy Library of Congress.*

Alcedo alcyon.—[100]
Oriolus Baltimorus.—[101]
Fringilla caudacuta.—[102]

Amphibia

Of these I can say but little.—The Alligator is found as high as this.—The soft shell turtle *(Testudo ferox)* is still abundant.—

Serpents I believe are very rare; I have seen some Vipers,[103] (*Coluber Rhomboideus*)[104] and one Rattle snake only (*Crotalus durissus*).[105]

---

his palm to the bone. He described and named the kite in his *American Ornithology* volume of 1811, rendering from his captive bird a famous plate that Audubon later plagiarized. Intriguingly, kites have responded well to modern human manipulation of the Southwest, shifting their range westward in the twentieth century. T. M. Brewer, *Wilson's American Ornithology*, 241–42; *A. O. U. Check-List*, 101; Eric Bolen and Dan Flores, *The Mississippi Kite* (Austin: Univ. of Texas Press, 1993): 18–32.

[100] The eastern belted kingfisher (*Megaceryle alcyon alcyon* [L.]). Other Southwestern kingfishes are out of range here. Oberholser, *Bird Life of Texas*, 1:501–505; Lowery, *Louisiana Birds*, pp. 406–407.

[101] Custis uses the American term first utilized by Mark Catesby and later by both Bartram and Barton rather than the Linnaean name (*Icterus galbula* [L.]) now accepted. The bird is a summer resident throughout the eastern United States, although today it is only infrequently seen in the region Custis has explored in this report. Oberholser, *Bird Life of Texas*, 2:823; Lowery, *Louisiana Birds*, p. 543

[102] *Fringella caudacuta* Gmelin, the sharp-tailed finch, in Brewer, *Wilson's American Ornithology*, p. 704. Now classified *Ammospiza cauducuta* and popularly known as the sharp-tailed sparrow, Oberholser, *Bird Life of Texas*, 2:908–909.

[103] This is obviously little other than a non-specific mention rather than a description, but there are several pit-vipers native to the country covered by the expedition. Custis must have seen the copperhead, in this stretch, *Ancistrodon contortrix contortrix* (L.). In the cypress swamps traversed by the expedition, the western cottonmouth moccasin (*A. piscivorus leucostoma* Lacépède) would certainly have been in evidence. Albert Hazen Wright and Anna Allen Wright, *Handbook of Snakes of the United States and Canada* 2:903–15, 921–25.

[104] The reference is to a species of eastern king snake, but in the Red River valley Custis was seeing a new and entirely different snake possessing the familiar red, black, and yellow markings. This was the beautiful Louisiana milk snake (*Lampropeltis triangulum amaura* Cope), a species of Louisiana and East Texas which has entered Arkansas and Oklahoma via the Red River bottomland. Ibid. 2:890–99; Kenneth L. Williams, *Systematics and Natural History of the American*

Custis saw, but failed to recognize as new, the striking Louisiana milk snake (Lampropeltis triangulum amaura). *Photograph by Joseph Collins, with the cooperation of the Audubon Park Zoo.*

Fishes

Catfish *(Silurus catus)* very abundant and of a large size.—We have caught some that weighed 59 lbs.

Gar & Alligator fish are also plenty.

Shrimps *(Cancer crangon)* are plenty.—[106]

Milk Snake, Lampropeltis triangulum, pp. 138–43. This snake is evidently the species whose brightly-colored skins the early Spanish chroniclers reported were worn as necklaces by Caddo shamans. Mildred Gleason, *Caddo: A Survey of the Caddo Indian in Northeast Texas and Marion County,* p. 28.

[105] More specifically, a western pygmy rattler, *Sistrurus miliarius streckeri* Gloyd, indigenous to Louisiana and East Texas. Wright and Wright, *Handbook of Snakes,* 2:1058.

[106] In Custis's day classification of the order Decapoda was in an embryonic

Minerals

You will receive a small Box containing a few minerals.—

No. 1 a pumice stone found on the edge of the River where it was
undoubtedly brought by the current.—It serves to strengthen
the report of there being Volcanoes on some of the waters of this
River.—[107]

No. 3 & 4 Specimens of the marl which I have before mentioned as
giving the Color to the River.—No. 3 was taken from the bank
at the Avoyelles, 4 from the banks at the Apalaches [village].—
There is also a specimen of sand stone from Cane River and
some Ore taken from a small Bayou back of [Natchitoches].

No. 2 a clay taken from a hill back of [Natchitoches]. This is sometimes found covering considerable portions of land.—I have seen
a small Prairie on Bayou Badtka covered with it.—

There are two small papers of seed contained in the Box.—

A List of Vegetables

Bignonia radicans in flower on the 4th of June.[108]
Hibiscus fraternus very plenty on the borders of the River in flower
on the 6th.[109]

---

stage. *Crangon* is the generic name of the marine shrimps, but no doubt what
Custis is seeing are fresh-water crayfish rather than shrimps. They must have
been species of the genus *Cambarus* (not yet designated in 1806), endemic to
moving rivers and streams of eastern North America. G. Smith and W F. R.
Weldon, "Crustacea," in Harmer and Shipley, *The Cambridge Natural History*
4:152–54, 213.

[107] There are no volcanoes specifically near the headwaters of the Red River,
which takes its sources on the Llano Estacado. But tectonic geology is not far
distant. Today's Capulin Volcano National Monument along the Canadian River
in nearby New Mexico is a testament to lava flows that once spilled across the
southern High Plains. Custis's specimen may well have been transported to the
Red from this source by human hands.

[108] The common trumpet creeper, whose habitat is streambanks and thickets
from Texas to Florida, and north to Pennsylvania and Missouri. Vines, *Trees,
Shrubs and Woody Vines*, p. 925.

[109] Most likely this was *H. moscheutos* (L.), the swamp rose-mallow; found in wet
meadows and moist woods from Texas to Florida, north to Maryland and

Mercurialis annua above the first Raft in flower the 6th[110]
Sida occidentalis in flower the 6th.[111]
Rhus coriaria[112] and *radicans*[113]
Smilax china[114] & *Sarsaparilla*.[115]
Rudbeckia purpurea in flower the 8th. — [116]
Podophyllum peltatum every where abundant[117]
Nymphaea nelumbo[118] and *alba*.[119] These cover the Lakes. The

Indiana, but see footnotes 229 and 235. Correll and Johnston, *Vascular Plants of Texas*, pp. 1031–32.

[110] This species of Euphorbiaceae is a European weed, probably correctly identified, since the party was still traversing settled strips of river here. See Rickett, 3:90–95.

[111] Probably the prickly-mallow (*S. spinosa* [L.]), ranging from Texas to Florida, north to Massachusetts and Nebraska. Ibid., 2:204.

[112] Instead, the American species called the smooth sumac (*R. glabra* [L.]), widely distributed in North America. Lundell, *Flora of Texas* 3:94.

[113] With this entry Custis probably refers to the poison ivy, *Toxicodendron radicans* (L.) Kuntze., found from Oaxaca, Mexico to Florida, north to Nova Scotia and British Columbia. Ibid., 3:107.

[114] Morton identifies this as the China-rose (*S. tamnoides* [L.]), found from Texas to Florida, north to Nova Scotia and South Dakota. Morton, "An Overlooked Publication of Botanical Interest," p. 452. The choices in *Vines, Trees, Shrubs and Woody Vines*, pp. 72–75, cause me to think the laurel greenbrier (*S. rotundifolia* [L.]) is also a possibility.

[115] Rather than the true wild sarsaparilla, which is tropical and out of range here, Custis saw a similar native type. Morton believes, because the stems of both plants are quadrangular, that this was the saw greenbrier (*S. bona-nox* [L.]), and that Custis missed it because of an incorrect description of the leaves in Linnaeus's *Systema*. It is found from Texas to Florida, north to Massachusetts and Nebraska. Morton, "An Overlooked Publication of Botanical Interest," p. 452; *Vines, Trees, Shrubs and Woody Vines*, pp. 72–75.

[116] Now known as *R. bicolor* Nutt., this species of black-eyed Susan was new, not published by Thomas Nuttall until 1834. The base of the ray-flowers is tinted purple. In dry soil from Texas to Alabama and northward. Rickett, 2:578; *Index Kewensis* 2:758. Beginning with this plant, the next forty entries (until June 24) come from observations made during the exploration's tour through the Great Swamp, in present Red River, Bienville, Webster, and Bossier parishes, Louisiana.

[117] See note 57.

[118] The nelumbo is a lotus known as the water chinquapin (*Nelumbo lutea* [Willd.] Pers.), endemic to rivers and lakes from Texas to Florida, north to New England and Minnesota. Rickett, 2:155–56.

[119] He names the white waterlily of Eurasia; on Lake Bisteneau and others

leaves of the *nelumbo* are of a very large size. I have seen them to measure 9 feet in circumference. In flower on the 8th.

Jussieua repens in flower the 10th.[120]

Aretium Lappa[121]

Solanum Virginianum on Lake Bistino—[122]

Hypericum proliferum in flower the 10th.[123]

Tradescantia Virginica every where abundant nearly out of flower on the 10th.[124]

Cassia chamaecrista beginning to put forth its flower on the 5th of June.—This plant was first seen at Campté and becomes more abundant as you ascend the River. It abounds in the Prairies & even throughout the Woods extending quite to the Rivers side.—In Virginia this vegetable is thought very advantageous to poor lands & answers by the name of Magotty Bay Bean because it was first discovered at that place.—Dr. James Greenway of Virginia, I believe, has given an account

---

here, was actually seeing the related fragrant waterlily (*Nymphaea odorata* Ait.), a ubiquitous species in the eastern United States, and popularly known in the South as the alligator bonnet. Ibid.

[120] Now taxonomically rendered *Ludwigia repens* Sw., this was a species of marsh purslane found from New Mexico to Florida, north to North Carolina and Missouri. Ibid., 2:312.

[121] Another genus that has been re-classified, this must have been the diminutive *Androsace occidentalis* Pursh, or rock jasmine. It would have been a new species, and in northwestern Louisiana would be at the southeastern edge of its range, now given as Arizona to Texas and Arkansas, and north to Ontario and British Columbia. It is a plant of the banks of streams. Ibid., 3:276; Correll and Johnston, *Vascular Plants of Texas*, p. 1183.

[122] This was probably *Solanum carolinense* (L.), the horse nettle. It could possibly have been the western horse nettle (*S. dimidiatum* Raf.), however, a new species that would have been at the perimeter of its range in northwestern Louisiana. I lean toward *carolinense*, found from Texas to Florida, north to New England and Washington. Ibid., p. 1396.

[123] A St. John's Wort, evidently a southern variety of *H. prolificum*, and most probably *H. fasciculatum* Lam., the sand-weed. Its range is Louisiana to Florida, north to South Carolina. Rickett, 2:210.

[124] This spiderwort was not the *virginiana* species, but a new plant, later recognized by Rafinesque and thus named *T. ohioensis* Raf. It is very similar to *virginiana*, but is more a southern variety, found from Texas to Florida, north to Massachusetts and Nebraska. Ibid., 2:62; Correll and Johnston, *Vascular Plants of Texas*, p. 363.

Louisiana yucca (Yucca louisianensis), *a typical specimen of the plant collected by Custis.*

of it in the Philosophical transactions.—There is also a paper on its properties as a manure in one of the numbers of the Medical Repository.—[125]

[125] Custis is seeing here a relative of the Virginia "Magotty Bay Bean." Probably this plant is a variety of the partridge pea, or prairie senna, either *C. fasciculata* var. *fasciculata* Michx., or *C. fasciculata* var. *robusta* (Pollard) Macbr. The former ranges from Texas to Florida, north to Massachusetts and South Dakota; the latter, a new variety in 1806, is found from East Texas to Florida and north to Ohio. Rickett, 2:320, 3:207; Correll and Johnston, *Vascular Plants of Texas*, pp. 790–92. The Greenway article referred to by Custis is: "An account of the beneficial effects of the CASSIA CHAMAECRISTA, in recruiting worn-out lands, and in enriching such as are naturally poor; together with a botanical description of the plant," *Transactions of the American Philosophical Society* 3 (1793): 226–30. The latter—and an indication that Custis kept up with the scientific journals—was John Dennis's article, "An Account of a Plant called the Magathy-

Myrica cerifera plenty on Lake Bistino. — [126]

Polygonum lapathifolium in flower on the 13th.[127]

Erythrina herbacea which I mentioned in my last [catalogues] as having [been] seen only at Rapide is very abundant after passing Nachitoches. — You will receive some of the seed. — [128]

Fragaria vesca plenty in Prairies[129]

Passiflora minima abundant in flower the 15th.[130]

Silphium laciniatum in Prairies in flower 15th.[131]

Satureia capitata[132]

Asclepias lactifera[133]

Bay Bean, or Accomac-Pea, cultivated for fertilizing lands," *The Medical Repository*, Hex. 1, 6 (1803): 273–76. These are very early references to the use of nitrogen-fixing legumes as natural fertilizers.

[126] The southern wax-myrtle, an evergreen shrub found in sandy swamps and low, acidic prairies from East Texas to Florida, north to New Jersey. Vines, *Trees, Shrubs and Woody Vines*, p. 118.

[127] The collections and observations made for the two dates appearing next in the catalogue were apparently done by Custis during a layover at Grappe's *vacherie* on Lake Bisteneau. Thus several European immigrant species will appear. This plant is a species of smartweed, now rendered *Persicaria lapathifolia* (L.) Small, a European immigrant found in wet or disturbed areas over most of the country now. Correll and Johnston, *Vascular Plants of Texas*, p. 525.

[128] See note 28.

[129] The entry refers to the northern wood strawberry, which is out of range here. He must have seen these Louisiana prairies covered with *F. virginiana* Duch., the wild strawberry, instead. It ranges from central Texas to Georgia, and north to Newfoundland and Alberta. Rickett, 2:194, 3:116. Three-quarters of a century earlier, Du Pratz had written of the strawberries in this region that they were ". . . of an excellent flavor, and so plentiful, that from the beginning of April the savannahs or meadows appear quite red with them." Du Pratz, *The History of Louisiana*, p. 238.

[130] See note 41.

[131] The compass plant, a bristly prairie species with sunflower-like flowers found from Texas to Alabama, north to Ohio and North Dakota. Rickett, 2: 581.

[132] Apparently a member of the genus *Satureja*, which includes the savories and calamints and probably the new species *Satureja arkansana* (Nutt.) Briq., or a related variety. It is found in ravines and on banks from central Texas to Ontario and Minnesota. Correll and Johnston, *Vascular Plants of Texas*, p. 1384.

[133] This is too general a designation for me to be able to determine which member of the three genera of milkweeds found in this range the entry refers to. See below.

Custis was unable to name the endemic bois d'arc (Maclura pomifera) *because the tree he saw was not in flower. Photograph by Katie Dowdy.*

———— *filiformis*[134]
———— *incarnata*[135]
Ascyrum Hypericoides in flower 15th.[136]
Achillea Santolina[137]

[134] Since "filiformis" means threadlike, this must have been *A. lanceolata* Walt., found in marshes from Texas to Florida and New Jersey, or *A. verticillata* (L.), ranging from Mexico to Florida, north to Ontario and Sasketchewan. Rickett, 2:405–406.
[135] The swamp milkweed, abundant in moist soil from New Mexico to Florida, north to Maine and Manitoba. Ibid., 2:402.
[136] The St. Andrew's cross, found in sandy soil from Mexico to Florida and north to New England and Kansas. Ibid., 2:207. See note 20.
[137] Custis is using the Linnean name for an East African plant; this was actually a new species of yarrow. *A lanulosa* Nutt. is the native species most like *santolina*, but Custis's plant could also have been *A. occidentalis* Raf. in this range. The former ranges throughout the United States; the latter from Arkansas to Florida

243

Plantago major[138]

Periploca secamone[139]

Coreopsis lanceolata in flower 15th.[140]

Crotalaria latifolia[141]

Astragalus carolinianus[142]

Euonymus americanus on the Banks of the River[143]

Drosera cuneifolia in flower the 16th.[144]

Tricosanthes cucumerina near the upper end of great Raft in flower 22nd.[145]

---

and northward. Ibid., 2:602; Correll and Johnston, *Vascular Plants of Texas*, p. 1705; Usher, *A Dictionary of plants used by man*, p. 16.

[138] A weed from the Old World, this was the common dooryard plantain, an intruder the Indians called, descriptively, "White Man's Footsteps." Rickett, 3:302.

[139] The Grecian silk vine (*P. graeca* [L.]), or a related woody vine of the milkweed family. This would have been another cultivated immigrant from Europe, the fourteenth thus far. Vines, *Trees, Shrubs and Woody Vines*, p. 879.

[140] A species of tickseed found in dry soil from New Mexico to Florida, north to New England and Michigan. Rickett, 2:557.

[141] The entry refers to a native of Jamaica. What Custis saw here was the native species of *Crotalaria, C. sagittalis* (L.), found in sandy soil in the eastern and central United States. Correll and Johnston, *Vascular Plants of Texas*, p. 802.

[142] *Carolinianus* is a synonym for *A. canadensis* (L.), the rattle-vetch, found from New Mexico to Georgia, north to Quebec and British Columbia. Ibid., p. 843; Rickett, 2:359.

[143] The strawberry bush, found in mud along streams and river bottoms from East Texas to Florida and north to Pennsylvania and Illinois. Correll and Johnston, *Vascular Plants of Texas*, p. 999.

[144] Custis is at this point examining the country along Bayou Bodcau, Bossier Parish, La. This was a species of insect-catching sundew. Two different species are found in this range which have the wedge-shaped leaves suggested by *cuneifolia*. Both were new. Custis is seeing either or both *D. intermedia* Hayne, found in wet sands and peaty areas from Texas to Florida, north to Newfoundland and Minnesota; and *D. brevifolia* Pursh, in the damp sands of pinelands or mixed forests from East Texas to Alabama and north to Tennessee. I think it quite likely that the latter plant was included in Custis's collection of specimens (perhaps No. 16?), thus enabling Frederick Pursh to publish it in his *Flora Americae Septentrionalis* (1814). See the headnote to the Botanical Specimens for additional information.

[145] The plant named is a vine of tropical Asia and Australia. Professor Joseph Ewan thinks this might have been the balsam apple (*Momordica charantia* L.), a similar cultivar brought by European settlers to the Ohio valley as early as the middle of the eighteenth century. Morton suggests that this might have been

Polygonum scandens in flower 22nd.[146]

Palmetto (   ) The root is used by the natives in the cure of *Lues venera*. They use it in the form of decoction.[147]

Arbutus Uva Ursi on Bayou Badtka. — [148]

Cassia marylandica on Bayou Badtka. — [149]

Sagittaria lancifolia in a lake near the upper end of the Raft.[150]

Hedera quinquefolia.[151]

Commelina vaginata every where abundant in flower 1st of June at Nachitoches. — [152]

---

the native bur cucumber (*Sicyos angulata* [L.]) instead. Morton, "An Overlooked Publication of Botanical Interest," 454.

[146] A weedy vine known as the climbing false buckwheat, extending from East Texas throughout most of the eastern United States. Rickett, 3:76.

[147] Almost certainly the saw palmetto (*Serena repens* [Bartr.] Small), found in prairies and sandy pinelands from Louisiana eastward to Florida and north to South Carolina. This is the first of several Native American ethnobotanical entries Custis makes. Saw palmetto was a traditionally-utilized medicinal plant for Southeastern Indians; it exerts a stimulant action upon the mucous membrane of the genito-urinary tract. Vines, *Trees, Shrubs and Woody Vines*, pp. 48–49; Vogel, *American Indian Medicine*, pp. 365–66; Usher, *A Dictionary of plants used by man*, p. 535.

[148] Today rendered *Arctostaphylos uva ursi* (L.) Spreng., the bearberry. But this species is not known to range into the Red River valley today. Professor Clair Brown believes Custis instead was seeing the tree huckleberry (*Vaccinium arboreum* Marsh.), a common and somewhat similar species found on Bayou Bodcau. Morton, "An Overlooked Publication of Botanical Interest," p. 455.

[149] The wild senna, found in dry thickets from Texas to Florida, to Pennsylvania and Iowa. Rickett, 2:320.

[150] A species of arrowhead plant, ranging from Texas to Florida in swamps and along streams. The lake mentioned in this entry is probably Swan Lake, Bossier Parish, Louisiana. Ibid., 2:58.

[151] Ivy plants were classified in the genus *Hedera* in the early Linnean system. What Custis is observing here is a grapevine known as the Virginia creeper (*Parthenocissus quinquefolia* [L.]), a climber widespread in North America from Mexico northward and eastward. Vines, *Trees, Shrubs and Woody Vines*, p. 711; Willis, *A Dictionary of the Flowering Plants and Ferns*, p. 537.

[152] This is a species of Old World herb known as the false flax, one much cultivated for its oily seeds. The *C. sylvestris* Wallr. and *C. microcarpa* Andrz. types are the varieties most often introduced to America by Europeans, and are now found in waste places throughout North America. Evidently what Custis has seen is the common dayflower (*C. virginica* [L.]), found widely in the eastern United States. Rickett, 2:226; *Index Kewensis* 1:401; Correll and Johnston, *Vascular Plants of Texas*, p. 704.

The only surviving specimens from the Red River survey, both collected in present Caddo Parish, Louisiana. the prairie-gentian (Eustoma grandiflorum) was a new plant of the western prairies; this is the first specimen of it ever collected. The eastern culver's root (Veroni-

castrum virginicum) *was probably collected as a typical medicinal herb of the country above the Great Raft. Rafinesque's variety,* villosum, *is no longer valid. Photographs courtesy the Academy of Natural Sciences, Philadelphia.*

Morea vegeta in flower 24th.[153]

Sison ammi near the upper end of Raft.[154]

Helianthus strumosus in flower 24th.[155]

Aristolochia pistolochia in flower 26th.[156]

Ranunculus hederaceus in little Prairie[157]

Arum pentaphyllum near Coashatta village[158]

Delpinium Staphisagria   Do.   Do. — [159]

Jatropha Urens (Stinging Cassava) in flower on the 12th every where abundant. — [160]

[153] Almost certainly the celestial lily, a member of a new genus. The species was a plant named after Thomas Nuttall, *Nemastylis nuttallii* Pick., which is found along streams from northeast Texas (and, in 1806, Louisiana) northward through Arkansas to Missouri. Correll and Johnston, *Vascular Plants of Texas*, p. 431.

[154] Still another European immigrant, this is an Old World herb of the parsley family which now grows wild in the United States. First described in Australia, it is now reclassified, and taxonomically rendered *Apium leptophyllum* Muell. & Benth. Rickett, 2:276; *Index Kewensis* 1:161.

[155] A type of sunflower similar to the Jerusalem artichoke; it is found from Texas to Florida, north to Maine and South Dakota. Rickett, 2:569-70.

[156] See note 33. This possibly could have been a new variety, however, *A.* var. *hastata* (Nutt.) Ducharte, found only from Louisiana to Florida, and north to Virginia. Ibid., 2:139; Correll and Johnston, *Vascular Plants of Texas*, p. 508. Having completed the detour through the Great Swamp, the exploring party is at this point back on the Red, and Custis is examining the region just north of Shreveport, in present Caddo and Bossier parishes.

[157] A species of buttercup, but rather than the *beteroanus*, probably *R. trisepaulus* Gill. ex Hook, a new species found in most of Eastern North America. *Index Kewensis* 2:689.

[158] See note 18. The exploring expedition remained more than two weeks at the Alabama-Coushatta village, but Custis catalogued fewer than ten additional species during the period. Instead, he utilized his time in ethnological studies of the Caddos (see part 3), and in preparing a collection of botanical specimens, all of which appear to have been gathered in this locality, between the head of the Great Raft and the present southern boundary of Arkansas.

[159] Three species of poisonous larkspurs *(Delphinium)* are possible, one of which would have been new. *D. tricorne* Michx. and *D. carolinianum* Walt. are found in the eastern half of the continent, while the white, or plains, larkspur (*D. virescens* Nutt.), later credited to Thomas Nuttall, is a species of the central prairies and is found here. Rickett, 2:160-61; Correll and Johnston, *Vascular Plants of Texas*, pp. 639-40.

[160] This is unquestionably the plant within the Euphorbiaceae family (in which *Jatropha* is a genus) known today as the bull-nettle (*Cnidoscolus texana* [Muell. Arg.] Small). A new species in 1806, the bull-nettle is widely distributed in the

Ilex cassine near the coashatta village[161]
Polypodium   every where plenty[162]
Fungi abundant
Cardicus virginicus in flower the 27th. — [163]

---❧ BOTANICAL SPECIMENS FROM ABOVE THE GREAT RAFT ❧---

EDITOR'S NOTE: The following entries refer to plant specimens collected by Custis in present Bossier and Caddo parishes, La., from June 23 to July 1, 1806, on Bayou Bodcau, in Caddo Prairie, and from the bluff hills east of the river in the vicinity of the Alabama-Coushatta village. Taken from several ecological settings, these must have been plants Custis regarded as typical of the wilderness above the Raft, or which he was unable to identify with his texts. See the Epilogue for the fate of this collection.

No. 1 & 2 & 4 at the Coashatta [village]
No. 3 in Prairies.[164] No. 5 every where plenty. The Coashatta
   Indians make a decoction of this which they drink at their
   green corn dance previous to taking the *Black drink.* — It pukes

sandy upland hills of northwestern Louisiana, Arkansas, Oklahoma, and Texas. Correll and Johnston, *Vascular Plants of Texas*, p. 954.

[161] The dahoon holly, found in sandy soils and pine barrens from Louisiana to Florida, and north to Virginia. Vines, *Trees, Shrubs and Woody Vines*, p. 650.

[162] Probably the resurrection fern (*P. polypodioides* [L.] Watt. var. *michauxianum* Weath.), endemic to rock ledges and mossy banks from Mexico to Florida, north to Maryland and Missouri. Correll and Johnston, *Vascular Plants of Texas*, p. 63.

[163] Rather than the plant he indicates, which does not occur in the Red River valley, Custis was seeing a related local thistle, probably *Cirsium carolinianum* (Walt.) Fern and Schub, in sandy forests from East Texas to Georgia, north to North Carolina and Indiana. Ibid., p. 1719.

[164] A new examination of the Barton Herbarium in the Academy of Natural Sciences, Philadelphia, during the spring of 1983, yielded two surviving botanical specimens from the Red River exploration. One has been identified as the eastern culver's root, a medicinal herb. Custis named it correctly on the note attached to the specimen (see photograph), although the plant is now called *Veronicastrum virginicum* (L.). Custis's note describes it as having been collected "about 450 miles up the Red River, in a large prairie"—undoubtedly Caddo Prairie. The specimen is large, and has been segmented. In fact, twenty-six dried plants the size of these must have made up a considerable and awkward bundle for wilderness transport.

them violently immediately after drinking it. — Whether it is the emetic property of the plant or the great quantity of warm water which they drink, that causes it to operate so soon I am unable to say. — [165]

No. 6 very plenty, particularly on the declivities of hills

No. 7. The poor people are said to use the root as a substitute for soap. The leaves are what the people of Campeachy make their cordage of. — [166]

The second Custis specimen, which Pursh saw and speculated on the attached note "Chironia?" might be a member of the family Gentianae, evidently was also cut down in Caddo Prairie. The plant is the prairie-gentian, or bluebell (now *Eustoma grandiflorum* [Raf.] Shinners). The genus was set up in 1806 by the British botanist R. A. Salisbury; the species, *grandiflorum*, was eventually described by Rafinesque in 1836. But Custis's collection of this plant is the earliest on record of what is essentially a western plains species. Its modern range is said to begin in the Texas Blackland Prairie, west to New Mexico and north to Colorado and Nebraska (Correll and Johnston, *Vascular Plants of Texas*, p. 1208). Its presence in northwestern Louisiana in 1806 is intriguing; probably it was native.

I am indebted to James Mears of the Academy's botany department for finding and photographing the Custis Red River specimens.

[165] The Green Corn Dance was a religious dance performed by the Alabama-Coushattas and other Creek tribes when the first corn shoots appeared above the ground. Its purpose was to placate the corn entities. Participants had to be cleansed and purified, and it was in this context that an emetic drink was consumed. The Black Drink itself, usually made from one of the hollies, either *Ilex cassine* (L.), or, more likely in this region, the yaupon, *I. vomitoria* Ait., was a magical broth of central importance to the tribes of the Southeastern United States and remains so even today in Seminole shamanistic training. Since Custis has collected a plant consumed before taking the Black Drink, this must have been the great blue lobelia (*Lobelia siphilitica* L.), a plant he will identify as growing at this village in his Report of October 1. It contains alkaloids that induce immediate vomiting when taken internally. John R. Swanton, *Early History of the Creek Indians and Their Neighbors*, Bureau of American Ethnology, *Bulletin 73*, pp. 226–30; Vogel, *American Indian Medicine*, pp. 78–79; Clair A. Brown, *Wildflowers of Louisiana and Adjoining States*, p. 106.

[166] References to Campeche and the uses he describes for this plant quite certainly point to a *Yucca*. The native soapweed here is the Louisiana yucca, not yet classified in Custis's day, but today scientifically rendered *Yucca louisianensis* Trel. It is a common plant of the pine uplands of this country, and it is a humid-land relative of *Agave lecheguilla* and *Yucca carnerosana*, both which are used in Mexico to make rope and for many other uses. Custis must have regarded this yucca as a characteristic species, as indeed it is, of the middle Red — evidence that his collection was of "typical" plants. Ricket, 3:34; Correll

No. 8. Abundant in Prairies. — The root is a Caddo remedy for the convulsions of Children. If at all useful, I think, it must be, in such cases as arise from worms, by its anthelmintic properties. — [167]

No. 10 a species of *mimosa* abundant in Prairies. — [168]

No. 9 at Coashatta. No. 11 abundant in Prairies. —

No. 12 a climber. — No. 13 on the banks of the River. — The leaves were feathered with an odd one.

No. 14 abundant in Prairies. —

No. 15 Coashatta village.

No. 16 On Lake Badtka. No. 17 plenty in Prairies

No. 18 In Prairies. No. 19 *Polypodium* every where abundant. [169]

No. 20. One of the most abundant vegetables in this country, being found in every situation high & low. No. 21 plenty in Prairies. —

No. 22 a small shrub growing near the head of great Raft. No. 23 found in Prairies. —

No. 24. I take it to be a species of *Lonicera*. Grows near Coashatta Village. — [170]

No. 25 very abundant No. 26 Coashatta village

---

and Johnston, *Vascular Plants of Texas*, p. 401; Sam Sheldon, "Ethnobotany of *Agave lecheguilla* and *Yucca carnerosana* in Mexico's Zona Ixtlera," *Economic Botany* 34 (October 1980): 376–90.

[167] The ethnobotanical reference to a Caddo anthelmintic may refer to the widely-used wormgrass, *Spigelia marylandica* (L.), probably the best-known Indian vermifuge in the South. The Cherokees sold it in such great quantities to the settlers that in some areas it became very rare. However, since its use was familiar, I wonder if this might instead be the Jerusalem oak, or Mexican tea (*Chenopodium ambrosioides* var. *anthelminticum* [L.] Gray). A Mexican native, it must have been introduced into this country very early, for its use was reported by the Natchez. Vogel, *American Indian Medicine*, pp. 175–76, 348.

[168] *M. strigillosa*, a prairie species, was new, but had been catalogued under the name *Mimosa punctata* in the Report on June 1. See Note 17. Obviously he suspected that this might be a new plant, for the abbreviated descriptions in Linnaeus's *Species Vegetibilium* simply were not enough to make a hard and fast literary decision.

[169] The resurrection fern (see note 162) is the dominant fern species of this part of the Red River valley.

[170] He must refer here to the trumpet honeysuckle, the only species of *Lonicera* in this range, and one that he had correctly identified in his June 1 Report.

—◆{ The Report of October 1: Alabama–Coushatta Village to the Spanish Camp, and Return }◆—

A List of Trees & Shrubs growing on R River

1. Cotton tree a species of *Populus* growing on the borders of the River as high as the Spanish camp. — [171]

2. Pecan *(Juglans petiolata)* abundant as high as Nachitoches after which it is very rare for 500 miles and is said to be plenty again. — [172]

3. Plane tree *(Platanus Occidentalis)*, plenty on the borders of the River as high as the Spanish Camp. — [173]

4. Hagberry *(Prunus padus)* plenty. — [174]

5. Persimmon *(Dyospyros Virginiana)* every where plenty. — [175]

6. Honey Locusts *(Gleditsia triacanthos* and *monosperma)* very abundant. — [176]

[171] Three possibilities exist in the region traversed by the explorers: the common eastern cottonwood (*Populus deltoides* Marsh.) found east of the Rockies; the swamp cottonwood (*P. heterophylla* [L.]) of alluvial lands along the entire Atlantic Coast, but particularly in the Mississippi valley; and a new subspecies of the eastern cottonwood known as the hairy cottonwood (*P. d.* var. *pilosa* [Sarg.] Sudw.), which occurs only in Louisiana, Georgia, Oklahoma, and Kansas. Vines, *Trees, Shrubs and Woody Vines*, pp. 90–92.

[172] Now *Carya illinoinensis* (Wangh.) K. Koch. It is found in rich river-bottom soils from Texas to Alabama, and north to Indiana. Ibid., p. 127.

[173] The sycamore, found in rich bottomland soils from Texas east to Florida, and north to Maine, Ontario, Nebraska. Ibid., p. 326.

[174] Probably not the European *Prunus padus* of Linnaeus, but more likely some species of southwestern wild cherry, perhaps the black cherry (*Prunus serotina* Ehrh.) or one of its varieties. Harper, *Bartram's Travels*, p. 602; Vines, *Trees, Shrubs and Woody Vines*, pp. 390–91.

[175] The common persimmon (*Diospyros virginiana* [L.]) is the only persimmon in range here. Found from central Texas to the Carolinas and north to Connecticut and Iowa. Robert A. Vines, *Trees of East Texas*, p. 443.

[176] *Triacanthos* is the common honey-locust, which ranges from Texas to Florida, north to Pennsylvania and Nebraska. *Monosperma* is a synonym for the water locust (*G. aquatica* Marsh.), found in swamps from East Texas across to Florida, north to South Carolina and Illinois. Ibid., pp. 279–85; Harper, *Bartram's Travels*, p. 517.

7. Oaks *(Quercus rubra,*[177] *alba,*[178] *phellos,*[179] *nigra*[180] and *esculus. —*[181]

8. Box elder.[182]

9. Sweet Gum *(Liquidambar styraciflua)* plenty. —[183]

10. Pines *(Pinus Sylvestris*[184] & *Taeda)* the *Taeda* is in great abundance and of a very large size. —[185]

11. Cypress *(Cypressus disticha* & *thyoides)* The *disticha* is met with as high as we ascended.[186] — The other I have only noticed

---

[177]"Rubra" is no longer in use, but in Custis's day was a catch-all for the many varieties of red oaks. He must have observed varieties of the southern red oak (*Q. falcata* Michx.), which in its various forms ranges from the Brazos River to Florida and north to Pennsylvania. Vines, *Trees of East Texas,* pp. 111-15.

[178]The white oak, common to most of the Eastern timberlands. Ibid., pp. 76-78.

[179]The willow oak, found in the Eastern woodlands as far north as New York and in this range often mistakenly called the "pin oak." Ibid., pp. 101-102.

[180]The water oak, which ranges north from the Texas-Louisiana area to New Jersey in swamps and along the Coastal Plain. Ibid., pp. 108-10.

[181]A misidentification of a new species now credited to Thomas Nuttall. This was the swamp chestnut oak (*Q. michauxii* Nutt.), found in moist conditions bordering swamps and rivers from Texas to Florida, north to Delaware and Indiana. Ibid., pp. 82-83. On these southern oaks, see also Harper, *Bartram's Travels,* pp. 603-606.

[182]The elder (*Sambucus canadensis* [L.]) is a member of the honeysuckle family, and ranges from Texas to Florida, north to Nova Scotia and Manitoba. Vines, *Trees of East Texas,* pp. 494-95.

[183]The American sweetgum, which ranges from East Texas to Florida and north to Connecticut and Illinois. Vines, *Trees of East Texas,* pp. 171-72.

[184]Evidently Custis was using *sylvestris,* a European pine, for the longleaf pine (*P. palustris* Mill.), the lofty pine tree bearing giant cones found in deep, sandy loams from Texas to Florida, north to Virginia. Between the Rapids and Natchitoches, the Red River wends its way through an almost pure stand of longleaf pine that stretches for almost 500 miles across East Texas and Louisiana. Nourished and preserved as a sub-climax by fires, the virgin stands tolerated little understory, and those seen by the explorers must have been beautifully parklike. Ibid., pp. 10-11; Shelford, *Ecology of North America,* p. 56.

[185]He refers to the loblolly pine, the largest of the Red River valley pines, and, as he notes, some of the virgin loblollies were gigantic, reaching heights of more than 170 feet. I find it remarkable that he did not distinguish the very common shortleaf pine (*P. echinata* Mill.); perhaps this *taeda* entry is a composite, and he thought the shortleafs he was seeing were immature loblollies. See Vines, *Trees of East Texas,* pp. 7-10.

[186]The bald cypress (now *Taxodium distichum* Rich.), the southern representative of the redwoods, is the most characteristic tree in the lowlands of the lower half of the Red River. Attaining a height of 130 feet and living as long as 1,200

below Nachitoches. — [187]

12. *Celtis Occidentalis*[188]

13. Ash *(Fraxinus Americana*[189] & *excelsior)*[190]

14. Sour Gum *(Nyssa Americana)*[191]

15. Elm *(Ulmus Americana).*[192]

16. Sassafras *(Laurus Sassafras)* every where plenty. — [193]

---

years, they are found from Texas to Florida, north to Missouri and to Massachusetts on the coastal plain. Vines, *Trees, Shrubs and Woody Vines*, pp. 8–14. William Bartram, in his *Travels*, wrote of the bald cypress: "The Cupressus disticha stands in the first order of North American trees" (Harper, *Bartram's Travels*, p. 58), but even in Du Pratz's day the Louisiana groves had been "wasted so imprudently," as he put it, that virgin trees already were "somewhat rare" (*History of Louisiana*, p. 217). Interestingly, Thomas Freeman, in 1811, would become the first American to my knowledge to complain of the destruction of these trees on the public domain. Writing to Secretary of the Treasury Albert Gallatin, he reported that illegal cutting was taking place in the virgin cypress swamps along the Mississippi, and that: "When the timber of these swamps is once destroyed, the land not only becomes useless but offensive." Freeman to Gallatin, Washington, Miss. Territory, July 9, 1811. Carter, *The Territory of Mississippi* 5:205–206. The enormous virgin trees are now quite rare in the Red River valley, although occasionally the enduring skeleton of one long dead may be seen towering above the surrounding forest.

[187] This must have been the white cedar (now *Chamaecyparis thyoides* [L.]B.S.P.), a tree which is now extinct on the Red River. Custis's entry here is the only substantial evidence that it once grew along the lower Red. It is found in acidic swamps from eastern Louisiana across to Florida on the coastal plain. Vines, *Trees, Shrubs and Woody Vines*, pp. 8–14.

[188] The common hackberry is what the entry refers to, but this is probably the similar sugarberry (*C. laevigata* Willd.) instead. It replaces the hackberry in the southern forests and is found in alluvial soil along streams or in woodlands from Texas and Florida north to Virginia and Kansas. Vines, *Trees of East Texas*, pp. 123–26.

[189] The white ash, found from Texas to Florida to Nova Scotia and Nebraska. Ibid., pp. 469–73.

[190] The *excelsior* of Europe is not found here; what Custis was seeing was probably the Carolina ash (*F. caroliniana* Mill.), a swampland ash confined to the Southeast, from Texas to Florida and north to Virginia and Missouri. William Bartram made the same mistake. Ibid.; Harper, *Bartram's Travels*, p. 511.

[191] Perhaps the water tupelo (*Nyssa aquatica* [L.]), but more likely the black tupelo (*N. sylvatica* Marsh.). The latter is found from Texas to Florida, north to Maine and Michigan. Vines, *Trees of East Texas*, pp. 428–31.

[192] The American elm, found throughout the United States east of the Rockies.

[193] The common sassafras (*Sassafras albidum* [Nutt.] Nees) is found from Texas to Florida, north to Maine and Ontario. In this range Custis possibly met with

17. Hickory *(Juglans alba)* very abundant. — [194]

18. Maple *(Acer pennsylvanicum*[195] and *Saccharinum). —* [196]

19. Mulberry *(Morus nigra). —* [197]

20. *Sideroxylon mite)*[198]

21. Redbud *(Cercis siliquastrum)*[199]

22. Dogwood *(Cornus florida*[200] & *Sericea)*[201]

23. Papaw *(Anno Glabra)* every where abundant. — [202]

the silky sassafras (*S. a.* var. *molle* Raf.), a new subspecies that Rafinesque added to science. Ibid., pp. 166–68.

[194] The hickories have been re-classified since Custis's time. Harper believes Bartram used "Juglans alba" to refer to the white-heart hickory (*Carya tomentosa* Nutt.); Custis could have been referring to this tree, but my speculation is that he was observing the more common shagbark hickory (*C. ovata* [Mill.] K. Koch). It ranges from Texas east to Florida, and north to Quebec and Nebraska. Ibid., pp. 365–66; Harper, *Bartram's Travels,* p. 544.

[195] The tree he identifies as the mountain maple of the Alleghanies must actually have been either the Florida sugar maple (*A. barbatum* Michx.), or Drummond's red maple (*A. rubrum* var. *drummondii* [Hook & Arn.] Sarg.), the more common species in the Red River country. Its primary range is Texas, Louisiana, Arkansas, and Oklahoma. Vines, *Trees of East Texas,* pp. 358–65.

[196] *Saccharinum* is the silver maple, found from East Texas to Florida and north to New Brunswick and Ontario. Ibid., pp. 365–66.

[197] William Dunbar also made this mistake. The native mulberry is not the Eurasian *nigra,* but instead the red mulberry (*M. rubra* [L.]), endemic to moist, rich soil throughout the eastern timberlands. Ibid., pp. 142–43.

[198] Custis probably follows Bartram in using "Sideroxylon" to refer to the buckthorn family. Several species are possible in this range, the most likely being the woollybucket bumelia (*Bumelia lanuginosa* [Michx.] Pers.), or the Carolina buckthorn (*Rhamnus caroliniana* Walt.). Harper, *Bartram's Travels,* p. 626; Vines, *Trees, Shrubs and Woody Vines,* pp. 701–702, 832–33.

[199] Almost certainly the Eastern redbud (*Cercis canadensis* [L.]), found in moist, low soils from Texas to Florida, and north to Ontario and Nebraska. Vines, *Trees of East Texas,* pp. 273–74.

[200] The common flowering dogwood, found from Texas to Florida, north to Maine and Ontario, and usually on hillsides. Vines, *Trees, Shrubs and Woody Vines,* p. 96.

[201] Barton used *Sericea* to refer to the red willow (*Salix interior* Rowlee), and Custis may be so using it here, since the species occurs widely in the Red River valley. However, Morton believes, and I agree, that the roughleaf dogwood (*C. drummondii* C. A. Meyer), a new species in 1806, is more likely the plant Custis saw. It is found from Texas to Florida, and north to Ontario. Vines, *Trees of East Texas,* pp. 32, 427–28; Morton, "An Overlooked Botanical Publication of Interest," 443.

[202] Two pawpaws are possible here, but rather than the tropical species he identifies, they would have been the common pawpaw (now *Asimina triloba* [L.]

24. Walnut *(Juglans nigra)* becomes more abundant as you ascend the river & is found high up of a very large size. — [203]
25. Chinquepin *(Fagus pumila)* abundant all through the country as high as the 1st little River and probably much higher. — [204]
26. *Hamamelis Virginica).* — [205]
27. *Halesia Tetraptera.* — [206]
28. Lime tree *(Tilia Americana)*[207]
29. Locust *(Robinia Pseudacia)*[208]
30. Red cedar *(Juniperus virginiana)* becomes more abundant as you ascend above the Coashatta village. In many places this is the principal tree found on the borders of the River. — [209]

Dunal), a wide-ranging pawpaw found from East Texas to Florida and north to New York and Nebraska; and the small-flower pawpaw (*A. parviflora* [Michx.] Dunal), which is confined to the southeastern United States south of the Carolinas. Its preference for stream-bank soils makes it a likely choice here. Vines, *Trees of East Texas*, pp. 157–60; Harper, *Bartram's Travels*, p. 440.

[203] The eastern black walnut. Range: Texas to Florida, north to Ontario and Nebraska. It grows to a height of 125 feet. Vines, *Trees of East Texas*, p. 174.

[204] Four chinquapins are found in the region explored by the Freeman and Custis expedition: the common chinquapin (*Castanea alnifolia* Nutt.), East Texas to Florida, north to North Carolina and Arkansas; the Florida chinquapin (*C. a.* var. *floridana* Sarg.), found in the same range; the Allegheny chinquapin (*C. pumilia* [L.] Mill.), from East Texas to Florida, north to New Jersey and Missouri; and the ashe chinquapin (*C. ashei* Sudw.), East Texas and Oklahoma to Florida and Virginia. Ibid., pp. 67–73.

[205] The common witch hazel, found in rich, moist, sandy soil from Texas to Florida, and north to Nova Scotia and Ontario. Ibid., pp. 170–71.

[206] He identifies the "Tetraptera" of Bartram, or the Carolina silver-bell (*Halesia carolina* L.); what he is seeing instead on the lower Red River is the two-wing silverbell (*H. diptera* Ellis), found along swamplands and in the understory of forest here. The species is found south of 34° N., from Texas to Florida. Ibid., pp. 448–51; Harper, *Bartram's Travels*, p. 523.

[207] See Part 1, note 52; Part 2, note 42.

[208] In the Accounts, Custis says he noticed this tree "only on Bayou Badtka" (Part 2). Since the black locust does not range this far south, I am convinced that Custis instead became the first botanist to discover the rare Texas honey locust (*X Gleditsia triacanthos* var. *texana* Sarg.), a natural hybrid species. Vines says that a group of these trees has been found along the Red River near Shreveport, although they are primarily Texas trees. Vines, *Trees of East Texas*, pp. 283–85.

[209] The reference is to the eastern red cedar, a ubiquitous species whose range covers almost all of eastern North America. But in the region near the head of the Raft the party must have encountered specimens of the southern red cedar

31. *Magnolia Tripetala.* —[210]
32. Toothache tree *(Zanthoxylon Clava Herculis,*[211] & *fraxinifolia* of Marshall).* —[212]
33. Beech *(Fagus Sylvatica)*[213]
34. Holly *(Ilex Aquifolium)*[214]
35. Wild cherry *(Prunus Virginiana)*[215]

(*J. silicicola* [Small] Bailey) as well. A relict of these trees has been discovered on the Red, in northwestern Louisiana. It was still undescribed in 1806, although Bartram had probably encountered the tree. Ibid., pp. 12-15; Harper, *Bartram's Travels*, p. 545. One particular stretch of the river, the section between the Medicine Mount village and the Great Bend, was known as "the Cedars." According to the Sibley-Grappe account, here: ". . . the cedar begins on both sides, and is the principal growth on the wide, rich river bottom for 40 miles; in all the world there is scarcely to be found a more beautiful growth of cedar timber; they . . . are large, lofty and straight." Sibley, "Historical Sketches," p. 66. Floating through this stretch in 1977, we did not see a single mature tree (one of 50 to 60 feet, although the Red River cedars may have gone up to 70 feet in pure stands), and the species itself has largely been succeeded by cottonwoods. Flores, "A Final Journey Down the Wild Red," entry for May 24, 1977. For the account of an early nineteenth century observer, see Part 4, note 7.

[210] The umbrella magnolia, found both in swamps and on wooded hillsides from southwestern Arkansas to Georgia and north to Pennsylvania and Missouri. *Vines, Trees, Shrubs and Woody Vines*, pp. 282-83. He must have seen it near the termination of the exploration.

[211] The Hercules'-club, found from Texas to Florida and north to North Carolina. *Vines, Trees of East Texas*, pp. 312-14.

[212] The *fraxinifolia* of Humphrey Marshall is today's *Z. americanum* Mill., out of range here. He must have seen the Texas Hercules'-club (*Z. hirsutum* Buckl.), a new tree in 1806. It is primarily a central Texas plant, but stands have been discovered in southwestern Arkansas. Ibid.

[213] The American beech (and in this range the southern variety known among botanists as the Carolina beech, *Fagus grandifolia* var. *caroliniana* Fern & Rehd.) rather than the European *Fagus sylvatica* of Linnaeus. The beech is found from East Texas to Florida, north to Nova Scotia and Wisconsin. Harper, *Bartram's Travels*, p. 501; *Vines, Trees, Shrubs and Woody Vines*, pp. 198-99.

[214] Custis could have seen any number of different members of the holly family (Aquifoliaceae) in the lower Red River valley. Most likely would have been the yaupon holly (*Ilex vomitoria* Ait.), found in low, moist woods from Texas to Florida and north to Virginia; and the American holly (*I. opaca* Ait.), a more widespread holly found from the Texas-Oklahoma region to Florida and northward to Massachusetts and Illinois. *Vines, Trees of East Texas*, pp. 337-40.

[215] The common choke cherry is found on the middle Red, but rarely; this perhaps was instead the black cherry (*P. serotina* Ehrh.), found over most of eastern North America, and commonly in the Red River valley. Ibid., pp. 229-32.

A List of Trees & Shrubs growing on R River

1. Cotton tree a species of Populus growing on the borders of the River as high as the Spanish Camp. —

2. Pecan (Juglans petiolata) abundant as high as Nachitoches after which it is very rare for 500 miles and is said to be plenty again. —

3. Plane tree (Platanus Occidentalis) plenty on the borders of the River as high as the Spanish Camp. —

4. Hag berry (Prunus padus) plenty. —

5. Persimmon (Dyospyros Virginiana) every where plenty. —

6. Honey Locusts (Gleditsia triacanthos and monosperma) very abundant —

7. Oaks (Quercus rubra, alba, phellos, Nigra and esculus. —

8. Box elder (C-207(3)s) : —

A page from the manuscript report submitted by Custis on October 1, 1806. Original in the National Archives.

36. *Prunus Lauro-cerasus.* — [216]

37. A tree growing on the banks of the Bayaux between the Coashatta Village and Nachitoches and is probably new. — It resembles in its size & manner of putting forth its leaves the *Bignonia Catalpa.* — The leaves are very large & three lobed, lobes intire, acute. — Until more is known of it we will call it *Bignonia Triloba.* — [217]

38. *Cephalanthus Occidentalis.* — [218]

39. *Viburnum Prunifolium.* — [219]

40. *Cratagus aria.* — [220]

41. Spice wood *(Laurus Benzoin)* very abundant. — [221]

[216] Rather than *Prunus laurocerasus* of Linnaeus, Custis must have seen specimens of the half-dozen plum varieties endemic to the lower Red River valley. The bad-tasting plum found near the Upper Kadohadacho village (see Part 4) was probably the Oklahoma, or sour plum (*Prunus gracilis* Engelm. & Gray). It is common to dry, sandy soils in the area covered by the expedition, and would have been a new species. Likely possibilities for other types of Red River plums are the wildgoose plum (*P. munsoniana* Wight & Hedr.); the Mexican plum (*P. mexicanus* Wats.), both of which were new, and the flatwoods plum (*P. umbellata* Ell.) and the Chickasaw plum (*P. augustifolia* Marsh.). The latter, in particular, may have been found in the vicinity of the Indian villages, for it is a southwestern plum believed to have been widely introduced into the woodlands by the Caddos and other tribes. Ibid., pp. 233–41.

[217] This undoubtedly was the southern catalpa (*Catalpa bignoniodes* Walt.), native from Louisiana eastward to Florida and Georgia. It is indeed a different species from the northern *speciosa*, but Custis's tree seems to have been merely an individual with lobed leaves, something known to occur, albeit rarely, in this species, according to Correll and Johnston, *Vascular Plants of Texas*, p. 1445. Custis's binomial, *Bignonia triloba* Custis, ought now to go into synonymy.

[218] The common button-bush, an extremely widespread plant found throughout North America and in Eastern Asia. Vines, *Trees of East Texas*, pp. 491–92.

[219] He names the blackhaw viburnum, which is found along streams across the middle Red to Florida, but its principal range is farther north. Perhaps this was instead the commoner rusty blackhaw viburnum (*V. rufidulum* Raf.), a tree now credited to Custis's competitor for the naturalist post, Rafinesque. Ibid., pp. 497–99.

[220] *Crataegus aria* is a synonym for *Pyrus aria*, but that plant is not found in this range. Probably what Custis saw was the red chokeberry (*P. arbutifolia* [L.] L. F.), endemic to swamps and wet pine barrens from East Texas to Florida and north to Nova Scotia and Michigan. Correll and Johnston, *Vascular Plants of Texas*, p. 114.

[221] The common spice-bush (*Lindera benzoin* [L.] Blume), found in low woods and swamps from Central Texas to Florida, and north to Maine and Ontario.

42. Candleberry *(Myrica cerifera)* in great abundance all through the Country as high as the 1st little River & probably much higher. — [222]

43. *Prinos Verticillatus.* — [223]

44. Bois d'arc, of this tree you have already had a description. — It is probably a new Genus; but not having seen it while in blossom I am unable to say whether it be new or not. — It is said first to make its appearance about the 2nd little River and is very abundant on a creek called Bois d'arc. The tree which I saw was one growing within a mile of Nachitoches & was probably transplanted. — This is about 30 ft. high; its trunk 7 or 8 ft. in circumference & about 6 or 7 ft to where it begins to ramify. — Its general aspect is that of an apple tree. — Its fruit is about the size of the large sour Oranges and of a greenish yellow. — The fruit I have preserved in whiskey in order to forward. — You will also receive some of the branches & leaves. — [224]

The hairy common spice-bush (*L. b.* var. *pubescens* [Palmer & Steyermark] Rehder) and the southern spice-bush (*L. melissaefolia* [Walt.] Blume) are also possibilities in this range. Ibid., pp. 293–95.

[222] The southern wax myrtle, found in sandy swamps or low prairies from East Texas to Florida, north to New Jersey. The species is found in the Red River valley at least 100 miles beyond the exploration's deepest penetration into the Southwest. Vines, *Trees of East Texas*, pp. 37–38.

[223] Custis follows Bartram in using "Prinos" to designate certain types of hollies. This entry probably refers to the common winterberry holly (*Ilex verticillata* [L.] Gray), a popular, red-fruited deciduous holly found in swamps and wet woods from southeastern Louisiana to Florida, north to Connecticut and Minnesota. Harper, *Bartram's Travels*, p. 600; Vines, *Trees, Shrubs and Woody Vines*, pp. 655–56.

[224] Bois d'arc is French for bow-wood, the tree being thus designated by the early Europeans because the Caddos and Osages made from it a superior hunting bow that was highly valued as a trade item. The genus was indeed a new one, but Custis's use of the sexual system of classification and his belief that George Hunter had already described the tree in his Ouachita River journal caused him to lose credit for the discovery, even though his is the first published account of it. Instead, the bois d'arc (*Maclura pomifera* [Raf.] Schneid.) was added to science by Rafinesque. The reputation of this tree had preceded its scientific description. Under various names (principally "Osage Apple"), the bois d'arc

A List Of Vegetables

Digitalis flava in flower the 11th of July above the Coashatta village.[225]

Ipomaea solanifolia in flower the 15th of July.[226]

Jussieua erecta in flower the 17th of July on the Banks of the River. — [227]

Portulacca oleracea abundant on all the sand beaches. — [228]

had excited the interest of Americans as early as 1804. Sibley had provided Jefferson with a detailed description of it in one of their first exchanges, and Meriwether Lewis sent back a notice of it from St. Louis. Hunter had described the tree in some detail in his journal (which Custis obviously examined), but the short botanical list from the Dunbar and Hunter expedition was not published, either in the official report or in the newspapers. Had Custis offered a name here, he would be the discoverer of this exotic tree. Since the tree he saw was out of flower, however, he could not.

The original range of the bois d'arc has never been definitely fixed. The fact that Custis describes a cultivated rather than a wild tree argues for confining its natural range to the Blackland Prairies and Cross Timbers country, between (roughly) the 30th and 35th parallels, and centering on Bois d'Arc Creek of north central Texas. Scattered trees found farther east, in the vicinity of the Caddo settlements, quite possibly were transplanted by the Indians.

[225] Instead of the foxglove, which is out of range here, probably the false foxglove (*Aureolaria grandiflora* [Benth.] Penn.), reported in the sandy, oak woods of the Three States area. If so, this was a new genus, later credited to Rafinesque. The plant entered here *could* have been, however, *A. flava* (L.) Farw., found from Texas to Florida and north to Maine and Ontario. Correll and Johnston, *Vascular Plants of Texas*, p. 1430.

[226] Badly misstated and unidentifiable in King's published version, this was a morning glory, probably the wild potato *I. pandurata* (L.) Mey., found in thickets from East Texas across the southeastern United States. Ibid., 1253; Rickett, 2:430.

[227] Probably *Jussiaea* instead, and in that case a species of primrose willow (*Ludwigia leptocarpa* [Nutt.] Hara.) that was new. This is a tropical species, found from South America as far north as North Carolina and Missouri. Ibid., p. 1134; Rickett, 2:311–12.

[228] Rather than the European purslane, Custis must have seen either *P. umbraticola* H.B.K., or *P. parvula* Gray, both new and both found in gravelly, sandy soils and on clay banks from Arkansas and Oklahoma westward. The party was at this point travelling through present southwestern Arkansas. Ibid., p. 608.

Hibiscus hirtus[229] ⎫ In flower on the 19th of
Typha angustifolia[230] ⎬ July. These covered a Prairie near
Polygonum pennsylvanicum[231] ⎭ the old Caddo village. —
Helianthus multiflorus above the 2nd little River, in flower on the
24th of July. — [232]
Origanum Vulgare in flower on the 24th. — [233]
Datisca hirta at the old Caddo village[234]
A species of *Hibiscus* found above the 2nd little River and is
probably new. Its stem is erect, smooth, leaves obliquely egg-
lanced, saw'd; flowers axillary, peduncles as if jointed, larger

---

[229] Evidently the woolly rose mallow (*H. lasiocarpos* Cav.), found from Texas
to Georgia, and along streams and rivers in the Mississippi Basin to Indiana and
Illinois. Ibid., pp. 1031–32. The prairies covered with this plant and the two
following were located in present Lafayette County, Arkansas, about 6 miles
northeast of Garland City.

[230] Reference is to the narrow-leaved cattail, found in shallow water and along
streams from Texas to Florida, north to Nova Scotia and Nebraska. Ibid., p. 85.

[231] The prairies on which the former Lower Kadohadacho village stood were
also covered in pinkweed, a tall (4-foot high) smartweed found in moist prairies
from Texas to Florida, north to Quebec and South Dakota. Rickett, 2:142. With
these three plants, Custis has established for us an interesting seral stage in the
takeover of an Indian "old field" by wild plants. Custis does not mention peach
trees (*Prunus persica* L.) in the vicinity of these village sites, but the Caddos did
cultivate this exotic; Anthony Glass saw "many peach trees" near an old Indian
site in Caddo Prairie. Glass, "Copy of a Journal of a Voyage from Nackitosh
into the interior of Louisiana," entry for July 17, 1808.

[232] *Decapetalus* and *stromosus* are synonyms with *multiflorus*, but the plant does
not appear under any of these names in this range. The large number of choices
makes it impossible to determine which species of sunflower this is.

[233] The entry refers to the wild marjoram, a European herb brought to the
northeastern United States which escaped to grow wild. Rickett says it "has been
reported as far south as North Carolina." Custis's observation, of course, is on
the Arkansas-Texas border. It is intriguing that this plant, much used as a medicinal tea by Europeans, was observed the day before the party examined the site
of the abandoned Upper Kadohadacho village, a scene of much previous European activity. Ibid., 1:374, 2:479.

[234] A somewhat confusing entry, but one cleared up by Freeman's Account
passage for this day. Custis is mistakenly assigning this plant to the *Dastica* genus,
whose only American species are found in the Californian and Mexican deserts.
What he was seeing here was undoubtedly the Indian hemp (*Apocynum cannibinum* [L.]). The herbs of the Datiscaceae family do have many of the habits of
Cannabis. The Indian hemp is often found on riverbanks throughout the United
States and Canada, and it was used by tribal people to make cordage and fishing
nets, as a chewing gum, and as a heart stimulant. Ibid., 2:398; Willis, *A Dic-*

above the apparent joint; exterior calyx from 12 to 15 awl'd rays. In flower on the 26th of July. — [235]

Clitoria ternatea in flower 2nd of August[236]

Polygala vulgaris. — [237]

Lobelia cardinalis[238] } In flower the 8th

——— *syphililica*[239] } of August —

Agave virginica in flower the 9th of August.[240]

Sagittaria sagittifolia abundant on all the Bayoux[241]

Elephantopus scaber in flower all August, every where abundant. — [242]

---

tionary of the Flowering Plants and Ferns, p. 341; Usher, *A Dictionary of plants used by man*, p. 52; Henry Burlage, *Index of Plants of Texas*, p. 8.

[235] Dr. Paul Fryxell, Research Geneticist at Texas A&M University, and a Malvaceae specialist, has examined this entry and from Custis's description believes the plant in question could only have been *H. laevis* Allioni (already published before 1806 as *H. militaris* [L.]), but wonders why Custis was not familiar with it. It is a fairly common, if localized, hibiscus, preferring the locale of streams and swamps in eastern North America. Paul Fryxell to the editor, College Station, Feb. 9, 1981, in the editor's possession; Correll and Johnston, *Vascular Plants of Texas*, pp. 1031-32.

[236] The entry refers to a cultivated tropical plant of the Old World; probably Custis is seeing the native *C. mariana* (L.), or pigeon wings, found from Arizona to Florida, to New York and Iowa. Rickett, 3:243.

[237] A species of milkwort, most likely *P. incarnata* (L.), found from Mexico to Florida, north to Ontario and Michigan. Ibid., 2:529.

[238] The cardinal flower, found in wet woods or along streams from Texas to Florida, north to Quebec and Minnesota. Most botanists now place this genus with *Campanula* in the bluebell family. Ibid., 2:524.

[239] See note 165. A strikingly beautiful plant, the great blue lobelia is a denizen of streambanks from Texas to Alabama, Maine and Manitoba. Ibid. Its major use in Indian *materia medica* was for the treatment of syphilis—hence the Latin name. In a survey of North Louisiana plants done in 1892 by Thomas W. Vaughan (see "Botanical Notes," in Lerch, *A Preliminary Report upon the Hills of Louisiana*, 151-58), the cardinal flower is included in the list of medicinal herbs, but the great blue lobelia is not. Since Custis is back at the Alabama-Coushatta village at this point, it is possible that this plant was an Indian cultivar.

[240] The false aloe, *Polianthes virginica* (L.) Shinners found on dry slopes and in woods from Texas to Florida, north to Virginia and Missouri. Rickett, 2:66.

[241] Instead, the American arrowhead, *S. calycina* Engelm., a new species found from California to Alabama, north to Ohio and South Dakota. Ibid., 2:54-58.

[242] Custis is seeing one or more of these American members of the genus *Elephantopus*: *E. carolinianus* Raeusch., found from Texas to Florida, north to New Jersey and Missouri; *E. tomentosus* (L.), the devil's-grandmother, ranging from Texas to Florida, to Maryland and Kentucky; and a new species, *E. nudatus* Gray, the elephant's-foot, restricted to a range from Louisiana to Florida,

Bignonia sempervirens. —[243]

——— *Unguis.* —[244]

Cassia chamaechrista which I mentioned in my last communications as being very abundant, is found to overspread the whole country as far as we ascended. — It continues in blossom from the 5th of June until Sept.[245]

Cassia occidentalis[246] } In flower the 25th
——— *marylandica*[247] } of August. these are
found in the greatest abundance about Nachitoches. —

Cassia Tora is also met with. This plant infests the whole country about Fort Adams and Natchez.[248]

Prenanthes alba in flower 28th of August[249]

Chenopodium anthelminticum plenty about Nachitoches. —[250]

---

north to Delaware and Arkansas. Rickett, 2:634, 3:502; Correll and Johnston, *Vascular Plants of Texas*, p. 1538

[243] If he saw this plant in the same habitat as the *Elephantopus*, it was probably *Gelsemium rankinii* Small, a new species of yellow jasmine that prefers swampy, waterlogged soils from Louisiana to Florida, north to North Carolina. Rickett, 2:338.

[244] Evidently the cross vine, *B. capreolata* (L.), a semi-evergreen creeper found in rich, moist woods from East Texas to Florida, north to New Jersey and Illinois. Vines, *Trees, Shrubs and Woody Vines*, p. 924.

[245] John Dennis, in his "An Account of a Plant called the Magathy-Bay Bean," describes *C. chamaechrista* as a plant which "overshadows the land, suffocating and excluding all other weeds and grass." The fact that Custis's related plant seems to have been the principal undergrowth of the country along the middle Red is a further consequence of the fire ecology of the natural forest; almost all the *Cassia* species are primary-stage colonizers on burned lands.

[246] The coffee senna, a tropical invader found in pinelands from Texas to Florida, north to Virginia and Kansas. Rickett, 2:320, 3:207.

[247] See note 149.

[248] A tropical species invading the southern United States, this was actually *C. obtusifolia* L., found in moist woods from Texas to Florida, north to Pennsylvania and Kansas. Ibid., 2:320.

[249] A rattlesnake root. This could have been *P. altissima* (L.) in this range, but it is rare, even in the rich, moist beech woodlands from Texas to Georgia, north to Quebec and Manitoba that it prefers. More likely this was the new type *P. serpentaria* Pursh var. *barbata* (Torr. & Gray), restricted to sandy forests of the southeastern United States. Correll and Johnston, *Vascular Plants of Texas*, p. 1734.

[250] A species of goosefoot weed known as Mexican tea. It is a weedy and medicinal herb found in waste places and salt marshes throughout most of the

Solidago altissima in flower 1st of Sept. — [251]

Tillandsia usncaoides seen as high as 50 miles above the 1st little River — [252]

Borassus flabelliformis plenty. — [253]

The description of a plant found on a sand beach below the second little River. —

Class *Didynamia*. Order *Angiosperma*

Calyx. Perianth double: the exterior, two leaved; leaflets lance-awl'd nearly the length of the tube of the corol: the interior one-leav'd 5 parted, divisions subequal, the length of exterior perianth. —

Corol. One-petall'd, grinning. Tube rather longer than calyx, contracted above the germ; Border two-lip'd: upper lip two cleft, obtusish, reflected; under lip three cleft, more deeply divided; more acute, with a groove in the middle of each division as if they had been doubled lengthwise, reflected. —

United States. Ibid., p. 533. Its abundance in an area of known Indian antiquity, such as Natchitoches, again causes one to wonder whether its growth might not have been promoted by the Indians.

[251] A species of goldenrod found from Arizona to Florida, north to Quebec and North Dakota. Rickett, 3:80.

[252] Spanish moss (correctly *usneoides*) is infrequently seen this far north today. Bartram says it was found up to 35°N. in his *Travels* (p. 56 of the Harper edition), but Dunbar related that on the Ouachita no more long moss was seen above 32°52' latitude. Dunbar, "Journal Of A Voyage," entry for Nov. 17, 1804, in Rowland, *Dunbar Letters*, p. 243. It is found as high as 33°, on a western tributary of the Red, the Black Bayou, but not in well-developed clumps. Custis could have mistaken one of the lichens, perhaps *Usnea plicata* (L.) Wigg. or *U. barbata* (L.) Wigg. for Spanish moss, but I doubt it. I think his record of its occurrence this far north points rather to a greater number of swamps, and more humid conditions, in 1806. See Bruce Fink, *The Lichen Flora of the United States*, pp. 349-50.

[253] The palmyra palm is what the entry refers to, but this is a different species in this range. Since he says it is "in plenty," he is probably observing the dwarf palm (*Sabal minor* [Jacq.] Pers.), which is abundant in the river bottoms of southern Louisiana, and is found from Texas to North Carolina. There is a possibility that he could have seen the Louisiana palm (*S. louisiana* [Darby] Bomhard), however, which is restricted to southern Louisiana and southeastern Texas. Both were new species when Custis made this entry. I lean toward the former. Vines, *Trees, Shrubs and Woody Vines*, pp. 46-48.

Stam. Fil. four; awl'd, of which the two inferior are longer, shorter than the style, inserted into the bottom of the tube. Anthers roundish, pendulous. —

Pist. — Germ oblong. Style thread form extended along the upper part of the corol to the division of the upper lip. Stigma cleft, forming when expanded a flat orbicular surface, with a small oblong incision in the middle

Per. — Capsule oblong, two valv'd Seeds. Very numerous, small. — Its stem is erect, shooting up about 7 inches above the ground, entirely beset with flowers; furnished with Bractes; destitute of leaves. — This plant is most probably a new Genus, if so & there is not already a Bartonia I beg leave to call it *Bartonia Bracteata.* — There were two of these growing near each other and the only ones of the kind I have ever seen. — [254]

Minerals. —

You will receive 4 small boxes containing the following specimens. —

Coal taken from a high bluff below the mouth of 1st little River.

---

[254] Ironically, Custis's final botanical entry—and the one he obviously considered his prize discovery, since he named it after his mentor—is one of two Great Plains plants he catalogued. Morton has carefully identified it, "from the good and complete description of Custis," as a species of broom-rape "discovered" by Nuttall in 1818, and named by him *Orobanche ludoviciana* Nutt. Custis was in error about the genus. Linnaeus had already named it, so *Bartonia* Custis can be taken as merely a synonym of *Orobanche* L. Custis is clearly the discoverer of this species, which is a denizen of river sandbars and dunes on the Great Plains, but his *bracteata* cannot replace Nuttall's name because in 1830 *bracteata* was given to a European *Orobanche.* Morton, "An Overlooked Publication Of Botanical Interest," 458–59.

Actually, the genus name, *Bartonia*, had already been appropriated by 1806, by Muhlenberg, five years earlier. However, Custis can be forgiven for overlooking that, since even Barton seems to have been unaware of it. Barton must have recognized that Custis's plant was an *Orobanche*, for just before Barton's death in 1815 there occurred a subsequently famous dispute between his major protégés, Nuttall and Pursh, over which one should have the honor of applying *Bartonia* to a new genus. Pursh won, and we now have two *Bartonias*. The dispute (with, however, no mention of Custis's effort) is discussed in Pennell, "Benjamin Smith Barton as Naturalist," 120–22.

—Here we find a stratum of coal 18 inches through, running horizontally into the bank, 70 ft. below the surface. This stratum extends for more than two hundred yards along the bluff.—

Allum taken from the same bluff.—This is found intermixed with the clay & incrusted over the whole side of the bluff.—

Bituminous shale interspersed with small particles of mica taken from a bluff about 8 miles above the Coashatta village & was almost entirely composed of this shale.

Lime stone taken from the bank of Red River below the 2nd little River. It is probably a Gypsum.—

Petrifactions taken from same place.—

Oyster shells from the sand beaches.

Pipe clay from the bed of the River opposite the old Caddo Village

A List of Animals.—

Birds

Ardea Americana. Very abundant.—[255]
———— *Caerulea.*—[256]
Plotus Anhinga.—[257]

---

[255] A very exciting entry, for the source whence he derives the binomial, Linnaeus' *Systema Naturae Per Regna Tria Naturae,* ed. by J. F. Gmelin, 2:621, is quite clear that this is the "Hooping Crane." The whooper (now *Grus americana* [L.]) was not likely to have been confused with any kind of heron or egret. Custis's note that they were "very abundant" raises the question whether there was possibly a breeding population in the natural prairies along the middle Red. The bird's summer range is known to have once extended to the Texarkana area. There were never many whooping cranes—their total population between 1700 and 1860 probably did not go over 1,400 individuals. Lowery, pp. 256–58; Oberholser, 1:286–87.

[256] The little blue heron (now *Florida caerulea caerulea* [L.]). Lowery, pp. 140–41; Oberholser, 1:110.

[257] The American anhinga *(Anhinga anhinga colubrina* Bartram), more commonly known as the "snake-bird," or "water turkey," is a strange and rather striking swampland bird whose Pleistocene-like appearance excited the interest of early observers. It is a common nester in the swamp lakes of northern Louisiana. Brewer, *Wilson's American Ornithology,* pp. 644–48; Lowery, pp. 135–36; Harper, *Bartram's Travels,* p. 629.

Tantalus Loculator. — [258]

Corvus Corax. I am told there is on the Ouachitta a variety perfectly white. — [259]

Hirundo Rivaria. — [260]

Scolopax flavipes. — [261]

Falco Peregrinus first seen on the 24th of July. — [262]

[258] The *Tantalus loculator* of Linnaeus was known in Custis's day as the wood ibis. It has since been reclassified *Mycteria americana* (L.), since it is a true stork and not an ibis. William Bartram described it as a bird of "the banks of great rivers" and inundated meadows, where it fed on "serpents, young alligators, frogs, and other reptiles." Harper, *Bartram's Travels,* pp. 95, 642; Brewer, *Wilson's American Ornithology,* pp. 561-62; Lowery, p. 154.

[259] Apparently the common raven, and in the case of the white variety, perhaps the white-necked raven (*Corvus cryptoleucus* Couch), which has white bases to its breast and neck feathers. The white variety seems not to have been actually observed; if it was the white-necked raven it would have been a new species. Both of these ravens are slightly out of range on the middle and lower Red according to modern distribution-sightings maps; this entry ought to cause some re-interpretation of raven ranges in the early-day Southwest. Oberholser, 2:593-99.

[260] Custis's use of "Hirundo Rivaria" may point to the bank swallow (*Riparia riparia riparia* [L.]), and here he would be following both Bartram and Jefferson (although his mentor, Barton, insisted that the "Little Bank Martin" was not truly the *Hirundo riparia* of Linnaeus). The bank swallow would only have been a migrant on the Red during the last six weeks of the expedition. Custis must have seen, and with this entry is more likely referring to, the rather similar rough-winged swallow (*Stelgidopteryx ruficollis* Audubon), which is still today a common nester in the high banks of the Red River. This was a new species, not described until Audubon's collections in Louisiana. Harper, *Bartram's Travels,* p. 527; Jefferson, *Notes,* p. 70; Barton, *Fragments,* p. 17; Oberholser, 2:572-83; Lowery, pp. 440-48; Dan Flores, "A Final Journey down the Wild Red," entry for May 25, 1977.

[261] Probably the lesser yellowlegs sandpiper (*Totanus flavipes* Gmelin), a shorebird of the family Scolopacidae. Jefferson mentions it in *Notes,* p. 70, as the "Yellowlegged Snipe." It is a migrant sandpiper of the Western Hemisphere, found on wet, short-grass prairies, sandbars, and riverbanks throughout the year in the Southwest. Brewer, *Wilson's American Ornithology,* pp. 725-27; Oberholser, p. 343; Lowery, pp. 293-94, calls it *Tringa flavipes.*

[262] Custis does the first scientific natural history work in the present state of Texas, and this bird, "first seen" on July 24 (when the party was just north of today's Texarkana, on the border of Bowie County) evidently deserves priority in this category. Unfortunately, pesticide accumulation in waterfowl has made the peregrine an endangered species. It is rarely, or never, found on the middle Red today. Lowery, pp. 243-44.

Eastern wild turkey (Meleagris gallopavo), *painted by Titian Ramsey Peale, Courtesy Library of Congress.*

Exploring the edge of the Post-Oak Savannah, Custis's "Lepus Timidus *of a very large size" was evidently the black-tailed jackrabbit* (Lepus californicus melanotis).

Sterna minuta. — [263]
Trochilus (2 species)[264]
Turkeys *(Malaegris Gallipavo)* are in the greatest abundance high

[263] Most likely the interior least tern (*Sternula albifrons anthalassa* Burleigh & Lowery), a new subspecies that nests on inland river sandbars. Brewer, *Wilson's American Ornithology*, pp. 511–12; Oberholser, 1:400–402; Lowery, pp. 346–47.

[264] The ruby-throated hummingbird (*Archilochus colubris* [L.]) is one obvious candidate. The rufous hummingbird (*Selasphorus rufus* Gmelin) is the other likely species, though the broad-tailed hummingbird (*Platurornis platycercus* Swainson) is a possibility. Oberholser, 1:479–98; Lowery, pp. 399–404.

up the River.—[265]
Swans, Geese and many species of Ducks are said to abound in the
Lakes about Nachitoches during the winter season.—[266]

Quadrupeds.—

Foxes *(Canis Lycaon*[267] *and vulpes)*[268]
Tyger *(Felis concolor)*[269]

[265] Custis's note on food preferences of the wild turkey (p. 278) may be a
response to Barton's statement in "Miscellaneous Facts and Observations,"
Philadelphia Medical and Physical Journal 2 (1806):163, that wild turkeys fed exclusively upon shell-fish, serpents, and vegetables, a fact which was "generally not
known to naturalists." Shelford, in his *The Ecology of North America*, p. 59, estimates that there were from fifty to two hundred wild turkeys per 10 square miles
in the pre-settlement Eastern Forest. Although Custis found them "in the greatest
abundance" along the Red in 1806, the species was totally extirpated here in the
nineteenth century. I have identified these birds according to species earlier;
clearly the party did not penetrate to the range of the dryland, Rio Grande turkey
(*Meleagris gallopavo intermedia* Sennett).

[266] Also present from October to April would have been the enormous flocks of
passenger pigeons (*Ectopistes migratorius* [L.]) that wintered in this country, con-
spicuously absent here.

[267] A slip of the memory, for *Canis lupus lycaon* Schreber refers to the eastern
gray wolf, and not the gray fox (evidently intended), which is *Urocyon cinereoargenteus cinereoargenteus* (Schreber), the species found north of 33°, and over much of
the eastern United States. Hall and Kelson, 2:860–62. One other intriguing possibility exists: Custis may have seen coyotes in the prairies here. Two years earlier,
William Clark had shot a specimen of what members of the Lewis and Clark
party had been calling "foxes," only to decide after examining it that this really was
some kind of "prairie wolff" that in size was about like "a gray fox." "What has
been taken heretofore for the Fox was those wolves," Clark wrote, "and no Foxes
has been seen." In Cutright, *Lewis and Clark: Pioneering Naturalists*, p. 85. If these
were coyotes they were members of the subspecies *Canis latrans frustror* Woodhouse, named in 1851. Hall and Kelson (pp. 843–45) define its original range as
extending into the region covered on the last leg of the exploration.

[268] The red fox (now *Vulpes fulva fulva* [Desmarest]), and in this region the
species of the eastern United States. Ibid., pp. 855–56. It is worth noting that
Vulpes fulva is here a migrant from farther east; in fact, the red fox probably was
introduced into America by English colonists.

[269] The cougar, in all probability *Felis concolor coryi* Bangs, although beyond
the Great Bend the subspecies would have been *F. c. stanleyana* Goldman.
Both were new types. Custis clearly intends cougars here rather than jaguars,
which in the nineteenth century did range into East Texas as far north as 32°
latitude. However, most American naturalists of the period routinely employed

Buffaloes, (*Bos Americana*) are first met with about the second little River and become more numerous as you ascend the Red River. I am told by Hunters, that in the large plains about the Panis Villages many thousands may be seen at a view.— Some say they have seen Ten thousand at a sight; this is most probably an exaggeration.—The Indians pursue them on horses and kill them with Bows & arrows and Spears.—[70]

Lepus Timidus of a very large size.—[271]

"Tyger" ro refer to the cougar (see Harper, *Bartram's Travels*, pp. 5, 646), and Nuttall mentions in 1819 that "panthers" were numerous in the woods along the middle Red. Nuttall, *A Journal of Travels into the Arkansas Territory*, p. 168; Hall and Kelson 2:952–57; Lowery, *The Mammals of Louisiana*, pp. 452–53.

[270] If, as some ecologists have argued, the widespread extinction of large American grazers during the late Pleistocene created an "unnatural" vacancy on the plains, then the enomous numbers of the American bison (*Bison bison bison* [L.]) may be understood, as well as the rapid proliferation of the mustang. Ecologically, the Great Plains region was capable of supporting 20 to 25 million bison in conjunction with its other grazing species.

As elsewhere in the woodlands, some bison seem to have been found throughout the Red River valley when the first Europeans visited the river. Certainly they were sufficiently numerous to modify the southeastern woodland culture of the resident Caddos towards prairie bison hunting traits. By 1806, however, the large herds really began at the advent of the Blackland Prairie. Increasing human pressure had combined with the inundations of the lower prairie by the advancing Great Raft to steadily force the bison range farther upriver. Lowery follows a source in *Mammals of Louisiana* (p. 504) which indicates that bison no longer ranged into the present state of Louisiana after about 1803. Travelling overland two summers later, in the same region where the Red River party was stopped, Anthony Glass began encountering bison herds and bands of wild mustangs at the eastern edge of the Blackland Prairie, south of present Bogota, Texas, around 95° W. (about the same longitude as Pecan Point, a major bison crossing on the Red during these years). By the time Glass had reached the Grand Prairie, near the Taovaya-Wichita villages, he was recording in his journal that "Some of them [bison] seen in every direction. Saw droves of Buffalo." Glass, entry for August 9, 1808, in Flores, *Journal of an Indian Trader*, 45, 45n.34.

[271] Custis does not appear to have procured a specimen of this animal for descriptive purposes, but since he saw it on the final leg of the exploration it must be assumed that this was the black-tailed jackrabbit (*Lepus californicus melanotis* Mearns). The range of this hare begins around the great bend; probably they were much more numerous, in the original, regularly-burned Post Oak Savannah than they are there today. Glass offers another clue as to the rapid ecological change in the region where Freeman and Custis were stopped. In 1808 he encountered colonies of prairie dogs less than 60 miles west of Spanish Bluff. Glass,

American bison (Bison bison bison) *and elk* (Cervus elaphas merriami) *painted by George Catlin in the Red River Valley, 1834. Courtesy National Museum of American Art, Smithsonian Institution.*

Mus Ludovicianus. — Tail length of the body, ears large; fore feet 4 toed, hind 5; body reddish ash; belly white; eyes large, black; whiskers 5-rowed; size of *Mus Musculus.* Burrows in hollow trees. — [272]

"Copy of a Journal of a Voyage from Nackitosh into the interior of Louisiana," entry for July 31, 1808.

If this entry does refer to the black-tailed jackrabbit, Custis had seen a new species, not catalogued until 1837. In fact, the same situation exists if this, instead, refers to the swamp rabbit (*Sylvilagus aquaticus aquaticus* [Bachman]), although it seems that he would have noted this large rabbit in one of the earlier Reports. Hall and Kelson, 1:268–69, 281–84; Lowery, pp. 163–67.

[272] One of the few new scientific names he offered, *Mus ludovicianus* Custis has not been picked up by mammalogists because of the obscurity of the published Account. The name and description do designate a previously undiscovered mouse within a genus not set up until 1841. Lacking a specimen, however, it is

273

I am told there is a flying squirrel perfectly black.[273]

White wolves (I suppose the *Canis Mexicanus)* are said to be very numerous—They are perfectly white, except the feet and half of the legs. They are seen in large herds. —[274]

Castor Fiber[275]	Abundant on the tributary
Mustela Lutra[276]	streams of Red River. —

---

not now possible to identify the precise mouse Custis captured, using his description alone. An examination of the mouse collection in the Texas Tech Museum's Laboratory of Zoology indicates that Custis's description could apply to any of three mice of the middle Red: *Peromyscus leucopus leucopus* (Raf.), *P. gossypinus megacephalus* (Rhoads), and *Ochrotomys nuttalli flammeus* (Goldman). Despite the 1807 publication of *Mus ludovicianus* Custis, then, its nomenclatorial status must be that of a *nomen dubium*. My thanks to Robert Owen and J. Knox Jones of Texas Tech University Museum's Laboratory for their assistance on this entry.

[273] Undoubtedly a tantalizing early reference to a color phase of the southern flying squirrel (*Glaucomys volans saturatus* A. H. Howell), which is found in considerable numbers in the Ouachita Mountains of present eastern Oklahoma. Custis obviously did not examine a specimen, but only heard of the animal from the hunters and guides on the expedition. Hall and Kelson, 1:406–407; Lowery, pp. 198, 203.

[274] One of several references in the quadruped catalogue, October 1, to species of the southern plains. The wolves in question here were obviously plains gray, or lobo, wolves (*Canis lupus nubilus* Say), found on the Great Plains from Texas to Saskatchewan and known to plainsmen since Coronado as "white wolves." Custis's brief description is the first published reference to this species, credited to Thomas Say of the Long expedition in 1820. Custis's description evidently is second-hand, taken from hunters on the expedition—probably Lucas Talapoon. Interestingly, no mention is made of the only wolf now native to the area covered by the exploration, today's endangered red wolf (*C. niger gregoryi* Goldman). Evidently none were seen. Hall and Kelson, 2:849–52; Lowery, pp. 386–90.

[275] The American beaver, and in the last stretch explored, the subspecies *C. canadensis texensis* Bailey, a new type. Hall and Kelson, 2:547. Evidently, at the time of the exploration the Indians of the area had not yet discovered the possibilities of the beaver trade. But they would shortly. In 1812 Dehahuit of the Caddos entered a special request with Thomas Linnard at the Natchitoches factory to order 20 beaver traps for them, since, "the Beaver . . . trade would be beneficial [to them] as Beaver abound in & about their country." Natchitoches/Sulphur Fork Agency Ledgers, 1809–1821, ledger entry for June 12, 1812.

[276] The river otter, another undifferentiated subspecies in 1806 that is endemic to the Red River valley and adjacent area: *Lutra canadensis texensis* Goldman. Hall and Kelson, 2:44–47; Lowery, p. 449. As with the Lewis and Clark expedition, Anglo-American trapping voyages up the Red followed on the heels of the

"From the accounts of all the Indians, I have seen, it is probable there may be a species of Antilope near the head waters of R. River."

From the accounts of all the Indians, I have seen, it is probable there may be a species of Antilope near the head waters of R. River.[277]

Freeman and Custis expedition. Maley claimed his companions, Bradley and Cox, trapped with moderate success on the main river in 1812. But once they turned up the Kiamichi—a favorite trapping tributary on the Red—they took sixty-three beaver and eleven otter pelts from March to May. Flores, "The John Maley Journal," pp. 86-120.

[277] Observing bands of pronghorns two summers earlier, the members of the Lewis and Clark party had referred to them for several weeks as *cabra* or *cabri*—

Elks (*Cervus Wapiti* of Dr. Barton) are plenty also about the head of the River. — [278]

I am informed by Lieutenant Osburn[279] of a very curious animal found on the Arkansas. The following is his account of it. — "There is a rabbit in the upper parts of Arkansas about the size of a common Buck; but shaped like the common hare or

---

goats. It is not surprising that Custis, operating only on second-hand information from Indians and guides, correctly surmised that the descriptions indicated some type of antelope. Barton had probably discussed the possibility with him, for in a "Miscellaneous Facts and Observations" column in his *Philadelphia Medical and Physical Journal, Supplement* 2 (1807):194-95, he mentioned that there were at least two types of "antelope" in the West. One had been known for 150 years, he wrote, but there was supposedly a type on the Arkansas River which was little known (see note 280, below). The American pronghorn actually combines features of both antelopes and goats; to find an appropriate niche for it in taxonomy, zoologists had to create a new family, Antilocapridae, of which it is the sole member. Apparently there were some bands of these animals in eastern Texas in the natural setting. In 1687 Joutel described many "wild goats" in the meadows two days (50 miles?) travel southwest of the Red River Caddos, evidently in the natural bluestem prairie along the Sulphur River in present Morris County. From confirmed records, in the nineteenth century pronghorns still ranged as far eastward as Fannin County—only 100 miles beyond the termination of Custis's examination of the river. Stiles, *Joutel's Journal of La Salle's Last Voyage*, p. 164; Hall and Kelson 2:1021-23; Cutright, *Lewis and Clark: Pioneering Naturalists*, pp. 81-82.

[278] Custis is possibly referring to both Southwestern species of elk here: *Cervus elaphus canadensis* Erxleben is the widespread type whose original range stretched from the Appalachians to the Rockies, while the upper Red River was within the range of the distinctive Merriam's elk (*Cervus elaphus merriami* Nelson), found from the Wichita Mountains of southwestern Oklahoma across Texas and New Mexico and into Arizona. No elk were seen by members of the Freeman and Custis party, but during winters, when the wildlife of the plains dispersed into the sheltered woodlands, bands of elk did migrate down the Red River valley into the region the Americans explored. There is a report that put elk in the state of Louisiana in 1829, and as late as 1842 a large bull was killed in Madison Parish in that state. In 1820, members of the Long expedition shot an enormous bull near the mouth of the Canadian, about 100 miles north of the terminating point of the Red River exploration of 1806. Hall and Kelson, 2:1000-1003; Lowery, p. 486. Custis's reference is to Barton's paper on the elk, "Account of the Cervus Wapiti, or southern elk of North America," *Philadelphia Medical and Physical Journal, Supplement* (1806): 36-55.

[279] At some point following his return to Natchez, Custis obviously entered into a conversation regarding plains wildlife with First Lieutenant Robert W. Osburn, of the Regiment of Artillerists, who must have been transferred to the

rabbit, is of a light red colour, sometimes mixed with white, or spotted; its hair is uncommonly coarse and so thick as to render it almost impossible to discover the skin through it & is about 3 inches in length particularly about the hind quarters; the flesh is equal to Venison and a little like it in flavor, but rather more juicy.—It is described by John Frazier a Chicasaw Indian who has killed of them as having one horn in the middle of its forehead bending downwardly & inwardly. This animal is most generally found in the neighborhood of the Osages. —I have seen the skin of one of these animals which weighed 5 lbs. english wt.—The skin is now to be seen at Arkansas [Post] in the possession of a Mr. Hendry of that place."[280]

Fishes.—

Silurus catus very abundant as high as we ascended.

border country during the ferment of the summer of 1806. In 1805, Osburn had been stationed at Chickasaw Bluffs (near present Memphis), not far from the Arkansas Post. William H. Powell, *List Of Officers Of The Army of the United States From 1779 to 1900*, pp. 42–43.

[280] Hendry was probably John Hendry, who signed a squatter's petition from the Arkansas District of the Louisiana Territory in 1812. See "Petition To Congress By Inhabitants Of Arkansas District," [March 11, 1812], in Carter, *The Territory of Louisiana-Missouri, 1806–1814*, vol. 14 of *The Territorial Papers of the United States*, pp. 526–28.

This "unicorn" did not, of course, exist on the Arkansas River or anywhere else in the American West. But the story was an old one in this part of the world. Bienville heard early in the eighteenth century that there were unicorns in Louisiana, and in 1720 La Harpe had matter-of-factly "confirmed" it when, traversing what is today central Oklahoma, he wrote that he came upon a band of Indians smoking the meat of "Unicorns" *(Licornes):* "This is an animal as large as a middle-sized horse; it has red hair of the color and length of that of goats, the leg rather slender, and in the middle of the forehead a horn, without branch, of a half foot long." Later, in the same country, he wrote: "We saw many unicorns without being able to approach them." Smith, "Account of the Journey of Benard de La Harpe," 385, 534. La Harpe reports no "goats" in the country he travelled, and that, coupled with his description, makes it almost certain that the animals he thought were unicorns were actually pronghorn antelope.

Since La Harpe's journal had been discovered in Natchitoches in 1805, stories of his "unicorns" must have been widespread in that frontier town. But Custis perhaps was more naïve than Alexander Wilson, his fellow naturalist, learned to be. ". . . so general vague and incorrect are almost all the accounts of illiterate

Buffaloe fish *(Cyprinus Americana)* also very abundant. — [281]
Herring *(Clupea Thrissa)* seen as high as the first little river. —
Gar *(Esox osseus)* very abundant.
Spatula fish of Du Pratz also met with. — [282]

Amphibia. —

Alligator *(Lacerta Alligator)* seen as high as the Spanish camp. —
Crotalus horridus. — [283]
Coluber versicolor. — [284]

Insects. —

Locusts very abundant all June and July. — They were so numerous that the Turkeys *(Malaegris Gallipavo)* fed almost entirely
on them. — [285]

----

sportsmen . . . that I pay little attention to any accounts received from such
people relative to my pursuits," he once wrote. "Nine times in ten they will be
found altogether erroneous." Wilson to Dunbar, New Orleans, June 24, 1810.
Rowland, *Dunbar Letters,* pp. 205–206.

[281] There are at least three buffalo fishes in the Red River: the common buffalo
fish (*Ictiobus cyprinella* Cuvier & Valen.), and two new species, the black buffalo
(*I. urus* Agassiz), and the white buffalo (*I. bubalus* Raf.). Both of the latter range
in the large rivers of the Mississippi valley. Jordan and Evermann, *American
Food and Game Fishes,* pp. 39, 41.

[282] This was the spoonbill, or paddle-fish (*Polyodon spathula* Walb.), which
weighs up to 150 pounds and is found in larger streams from the lower Mississippi
upriver to Lake Erie. Pratt, *Vertebrate Animals,* p. 29.

[283] Custis no doubt encountered a canebrake rattlesnake (*C. h. atricaudatus* La-
trielle), the subspecies of the midsouth, as his examination of the river was
stopped a bit short of the eastern perimeter of the range of the still undiscovered western diamondback (*C. atrox* Baird & Girard). Wright and Wright,
Handbook of Snakes, 2:962, 965.

[284] Custis could have been referring to one or several of a large number of
striped, ribbon, or garter snakes in this range.

[285] Barton was probably at work on his "Additional Facts and Observations
relative to the American Locust," which appeared in the *Philadelphia Medical
and Physical Journal, Supplement 2* (1806):186–87, at the time Custis was appointed
to the expedition, hence this entry. More than 600 species of locusts (grasshop-
pers) have been classified in America north of the Río Grande, rendering the field
of possible choices too vast for any precision. See Lester A. Swann and Charles
S. Papp, *The Common Insects of North America,* p. 70.

Lytta atrata *(Meloe pennsylvanica)* abundant on the young Willows and cotton trees which they entirely strip of their leaves. —I collected nearly a quart from one small willow branch.[286]

Lytta vittata very abundant. These have lately been used in the U. States as a substitute for the *Cantharides* and are found superior to them. —[287]

[286] Most likely the black blister beetle (*Epicauta pennsylvanica* DeGeer) of the family *Meloidae,* a species common everywhere in the United States. Ibid., p. 382; Ross H. Arnett, Jr., *The Beetles of the United States,* p. 621.

[287] Probably *Epicauta vittata* DeGeer, the striped blister beetle, endemic to the central and northeastern parts of the United States and Canada, but quite possibly any one of the variety of widely-distributed species of the genus *Lytta,* or the subgenera *Pomphopoea, Poreospasta, Paralytta,* or *Adicolytta.* Many Americans, including the great early entomologist, Thomas Say, were convinced that American blister beetles would eventually replace the European *Lytta vesicatoria* (L.) ("Spanish Fly") for medical uses. Although this did not happen, some of the *Epicauta* and *Lytta* species have become sources of cantharidin. Ibid., p. 625; Swann and Papp, *Common Insects of North America,* p. 382.

Editor's Epilogue
The Last Jeffersonian Exploration

PRECEDED by messengers bearing news of the confrontation on the river, during the last week of August, 1806, the disappointed members of the Exploring Expedition of Red River straggled into Natchitoches on borrowed Indian ponies. They found that frontier town virtually seething with excitement and outrage over the incident at Nanatsoho (soon "Spanish") Bluff. On August 17, Territorial Governor Claiborne, visiting in Natchez, received word that the exploring party had been stopped and that the Spaniards not only were east of the Sabine, but also were encamped within easy striking distance of Natchitoches. Issuing a call for a general mobilization, Claiborne departed for Natchitoches on horseback the next day, and arrived on the twenty-fifth, two days after Freeman's own arrival there.[1] Already, Cushing at Fort Claiborne had sent word for Colonel Jacob Kingsbury at Fort Adams to march his entire garrison of (now) three companies to Natchitoches.[2] The day following Claiborne's arrival, Captain Bower of the Opelousas Post arrived with an additional contingent of American soldiers. To both Americans and Spaniards, the war that had been looming like a storm cloud since the purchase of 1803, now seemed an imminent reality. As the *Richmond Enquirer,* reporting the fate of

[1] *Mississippi Messenger,* August 19, 1806; Abernethy, *The Burr Conspiracy,* pp. 51–52.
[2] Abernethy, *The Burr Conspiracy,* p. 52.

281

Jefferson's exploring party put it, "Something energetic will take place at no great distance of time."[3]

For a number of reasons, some of which will emerge presently, historians of the Louisiana-Texas frontier heretofore have missed the significance of the exploration in the events of 1806. On-the-scene observers, however, appear to have believed the event was a major catalyst in the crisis. John Sibley's assignation of causes is quite clear on this point, as is evident by his letter to one of his sons in September:

> The Spaniards resenting being removed over the River Sabine by the Officer Commanding here last winter have returned, taken their old Ground in force about 1200, Under the Command of two Officers of Rank & Experience, Equipt. with Cannon &c. . . . They frequently Patrolle within five or Six Miles of Natchitoches have turned back an Exploring party ascending Red River by Order of the President . . . have Cut down & carried away the flag of the United States that with Other Insults & outrages not to be borne with. —[4]

For several days in late August and early September, Claiborne and Spanish troop commander Herrera, with Ensign DuForest acting as interpreter and dispatch-bearer, engaged in a sharp diplomatic exchange, the major points of which were the stopping of the exploring party, the particular spot on the river where the incident took place, and the movement of Spanish troops east of the Sabine. In reference to arresting the progress of the exploring party, Herrera informed Claiborne that the Americans repeatedly had been warned that this would be Spain's course of action if Jefferson attempted to have the Southwest explored before the Louisiana boundary was settled, and that the request for a passport had been refused for this reason. The Spanish troop movements, he insisted, were a *response* to the American move of sending a military-escorted party into the Provincias Internas.[5]

[3] *Richmond Enquirer*, October 10, 1806.

[4] Sibley to Samuel Sibley, Natchitoches, September 26, 1806. In Whittington, "Dr. John Sibley Of Natchitoches," 500–501.

[5] Herrera to Claiborne, Spanish Camp [near Bayou Pierre], August 28, 1806. Rowland, *Official Letter Books of W. C. C. Claiborne* 3:392. This exchange is also available in the *American State Papers*.

The definition of just where the Provincias Internas ended and Louisiana began was, of course, the problem. As Wilkinson explained to Nemecio Salcedo a few months later, despite his wish to procure a part of Texas, Jefferson had no wish to violate territory claimed by Spain. Nonetheless: "The Red River and all its channels belonged to France . . . she set up various towns on that river and owned them as a part of Luisiana until the latter Territory was delivered to Spain, and . . . on the other hand, Spain did not set up a single town along that River. . . ."[6]

Claiborne articulated an even more expansive definition. Despite Freeman's own report that he believed he had found the remains of La Harpe's Post two days before his progress had been blocked by Viana, Claiborne insisted in his letters to Herrera that the American explorers had been forcibly detained below the earlier French perimeter, and thus *on American soil.* Evidently Claiborne based this interpretation not on the location of posts, but on the upriver activity of French traders among the Taovaya-Wichitas and Comanches. As a further point of national honor, Claiborne objected hotly to the Spanish treatment of the American flag the Caddos were flying in their village. The Caddos had been French, and were now American, Indians, he maintained, and such an outrage demonstrated a lack of respect for the United States that Spain would learn to regret.[7]

Herrera, a man of continental grace and manners, sought to ease the emotion-charged atmosphere, but he was firm. Disregarding the activity of traders, he chose to base his interpretation of the French perimeter in the Southwest on the actual military presence. The American explorers, he explained, had been allowed to examine the Red River to and beyond that line. It was only after they passed out of Louisiana that Captain Viana had blocked them and asked them "to retrograde to American territory." As for the Caddos, he conceded that they had once been under French control.

---

[6] Wilkinson to Salcedo, Washington, July 1, 1807. Jackson, *The Journals of Zebulon Montgomery Pike* 2:236.

[7] Claiborne to Herrera, Natchitoches, August 26, 1806. Rowland, *Official Letter Books of W. C. C. Claiborne* 3:383–84.

But, he continued, as Governor Claiborne "surely must know" (Claiborne probably did not), a decade before, the Caddos had transferred from their former locations on the Red to a new location, and "the place which they [now] inhabit is very far from [Louisiana] and belongs to Spain. . . ." If the Caddos had moved to Mexico City, could the Americans claim that the French (and thus they) had a right to it? If the Caddos wanted to befriend the Americans they could move, but in their present location they could not fly an American flag.[8] A few weeks later Claiborne called Dehahuit and a body of Caddo warriors to Natchitoches to discuss the situation of these Indians. But Sᵏɔ'-childni'ni was not moved.

In mid-September (some four and a half *months* after receiving his orders from Dearborn), the prime mover of the Southwest stepped into this stormy situation, his mind apparently awhirl with plots and counterplots. Here was the lighted match for the powderkeg. Wilkinson already had sent urgent word to Cushing for Claiborne to await his arrival before engaging the Spaniards. And now, the incident he had labored for achieved, with nearly 1,500 frontier militia assembled in Natchitoches under his command, the general translated Burr's "cipher letter" of July 22, revealing both opportunity and objectives in no uncertain terms:

Our project my dear friend is brought to the point so long desired. . . . The people of the country to which we are go [ing?] are prepared to receive us—their agents, now with me, say that if we will protect their religion and will not subject them to a foreign power, that in three weeks time all will be settled.

The gods invite us to glory and fortune. It remains to be seen whether we deserve the boons.[9]

Although Wilkinson's subsequent decisions and movements are well known, and only indirectly concern us here, a brief summary

[8] Herrera to Claiborne, Spanish Camp [near Bayou Pierre], August 28, 1806. Ibid., p. 392.

[9] Burr to Wilkinson, July 22, 1806. This letter, widely available in forms known as the "Swartwout" and "Bollman" letter, is quoted here as it appears in the new The Papers of Aaron Burr, Series 1.

is necessary. Bristling with military importance, on September 24 he wrote Governor Cordero of Texas (now directing the Spanish response from Nacogdoches) that President Jefferson had commanded him to inform Spanish officials that all the country east of the Sabine was considered to lie within the jurisdiction of the United States. Before he could receive a reply, however, something totally unexpected happened. Herrera's force of more than six hundred men was not well-equipped, and many of the troops, including Herrera, were ill. Thus, obeying earlier orders from Salcedo (and not disobeying orders, as some historians have claimed), on the twenty-seventh Herrera pulled his army out of Bayou Pierre and back across the Sabine, where it began to put up barracks. The next chess move was provided by Wilkinson, who notified Cordero that he was moving his force to the east bank of that river. From Nacogdoches, Cordero replied that since Spain claimed to the Arroyo Hondo, he must oppose any American advance to the Sabine. In reality, Herrera's move west of the Sabine had stalemated Wilkinson. Now he could not get at the Spaniards unless he crossed the river the Americans were advancing as the boundary.[10]

Meanwhile, the general had other problems. A week into October he received the most famous of the cipher letters from Burr, detailing the plan for descending the Mississippi to New Orleans with a force later in the fall. "After a sleepless night," according to Abernethy, on the morning of the ninth Wilkinson informed Colonel Cushing of the "Burr" Conspiracy—omitting his own role, of course—and announced that he planned on marching at once to the Sabine to make terms with Herrera. On the twentieth, still in Natchitoches, Wilkinson wrapped himself in the flag and wrote two letters to President Jefferson, in which he vaguely outlined a "Western Conspiracy" and advised that he was in a splendid position to save the country by terminating this business with

---

[10] Wilkinson to Cordero, Natchitoches, September 24, 1806; Cordero to Salcedo, near Nacogdoches, September 27, 1806; Salcedo to Cordero, en route to Texas, October 24, 1806. The Bexar Archives.

the Spaniards and Louisiana, freeing him "to throw myself with my little Band into New Orleans, to be ready to defend that capital against usurpation. . . ."[11] Historians are convinced that public linking of his name with the plot in the rash of newspaper stories that summer, coupled with Wilkinson's weakness of character and perhaps a growing conviction that the plan was really an impossible one, led him to this decision to double-cross Burr. It may be, however, that the peaceful conclusion of the confrontation between Viana and Freeman on the river had robbed Wilkinson of the "incident" he believed necessary to trigger a war.

Three days later, Wilkinson set out with his army—about half and half militiamen to regulars, with a sprinkling of people from the exploring expedition—crossed the Arroyo Hondo, and proceeded through the pine-clad hills to the Sabine. On November 1, with only the muddy little woodland stream separating the two armies, Wilkinson sent an emissary to Cordero proposing a "neutral ground" settlement. Since Salcedo (who was at this moment hurrying to Texas) had ordered Herrera not to engage the Americans without an "absolute and positive certainty" of being able to defeat them, the latter seized the initiative. He ignored Cordero's evasive reply to Wilkinson and decided himself to accept the American offer. On the fifth, Viana was dispatched to the American camp (where he was grudgingly congratulated by the Freeman and Custis men in Wilkinson's army) and the Neutral Ground Agreement of 1806 was signed, establishing a neutral buffer strip, claimed by both countries but governed by neither. Its western boundary was the Sabine and that on the east a line drawn from the mouth of the "Mermento" (the Calcasieu) on the Gulf north through the Arroyo Hondo to the thirty-second parallel.[12]

---

[11] The letters are widely available, but most readily in Abernethy, *The Burr Conspiracy*, pp. 150–52. An edited selection of Burr papers, prepared by Mary Jo Kline, is currently in the process of being published by Princeton University Press.

[12] Salcedo to Cordero, en route to Texas, October 24, 1806; Herrera to Cordero, Sabine Camp, November 6, 1806. The Bexar Archives. The historian of the Neutral Ground, J. Villasana Haggard, in his "The Neutral Ground Between Louisiana and Texas, 1806–1821," *The Louisiana Historical Quarterly* 28 (October 1945), reprints the only extant map of the Neutral Ground, drawn, however,

Obviously avoided and unresolved by this settlement were the extent of the American claim to the Red and the disposition of Dehahuit's Caddos. Although the settlement seemed on its face to be a victory for Spain, and was a far cry from the original proposals of the American diplomats in Aranjuez to have most of Texas proclaimed a "neutral zone," events would prove the omissions to be important victories for the United States.

As for Wilkinson, he was not even a party to the ceremony. He had departed at 5 a.m. that morning, and the next day he left Natchitoches for New Orleans. The contrived war was not to be. Yet, astonishingly, even for Wilkinson, while Burr was descending the Mississippi into a fiasco that would end with his capture early in 1807, Wilkinson sent an aide, Walter Burling, on a secret mission to Mexico City to ask for a payment of some $111,000 from the Spaniards for "saving your country." He informed Yturrigaray that he had risked his life "by the change I have made in the military arrangements without the knowledge of my government."[13] Suspecting that they had been maneuvered, the disgusted Spaniards never paid.

after 1819, which shows the eastern boundary extending beyond the thirty-second parallel to the Red River. Haggard is convincing in his contention that the map errs in this regard. See 1038–40, 1040n.78, 1045.

[13] Herrera to Cordero, Nacogdoches, December 1, 1806. The Bexar Archives; Royal Ornan Shreve, *The Finished Scoundrel*, pp. 223–27; Gerald Ashford, *Spanish Texas: Yesterday and Today*, p. 195. Wilkinson had no luck convincing Yturrigaray, who sent Burling back with the reply that he wished Wilkinson "happiness in pursuit of [your] righteous intentions." The Spanish government, of course, had already paid the American general some $10,000 for his "Reflections on Louisiana." As a bizarre footnote, Wilkinson effectively played both sides against the middle by talking the Jefferson administration into reimbursing him for Burling's mission to the amount of $1,750. In fact, Wilkinson was eventually paid nearly $11,000 by the Jefferson and Madison administrations to cover his expenses in "crushing the conspiracy." Cox, in "General James Wilkinson And His Later Intrigues With The Spaniards," points out the obvious: that Wilkinson's chief motive in all his plots was not ideology (he was certainly no friend of republican revolution), nor even power, but simple pecuniary gain.

The positions of previous scholars respecting the Burr-Wilkinson plot and government exploration are interesting. Most, of course, have believed that Pike was a spy against the Spaniards; William Goetzmann, in his *Exploration and Empire: The Explorer and the Scientist in the Winning of the American West*, pp. 42–49, devotes only two sentences to what he calls the "Captain Thomas Sparks"

In actual fact, we now know that Wilkinson's peace with Spain was in keeping with the administration's wishes, although he and Jefferson evidently came to this conclusion independently. On November 8, two days *after* the signing of the Neutral Ground Agreement, Dearborn wrote to the general explaining that it was Jefferson's desire that the crisis with Spain be settled pacifically and transmitting the administration's own six-point plan based upon the Sabine as a temporary boundary, with Spain retaining Bayou Pierre. Neither power was to be permitted to occupy a point on the Red above Natchitoches, and all but three-hundred American troops would be withdrawn from the river.[14]

Despite the urging of his diplomats and a number of rather menacing public statements, there is virtually no evidence that Jefferson ever developed a plan for the invasion of Texas. The most aggressive action he ever took in the Southwest, notwithstanding his territorial claims, was the exploring probe sent up the Red. And though scientific, economic, and diplomatic objectives for the expedition can be documented, whatever military orders (if any) Freeman received can only be speculated upon.

FREEMAN AND PIKE

There may have been an intended relationship between Sparks's military escort and Zebulon M. Pike's party, but what is known is sketchy and somewhat dubious. Historians still divide over the true nature of the Pike exploration, and with good reason. What

---

expedition, but discusses Wilkinson's conspiracy at some length with regard to Pike. Donald Jackson has carried his interpretation only to the point of writing that Wilkinson had "a plan with Burr for some kind of operation against the Spanish," and to conclude it "he must get a war going." Jackson, *The Journals of Zebulon Montgomery Pike* 2:103n. Cox, early in his career, did research on the Freeman and Custis expedition as part of a synthesis on Louisiana exploration. In his later years he unearthed much of the evidence implicating Wilkinson in a Southwestern conspiracy, but he never returned to the Red River exploration in the context of his new material.

[14] Dearborn to Wilkinson, Washington, November 8, 1806. War Department, Letters Sent, Main Series.

is evident is that some two months after the president's exploring party had already entered the mouth of the Red River, with instructions to traverse that stream to its headwaters, Wilkinson on his own initiative launched Pike overland on a second expedition aimed (ostensibly) at the same river. Starting from St. Louis, Pike was to return to their villages a number of Indians from the 1805 Osage delegation to Washington. After endeavoring to make peace between the disaffected tribes of their country and sending Lieutenant James B. Wilkinson (the general's son) down the Arkansas, Pike was to proceed to establish good relations with the "Ietans" (the Comanches). Since accomplishing the latter "will probably lead you to the Head Branches of the Arkansaw, and Red Rivers" Pike would no doubt find himself near the New Mexico settlements, where he "should move with great circumspection." The general then instructed Pike in the "primary" scientific objectives (i.e., geography and natural history) of the journey, primary aspects Pike felt at liberty to virtually ignore. Finally, in pursuit of good Indian relations and scientific knowledge, "you, yourself may descend the Red River. . . ."[15]

Exactly what Wilkinson had in mind by essentially duplicating the scientific and diplomatic objectives of an expedition already underway it is not possible to say with conviction. Given his timing and the effort he had put into promoting a confrontation, it is logical to assume that he was relatively certain that the Spaniards would move against Jefferson's party, although he could not have been certain of their success. But a confrontation, and particularly a battle, between Americans and Spaniards on the Red River was quite likely to lead to a war, and in this context it begins to be more and more certain that Pike's expedition really was a spying

---

[15] Wilkinson to Pike, St. Louis, June 28, 1806. Jackson, *The Journals of Zebulon Montgomery Pike* 1:285–87. Since Pike was on the Arkansas and, as Wilkinson put it, had determined "himself to descend Red River, you may therefore expect pretty correct charts of both those Rivers next spring, should no misfortune happen to the parties." Wilkinson to Dearborn, October 17, 1806. Ibid, 2:153. Relative to natural history, Pike notes in the preface to his published account (1:xxiv): "With respect to the great acquisitions which might have been made to the sciences of botany and zoology, I can only observe, that neither my education nor taste led me to the pursuit. . . ."

mission against a principal Anglo objective: the highway to Santa Fe. The attachment of Dr. John Robinson to the party and his subsequent strange behavior in New Mexico have caused historians to believe Wilkinson was endeavoring to make contact with certain officials in New Mexico.[16]

There was always the chance that the Spaniards would botch the capture of Freeman and Custis, of course. And it is here that two comments seemingly pulled out of the air by a pair of Pike's less loyal followers begin to make sense. After the capture of Pike's party north of Santa Fe in late February, 1807 (he was on the Río Grande, and professed shock when the Spaniards told him it was not the Red), the expedition members were closely questioned by Spanish officials. One of them, Private John Sparks, told Joaquín del Real Alencaster that a hitherto unrevealed objective for the expedition had surfaced once it was underway. Alencaster related the exchange to Nemecio Salcedo thus:

He says they left San Luis . . . believing that the expedition had as its object the reconnaissance of the Colorado [Red] River, but that when they reached the point of crossing the mountains in February they asked various questions of their commander about where they were going, since they were already in Spanish territory, and he answered them that they should advance, for on the Colorado they would meet a Captain with an expedition of a considerable party of Anglo-American soldiers. . . .[17]

This could have been no other than Captain Richard Sparks and the forty-six-man military escort accompanying Freeman and Custis.

A week later, Alencaster received corroboration of the story from Thomas Daugherty, a twenty-six-year-old Pennsylvanian who had been Pike's orderly on the expedition. According to Daugherty, Wilkinson had told Pike that if he were captured, an American force should be on hand to rescue him, and "that

---

[16] See especially Abernethy, *The Burr Conspiracy*, p. 279. W. Eugene Hollon, in *The Lost Pathfinder: Zebulon Montgomery Pike*, ventures no real opinion on Robinson. The master Pike scholar, Jackson, finds no real evidence to support Abernethy's contentions.

[17] Alencaster to Salcedo, Santa Fe, April 7, 1807. Jackson, *The Journals of Zebulon Montgomery Pike* 2:181.

they would go along the principal rivers. . . ."[18] Perhaps Sparks and Daugherty were confused, traitorous, or "Dam'd rascels," as Pike put it, but they certainly did seem to possess some knowledge of a connection between their own expedition and another American probe up the Red. There is no other evidence for a rendezvous of the two exploring parties, unless it lies in a logical extension of the one-plus-one principle to Wilkinson's reply to Salcedo's questions about the Sparks-Daugherty testimony, that the Americans had indeed attempted to explore the Red "by sending Mr. Freeman to follow it from its mouth upwards, and Lieut. Pike, from its sources downwards."[19]

COVER-UP?

The question of just how much Jefferson really knew about events in the Southwest in 1806 is unavoidable. It has already been noted that the president's Red River expedition was viewed with some suspicion in his day, one newspaper editor pointedly linking it to Jefferson's wish to liberate and revolutionize Texas, and New and Old Mexico. Aaron Burr always insisted that the "conspiracy" was fully disclosed to Jefferson, and general supposition held that the president was the mastermind. Indeed, Dearborn told Wilkinson in January, 1807, that the common interpretation was that the conspiracy was to have featured

an attack on Mexico and a revolution of that Country . . . but to be under the direction of the Government of the United States. . . . honor, glory and riches awaited every individual who would thus engage in the service of his country. Many honest and respectable men . . . kept the Executive informed from time to time of the general movement.[20]

In addition, Jefferson's unwavering support (Dumas Malone calls it a "whitewash") of the unsavory Wilkinson during the Burr

---

[18] Alencaster to Salcedo, Santa Fe, April 15, 1807. Ibid., pp. 198, 201n.2. Jackson asserts that there "is every reason to believe that Daugherty was telling the truth."

[19] Wilkinson to Salcedo, St. Louis, July 1, 1807. Ibid., p. 236.

[20] Dearborn to Wilkinson, Washington, January 21, 1807. War Department, Letters Sent, Main Series.

Conspiracy trials (Wilkinson was acquited of the charge that he was a Spanish agent in his court-of-inquiry, as well as of duplicity in the plot in his court-martial in 1811) has likewise raised eyebrows, particularly since it is known that he had twice received evidence of Wilkinson's machinations before 1806.

Although we may never know the answer to this question, it is worth noting that Thomas Hart Benton, the torchbearer of the mid-nineteenth-century American drive to the west, never looked to the disgraced Aaron Burr as his spiritual antecedent. Instead, a conversation with the Sage of Monticello in the 1820s imbued Benton with the idea that he was the executor of Jefferson's plans for western North America. It appears that the Anglo-American desire for Texas, in particular, is a historical theme which ought to be closely examined from a scholarly perspective. Beginning with Jefferson's claims in 1803, it coursed through tacit approval of the filibusters into Texas by President Madison during the Mexican Revolution, continued in attempts by presidents John Quincy Adams and Andrew Jackson to *purchase* Texas, and culminated with American support for the Texas Revolution and eventual annexation in 1845. Fuller knowledge of the events surrounding the Southwestern exploration of 1806 would seem to give us a fresh perspective from which to view this subsequent matrix of events.

One thing that is certain from the evidence is that Jefferson, whatever the extent of his interest in a liberal revolution in Mexico, cannot be charged with sacrificing his scientific probe into the Southwest for such an end. His insistence that Dunbar send the party up the Red rather than the Arkansas was an unfortunate mistake in exploration terms, but it was a move made for territorial and diplomatic considerations. Clearly, Jefferson never believed that the capture of his expedition was inevitable, nor does he seem to have suspected Wilkinson's role. Exploring the Southwest had been a hazardous proposition from the first; he must have interpreted it as a chance taken, but lost.

Even so, the play of circumstances that conspired to almost completely obscure the Red River expedition hints at more than simple political embarrassment; it may indicate that Jefferson wished to prevent a connection in the public mind between the exploration and the Burr-Wilkinson plot. It is true that in late 1806 and early 1807 he was concerned with weightier issues: the triumphant return of Lewis and Clark, the Burr plot and trial, the embargo. Yet the expedition had been a personal project, the nature of which keenly interested him. And however embarrassing its early abortion at the hands of Spain, it had been a probe conducted by civilian scientists who had assembled scientific data on nearly 650 miles of unfamiliar Louisiana terrain, with a great factor of accuracy.

Although cover-up is perhaps too strong a word, the facts clearly show that the administration wanted as little attention drawn to this Southwestern expedition as possible. Freeman's account to the president of the incident with Viana's army, after being suspiciously intercepted and detained by Colonel Cushing, finally had been taken by military messenger to an angry Dunbar, who in October forwarded the second half of the Freeman journal to the president.[21] As has been indicated previously, after his perusal of the documents Jefferson passed them on, for redaction, to Nicholas King. Apparently he included instructions for King to delete from the accounts several references implying that the expedition was attempting to win the Indians and was preparing for a military showdown with the Spaniards. While King was thus engaged, Jefferson had occasion to deliver his annual message to Congress. He mentioned both of his Louisiana explorations, lingering of course on Lewis and Clark, but noting of Freeman and Custis that they had examined the Red River "nearly as far as the French settlements had extended," and that although the tour had been conducted with "a zeal and prudence meriting entire approbation," it had "not been so successful" as that of Lewis and Clark.[22]

---

[21] Dunbar protested to Dearborn that he considered Cushing's action improper. Dunbar to Dearborn, Natchez, September 6, 1806. Rowland, *Dunbar Letters*, p. 348.

[22] Jefferson's State of the Union Address, 1806. In Ford, *The Writings of Thomas Jefferson* 8:492. Attached is a memorandum written by Secretary of State Madison

That, in fact, was about all Jefferson was willing to say about what must have been one of the significant disappointments of his second term in office. That this contrasts with his attitude regarding the Lewis and Clark exploration is self-evident and understandable, but a suspicion persists that perhaps Jefferson was content to have the American public assume that the Burr Conspiracy was actually responsible for the uproar in Texas.

Thus the Freeman and Custis Account was not serialized in the *National Intelligencer*, nor did it appear in the *Annals of Congress*. When Hopkins and Seymour Press of New York published from the congressional documents its *Message From the President of the United States, Communicating Discoveries Made in Exploring the Missouri, Red River, and Washita*, virtually the only source of information on Louisiana exploration available to the public for several years, it featured Sibley's second-hand account rather than the report of Jefferson's exploring party. Despite his early role in promoting the exploration, the president's friend and fellow Republican Samuel L. Mitchill, publisher of the major scientific journal, the *Medical Repository*, never once mentioned the Freeman and Custis expedition in those pages, while doing lengthy articles on all of the other American explorations of the time.[23] Finally, in January, 1807, the *National Intelligencer*, the official voice of the administration, ran a detailed front-page article explaining the crisis in the Southwest, alluding to the troop movements (without explaining *why* there had been a Spanish mobilization), the diplomatic correspondence, and the Neutral Ground Agreement, *without a single reference to the President's exploring expedition or its con-*

(p. 484) questioning whether Jefferson should mention the French *settlements* in connection with the expedition, since that might imply that these defined the limit of the American claim.

[23] Mitchill reviewed and summarized the Dunbar and Hunter probe in vol. 3, no. 3 (1806), pp. 305–308; Pike's Mississippi River expedition in vol. 4, no. 4 (1807), pp. 376–89; Gass's journal of the Lewis and Clark expedition in vol. 5, no. 3 (1808), pp. 185–90; and Pike's western exploration in vol. 6, no. 3 (1809), pp. 297–300. In fairness to him, perhaps it was the mangled natural history of the King publication, or an assumption that the Southwestern expedition had made no new geographical discoveries which caused him to ignore it, but neither reason really seems satisfactory as an explanation.

frontation with the Spanish army.[24] That newspaper, in fact, never published a notice at all relative to the Red River expedition. And despite Jefferson's continuing insistence that the Río Grande was the true boundary and that all the affluents of the Mississippi were within Louisiana (he suggested to John Melish that he so draw his maps as late as 1816), the administration never formally protested the stopping of its Southwestern expedition, a venture which had cost it some $8,000.[25]

ACCOMPLISHMENTS OF A "FAILED" EXPEDITION

The passing of nearly two centuries has led to a reappraisal of the scientific value of the Freeman and Custis exploration. Today it is the ethnological data and the ecological references that hold the most historical interest; in 1806 it was the geographical work

[24] *The National Intelligencer*, January 19, 1807. The typeset used in the publication of the King redaction is the same as that utilized by the *Intelligencer*, pointing to the conclusion that Jefferson had *An Account of The Red River, in Louisiana* printed in the offices of that newspaper. No records remain to show how many copies were printed; my figure of 200 in Editorial Procedures is based upon the assumption that Jefferson had a copy made for every member of Congress, but that is not certain, and thus the figure may be too high. Only ten originals are now extant in various libraries in the United States. Copies are known to be in the Yale Library of Western Americana; Bancroft Library, University of California, Berkeley; Howard-Tilton Memorial Library, Tulane University; Clements Library, University of Michigan; Maryland Historical Society, Baltimore; Harvard University; Streeter's Collection, Morristown, New Jersey; Boston Athenaeum; U.S. Geological Survey; and the Library of Congress, which also holds the manuscript copy. According to Wilburforce Eames, the copy presented to the Library of Congress in 1807 was bound to the *back* of King's redaction of Pike's 1805 Mississippi River account, and included a letter of presentation from Dearborn dated March 9, 1807. In Thomas W. Streeter, *Bibliography of Texas, 1795–1845*, item No. 1040. So obscure was the King publication of the expedition that only thirteen years later (1820) explorer and naturalist Edwin James was totally unaware of it.

[25] Documentation for tabulating the full cost of the expedition is incomplete, and the figuring is complicated by virtue of the mid–journey cancellation of the project. Nonetheless, an estimate can be ventured, based principally upon the following documents: Dunbar to Dearborn, Natchez, March 18, April 1, May 6, 1806, Rowland, *Dunbar Letters*, pp. 331–33, 336–37, 341; Freeman to the War Department, New Orleans, May 20, 1806; Sibley to Dearborn, Natchi-

that seemed most important. Initially, King's superb *Map of the Red River In Louisiana* (1806), a definitive chart of the lower 615 miles of the river drawn up from the survey notes of the party, suffered the same obscurity as the published account to which it was appended. But in 1807 its findings were somewhat redrawn to include Wilkinson's and Herrera's troop movements and incorporated into Anthony Nau's *The First Part of Captn. Pike's Chart of the Internal Part of Louisiana.* This map, along with a second Nau map showing country farther west, summarized what was known

---

toches, November 10, 1806; Custis to the War Department, December 24, 1806, all in War Department, Letters Received, Main Series; Freeman to Jefferson, Philadelphia, November 25, 1805, The Thomas Jefferson Papers, 1st Ser.

The expedition's expenses can be broken down thus:

Salaries:

Freeman at $4 a day, November 16, 1805 through October 1, 1806	$1400
Custis at $3 a day, January 17 to December 24, 1806	1020
Sparks and Humphreys at $3 a day (combined), April 19 through August 25, 1806	402
François Grappe's guide services	70

Supplies & Expenses:

Cabin Stores for the leaders	$ 300
Cash for contingency expenses	150
Advance to the leaders	200
Payment for an Indian messenger	50
Supplies in New Orleans	820
Chronometer in Philadelphia	265
Camera obscura in Philadelphia	60
Perogue at Natchez	130
Dunbar's "exegencies" cash*	1000
Subtotal	$5867

*Included purchase of two dozen barrels of flour at Natchitoches and payment to Talapoon, Cut Finger, and Grand Ozages?

Estimated expenses for which figures do not exist:

Two specially-constructed flatboats	$ 800 ?
Telescope for observing Jupiter's moons	250 ?
Expenses for the two leaders in 1806	1000 ?
Goods left from Ouachita expedition	200 ?
Indian presents from Sibley and Linnard	600 ?
Subtotal	$2850 ?
Total estimated expenses for expedition	$8717

of the Southwest as a consequence of the American explorations of 1804–1807. Nau sent the Red River beyond Spanish Bluff careening off far southwest of its actual course and followed Von Humboldt's error (plagiarized by Pike) in showing the origins of the "Red River of the Mississippi" near Santa Fe. The second Nau map likewise shows Melgares's route down the "Red" (it may have been the Canadian), labeling it "The Route pursued by the Spanish cavalry when going out from S[ta.] Fee in Search of the American Exploring Parties commanded by major Sparks and Capt. Pike in the Year 1806." Viana's route, shown on Spanish maps of the period, does not appear.

Still later the mapwork from the expedition was picked up and included in William Clark's 1809 manuscript map of the West, though all the southern portions were omitted when this map was published in 1814. Even later it was used by John Melish in the numerous editions of his *Map of the United States.* Today, a comparison of the King-Freeman map with later survey and topo maps of the Red River points up an amazing degree of precision in the geographical field work performed by Freeman, Humphreys, and Custis. Along with that done by Dunbar and Hunter, their mapwork far excelled in accuracy that done by the other explorers of the period. But publicly, of course, it has always been the more dramatic and extensive geographical discoveries of Lewis and Pike that have caught the fancy of the nation.[26]

Peter Custis's natural history work is more difficult to assess. Today, working from his manuscript reports and carefully correcting his misidentifications, the result of his survey is a valuable and intriguing ecological investigation of the early Red River valley's natural history. But to contemporaries, his contributions to science were far less compelling. Discerning why this impression prevailed requires much explanation and some speculation, but it is important to understand it, for Custis was the first American-trained naturalist to accompany an exploring expedition to the

[26] The Nau maps are reproduced in full in Jackson, *The Journals of Zebulon Pike* 1. For Clark's two maps (the manuscript version showing a piece of Freeman's survey), see Wheat, *Mapping the Transmississippi West* 2, maps 291 and 316. The Melish maps are widely reproduced today.

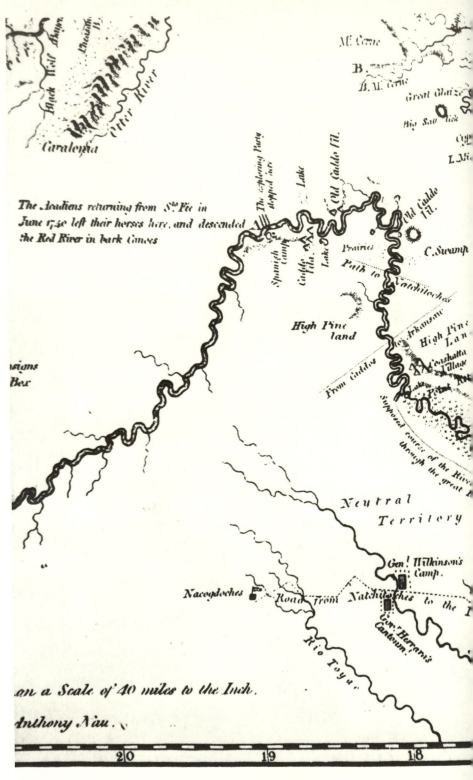

Portion of Nau's map, The First Part of Captn. Pike's Chart of the Internal Part of Louisiana, *1807, showing Freeman and Custis, Dunbar and Hunter discoveries, and the Wilkinson-Herrera confrontation.*

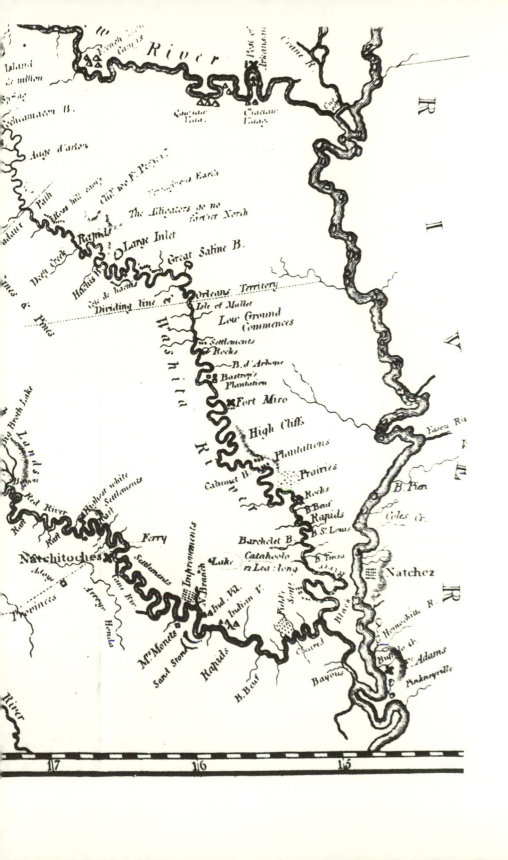

West. As Barton's own student, he represented the best the Americans had to offer at the time.

Custis's performance as a naturalist must be understood in context. Unlike later explorations, which normally included several diverse natural science specialists, the Southwestern party had to make do with a single individual, who obviously was called upon to make meaningful observations in half a dozen fields. That kind of effort would have taxed even an experienced naturalist, and at only twenty-five, not yet having completed his academic training, Custis was anything but experienced. His major difficulties can be traced to the inadequacy of his references—critical, since his identifications came from literary discriptions rather than a comparison of specimens—and a general failure to grasp the principles of geographic distribution of species. Custis had an enviable opportunity to transfix his name permanently and widely in natural history nomenclature, yet time and time again he assigned known names to species which actually were new, and which he was the first to examine. Many, it is true, could not have been so identified (and often were not until the twentieth century) until specimen comparisons could be made. So Custis, perhaps with encouragement from Barton, was quite conservative about declaring new species and assigning new names. Unfortunately, rather than working up his twenty-six botanical specimens collected above the Great Raft himself, he allowed them to go to the Barton Herbarium, where those specimens that were not damaged (some perhaps were) almost certainly fell into the hands of Frederick Pursh. Thus, like those of both Lewis and Dunbar, whose new plants Pursh received credit for, Custis's Red River collection probably produced new species now credited to Pursh.[27]

[27] Pursh's work with the Lewis and Clark collections (a task Barton had taken on, but never performed) is well known. See Cutright, *Lewis and Clark: Pioneering Naturalists.* Unknown is his publication of the only new plant from the Dunbar and Hunter collection, the southeastern licorice (*Glycyrrhiza lepidota* Pursh). Muhlenberg had identified a specimen of this plant as a new species in his correspondence with Dunbar of July 5, 1808 (Rowland, *Dunbar Letters*, pp. 201–203). Custis's collection, according to Dunbar, "received some wet or dampness from rain on the way from Nachitosh." Although he carefully dried them, some of the specimens were probably damaged. Dunbar to Dearborn, Natchez, September 6, 1806, ibid., p. 348.

From his Red River examination Custis published only one article, in effect the account of the lower (and settled) Red he had transmitted to Barton, which Barton got into print later that fall as "Observations relative to the Geography, Natural History, & etc., of the Country along the Red-River, in Louisiana," in his *Philadelphia Medical and Physical Journal.* And Barton omitted from it the description of Custis's prize discovery, the amphiuma he had named "Syren quadrupeda." In many ways Custis's last two reports, on the Great Swamp and the wilderness above the Raft, were even more interesting, and they included detailed descriptions (and in four instances new Latin names) for eighteen plants and animals he considered new. Too, these sections included his ethnological and ethnobotanical references and his completed list of some fifty-six species of trees growing along the Red. Most of this, of course, was published in the King version of the journals in 1807, but the Latin names of Custis's carefully-prepared reports, as well as the organization, were so garbled, and the publication so obscure, that rather than receiving credit, Custis must have seen his reputation as a naturalist suffer in consequence. Perhaps it was discouragement at the lack of recognition, perhaps the press of completing his doctoral thesis and finding employment, but Custis never worked up and re-published any of his major discoveries (such as the Mississippi kite) from the exploration.

Now that Custis's work has come to light, a comparison with the work of Meriwether Lewis is almost inevitable. Donald Jackson, in fact, has tentatively already done it, and clearly gives the edge to Lewis. Conrad Morton does not compare the two, but he is far more sympathetic to Custis, although like Jackson's, his appraisal is not based upon the full story.[28] In reality, assessing Custis and Lewis side by side is a bit unfair to both. Lewis not

[28] Jackson, *Thomas Jefferson & the Stony Mountains*, pp. 233, 240n.20, writes, however, that "Custis must not be dismissed as an unimpressive figure in the scientific investigation of the West . . . until a detailed analysis of his work can be made." Morton, in "An Overlooked Publication Of Botanical Interest," p. 441, finds Custis's work effective considering the trying circumstances. "I can picture Custis sitting in the open flat boat while it was proceeding up the river at a snail's pace," he writes, "trying to match up his specimens with those brief

only explored regions which were "new" and manifestly different from the Atlantic states, he also led his party, and could botanize or hunt when he wished. Stopped short of the prairies, Custis examined a country only subtly different from the East and was, as he tells us, "subject to the movements of another." Custis felt confident enough in his training that he was able systematically to use Latin nomenclature, to rely primarily upon literary identification, and to describe professionally new species and propose new binomials. Lewis, on the other hand, was almost completely unfamiliar with scientific binomials, and thus could not name new species. Perhaps as a result, his descriptions are often fuller than those by Custis, if not as scientifically correct. But Lewis's methodology of collecting specimens of all unusual or dubious plants so that more capable naturalists could later examine and name them was more productive of new discoveries. A final impression emerging from the exercise is that on such wilderness treks, more than anything else a naturalist needed to be a zealous outdoorsman, and in this respect Lewis may have exceeded his better-educated contemporary explorer of southern Louisiana.

To Americans of that day, it may have seemed of minor importance that the explorers had established a rapport with the native groups on the lower half of the Red, but subsequent events proved this fact to have been of great significance to the Americans. Freeman's respect and friendliness for them clearly impressed Dehahuit of the Caddos and Echean of the Red River Alabama-Coushattas. In contrast to Spanish actions, the ultimate effect of the American expedition was to cement the allegiance of both tribes to the United States. As events soon proved, this was by no means inconsequential. The Caddos, in particular, continued to exert a strong influence over the Taovaya-Wichitas upriver, and through them, the myriad Comanche bands of the plains. Fortunately, in Dr. Sibley the Jefferson administration had an Indian agent who actively exploited the borderland situation to win Indians to the United States. Through the Caddos, in August,

Linnaean diagnoses, throwing up his hands at the impossiblity, and finally tossing a coin as to which name to enter into the list."

1807, Sibley successfully held a "Grand Council" in Natchitoches that attracted thirty nations of the near Southwest—including the Comanches, whom both Freeman and Pike had been unable to reach. The high point of the council, in fact, came when a Penateka Comanche chief exchanged his Spanish flag for an American one that Freeman had left with Sibley for this purpose after the exploration was aborted.[29]

As for the Red River Alabama-Coushattas, a steady accretion in population quickly made them one of the most important Indian divisions on the lower Red (by 1820 their river-bluff village had attracted more than 350 of their kinsmen).[30] Following the visit by the American exploring party, Echean and his Red River village remained firm in their loyalty to the Americans. In this relationship they broke with their kinsmen in the Sabine River villages, who remained loyal to Spain, and who even sent the influential Coushatta chief Pia Mingo to entreat them to forsake the Americans. Eventually the Alabama-Coushattas even formed with the Caddos a North Louisiana Indian battalion that Sibley planned to march to the defense of New Orleans in 1815. (When the 150 warriors were finally assembled at Natchitoches in mid-January, the Battle of New Orleans was already over.)[31]

As were Lewis and Clark, Freeman and Custis also were indirectly responsible for opening to Americans a major waterway route into the interior. As indicated in the Introduction, in the pre-exploration period Spanish patrols frequently were dispatched to capture American hunters and traders to the river tribes. Indeed, since Philip Nolan, Spanish officials had been prone to take an unyielding position toward Americans on the Southwestern rivers.

[29]Sibley, *A Report from Natchitoches in 1807*, entries for August 9 through 18, pp. 48–67.

[30]Jedidiah Morse, *A Report to the Secretary of War of the United States on Indian Affairs, Comprising a Narrative of a Tour Performed in the Summer of 1820, under a Commission from the President of the United States*, p. 373; Flores, "The Red River Branch Of The Alabama-Coushatta Indians," pp. 68–71.

[31]Sibley to James Monroe, Natchitoches, January 10, 1815. Garrett, "Doctor John Sibley and The Louisiana–Texas Frontier," 49:610–11.

This situation changed in the period immediately following the crisis of 1806. Early the next year, Cordero cautioned Spanish frontier officials that they must judiciously avoid "any noisy disturbances which might create new cause for friction between the two govnts," and noted that retaliatory actions ought to be directed against the Indians who dealt with the Americans rather than against the American traders—a policy of dubious wisdom, it would seem, but one that would keep the peace.[32]

Given this new policy, it did not take long for the general line of the Red to become the Southern frontiersman's favorite artery into the Southwestern hinterland. Indeed, fewer than six weeks after Freeman was forced back at Spanish Bluff, six American traders, led by John S. Lewis and William C. Alexander and guided by Lucas Talapoon, set out from Natchitoches on horseback to follow the river to the plains. After delivering to the Taovaya village the American flag Freeman had brought for them, the Lewis and Alexander party caught mustangs, made contact with a large band of Southern Comanches, and stayed on the upper Red without harrassment until the summer of 1807.[33]

John Sibley, for one, thought he understood what Jefferson expected of him as a response to the Freeman incident. He not only held the great council at Natchitoches in 1807 (toward which end he seems to have enlisted Lewis and Alexander), but also, the following year, actively promoted an expedition that in Indian diplomacy may be regarded as a semi-official, secret attempt to realize Red River exploration objectives. In July of 1808, Natchez planter and trader Anthony Glass and ten companions (including Alexan-

[32] Cordero to Salcedo, San Antonio, February 4, 1807; Viana to Cordero, Nacogdoches, July 9, 1807; Salcedo to Cordero, Chihuahua, July 12, 1807. The Bexar Archives. As the new policy was put into effect, Viana could not suppress his alarm to his superiors, writing that: ". . . the number of unknown men moving into the disputed territory is growing. . . . they do not approach dwellings, avoid the whites, deal solely with the Indians, and . . . are completely equipped with muskets, pistols, and swords."

[33] On the Lewis and Alexander trading expedition, see Sibley, *A Report from Natchitoches in 1807*, entries for February 13, June 25, pp. 13, 40–42; Sibley to Dearborn, Natchitoches, July 3, 1807, and November 20, 1808, in Garrett, "Doctor John Sibley and The Louisiana-Texas Frontier," 45:381–82, 47:50.

der and Talapoon), provisioned with upwards of $3,000 worth of goods loaded on sixteen packhorses and with an additional remuda of thirty animals, set out to completely win the upriver tribes to American trade. Donning a military coat and sword and travelling under an American flag, carrying a scarlet officer's coat from Sibley to present as a token of American friendship to Awahakei of the Taovayas, Glass titled himself "Captain," and Sibley so styled him in his official correspondence about the expedition. Yet Governor Claiborne, whose own confidence in the American interpretation of the Red River boundary seems to have eroded considerably, was suspicious from the beginning. He wrote to several officials, including Secretary of State Madison, that rumor had it that Glass intended to look for a "silver mine" in the Red River country, among Indians who were subjects of Spain. Further, he told Madison: ". . . it may be a prelude to a project of greater moment: — It has a squinting toward Burrism."[34]

Actually, by establishing the American presence in the upper drainage of the Red, Glass was enacting a Jeffersonian plan which dated all the way back to April, 1804. Journeying from the Natchitoches Salt Works eastward around Lake Bisteneau and the Great Swamp, Glass's party crossed the Red at the Alabama-Coushatta village, and then set out across the highlands paralleling the Sulphur River on the "Pani-Conchetta Trace." By the end of July they were among wild horses and killing bison from horseback, Indian-style, in the Blackland Prairie near present Paris, Texas. Five weeks after leaving Natchitoches, Glass arrived at the Taovaya-Wichita villages, where he hoisted his American flag and helped them fight the Osages. Eventually he persuaded them to take him among "the Hietans" (Comanches), and both tribes finally agreed to show the American party their sacred healing shrine, a metallic mass the Comanches called Po-a-cat-le-pi-le-carre. After visiting the mysterious metal, evidently near present Albany, in Shackleford County, Texas, the Glass party split. With Talapoon and his Indian entourage, Glass continued travelling

---

[34] Claiborne to Madison, New Orleans, August 31, 1808. Rowland, *Official Letter Books of W. C. C. Claiborne* 4:199–200.

south to the Colorado River, trading guns for horses with both
Penatekas and representatives from other Comanche bands, and
apparently mistaking the uplift of the Callahan Divide, looming to
illusory heights on the horizon to the west, for "the Great Rocky
Mountains." When Glass returned to Natchitoches after eight
months of travel among the Indians of Texas, many of the plains
bands were firmly in the American camp. In 1809, the Taovayas
and Comanches even agreed to sell their sacred metal to George
Schamp and others of the Glass party, who assumed the meteorite
to be an immense nugget of platinum, and whose efforts to retrieve
it from the middle Brazos River country attracted so much attention that the Spaniards could not feign ignorance and finally did
send a patrol under Captain José Goseascoechea to investigate.
Goseascoechea never saw the Americans.[35]

Although the Spaniards knew about these forays along their
borders, their efforts to deal with them had now become impaired
by caution. The best idea Texas officials could manage was to

[35] My account of the Glass and Schamp trading expeditions here is summarized
from Flores, *Journal of an Indian Trader*, which reproduces and annotates the Glass
journal. Glass, who in many ways is the Southwestern analogue of contemporary
John Colter, has been even more obscure than Freeman and Custis. Extracts of his
journal of the 1808–1809 sojourn onto the plains are published here, with permission, for the first time. On the Spanish response to the Glass and Schamp expeditions, the critical letters are: Salcedo to Cordero, Chihuahua, August 16 and 31,
1808, and Bernard Bonavía to José Goseascoechea, San Antonio, October 4, 1809,
togther with the latter's diary of his expedition in search of the Americans, kept
from October 5 to November 21, 1809, all in The Bexar Archives.
Floated down the Red to Natchitoches by the Schamp party in 1810, the
1,635-pound meteorite created a sensation in Louisiana. Most observers were
convinced that it was platinum, and Thomas Linnard of the Natchitoches Indian
Factory remarked that undoubtedly "this is what was said to be the silver ore that
abounds in the tract of country occupied by the Panies . . ." Natchitoches-Sulphur
Fork Agency Ledgers, 1809–1821, ledger entry for August 26, 1809. On behalf of
the traders, Sibley dispatched the meteorite to New York, where Colonel George
Gibbs of the New York Lyceum recognized it as meteoric iron and acquired it for
his collection. At his death it was bequeathed to Benjamin Silliman, long a student of meteors and meteorites, at Yale. For most of the nineteenth century it was
the largest meteorite in any collection in the world and was written up many times
in Silliman's *American Journal of Science and Arts*. Today it is housed in the Peabody Museum of Natural History at Yale, where it is known as "Red River." For an

set up an Indian trading factory under Marcel Soto at Bayou Pierre in hopes of retaining the Red River trade, and, early in 1808, to dispatch from San Antonio a 200-man force led by Captain Don Francisco Amangual to reconnoiter the headwaters of the Red in order to insure the loyalty of the Comanches and other tribes.[36] These measures were not enough. Americans who were foolish enough to actually approach Santa Fe were still captured, but the events of 1806 appear to have effected a practical transfer of control of the Red River valley to the Americans.

While Anglo traders and hunters began to utilize the Red and its tributaries immediately, actual settlement proceeded much more slowly, despite the glowing reports of the country Freeman and Custis had sent back. There were two reasons. First, until the Great Raft was removed and the river made navigable, north of Campti the river valley could hold little inducement to farmers, and second, as long as the Raft existed it served as an effective environmental barrier between white settlements on the lower river and the Indian communities above. This natural barrier was used to advantage by the American government after the breakup of many of the Eastern tribes during the War of 1812. Perhaps Custis's report of the game-rich river valley was remembered by the War Department, but at the outset of the government's "removal solution" the middle Red was selected as an initial relocation site. This prototype Indian Territory within two decades was so filled with refugee Indians that agent George Gray of the Caddo

account of this meteorite, and others venerated by southern Plains Indians, see Flores, epilogue to *Journal of an Indian Trader.*

[36] Marcel Soto's trading house at Bayou Pierre was established in the spring of 1808 expressly to win the trade of the Caddos and Taovaya-Wichitas. By late 1809, however, Soto had yet to win these tribes back to Spain. Critical letters on the Bayou Pierre post are Cordero to Salcedo, San Antonio, February 5, 1808; Salcedo to Cordero, Chihuahua, June 14, 1808; Guadiana to Cordero, Nacogdoches, March 19, 1809; Manuel Salcedo to Bonavia, San Antonio, November 29, 1809, all in The Bexar Archives. On Amangual's expedition, which started from San Antonio on March 30 and returned from Santa Fe to the point of origin on December 23, see Loomis and Nasatir, *Pedro Vial and the Roads to Santa Fe.* Amangual's journal, assembled from the several versions which exist in manuscript, is reprinted on pp. 461–533 of this work, although without much effort at annotation.

Prairie Agency lamented that the area "appears to be the whirlpool that is sucking within its bosom the restless and dissatisfied, of all nations and languages. . . ."[37]

Despite government wishes, the early records reveal that illegal white squatters—mostly the type of frontiersmen who hunted and ran stock rather than farmed—entered the area with dogged persistence. These intruders rarely came upriver, instead journeying overland from the east and north and settling on the river-bottom prairies above the Sulphur River and near Pecan Point (a favorite game crossing of the Indians), in what is now southeastern Oklahoma. As with the American traders on the river, Spanish officials in Texas pointedly looked the other way, even when the Anglo backwoodsmen set up on the south side of the river. Indian complaints periodically brought American soldiers from Natchitoches and Fort Smith to drive the squatters away, but with little lasting success.[38] After the Adams-Onís Treaty of 1819 made the Red River the international boundary, and particularly after Mexico finally threw off the yoke of Spanish imperial rule two years later, Anglo-Americans quickly poured into northeast Texas, preserving the name "Spanish Bluff" in their local folklore, but almost nothing else relative to Jefferson's exploration of 1806. Farther downriver, it was not until Dehahuit's death in 1833 that the Americans were able to pressure the Caddo chiefs Tarshar, Tehowahimmo, Mattan, and Tooeksoach into ceding their homelands to the United States.[39] After July 1, 1835, the region between the Great Raft

[37] George Gray to Secretary of War James Barbour, Caddo Prairie Agency, June 13, 1827. Carter, *The Territory of Arkansas, 1819–1836*, vol. 20, *The Territorial Papers of the United States*, pp. 479–81.

[38] See Stephen H. Long to Brigadier-General Thomas Smith, Fort Smith, January 30, 1818, and Arkansas Territorial Governor James Miller to Secretary of of War John C. Calhoun, Fort Smith, June 20, 1820, Ibid., 19:4–10, 191–95. Long reported that 3,000 settlers from Indiana, Kentucky, Tennessee, and Illinois, had squatted illegally along the middle Red from the Great Bend to the Kiamichi. For the Indian disapproval, see Sibley to Secretary of War William Eustis, Natchitoches, July 17, December 31, 1811, in Garrett, "Doctor John Sibley and The Louisiana-Texas Frontier," 49:116–18, 403–405.

[39] Glover, "A History of the Caddo Indians," pp. 929–30. Dehahuit, according to Indian tradition, was buried atop Stormy Point, overlooking Caddo Lake. About 1870, a bluff on the southwestern corner of the point washed out to

and the Great Bend was finally open to legal white settlement. By the early 1840s, the tribes that had called the Red River valley their home for thousands of years were scattered across Texas and the Indian Territory, relinquishing their former homes and sacred places to the relentless avalanche of whites.

Despite the failure of the exploration to realize its objectives, participation in the Jefferson expedition proved a boon to the subsequent careers of most of the leaders. Richard Sparks was promoted to the rank of major as a result of his defensive actions to protect the party at Spanish Bluff. At the outset of the War of 1812 he was thus in a good position for promotion to the rank of colonel, and a command. Serving with distinction in that conflict, Sparks was discharged from the service with honors in June, 1815. Two weeks later he died.[40]

Custis's subsequent career is more puzzling. He completed his final work for the government in October, telling Dearborn: "I have to return my most sincere thanks for the appointment with which you honored me, & to regret the failure of the expedition." Returning to the University of Pennsylvania, he completed his M.D. examination by May, submitting a thesis on "Bilious Fever of Albermarle County [Va.]," a topic that anticipated the focus of his later career. In 1807, however, his interest in natural history remained high. He worked on a botanical collection from Virginia for Barton's herbarium that summer, and his work on the Red was alluded to by Barton in an address before the Philadelphia Linnaean Society.[41]

For what appears to have been a variety of reasons, Custis increasingly found himself drawn away from natural history towards medicine. One factor was obviously financial: having sacrificed

reveal a skeleton decorated with copper epaulets and a headpiece of virgin silver. Veatch, "The Shreveport Area," 202-203.

[40] Heitman, *Historical Register and Dictionary of the United States Army* 1:909.

[41] Custis to Dearborn, Natchez, October 1, 1806. War Department, Letters Received, Unregistered Series. Louise R. Coursey, Charles Patterson Van Pelt Library, the University of Pennsylvania, to the editor, Philadelphia, April 25, 1979; John Hendley Barnhart, "Brief Sketches of some Collectors of Specimens in the Barton Herbarium," *Proceedings of the Philadelphia Botanical Club* 9 (1926): 35; Barton, "A Discourse on Some of the Principal Desiderata in Natural His-

his share of the family estate to advance his education, by 1807 Custis found himself back in Drummond Town without adequate means of support. Custis's experience with Jefferson's reticence about the exploration must have bothered him; that the scientific community ignored the expedition surely disheartened. The net result was that instead of promoting his Red River discoveries and continuing natural history, by 1808 Custis settled in as a doctor in New Bern, North Carolina. There he successively married the daughters of two fellow physicians, Mary Pasteur in 1809, Katherine Carthy in 1818. Although he named his eldest after Linnaeus and his second-born Peter Barton, after the mentor who had sent him off to the West, Custis never seems to have published in natural history again. In 1808 Thomas Nuttall arrived from England to become Barton's new protégé in the West, and Nuttall, Pursh, Wilson, and Rafinesque went on to rediscover many of the plants and animals Custis had seen first on the Red River in 1806. Peter Custis lived a long life. Thought "somewhat blunt and caustic" by contemporaries, he was also "highly popular" in Carolina society. He died on May 1, 1842, having outlived all the other principals of the exploration.[42]

---

tory," p. 23; Custis to Barton, Drummond Town, Virginia, May 21, 1807. Benjamin Smith Barton Collection.

[42] On Custis's life after the exploration, see (on his move from Virginia to New Bern), Custis to Barton, New Bern, October 29, 1808, Barton Collection; Notice of marriage, Dr. Peter Custis to Mary Pasteur, daughter of Dr. Edward Pasteur, April 20, 1809, in *Raleigh Register*, April 27, 1809; Alan Watson, *A History of New Bern and Craven County* (New Bern: Tryon Palace Comm., 1987), 323. On his later (1818) marriage to Katherine Carthy, daughter of Dr. Daniel Carthy, see Craven County Marriage Bonds, North Carolina State Archives, Raleigh, North Carolina.

The characterization of his personality is in the Stephen Miller Memoir, Collection no. 371, East Carolina Manuscript Collection, J. Y. Joyner Library, East Carolina University, Greenville, North Carolina: "Recollections of Physicians in Early North Carolina."

Other sources on Dr. Custis's post-exploration life include: Peter Custis Will and Testament, Craven County Original Wills, North Carolina State Archives, Raleigh, North Carolina, June 30, 1840. (The will lists as his children: Linnaeus, Peter Barton, Sally, Betsey, Pennan, and Park.) The Custis family Bible survives in the New Bern Historical Society. On his death see: Dr. Peter Custis, Certificate of Death, May 1, 1842, Craven County, N.C., Superior Court, "Will Book D," pp. 54–55. The only biographical sketch that currently

The Arkansas River Expedition

As for Thomas Freeman, his work on the Red River had sufficiently impressed Jefferson for the president to retain him in
the border country for one more attempt at scientific exploration
of the West—up the Arkansas River in the spring of 1807. A committee of the House, chaired by John Alston of South Carolina,
took up this question, mentioning favorably the work of Freeman
on the Red, and endorsing the president's plan for resuming the
exploration of the Southwest.[43] During the winter and spring of
1806–1807, Freeman was apparently at The Forest where he and
Dunbar planned the Arkansas River expedition and conferred
with Lieutenant James B. Wilkinson, who had come down that
river the previous fall, arriving in Natchez in February.[44]

As late as March this expedition was still on. Although Dearborn assumed the responsibility for implementation, the basic plan
seems to have been Jefferson's. Since no naturalist could be
found, Freeman was given the sole field command, and Lieutenant
Wilkinson, Lieutenant Thomas A. Smith, and thirty-five troops
were to provide the military escort. The exploration was to in-
volve a spring ascent of the Arkansas, a winter encampment at
the Osage villages, and then a complete geographic examination
of the river to its sources in the Rockies, with the opportunity for
Freeman to explore in a northwesterly direction from there. In
February, Jefferson sent to Dearborn, for forwarding to Freeman,
a list of trade items Meriwether Lewis had found most desired by
the Indian nations of the West, expressing hope that the list "may
be useful to Colo. Freeman and our future explorers."[45] While

exists on Custis is one done by the editor for Sterling's *Biographical Dictionary
of North American Environmentalists.*

[43] Isaac J. Cox, "The Early Exploration of Louisiana," (Ph.D. diss., the University of Pennsylvania, 1906), p. 90.

[44] For letters and other pertinent information, see Jackson, *The Journals of
Zebulon Montgomery Pike* 1:287, 340, 2:142-44, 174. Lieutenant Wilkinson's
sketchy journal of his descent of the Arkansas is in 2:3-19. Just how good a companion explorer the younger Wilkinson would have been is open to question.
His health was not good, he and Pike had quarreled at their departure, and
half of his men had deserted during the descent of the Arkansas.

[45] Jefferson to Dearborn, Washington, February 14, 1807. The Thomas Jeffer-

Dunbar worried that the party was becoming too military and might threaten Spain, Spanish officials took no action, and, early in April, Freeman proceeded to the next step: writing Sibley to have his Red River flatboats retrieved from the Alabama-Coushatta village posthaste and sent downriver to Natchez. Within three weeks a Mr. Philebare, one of Sibley's Indian interpreters, had the flatboats back in Natchitoches, freshly-caulked and in good shape.[46] That May, in one of the more interesting developments concerning this expedition, Dunbar penned a letter to Wilkinson (the only missive Dunbar is known to have written the general) relative to the possiblity that this expedition, too, might be interfered with, in this case by the Osages. It asked for Wilkinson's personal protection, and closed with the sarcastic admonishment that: ". . . there are moments when . . . the ultimate good of our Country ought to be the object perpetually in view."[47]

Unfortunately, even while Dunbar and Freeman were making their final plans, in Washington the expedition had already been cancelled. On March 30, Dearborn wrote Dunbar that "by some mistake or inattention," no appropriation had been made in Congress for financing the Arkansas exploration, and consequently that "Mr. Freeman's services in the exploring line are at an end, at present. . . ."[48] Away in New Orleans selecting men and supplies, Freeman did not discover that the tour had been called off until after his arrival at The Forest in June, with "a detachment of 40 men well chosen and well provided for the expedition up the Arkansas." Aware now that he was not destined to become the Meriwether Lewis of the Southwest, Freeman wrote Dearborn with just a trace of bitterness that suspension of the probe "has been a very great disappointment to all Americans in the

son Papers, Ser. 1; Wilkinson to Pike, New Orleans, May 20, 1807. Jackson, *The Journals of Zebulon Montgomery Pike* 2:18n.20, 229.

[46]Sibley to Dearborn, Natchitoches, April 3 and 20, 1807. Garrett, "Doctor John Sibley and The Louisiana–Texas Frontier," 45:299, 378.

[47]Dunbar to Wilkinson, Natchez, May 3, 1807. Rowland, *Dunbar Letters*, p. 354.

[48]Dearborn to Dunbar, Washington, March 30, 1807. Ibid., pp.197–98.

enterprise, but peculiarly so to me, having flattered myself with the most sanguine hope of complete success."[49]

What had happened seems obvious. Congress, despite Alston's recommendations, was fully cognizant of the perilous nature of Southwestern exploration. It thus ended Jefferson's cherished dream of sending scientific expeditions up all the major rivers of the West by the very effective withholding of funds. It would not be until the Stephen Long expedition of 1819–20 that another American exploration of the West would be attempted. The heyday of Jeffersonian exploration had come to an end.

THOMAS FREEMAN, 1807–21

In the summer of 1807, then, Thomas Freeman joined Meriwether Lewis and William Clark in the ranks of former explorers to whom Jefferson felt he owed a debt. Fulfilling his expectations, all of the Republican administrations to follow assigned Freeman important and influential positions, eventually to the point of arousing suspicion that appeared in an editorial from the New Orleans *Louisiana Gazette.* "Mr. Freeman, altho' a foreigner . . . continues a favourite of government," it read, adding pointedly that "cabinet secrets relating to the expedition were entirely confided to Mr. Freeman," and that, remarkably, knowledge of "those secret expeditions, secret orders, and secret plans wonderfully enhance [his] talents, respectability, and worth. . . ."[50]

---

[49] Freeman to Dearborn, Natchez, June 15, 1807. War Department, Letters Received, Main Series. There are some developments worth taking note of with respect to this expedition. One is that Jefferson allowed Dearborn to assume virtually sole responsibility for it, which may explain why Congress was allowed to "overlook" the appropriation for it. A second is Jefferson's strange failure to personally notify Dunbar, a correspondent for most of the preceding decade, of the cancellation. In fact, Jefferson and Dunbar *never* corresponded again after the failure of the Red River expedition in 1806.

Finally, modern aficionados of early American exploration in the Southwest are soon to be treated to a new novel, by Professor Donald Jackson, that will deal with Freeman's 1807 Arkansas River expedition as if it actually were carried to fruition.

[50] *The Louisiana Gazette,* May 16, 1811.

The focus of Freeman's remaining life's work was in the Southeast. Following the decision to cancel the Arkansas tour, Secretary of the Treasury Albert Gallatin requested that Seth Pease, surveyor general of the lands south of Tennessee, appoint Freeman surveyor of the boundaries for the new Chickasaw Treaty, for precision was required and the explorer was "very well qualified."[51] Over the next two years, Freeman won mounting respect from both Gallatin and Jefferson for his support of squatter's rights in Tennessee and his census work in the Mississippi Territory.[52] In the autumn of 1809 he had occasion to perform a more personal service for Jefferson. The second week of October, Meriwether Lewis, suffering from depression, evidently committed suicide at Grinder's Tavern on the Natchez Trace. Arriving soon afterward at the scene of this tragedy, Freeman was charged with conveying his fellow explorer's personal effects to Virginia, where he presented them to Jefferson. Among them was Lewis's journal of the epic exploration of northern Louisiana.[53]

In 1810, when Seth Pease resigned his surveyor general's post, President Madison informed Gallatin that he intended to reward Freeman with the appointment. Nominated on January 7, 1811, he was confirmed two days later.[54] At long last, Freeman had "flowed into a permanency."

It was a satisfying year in another respect. General Wilkinson's long-delayed court-martial for complicity in the Burr Conspiracy at last got underway, prompted by the publication in 1809 of Daniel Clark's *Proofs Of The Corruption Of General James Wilkin-*

[51] Albert Gallatin to Seth Pease, Washington, March 30, 1807. Carter, *The Territory of Mississippi, 1798–1817*, vol. 5, *The Territorial Papers of the United States*, pp. 540–41.

[52] Dearborn to Freeman, Washington, October 25, 1808; Freeman to Gallatin, Madison County, Mississippi Territory, January [?], 1809; Freeman to Gallatin, Nashville, March 4, 1809, with marginal note by Gallatin; Ibid., pp. 658–59, 692, 720–22.

[53] Thomas Freeman and William C. Anderson, Memorandum of Lewis' Personal Effects, Nashville, November 23, 1809. Jackson, *Letters of the Lewis and Clark Expedition*, p. 470.

[54] Pease To Madison, Washington, July 23, 1810; Freeman to Gallatin, Washington, Mississippi Territory, August 8, 1810, Carter, *The Territory of Mississippi* 6:84, 95–97n.12.

son, And Of His Connexion With Aaron Burr. A star witness for the prosecution was Freeman's old nemesis, Andrew Ellicott, and when Wilkinson asked Freeman to appear as a counter witness, the former explorer never hesitated. In response to Wilkinson's questioning, Freeman's testimony not only cast doubt on Ellicott's honesty, but made the Philadelphia mathematician appear morally bankrupt as well. On the boat trip down the Mississippi with Ellicott in 1798, he told the jurors, talk was that Ellicott, his washerwoman Betsy (whose "known character was that of a prostitute, and of the lowest grade"), and young Andy Ellicott shared a nightly bed, and that "I was even pressed myself by the old sinner Ellicott, to take part of his bed with his washerwoman and himself for the night."[55] Freeman's testimony against the man who had once described him to the government as possessing a "want of information, extreme pride, and [an] ungovernable temper,"[56] seriously impaired the prosecution's case, but the irony was double-edged. By helping to acquit Wilkinson, Freeman had unknowingly assisted the man who, more than anyone else, was responsible for the failure of the Red River expedition five years earlier.

Freeman's confident and somewhat intense letters during the last decade of his life reveal a man who handled considerable power well and fairly. Whether he was reporting illegal timber cutting on the public lands, submitting maps of Natchez and of the Choctaw Purchase, or supervising the running of the boundaries of the Creek land cession of 1814 (during which his surveyors had to be protected by Andrew Jackson's army), Freeman continued to impress government officials, who viewed his work as detailed, experienced, and "generally very correct."[57]

[55] Wilkinson explained to the jury that it was his befriending of Freeman in 1798 that was the actual origin of Ellicott's hatred towards him—and the source of his "lies" about the Spanish pension. Freeman's testimony is in Wilkinson, *Memoirs of My Own Time* 2: appendix 32, p. 183.

[56] Ellicott to Timothy Pickering, Darling's Creek, November 8, 1798. *American State Papers, Miscellaneous,* Class 10, 1:710–11.

[57] Freeman to Gallatin, Washington, Mississippi Territory, July 9, July 15, 1811; Freeman to Josiah Meigs, Washington, Mississippi Territory, March 4, 1816; Freeman to Meigs, St. Stephen, Alabama District, April 12, 1816; Meigs

By 1816, however, constant wilderness travel had begun to take its toll. That summer he must have become very ill, for he delayed running the Creek boundaries until he had "recovered sufficiently from the extreme fatigue of traveling in the wilderness annoyed by flies and heat. . . ." By September, rumors reached Washington that Freeman had died. But the rumors were false, and he recovered enough to comply with a request that he move the surveyor general's office from Washington, in the Mississippi Territory, to the Alabama District. Setting up in St. Stephens in 1817, he worked on the northern boundary of the Creek cession and explored the rivers of the area.[58]

In 1820, Freeman was back in the Natchez area, briefly, in preparation for running the boundary between Mississippi and Alabama. Later that spring he signed an agreement with General John Coffee at the mouth of the Pascagoula, on the Gulf, relative to the Choctaw boundary.[59] On November 8, 1821, Freeman died suddenly in Huntsville, Alabama. That his death was deeply lamented in the society through which he moved is demonstrated by this notice which appeared in the *Mississippi Gazette:*

> The urbanity of his manner, the amiability of his disposition, and the honorable uprightness of his deportment, endeared him to all his acquaintances. To the country the loss is most serious, for few men are to be found who are as well qualified to fill the important office which he held—scientific and judicious. The most perservering industry and rigid integrity, were the strongest traits of his public character, and enabled him to afford the highest degree of usefulness.[60]

---

to Israel Pickens, Washington, August 18, 1817, in Carter, *The Territory of Mississippi* 6:205–206, 210–11, 528–30, 677–78, 799.

[58] Freeman to Meigs, St. Stephen, Alabama District, June 30, 1816; David Holmes to Judge Harry Toulmin, Washington, Mississippi Territory, September 16, 1816; Meigs to Freeman, Washington, May 26, 1817; Freeman to Meigs, Washington, Mississippi Territory, July [?], 1817. All in Carter, *The Territory of Alabama*, 1817–19, vol. 18 of *The Territorial Papers of the United States*, pp. 694–95, 704, 792, 338.

[59] Freeman to General John Coffee, Washington, Mississippi, April 23, 1820; Thomas Freeman and John Coffee, Agreement, May 29 and June 18, 1820. The John Coffee Papers. Alabama Department of Archives and History, Maps and Manuscripts Division.

[60] *Mississippi Gazette*, November 24, 1821. Freeman, who was in his middle thirties at the time he led the Red River expedition, was near fifty at his death.

History & The Forgotten Expedition

In the final analysis, it is to be regretted that what history will remember about the Freeman and Custis expedition is that it was forcefully aborted short of its objectives and that its failure, along with the arrest of Pike, effectively ended the first phase of scientific exploration of the American West. Freeman and Custis did make significant scientific and diplomatic contributions. In the present day, their Accounts have become the most valuable primary source for policy makers attempting to restore the Indian-shaped valley and original environmental setting of the lower half of the Red River valley. Overshadowed by the fabled Lewis and Clark exploration to the Pacific and back, their story largely suppressed by the government for political ends, the "Exploring Expedition of Red River" has been for a long time lost to American history. And when it has not been overlooked, it has been thought of only in terms of failure—failure to evade the Spaniards and contact the upriver Indian tribes, failure to reach the headwaters of the river and thus discover the great geographical error of the Southwest, failure to reach Santa Fe, and failure in the realization of whatever relationship it had to the Pike expedition.

Imagination is now the only means of considering America's second great exploration westward in terms of what might have been had the world been a different place in 1806. Such speculation is fruitless for the literal-minded, but I have found it impossible not to imagine Freeman and Custis among the Comanches, or marveling at the great multihued desert canyonlands (as their successors, Randolph Marcy in 1852 and Ernest Ruffner in 1876, assuredly did) of the Llano Estacado. But of course fiction is now the only way to entertain their, or Jeffersonian America's, reactions to the bright badlands, the mirages, the great yellowed horizontal sweeps, and the astonishing wildlife panoramas of the southern High Plains. It could be, had Jefferson's Red River probe been a success, that we'd have only exchanged Peter Custis for Stephen Long as the inventor of the "Great American Desert."

Relying upon consummate woodcraft and unflagging energy, Lewis and Clark had traversed the northern Louisiana Purchase almost without mishap. Those same traits also served the Red River party well, enabling them to surmount obstacles such as the Great Raft and Great Swamp. But of course in the Spanish Borderlands, nature was never the sole obstacle to U.S. hopes for exploration. In some respects Freeman and Custis were a "first sacrifice" to an imperial—now cultural—encounter still going on in the American Southwest. In 1806 their failure was New Spain's success. Now, as with Lewis and Clark, the story of Jefferson's effort to explore the river he viewed as "next to the Missouri, the most interesting water of the Mississippi" belongs to all of us.

--⋅≫⊰ *Jefferson's Letter of Exploring Instructions* ⊱≪⋅--

EDITOR'S NOTE: The Jefferson exploration letter, never published until now, is a transcript of Freeman's personal copy, now housed in the Peter Force Collection of the Library of Congress. It was originally written in the spring of 1804, and for nearly eighteen months—while Jefferson and Dunbar considered and rejected a plethora of leaders, and eventually dropped the Arkansas River and (by his choice) Dr. Hunter from the exploration—it did not carry an addressee's name. In fact, the second copy, preserved in the Jefferson Papers of the Library of Congress, never was addressed. Freeman's copy is addressed to him in Jefferson's hand, and evidently was presented to him at his private dinner with Jefferson in November, 1805. Freeman carefully safeguarded his copy, and after his death in 1821 the letter passed into the hands of the Historical Society of Mississippi. In 1859 the president of that body, Colonel B. L. C. Wailes, forwarded the letter to Peter Force, who had obtained for his collection of documents King's manuscript redaction of the Freeman and Custis journals and reports.

By far the most outstanding feature of this letter of classic exploring instructions is the remarkable similarity it bears to Jefferson's June 20, 1803, letter to Meriwether Lewis. Except for the details of the prospective routes, there are only minor differences (indicated in the accompanying annotation) between the two.

As elsewhere, no changes have been made in the original spelling and punctuation of this document.

To Thomas Freeman Esquire

The government of the US. being desirous of informing itself of the extent of the Country lately ceded to them under the name of Louisiana to have the same with its principal rivers geographically delineated, to learn the character of the soil climate productions & inhabitants, you are appointed to explore for these purposes the interesting portion of it which lies on the Arkansas and Red Rivers, from their confluence with the Mississippi to the remotest source of the main streams of each and the high lands connecting the same and forming a part of the boundary of the Province.

You will receive from the Secretary of War information and instructions as to the provision to be made of men arms, ammunition medicine substence clothing covering camp utensils instruments of observation and measuring boats light articles for barter and presents among the indians and other necessaries all of which are to be collected at Natchez which is to be considered the point of departure. From Natchez you are to proceed to ascend the Red river taking observations of longitude and latitude at its mouth, at all remarkable points in its course & especially at the mouths of rivers, at rapids, islands and other places & objects distinguished by such natural marks and characters of a durable kind as that they may with certainty be recognized thereafter. the courses of the rivers between these points of observation may be supplied by the compass the log line and by time corrected by the observations themselves. the variations of the Compass too in different places are to be noted.

In this way you will proceed to the remotest source of the main stream of the Red river and thence to that of the Arkansa along the high lands which divide their waters from those running into the Rio Norte or the Pacific Ocean ascertaining by the chain and compass with due corrections for variation, the courses and extent of said high lands, and by carefull and multiplied observations the longitude of the said remotest sources of the main streams of each River. You are then to descend the Arkansas from its source to its mouth ascertaining by like observations all remarkable points on the said river supplying its courses between these points by the Compass the log line and by time as directed for the Red River and using peculiar care to find with accuracy the latitude and longitude of the mouth of the river.

Although we have before said you are to ascend the Red river and descend the Arkansas on the presumption that the former is the least rapid yet if the fact be known to be otherwise or any other circumstances overweigh this you are at liberty to reverse this order and ascend the Arkansas and descend the Red river observing in the other points the instructions before given.

Your observations are to be taken with great pains and accuracy to be entered distinctly and intelligibly for others as well as yourself to comprehend all the elements necessary with the use of the usual tables to find the latitude and longitude of the places at which they were taken and are to be rendered to the War office for the purpose of having the calculations made concurrently by proper persons within the US. several copies of these as well as of your other notes should be made at leisure time and put into the care of the most trustworthy of your attendants to guard, by multiplying them against the accidental losses to which they will be exposed. a further guard perhaps would be that one of these copies should be on the paper of the birch as supposed less liable to injury from damp than common paper.

The following objects in the Country adjacent to the rivers along which you will pass will be worthy of notice. The soil and face of the Country, the growth and vegetable productions especially those not of the maritime states. the animals of the Country generally and especially those not known in the maritime states. the remains and accounts of any which may be deemed extinct. the mineral productions most worth notice but more particularly

> metals limestone, gypsum pitcoal, saltpetre, rock salt and salt springs and mineral waters, noting the temperature of the last and such circumstances as may indicate their characters.

Volcanic appearances.
Climate, as characterized by the thermometer by the

proportion of rainy cloudy and clear days, by lightning hail snow ice, by the access and recess of frost by the winds prevailing at different seasons the dates at which particular plants put forth or loose their flower or leaf times of appearances of particular birds, reptiles or insects. Most of these articles may be entered in a callendar or table so as to take little room or time in entering.

Court an intercourse with the natives as intensively as you can, treat them on all occasions in the most friendly and conciliatory manner which their conduct will admit. allay all jealousies as to the object of your journey make them acquainted with the position, intent, character peaceable and commercial dispositions of the US. inform them that their late fathers the Spaniards have agreed to withdraw all their troops from the Mississippi and Missouri and from all the countries watered by any rivers running into them; that they have delivered to us all their subjects, Spanish and French settled in those countries together with their posts and [illegible] in the same that henceforth we become their fathers and friends[1] that our first wish will be to be neighborly, friendly and useful to them and especially to carry on commerce with them on terms more reasonable and advantageous for them than any other nation ever did: Confer with them on the points most convenient as mutual frontiers for them and us say that we have sent you to enquire into the nature of the Country and the nations inhabiting it to know their wants and the supplies they will wish to dispose of and that after you shall have returned with the necessary information we shall take measures with their consent for setting trading houses among them at suitable places that in the mean time the same traders who reside among them or visit them and who are now become our citizens will continue to supply them as

[1] This passage furnishes one of the few paragraphs that has no counterpart in the letter to Lewis, and it reflects Jefferson's awareness that Spain might not be willing to accept his definition of the extent of Louisiana. Thus, his Southwestern explorers were to stress the American version of the boundaries to the Indian nations encountered, enlisting their allegiance by telling them that Spain had *voluntarily* delivered them over to the United States. In a diplomatic situation of much more explosive potential than that of Lewis and Clark, Jefferson's Red-Arkansas river leaders were intended to perform a diplomatic as well as scientific function.

usual & that they will find us in all things just and faithful friends and patrons.

You will endeavour as far as a dilligent pursuit of your journey will admit to learn the names and numbers of the nations through which your rout lies.

> the extent and limits of their possessions their relations with other tribes and nations their language, traditions, monuments their ordinary occupations in agriculture fishing hunting war arts and the implements of these their food clothing and domestic accomodations; the diseases prevalent among them and the remedies they use; moral and physical circumstances which distinguish them from other tribes we know. peculiarities in their laws customs and dispositions; And articles of commerce they may need or furnish & to what extent.

And Considering the interest which every nation has in extending and strengthening the authority of reason and justice among the people around them it will be useful to acquire what knowledge you can of the state of morality religion and information among them, as it may better enable those who may endeavour to civilize and instruct them to adapt their measures to the existing notions and practices of those on whom they are to operate.

As it is impossible for us to forsee in what manner you will be received by these people, whether with hospitality or hostility so it is impossible to describe the exact degree of perserverance with which you are to pursue your journey. We value too much the lives of citizens to offer them to probable destruction. Your numbers will be sufficient to secure you against the unauthorized opposition of individuals or of small parties. but if at any time a superior force authorized or not authorized by a nation should be arrayed against your further passage and inflexibly determined to arrest it, you must decline its further pursuit and return. in the loss of yourselves we should also loose the information you will have acquired. by returning safely with that you may enable us to renew the essay with better calculated means. to your own discretion therefore must be left the degree of danger you may risk and the point at which you should decline: only saying we wish you to err on the side of your safety and to bring back your party safe even with less information.[2]

As far up the rivers as the white settlements extend an intercourse probably exists with Natchez or New Orleans: and as far as traders go they may furnish a conveyance for your letters to either of those places; beyond that you may perhaps be able to engage Indians to bring letters for the government, on promising that they shall receive at either of those places such special compensation as you shall have stipulated with them, and measures will be taken there to insure a fulfilment of your stipulations. avail yourself of all these means to communicate to us at reasonable intervals copies of your journal notes and observations of every kind.

Doct.ʳ George Hunter of Philadelphia will accompany you as a fellow labourer and counsellor in the same service, while the ultimate direction of the expedition is left to yourself. he is to make observations to note courses and enquire into the same subjects recommended to you but seperately as it is supposed that the two different accounts may serve to corroborate or to correct each other. he is to participate with you in the conveniences and comforts provided and to receive from you what aid and facility you can yield for his pursuits consistently with due dilligence in the prosecution of your journey. shall the accident of death happen to you he is to succeed to the direction of the expedition and to all the powers which you possess. should he also die the officer attending you and subject to your orders will immediately return with his party in the way he shall deem best bringing the papers and other effects belonging to the mission.

As the great distance between this and the point of your departure leaves it impractical for these instructions or those of the Secretary of War to go into all the details which may be necessary to prepare and expedite your departure I have requested William Dunbar esquire of the [sic] Natchez to take on himself the direc-

[2] This same paragraph, with the change of only one or two words, also appears in the letter to Lewis, and thus originated in concept with the Lewis and Clark, not the Southwestern, expedition. For comparison of this letter to the one to Lewis, see Jefferson to Lewis, Washington, June 20, 1803, in Jackson, *Letters of the Lewis and Clark Expedition*, pp. 60–66.

tion of everything supplementary and additional to our instructions to superintend and take order in whatsoever may be further neessary in the course of your preparations, departure, going & returning. you will therefore consider his further instructions and proceedings as eminating from myself and conform to them accordingly: and you will make him during your journey the centre of communication between yourself and the government and on your return and arrival at the [*sic*] Natchez you will report yourself to him and receive from him the information and instructions proper for the occasion and which shall have been furnished by the government: these shall particularly provide for the immediate paiment of yourselves of what shall be due to you and of all arranged to the Officer and men which shall have incurred since their departure: and such as shall have faithfully and obediently performed their duty during the tour shall be recommended to the liberality of the legislature for the grant of a portion of land to each in proportion to his grade or condition ———

Given under my hand and seal at Monticello this 14th day of April 1804 & of the independence of the United States the twenty-eighth.

Th: Jefferson

A List of Notable Points on the Middle and Upper Red River

By Peter Custis

EDITOR'S NOTE: the chart of outstanding geographical features and distances on the Red is reproduced here from Peter Custis's letter to Benjamin Smith Barton, dated June 1, 1806, the day before the party left Natchitoches for the wilderness upriver. The manuscript original is in the Benjamin Smith Barton Collection of the library of the American Philosophical Society, Philadelphia. This chart was published on pages 48–50 of Custis's article, "Observations relative to the Geography, Natural History, & etc., of the Country Along the Red-River, in Louisiana," *The Philadelphia Medical and Physical Journal* (1806).

What this chart represents is not scientific measurements by Freeman and Humphreys, but the earthy, and, not surprisingly, accurate river knowledge of the Indian traders and hunters who followed the Red River into the game-rich prairies and plains of the early Southwest. These rough-hewn plainsmen, as Custis's chart demonstrates, were landmark oriented, and in this respect their accounts are reliable, for all the landmarks that appear here are readily identifiable today, either from maps or by observation from a boat in the current of the river itself. Custis does not specify who among the Natchitoches hunters provided him with this information, but from the close similarity this chart bears to the one accompanying Sibley's 1805 report on the river, François Grappe must have been responsible for much of it. Grappe, known to the expedition members as "Touline," guided the party into the Cadodoquia.

As elsewhere, no changes have been made in the original spelling and punctuation of this document.

The distance from Natchitoches to the source of the Red-River, according to the accounts of the best and most respectable hunters and traders. The distances have been curtailed in consequence of the Indian traders and hunters being apt to overrate them.

		Miles
1	To Grande Ecore	10
2	Campté	20
3	Bayou Chanuo[3]	15
4	Through do. into Lake Bristino [*sic*]	3
5	Through Lake Bristino to the upper end of do.	60
6	Through Bayou Dochette to Red River again	9
7	To Conchetta villages [*sic*] (where the Cadoux lived, 9 years ago)[4]	60
		——— 177
8	First Little-River, south side[5]	80
9	Long Prairie, north side	25
10	Upper end of do.	5
11	Little Prairie, south side	40
12	Upper end of do.	25
13	Pine Bluff, north side	12
14	Upper end of do.	5

[3] Sibley spells it "Channo" in his chart. From the abbreviated length, this would seem to be Bayou Pascagoula, although Loggy Bayou, Red River Parish, La., is a possibility.

[4] This is a mistake that Sibley also makes. During the course of the exploration, Custis will discover that the last Caddo occupation of the river valley had not been in the Caddo Prairie region, where the Alabama-Coushattas settled, but farther north, at the site of the Caddo Medicine Mount in present southwestern Arkansas.

[5] The Sulphur River, which drains the Blackland Prairie of northeast Texas and empties into the Red in Miller County, Ark. Like virtually all of the streams and tributaries Custis mentions here, it is no longer a free-flowing stream, but

		Miles
15	The Cedars[6]	15
16	Upper end of Cedars, and mouth of Little-River, north side[7]	40
17	Round Prairie, north side, and first fording place[8]	20
18	Lower end of Long Prairie, south side	25
19	Upper end of do.	40
20	Next Prairie, south side	12
21	Upper end of do.	20
22	Three mile Oak and Pine Bluff[9]	30
23	Pecan grove[10]	9
24	Upper end of do.	6
25	Next Prairie above the Pecans	40
26	Upper end of do.	25
27	Pine Bluff, south side	45
28	White Rock Bluff[11]	15
29	Next Prairie, north side	45
30	Upper end of do.	30

has been dammed. For other pertinent information, including Freeman's description of its mouth, see the Accounts, Part 4.

[6] The Cedars, named for the magnificent groves of eastern red cedar that once appeared here, growing along both banks of the Red between the present towns of Garland City and Fulton, Ark.

[7] Little River, which empties into the Red at the upper end of the Great Bend, in Hempstead County, Ark. Its four main affluents drain the southern Ouachita Mountains. For further information, see the Accounts, Part 4.

[8] Both prairie and gravel bar are just west of present Index, Little River County, Ark.

[9] Evidently Nanatsoho Bluff, soon named "Spanish Bluff" in consequence of its role in this exploration. This is the spot where the Freeman and Custis expedition was terminated.

[10] Pecan Point, in present McCurtain County, Okla., was a major buffalo crossing and landmark on the Red. It later became the site of very early Anglo-American settlements in this country.

[11] The chalk bluffs are a distinctive feature on the middle Red, stretching for several hundred yards, on the south bank, along the river nearly due south of today's Idabel, Okla.

		Miles	
31	Bayou Gatte, north side[12]	6	
32	To Kiomitchie, or Riviere la Mine[13]	25	
		───	640
33	Pine Bluff, south side	25	
34	Bois d'arc, or Bayou Kick, south side*[14]	40	
35	The Nazure, or Boggy-River, north side[15]	8	
36	Blue-River, same side[16]	50	

*Ancient village, or old fort, 20 miles from whence is a salt spring on Little River.

[12] At least three minor streams flow into the Red from the north between Pecan Point and the mouth of the Kiamichi. Bayou Gatte (which Sibley renders "Galle") was probably the westernmost of these, Cedar Creek. The other two possibilities are Buzzard Creek and Whitegrass Creek.

[13] The Kiamichi (from the French *kamichi*, meaning "Horned Screamer," a name given the river by the Arkansas Post voyageurs, who first saw ivory-bill woodpeckers in its valley) has its sources on Rich and Pine mountains on the Arkansas-Oklahoma border, and flows southwest between the Winding Stair and Kiamichi mountains before emptying into the Red. "Riviere la Mine" refers to a very early story that there was a silver mine on it. The Kiamichi was a favorite of the wilderness trappers because its mountainous terrain was prime beaver habitat, and its confluence with the Red became the site of the American Fort Towson in 1824.

[14] Bois d'Arc Creek, which empties into the Red River from the south in present Fannin County, Texas. The Indian name for it was Nahaucha (meaning "the thick," referring to the thick growth of bois d'arc along it). Sibley says the Natchitoches hunters thought it the best beaver stream on the Red. Custis's chart places it east of Boggy Creek; actually, it flows into the Red some 10 miles to the west of that river's mouth. His note referring to an "ancient village, or old fort" on this stream is evidently a reference to La Harpe's Post, but he has the location wrong, clearly so from the reference to Little River.

[15] Boggy Creek, which in two branches (the Muddy Boggy, which is 110 miles long, and the Clear Boggy, 70 miles long) drains some 2,520 square miles of present south central Oklahoma, joins the Red in western Choctaw County at mile 660 above the mouth.

[16] The Blue River, another relatively short stream (100 miles long, with a drainage of 660 square miles) was so named because of the extreme transparency

		Miles
37	Faux Anachitta, or Little Missouri, same side[17]	25
38	Panis Villages[18]	60
39	White Rock (old Panis Towns)[19]	120
40	From thence, as you ascend, the river divides into many branches,[20] and to the source is	

of the waters. It drains the region south of Oklahoma City and Norman, and comes in at mile 689, near the town of Wade, in present Bryant County, Okla.

[17] Sibley called this river "Fauxwacheta" (False Ouachita), but reported that some of the hunters referred to it as the Missouri Branch of the Red. It was (and is) a major river, taking its head on the Llano Estacado of the Texas Panhandle and swinging through modern southwestern Oklahoma in a 500-mile arc (with a drainage of more than 7,800 square miles) to join the Red in present Marshall County, at mile 759. Today the confluence of the two rivers, portrayed by George Catlin in a rare landscape in 1834 (see the Accounts, Part 4) is submerged beneath the waters of Lake Texoma, the first dammed, man-made reservoir on the main river.

[18] The "Pani" (Taovaya-Wichita) site on the Red River, the location of which is discussed in the Editor's Introduction, is considered to be the most important Indian site in the state of Oklahoma. Five years after the Freeman and Custis exploration, at the death of the Taovaya chief, Awahakei, the location was finally abandoned. Sibley to Eustis, Natchitoches, December 31, 1811, Garrett, "Doctor John Sibley and The Louisiana-Texas Frontier," 49:413. Anglo-Texans, upon seeing the ruins of these villages, erroneously though the site represented a Spanish occupation. They called the south bank sites "Spanish Fort," a name the spot still bears.

[19] A fascinating reference that points to the conclusion that the French hunters considered the North Fork (rather than Prairie Dog Town River) the main stream. "White Rock" evidently designates the bare, grayish-white Quartz Mountains of present southwestern Oklahoma. From various references (see the Editor's Introduction) we know that for a brief time in the 1760s or 1770s Osage pressure had forced the Taovaya-Wichitas to abandon their Cross Timbers location for a refuge in "broken country farther upstream." They remembered this "White Rock" refuge even after they returned to their traditional location, and after 1811 it became their last haven in the Southwest. George Catlin's painting of a mountain-girt "Pawnee-Pict" village (see the Accounts, Part 4) is of this location in Devil's Canyon (present Quartz Mountains State Park) on Elm Creek tributary of the North Fork.

[20] The four major forks, working from the south, would be the Pease, Prairie Dog Town Fork, the Salt Fork, and the North Fork. Prairie Dog Town Fork, designated by the United States Supreme Court in the Greer County case of

	Miles	
estimated at	300	
	───	628
After curtailing one third, the whole distance is		1445[21]

1896 as the main stream, drops off the Llano Estacado through the spectacular Palo Duro Canyon. But contrary to Randolph Marcy's belief during his 1852 exploration of the upper Red, its actual headwaters begin far to the west, in the remnant, Pleistocene channels of Palo Duro, Frio, and Tierra Blanca creeks, which flow (intermittently) across some 100 miles of slightly-inclined High Plain. Although the Frio is the longest, the early Spanish explorers usually followed Tierra Blanca ("Río Blanco"). With Marcy's failure to trace them, these streams were not mapped as the headwaters of the Red River until the present century.

[21] Sibley, who cites similar (although not identical) figures, but does not adjust the distance for exaggeration as Custis does, gives the distance from Natchitoches to the headwaters "in the mountains" as 1,885 miles. He puts the total length of the river at 2,151 miles. The actual length of the modern and considerably straightened river, according to the House Document "Red River, La., Ark., Okla., and Tex.," is 1,300 miles from the sources of Prairie Dog Town Fork in eastern New Mexico to the river's confluence with the Mississippi. The Custis estimate is thus much the more accurate, is indeed the first close approximation of the true length of the Red. I find it noteworthy that Custis makes no mention of a Rocky Mountain origin for the river. Perhaps too much can be made of such a negative; nonetheless, the omission flew in the face of accepted opinion of both hunters and cartographers. This Custis chart, which was published, may have aroused doubt in American minds concerning the true nature of the Red River, a doubt that must have deepened with Pike's inability to locate the headwaters of the Red in the Southern Rockies the following winter. The Spaniards actually made no better use of their maps, prepared by Vial, Walker, and others. When the Adams-Onís negotiations began in 1818, Onís argued against the American offer to run the boundary along the Red "to its source, touching the chain of the Snow Mountains," holding that the Arkansas would be a safer boundary since "This [Red] river rises within a few leagues of Santa Fe, the capital of New Mexico." This proposal, which led to the compromise of utilizing both rivers in the final settlement, is in John Quincy Adams to Don Luis de Onís, Washington, October 31, 1819; and Onís to Adams, Washington, February 1, 1819. *Annals of Congress*, 15th Cong., 2d sess., 2:1902–1906, 2111–113.

The earliest correct location for the sources of the Red by an American explorer came from Dr. Edwin James of the Long expedition—after that expedition had made the typical mistake of confusing the Canadian for the Red. James reported in 1820 that: "We are yet ignorant of the true position of the sources of Red river, but we are well assured the long received opinion . . . is erroneous. Several persons have recently arrived at St. Louis in Missouri, from Santa Fe, and, among others, the brother of Captain Shreeves, who gives information . . . that at a considerable distance to the south of this point in the high plain is the principal source of Red River." James, *Account of an Expedition from Pittsburgh to the Rocky Mountains*, 17, Pt. 4, p. 79. Henry S. Tanner's *Map of North America*, 1822, in Wheat, *Mapping the Transmississippi West* 2, map 350, is the first American map to locate the sources of the Red River in their approximate true location.

Meteorological observations made on Red River, 1806

EDITOR'S NOTE: This meteorological chart is Custis's work, and it appeared as an appendix to the published version. Jefferson had given somewhat vague instructions for such a chart in his letter of exploring instructions; Dunbar was much more specific, and the care and precision evident in these entires may be credited equally to him. In his last-minute missive to "Freeman Esqr. & his Associates," Natchez, April 28, 1806, Dunbar included this directive: "—the depth of the river may be sounded every morning by the Thermometer. Doctor Custis will no doubt keep a register of the weather[;] the degrees of the thermometer may be recorded 3 times a day, before sunrise [,] at 3 p. m. or the hottest time of the day & at 8 or 9 p. m.— . . . the direction & strength of the wind, with cloudy & clear days ought to be added. . . ."

Day of Month	Latt.	Temp. In Air	6 AM In River	Temp. In Air	3 PM In River	Temp. In Air	9 PM In River
May 2		71	72	85	76	76	76
3		72	74	85	76	78	76
4		74	76	84	77	78	77
5	31°.16′	70	77	85	76	77	77
6		76	78	82	79	74	78
7		72	78	82	79	78	78
8		76	78	83	80	66	78
9		62	78			60	78
10	31°.20′	50	78	80	79	66	78
11		62	77	81	78	78	77
12		72	78	73	77	68	76
13		73	76	76	77	74	77
14		72	75	85	86	77	76
15		76	76	70	76	69	75
16		69	73	74	78	72	74
17		67	73	65	75	68	74
18		64	73	75	75	70	74
19	31°.46′	65	73	84	74	78	74
20		72	73	90	76	76	76
21		70	75	90	77	74	77
22		71	77	88	79	78	79
23		74	80	88	80	72	80
24		69	80	86	82	76	82
25		73	82	84	82	76	82
26		72	82	72	82	70	80
27		69	80	76	80	72	79
28		69	79	79	79	74	79
29		72	79	85	80	78	79
30		80	78	87	80	74	79
31		74	78	84	84	74	79
June 1		72	70	90	80	79	80
2		76	80	89	81	82	80

Winds	Remarks on the Weather
South	A moderate breeze, and clear.
Variable	In the morning foggy, the rest of the day clear; gentle breezes.
SE & S	A gentle shower in the morning; rest of day clear; gentle breezes.
S & W	Clear. A strong breeze.
South	In forenoon cloudy; in afternoon clear.
South	Cloudy greater part of the day—A gentle rain in the afternoon—Very strong wind.
West	Clear—Wind very strong.
Var.	Clear—Wind very light.
East	Clear—Very light breeze.
E & SE	Cloudy—a fresh breeze—In the night rain with thunder and lightning.
E, NE	In the morning a great rain with thunder and lightning, and strong wind.
N, NE	Cloudy in forenoon; in afternoon rain with heavy thunder and lightning; in night a violent thunderstorm.
West	Clear; light wind.
W, NW	Excessive rain with severe thunder and lightning.
South	Cloudy, a gentle shower in the afternoon.
NE	Much rain with heavy thunder and lightning.
SW	Cloudy all day; light wind.
N, NE	Clear.
NW	In the evening cloudy with thunder and lightning; rest of the day clear.
W, NW	Clear greater part of the day; in the evening cloudy with thunder.
SE	Clear, light breeze; thunder in the evening.
S & N	In forenoon clear; afternoon a heavy shower with thunder and lightning.
NE	Clear; wind very light.
NE	In forenoon clear, rest of the day overcast; in the night rainy.
NE	Rainy all the day and night.
E, NE	Overcast; wind very light.
Variable	In the afternoon rain with thunder and lightning.
South	Clear; wind light; in the night rain with thunder and lightning.
S & NW	In the afternoon rain with thunder and lightning.
North	Cloudy greater part of the day.
North	Clear; wind very light.
East	Clear; wind very light.

Day of Month	Latt.	Temp. In Air (6 AM)	6 AM In River	Temp. In Air (3 PM)	3 PM In River	Temp. In Air (9 PM)	9 PM In River
June 3		76	82	84	80	76	80
4		79	80	83	84	78	80
5		76	82	84	82	74	82
6		74	82	86	83	80	82
7		78	83	88	82	82	82
8	31°.56'.27''	80	84	88	83	82	84
9		80	85	86	84	80	85
10		76	85	86	84	82	84
11		85	84	83	86	77	84
12		74	82	79	86	76	82
13		76	80	82	88	79	84
14		76	82	87	83	78	82
15	32°.26'	78	84	85	84	80	82
16		76	82	90	85	82	83
17		73	72	88	85	76	84
18		82	83	84	85	78	84
19	32°.34'	78	84	87	87	80	84
20		76	84	85	84	80	84
21		80	85	90	88	82	85
22		80	84	90	86	82	84
23		78	84	88	86	82	85
24		80	85	89	88	82	88
25		79	88	92	90	82	86
26	32°.47'	82	88	88	90	78	86
27		79	88	90	89	81	88
28		81	88	90	90	81	87
29		80	88	92	90	80	88
30		78	87	92	90	78	86
July 1		78	88	92	92	80	87
2		80	88	94	92	80	87
3		75	88	89	91	79	87
4		76	86	90	92	79	88
5		78	87	93	91	82	86
6		80	88	93	91	82	87

Winds	Remarks on the Weather
North	In afternoon rain with thunder.
Var.	Rain with thunder and lightning.
SE	Rain with thunder and lightning.
East	Clear; wind very light.
West	Clear; wind very light.
West	ditto
NW	ditto
West	ditto
N, NW	Rainy all the afternoon, with thunder and lightning; rain greater part of the night.
S, SE	Rainy greater part of the day with part of the night, with thunder.
North	Cloudy all day with a little rain.
N, NW	Cloudy with heavy thunder and lightning; a little rain in the afternoon.
North	Clear; wind very light.
SW	ditto
W, SW	Clear, wind light.
SE	Cloudy in the afternoon; wind fresh.
South	Cloudy greater part of the day; thunder in the evening.
SW	Cloudy—Thunder in the afternoon.
NW	Wind light—overcast.
NW	Wind light—clear.
South	Wind very light—clear.
SE	Wind very light—in the afternoon overcast.
SW	Wind very light—Gentle shower in the afternoon with thunder.
Var.	Fresh breeze; in afternoon cloudy with thunder.
South	Wind very light; rain in forenoon.
S, SW	Light breeze; in forenoon overcast.
S, SW	Fresh breeze; clear.
South	ditto
W, NW	ditto
N, NW	ditto
South	Rainy all the morning with thunder and lightning; rest of the day clear.
S, SW	Clear; wind very light.
S, SW	ditto
SW	Clear; wind fresh. In the fore part of the night rain with thunder and lightning.

Day of Month	Latt.	Temp. In Air (6 AM)	6 AM In River	Temp. In Air (3 PM)	3 PM In River	Temp. In Air (9 PM)	9 PM In River
July 7		80	88	96	93	80	88
8		75	88	92	93	82	88
9		78	88	92	92	79	88
10		78	83	83	89	78	88
11		77	87	89	90	79	86
12		83	86	90	98	82	87
13		83	87	89	88	77	86
14		80	85	92	90	83	88
15	33°.12'	84	88	93	92	83	86
16		84	88	92	92	81	88
17		83	89	89	92	85	91
18		84	89	92	92	83	90
19		81	90	93	92	83	89
20		80	89	92	94	82	89
21		80	88	91	91	84	88
22		81	87	86	90	80	86
23	33°.27'	76	86	83	89	75	84
24		69	83	81	87	72	86
25		73	81	85	86	78	83
26		70	83	88	90	80	83
27		79	84	90	91	79	85
28		78	84	?	87	79	85
29		80	83	86	88	85	83
30		76	83	90	86	78	84
31		78	84	90	?	80	82
Aug. 1		78	86	90	?	81	86
2		79	85	86	87	80	84
3		79	83	85	88	78	86
4		78	83	84	87	77	84
5		78	88	89	86	80	84
6		81	?	90	87	82	87
7		79	80	87	87	81	86
8		82	86	92	91	82	87
9		76	86	92	91	84	87
10	32°.47'	77	88	92	90	80	86

Winds	Remarks on the Weather
West	Clear; light breeze.
South	ditto
South	Fresh breeze; a gentle shower in the afternoon.
South	Fresh breeze; cloudy all day with rain in the evening.
SW	Cloudy greater part of the day; rain in the morning.
SW	Clear—fresh breeze.
West	ditto
W, SW	ditto
West	ditto
Var.	ditto
South	Wind very light; overcast.
Var.	Light breeze—part of the day overcast.
N, NE	Clear—light breeze.
Var.	Cloudy in the morning, rest of the day clear—fresh breeze.
S, SW	Fresh breeze—overcast in the forenoon.
East	Cloudy all day, with rain in the afternoon and night.
East	Clear—light breeze.
E, SE	ditto
Var.	ditto. Fresh breeze.
South	Overcast in the forenoon, rest of the day clear—fresh breeze.
East	Cloudy in the morning, rest of the day clear—fresh breeze.
South	Cloudy all the forenoon—fresh breeze all day.
Var.	Cloudy all the forenoon with some rain; rest of the day clear.
ditto	Cloudy in the forenoon—rest of the day clear—light breeze.
East	Cloudy greater part of the day—fresh breeze.
N, NE	Rain in the afternoon.
South	Rainy greater part of the day.
N, NE	Cloudy all day. Rain in the evening, with some thunder and lightning.
S, SW	Cloudy all day—light breeze.
South	Clear—fresh breeze.
SE	ditto. Light breeze.
East	ditto ditto
	ditto. Fresh breeze.
South	ditto ditto
West	ditto. Light breeze.

Day of Month	Latt.	Temp. 6 AM		Temp. 3 PM		Temp. 9 PM	
		In Air	In River	In Air	In River	In Air	In River
Aug. 11		72	87	92	90	78	86
12	At the Coashatta Village	78	88	93	93	79	87
13		80	88	84	88	80	86
14		76	84	76	84	75	82
15		74	82	83	87	76	86
16		76	84	76	84	74	82
17		72	82	86	88	76	82
18		70	83	87	89	75	82
19		72	82	?	?	?	?

Winds	Remarks on the Weather
East	Clear. Light breeze.
Var.	Overcast—light breeze.
East	Rainy all the afternoon and all the night.
Var.	Rainy the greater part of the day.
North	Clear—fresh breeze.
Var.	Rainy greater part of the day.
NW	Clear—light breeze.
South	ditto
SE	ditto

The following observations were made at Natchitoches

Date		6 A.M. In Air	3 P.M. In Air	9 P.M. In Air	Winds	
		Deg.	Deg.	Deg.		
Aug. 28	31° 46'		73	73	Calm	Cloudy all day.
29	"	74	78	78	Varia.	Rainy all day.
30	"	78	79	78	East	Cloudy all day, with some rain.
31	"	75	77	76	E, NE	Cloudy all day, with some rain.
Sept. 1	"	72	84	78	NW	Clear; fresh breeze.
2	"	79	88	79	Varia.	In the afternoon rain, with some thunder and lightning.
3	"	78	87	76	North	In the afternoon cloudy with thunder.
4	"	78	82	75	East	Cloudy all the afternoon, with some thunder.
5	"	78	83	75	E, NE	Cloudy all day; rain in the afternoon and greater part of the night.
6	"	76	79	73	NE	Cloudy greater part of the day, with rain in the afternoon.
7	"	76	83	80	North	Clear; fresh breeze.
8	"	78	85	81	Varia.	ditto

Bibliography

PRIMARY MATERIAL

Unpublished Documents and Letters Collections:

Accomac County (Virginia) Deeds for 1804.

Custis, Dr. Peter. Last Will and Testament, June 30, 1840; Certificate of Death, May 1, 1842. Craven County, North Carolina, Superior Court, "Will Book D."

Natchitoches–Sulphur Fork Agency Ledgers, 1809–1821. The National Archives.

The Benjamin Smith Barton Collection. Library of the American Philosophical Society, Philadelphia.

The Bexar Archives. Manuscripts and translations. Barker Texas History Center of the Sid Richardson Library, University of Texas-Austin.

The George Hunter Journals, with related documents. Miscellaneous Manuscripts Collection. Library of the American Philosophical Society, Philadelphia.

The John Coffee Papers. Alabama Department of Archives And History, Montgomery.

The John McKee Papers. Library of Congress, Manuscripts Division.

The Louis H. Pammel Papers. University Archives, Iowa State University Library, Ames.

The Nacogdoches Archives. Blake's transcriptions. Barker Texas History Center of the Sid Richardson Library, University of Texas-Austin.

The Papers of Aaron Burr. Series I, Correspondence. The New York Historical Society.

The Peter Force Collection. Library of Congress, Manuscripts Division.

The Records of the Adjutant General's Office, 1780–1917. National Archives.

The Spanish Archives of New Mexico. The Southwest Collection, Texas Tech University, Lubbock.

The Thomas Jefferson Papers. Library of Congress.

The William Dunbar Papers. Mississippi Department of Archives and History, Jackson.

War Department, Letters Received and Letters Sent. Main and Unregistered Series. National Archives.

War Department, Letters Sent to the President. National Archives.

Published Documents and Letters Collections:

American State Papers: Foreign Relations; Military Affairs; Public Lands; Miscellaneous.

Annals of the Congress of the United States, 1789–1824. 42 vols. Washington, D.C., 1834–56.

Bolton, Herbert E. *Athanase de Mézières and the Louisiana-Texas Frontier 1768–1780.* 2 vols. Cleveland: Arthur H. Clark, 1914.

————. *Guide to Materials for the History of the United States in the Principal Archives of Mexico.* Washington: Government Printing Office, 1913.

Carter, Clarence E., ed. *The Territory of Alabama, 1817–1819.* Vol. 18 of *The Territorial Papers of the United States.* 28 vols. Washington: Government Printing Office, continually since 1933.

————. *The Territory of Arkansas, 1819-1829,* vols. 19–20.

————. *The Territory of Louisiana-Missouri, 1806–1814,* vol. 14.

————. *The Territory of Mississippi, 1798–1817,* vols. 5–6.

————. *The Territory of Orleans, 1803-1812,* vol. 9.

Clark, Daniel. *Proofs of the Corruption of General James Wilkinson and of His Connexion with Aaron Burr.* Phila.: Wm. Hall Printers, 1809.

"[Documents] Concerning Philip Nolan." *The Quarterly of the Texas State Historical Association* 7 (April 1904), 308–17.

Ford, Paul L., ed. *The Works of Thomas Jefferson.* 12 vols. New York: G. P. Putnam's Sons, 1904–1905.

French, B. F. *Historical Collections of Louisiana.* Philadelphia: Daniels & Smith, 1850.

Garrett, Julia Kathryn, ed. "Doctor John Sibley and the Louisiana-Texas Frontier, 1803–1814." *Southwestern Historical Quarterly* 45–49 (1942–46).

Hackett, Charles Wilson, ed. and trans. *Pichardo's Treatise on the Limits of Louisiana and Texas.* 4 vols. Austin: University of Texas Press, 1931–46.

Jackson, Donald, ed. *Letters of the Lewis and Clark Expedition, with Re-*

lated Documents, 1783–1854. 1st ed. 1962. 2d ed. (2 vols.) Urbana: University of Illinois Press. 1978.

———. *The Journals of Zebulon Montgomery Pike: With Letters and Related Documents.* 2 vols. Norman: University of Oklahoma Press, 1966.

Jefferson, Thomas. "The Limits and Bounds of Louisiana." In *Documents Relating to the Purchase and Exploration of Louisiana.* Boston and New York: Houghton & Mifflin, 1904.

Kinnaird, Lawrence, ed. *Spain in the Mississippi Valley, 1765–1794.* 3 parts. Washington: Government Printing Office, 1946.

Mathews, Catherine Van Cortlandt. *Andrew Ellicott: His Life and Letters.* New York: The Grafton Press, 1908.

Mills, Elizabeth Shawn. *Natchitoches, 1729–1803: Abstracts of the Catholic Church Registers of the French and Spanish Post of St. Jean Baptiste des Natchitoches in Louisiana.* 2 vols. New Orleans: Polyanthos, 1977.

Nasatir, A. P., ed. *Before Lewis and Clark: Documents Illustrating the History of the Missouri, 1785–1804.* 2 vols. St. Louis: Historical Documents Foundation, 1952.

Nottingham, Stratton, ed. and comp. *Wills and Administrations of Accomack County, Virginia, 1663–1800.* Cottonport, Va.: Polyanthos, 1973.

Robertson, James, ed. *Louisiana under the Rule of Spain, France, and the United States, 1785–1807.* 2 vols. Cleveland: Arthur H. Clark, 1911.

Rowland, Dunbar, ed. *Official Letter Books of W. C. C. Claiborne, 1801–1816.* 6 vols. Jackson, Miss.: Printed for the State Department of Archives and History, 1917.

Rowland, Eron Dunbar, ed. *Life, Letters and Papers of William Dunbar: Of Elgin, Morayshire, Scotland, and Natchez, Mississippi. Pioneer Scientist of the Southern United States.* Jackson: Press of the Mississippi Historical Society, 1930.

Sibley, John. *A Report from Natchitoches in 1807.* Annie Heloise Abel, ed. New York: Museum of the American Indian, 1922.

Styrett, Harold C., ed. *The Papers of Alexander Hamilton.* 26 vols. New York: Columbia University Press, 1961–69.

Whittington, G. P., ed. "Dr. John Sibley of Natchitoches, 1757–1837." *The Louisiana Historical Quarterly* 10 (October 1927), 467–512.

Wilkinson, James. *Memoirs of My Own Time.* 4 vols. New York: AMS Press, reprint of the 1816 edition.

Exploring Journals and Travel Accounts:

Benson, Adolph, ed. and trans. *Peter Kalm's Travels in North America.* 2 vols. New York: n. p., 1937.

Cuming, Fortescue. *Sketches of a Tour to the Western Country . . . Commenced at Philadelphia in the Winter of 1807, and concluded in 1809.*

Vol. 4 of Reuben Gold Thwaites, ed., *Early Western Travels, 1748–1846.* 32 vols. Cleveland: The Arthur H. Clark Co., 1904–1907.

Custis, Peter. "Observations relative to the Geography, Natural History, & etc., of the Country along the Red-River, in Louisiana." *The Philadelphia Medical and Physical Journal* 2, Pt. 2 (1806), 43–50.

Darby, William. *The Emigrant's Guide to the Western and Southwestern States and Territories.* New York: Kirk and Mercein, 1818.

De Voto, Bernard, ed. *The Journals of Lewis and Clark.* Boston: Houghton-Mifflin, 1953.

Dunbar, William. "Journal of A Voyage." In Rowland, *Life, Letters and Papers of William Dunbar.*

Ellicott, Andrew. *The Journal of Andrew Ellicott.* Chicago: Quadrangle Books, 1962 reprint of the 1803 edition.

Flores, Dan. "A Final Journey Down the Wild Red." *The Shreveport Times Sunday Magazine,* August 14, 1977.

———, ed. "The John Maley Journal: Travels and Adventures in the American Southwest, 1810–1813." Unpublished master's thesis, Northwestern State University of Louisiana, Natchitoches, 1972.

———, ed. *Journal of an Indian Trader: Anthony Glass & the Texas Trading Frontier, 1790–1810.* College Station: Texas A&M University Press, 1985.

Folmer, Henry. "The Mallet Expedition of 1739 Through Nebraska, Kansas and Colorado to Santa Fe." *The Colorado Magazine* 16 (September 1939): 161–73.

Gaignard, J. "Journal of an Expedition up the Red River, 1773–1774." In vol. 2 of Bolton, *Athanase de Mézières and the Louisiana-Texas Frontier, 1768-1780.*

Harper, Francis, ed. *The Travels ef William Bartram.* New Haven: Yale University Press, 1958.

Hatcher, Mattie Austin, trans. "The Expedition of Don Domingo Terán de Los Rios into Texas." *Preliminary Studies of the Texas Catholic Historical Society* 2 (January 1932): 1–67.

Hunter, Clark, ed. *The Life and Letters of Alexander Wilson.* Philadelphia: American Philosophical Society, 1983.

James, Edwin. *Account of an Expedition from Pittsburgh to the Rocky Mountains Performed in the Years 1819, 1820.* Vol. 17 of Reuben Gold Thwaites, ed. *Early Western Travels, 1748–1846.*

McDermott, John Francis, ed. "The Western Journals of Dr. George Hunter, 1796-1805." *Transactions of the American Philosophical Society* 53 (1963).

Marcy, Randolph B., and G. B. McClellan. *Adventure on Red River: Report on the Exploration of the Headwaters of the Red River by Captain Randolph B. Marcy and Captain G. B. McClellan.* Grant Foreman, ed. Norman: University of Oklahoma Press, 1937.

Morse, Jedediah. *A Report to the Secretary of War of the United States on Indian Affairs, Comprising a Narrative of a Tour Performed in the Summer of 1820, under a Commission from the President of the United States.* New Haven: Printed for S. Converse, 1822.

Nuttall, Thomas. *A Journal of Travels into the Arkansas Territory During the Year 1819.* Savoie Lottinville, ed. Norman: University of Oklahoma Press, 1979.

Sibley, John. "Historical Sketches of the Several Tribes in Louisiana South of the Arkansas River and Between the Mississippi and the River Grand." In Thomas Jefferson, *Message from the President of the United States, Communicating Discoveries Made in Exploring the Missouri, Red River, and Washita, by Captains Lewis and Clark, Doctor Sibley and Mr. Dunbar.* New York: Hopkins and Seymour, 1806.

Smith, Ralph, ed. and trans. "Account of the Journey of Benard de La Harpe: Discovery Made by Him of Several Indian Nations Situated in the West." *Southwestern Historical Quarterly* 62 (July 1958–October 1959): 75–86, 246–59, 371–85, 525–41.

Stiles, Henry Reed, ed. *Joutel's Journal of La Salle's Last Voyage, 1684–7.* Albany: By Joseph McDonough, 1906.

Stoddard, Major Amos. *Sketches, Historical and Descriptive, of Louisiana.* Philadelphia: Mathew Carey, 1812.

Tonty, Henri de. "Memoir by the Sieur de la Tonty." In vol. 2 of Isaac J. Cox, ed. *The Journeys of Rene Robert Cavelier Sieur de La Salle.* 2 vols. New York: Allerton Book Co., 1922.

Thwaites, Reuben Gold, ed. *Original Journals of the Lewis and Clark Expedition.* 8 vols. New York: Dodd, Mead and Co., 1904–1905.

Other Contemporary Primary Works:

Atwater, Caleb. "On the Prairies and Barrens of the West." *American Journal of Science and Arts* 1 (1818): 116–25.

Barton, Benjamin Smith. "Account of the Cervus Wapiti, or southern elk of North America." *The Philadelphia Medical and Physical Journal, Supplement* (1806), 36–55.

———. "Additional Facts and Observations relative to the American Locust." *Philadelphia Medical and Physical Journal, Supplement 2* (1806), 181–87.

———. "A Discourse on Some of the Principal Desiderata in Natural History, and on the Best Means of Promoting the Study of this Science, in the United States." (1807) In Keir B. Sterling, ed. *Contributions to the History of American Natural History.* New York: Arno Press, 1974.

———. *Fragments of the Natural History of Pennsylvania.* In Keir B. Sterling, ed. *Selected Works by Eighteenth Century Naturalists and Travellers.* New York: Arno Press, 1974.

———. "Miscellaneous Facts and Observations." *Philadelphia Medical and Physical Journal: Supplement 1* (1805), 66–67; vol. 2 (1806), 159–60, 163; *Supplement 2* (1806), 194–95.

———. *New Views of the Origins of the Tribes and Nations of America.* Philadelphia: By the author, 1797.

———. "On the Siren Lacertina." *The Philadelphia Medical and Physical Journal, Supplement* (1808), 69.

Brewer, T. M. *Wilson's American Ornithology.* New York: Arno Press, 1970 reprint of the 1840 edition.

De Ferrer, Jóse Joaquin. "Astronomical Observations made by Jóse Joaquin de Ferrer, chiefly for the Purpose of determining the Geographical Position of various Places in the United States, and other Parts of North America." *Transactions of the American Philosophical Society* 6 (1809), 158–64.

Dennis, John. "An Account of a Plant called the Magathy-Bay Bean, or Accomac-Pea, Cultivated for fertilizing Lands." *The Medical Repository*, Hex. I, 4 (1803), 273–76.

Du Pratz, M. Le Page. *The History of Louisiana, or of the Western Parts of Virginia, and Carolina.* Introduction by Henry Clay Dethloff. Baton Rouge: Claitor's Publishing Division, 1972 reprint of the 1774 edition.

Greenway, James. "An account of the beneficial effects of the CASSIA CHAMAECRISTA, in recruiting worn-out lands, and in enriching such as are naturally poor; together with a botanical description of the plant." *Transactions of the American Philosophical Society* 3 (1793): 226–30.

Jefferson, Thomas. *Notes on the State of Virginia.* William Pedin, ed. Chapel Hill: University of North Carolina Press, 1954 reprint of the 1787 edition.

Linné, Caroli A. [Carolas Linnaeus] *Systema Naturae Per Regna Tria Naturae.* Edited by J. F. Gmelin. 4 vols.; London: J. B. Delamolliere, 13th edition, 1789.

———. *Systema Vegetabilium.* Edited by Andrea Murray. Gottingae: J. C. Dieterich, 14th edition, 1784.

Muhlenberg, Henry. "Index Florae Lancastriensis." *Transactions of the American Philosophical Society* 3 (1793): 157–84.

Nuttall, Thomas. "Collections towards a flora of the territory of Arkansas." *Transactions of the American Philosophical Society* 5, new series (1835–36).

Pursh, Frederick. *Flora Americae Septentrionalis.* 2 vols. London: White, Cochrane & Co., 1814.

Rafinesque, C. S. "An Essay on the Exotic Plants, Mostly European, which have been naturalized and now grow spontaneously in the Middle States of North America." *The Medical Repository* 8 (1811): 330–45.

Bibliography

Contemporary Newspapers:

Columbian Centinel (Boston, Massachusetts).
Courrier des Natchitoches (Natchitoches, Louisiana).
Mississippi Gazette (Natchez, Mississippi).
Mississippi Messenger (Natchez, Mississippi).
Richmond Enquirer (Richmond, Virginia).
The Louisiana Gazette (New Orleans, Louisiana).
The National Intelligencer (Washington, D.C.)

Government Publications:

Dane, Carl H. "Upper Cretaceous Formations of Southwestern Arkansas." *Bulletin of the Arkansas Geological Survey*. Little Rock: Government Printing Office, 1929.

Durham, Clarence O. *Iron Ore of Central North Louisiana*. Louisiana Geological Survey *Bulletin* No. 41. Baton Rouge: Louisiana Department of Conservation, 1964.

Fisk, H. N. *Geology of Avoyelles and Rapides Parishes*. Louisiana Geological *Bulletin* No. 18. New Orleans: Louisiana Department of Conservation, 1940.

Harris, G. D. "Natchitoches Area." Special Report No. 1 in Gilbert D. Harris and A. C. Veatch, *A Preliminary Report on the Geology of Louisiana*. Baton Rouge: Louisiana State University and the State Office of Experiment Stations, 1899, 140–48.

———. "The Cretaceous and Lower Eocene Faunas of Louisiana." Special Report No. 6 in Harris and Veatch, 289–309.

Heitman, Francis B. *Historical Register and Dictionary of the United States Army*. 2 vols. Washington: Government Printing Office, 1903.

Hodge, Frederick Webb, ed. *Handbook of American Indians North of Mexico*. Bureau of American Ethnology *Bulletin* 30. 2 vols. Washington: Government Printing Office, 1907.

Lerch, Otto. *A Preliminary Report upon the Hills of Louisiana, North of the Vicksburg, Shreveport and Pacific Railroad*. Baton Rouge: Louisiana State University and the State Office of Experiment Stations, 1892.

Murray, Grover E. *Geology of DeSoto and Red River Parishes*. Louisiana Geological Survey *Bulletin* No. 25. Baton Rouge: Louisiana Department of Conservation, 1948.

Paxton, Dr. Joseph. Letter to A. H. Sevier, Mount Prairie, Arkansas Territory, August 1, 1828. *House Doc. 78*, 20th Cong., 2nd sess., 1830.

"Red River, La., Ark., Okla., and Tex." *House Doc. 378*, 74th Cong., 2nd sess., 1936.

"Report of Preliminary Examination of Red River, Tex. and Okla., from Mouth of the Washita to Mouth of the Big Wichita River." *House Doc. 193*, 63rd Cong., 1st. sess., 1913.

"Report of Survey of Cypress Bayou and Channels Connecting Shreveport, La., with Jefferson, Tex." *House Doc. 785*, 59th Cong., 1st sess., 1906.

Swanton, John R. *Early History of the Creek Indians and Their Neighbors.* Bureau of American Ethnology *Bulletin 73.* Washington: Government Printing Office, 1922.

———. *Source Material on the History and Ethnology of the Caddo Indians.* Bureau of American Ethnology *Bulletin* 132. Washington: Government Printing Office, 1942.

———. *The Indians of the Southeastern United States.* Bureau of American Ethnology *Bulletin* 137. Washington: Government Printing Office, 1946.

———. *The Indian Tribes of North America.* Bureau of American Ethnology *Bulletin* 145. Washington: Government Printing Office, 1952.

Veatch, Arthur C. "The Shreveport Area." Special Report No. 2 in Harris and Veatch, *A Preliminary Report on the Geology of Louisiana,* 149–208.

Cited Personal Communications:

Coursey, Louise R., to Dan Flores. Charles Patterson Van Pelt Library, University of Pennsylvania, Philadelphia, April 25, 1979.

Ewan, Joseph, to Dan Flores. Tulane University, New Orleans, March 12, 1982.

Fogarasi, Kasia, to Dan Flores. The Academy of Natural Sciences of Philadelphia, April 27, 1981.

Fryxell, Paul, to Dan Flores. Texas A&M Agricultural Extension Service, College Station, February 9, 1981.

Gregory, Hiram, to Dan Flores. Laboratory of Anthropology, Northwestern State University of Louisiana, Natchitoches, April 15, 1975.

Harris, R. King, to Dan Flores. Dallas, March 16, 1979.

Musick, Michael P., to Dan Flores. Military Archives Division, National Archives, Washington, May 8, 1979.

Scurlock, J. Dan, to Dan Flores. Texas State Archeological Commission, Austin, May 2, 1975.

Thomas, R. Dale, to Dan Flores. Department of Biology, Northeast Louisiana University, Monroe, La., April 3, 1981.

Webb, Dr. Clarence, to Dan Flores. Shreveport, April 26, 1979.

Maps:

Darby, William. *Map of Louisiana* (1812). Photocopy in the Louisiana Room of the Watson Library, Northwestern State University, Natchitoches.

Hardee, T. S. *Hardee's Geographical, Historical and Statistical Map of Louisiana Embracing Portions of Arkansas, Alabama, Mississippi and Texas from Recent Surveys and Investigations and Officially Compiled under Authority from the* [Louisiana] *State Legislature* (1871). Photocopy in the Louisiana Room of the Watson Library, Northwestern State University, Natchitoches.

King, Nicholas. *Map of the Red River in Louisiana. From the Spanish Camp where the exploring party of the U. S. was met by the Spanish Troops to where it enters the Mississippi* (1806). Redrawn, and addendum to this volume. Original in Library of Congress.

Marcotte, P. H. *Map of the Parishes of Caddo, Claiborne, Natchitoches with Part of Rapides Louisiana.* General Land Office, *circa* 1840. Louisiana Room of the Watson Library, Northwestern State University, Natchitoches.

Miera Y Pacheco, Bernardo. "Map of the Dominguez-Escalante Expedition, 1776." In volume 1 of Carl I. Wheat, comp. *1540–1861: Mapping the Transmississippi West.* 2 vols. San Francisco: The Institute of Historical Cartography, 1957–58.

Nau, Anthony. *The First Part of Captn. Pike's Chart of the Internal Part of Louisiana* (1807). The section showing the Freeman & Custis exploration addendum to this volume.

Puelles, Fray José María de Jesús. *Mapa Geographica de la Provincias Septentrionales de esta Nueva España* (1807). Map Collection, Barker Texas History Center. University of Texas–Austin.

Raisz, Erwin. "Landforms of the United States." In Wallace W. Atwood, *The Physiographic Provinces of North America.* Boston: Ginn and Co., 1940.

Shreve, Henry Miller. *Rough Sketch of that part of Red Rivir* [*sic*] *in which the Great Raft is situated and* [of] *the bayous, lakes, swamps, &c. belonging to or in its vicinity. 31.50' to 32.20'; 93.10' to 93.40', 1833.* Louisiana *House Doc. 98,* Ser. 256, p. [14]. Addendum to this volume, as redrawn by E. M. Parker.

Tanner, H. S. *Map of Louisiana and Mississippi* (1820). Photocopy in the Louisiana Room of the Watson Library, Northwestern State University, Natchitoches.

United States Geological Survey Maps, Topographical, for the Red River Valley. Mississippi, Louisiana, Arkansas, Texas Quadrangles.

Veatch, A. C. "Map of Northern Caddo parish in 1839. Compiled from Public Land Surveys." Addendum to this volume.

Von Humboldt, Alexander. *Carte Generale Du Royaume De La Nouvelle Espagne* (1810)," Portion dealing with the Southern Rockies addendum to this volume. Original in Library of the University of Illinois, Urbana-Champaign.

Secondary Material

Books:

Abernethy, Thomas Perkins. *The Burr Conspiracy*. New York: Oxford University Press, 1954.

Almaráz, Félix D., Jr. *Tragic Cavalier: Governor Manuel Salcedo of Texas, 1808–1813*. Austin: University of Texas Press, 1971.

Archer, Sellers G., and Clarence Bunch. *The American Grass Book*. Norman: University of Oklahoma Press, 1953.

A. O. U. Checklist of North American Birds, 5th ed. Baltimore: Port City Press, 1957.

Arnett, Ross H., Jr. *The Beetles of the United States*. Ann Arbor: American Entomological Institute, 1973.

Arthur, Joseph C. *Manual of the Rusts in the United States and Canada*. New York: Hafner Publishing Co., 1962.

Ashford, Gerald. *Spanish Texas. Yesterday and Today*. Austin and New York: The Pemberton Press, 1971.

Audubon, John James. *The Birds of America, 1827–1830*. Quarto. New York: The MacMillan Co., 1937.

Bell, Robert E., Edward B. Jelks, and W. W. Newcomb. *A Pilot Study of Wichita Indian Archeology and Ethnohistory*. Dallas: National Science Foundation Final Report, 1967.

Biographical and Historical Memoirs of Northwest Louisiana. Nashville: The Southern Publishing Co., 1890.

Bishop, Sherman C. *Handbook of Salamanders: The Salamanders of the United States of Canada, and of Lower California*. Ithaca: Comstock Publishing Co., 1947.

Bolen, Eric, and Dan Flores. *The Mississippi Kite: Portrait of a Southern Hawk*. Austin: University of Texas Press, 1993.

Bolton, Herbert Eugene. *Coronado: Knight of Pueblos and Plains*. Albuquerque: University of New Mexico Press, 1964 edition.

———. *Texas in the Middle Eighteenth Century*. Austin: University of Texas, 1970 reprint of the 1915 edition.

Bowers, Claude. *Jefferson in Power: The Death Struggle of the Federalists*. Boston: Houghton Mifflin Co., 1936.

Brown, Clair A. *Wildflowers of Louisiana and Adjoining States.* Baton Rouge: Louisiana State University Press, 1972.

Bryan, W. B. *A History of fhe National Capital, from Its Foundations Through the Period of the Adoption of the Organic Act.* 2 vols. New York: MacMillan Co., 1914–16.

Carter, George. *Earlier Than You Think.* College Station: Texas A&M University Press, 1980.

Chandler, Barbara O., and J. Ed Howe. *History of Texarkana and Bowie and Miller Counties, Texas-Arkansas.* Texarkana: n. p., 1939.

Claiborne, J. F. H. *Mississippi as a Province, Territory and State, with Biographical Notices of Eminent Citizens.* Jackson: Power and Barksdale, 1880.

Cochran, Doris M., and Coleman J. Goin. *The New Field Book of Reptiles and Amphibians.* New York: G. P. Putnam's Sons, 1970.

Cook, Warren. *Flood Tide of Empire: Spain and the Pacific Northwest, 1543–1819.* New Haven and London: Yale University Press, 1973.

Correll, Donovan Stewart, and Marshall Conring Johnston. *Manual of Vascular Plants of Texas.* Volume 6 of *Contributions from the Texas Research Foundation.* Renner, Texas: Texas Research Foundation, 1970.

Cutright, Paul Russell. *Lewis and Clark: Pioneering Naturalists.* Urbana: University of Illinois Press, 1969.

Dorsey, George A. *The Mythology of the Wichita.* Washington: Carnegie Institution of Washington Publication No. 40, 1904.

———. *Traditions of the Caddo.* Washington: Carnegie Institution of Washington Publication No. 41, 1905.

Duncan, Wilbur H. *Woody Vines of the Southeastern United States.* Athens: University of Georgia Press, 1975.

Fink, Bruce. *The Lichen Flora of the United States.* Ann Arbor: University of Michigan Press, 1935.

Flores, Dan. *Horizontal Yellow: Nature and History in the Near Southwest.* Albuquerque: University of New Mexico Press, 1999.

Folmer, Henry D. *Franco-Spanish Rivalry in North America, 1524–1763.* Glendale: Arthur H. Clark Co., 1953.

Fortier, Alcee, ed. *Louisiana: Comprising Sketches of Parishes, Towns, Events, Institutions, and Persons, Arranged in Cyclopedic Forrn.* 2 vols. New Orleans: Century Historical Association, 1914.

Freeman, Douglas Southall, J. A. Carroll, et al. *George Washington: A Biography.* 7 vols. New York: Charles Scribner's Sons, 1948–57.

Garrett, Julia Kathryn. *Green Flag over Texas.* New York: Cordova Press, 1939.

Geiser, Samuel W. *Naturalists of the Frontier.* Dallas: Southern Methodist University Press, 1937.

Gilbert, Bill. *The Trailblazers.* New York: Time-Life, 1973.

Gleason, Mildred S. *Caddo: A Survey of Caddo Indians in Northeast Texas and*

Marion County, 1541–1840. Jefferson, Texas: Marion County Historical Commission, 1981.

Goetzmann, William. *Exploration and Empire: The Explorer and the Scientist in the Winning of the American West.* New York: W. W. Norton &
Co., 1966.

Hall, E. Raymond, and Keith R. Kelson. *The Mammals of North America.*
2 vols. New York: The Ronald Press, 1959.

Hallenbeck, Cleve. *Alvar Núñez Cabeza de Vaca: The Journey and Route of
the First European to Cross the Continent of North America, 1534–1536.*
Port Washington, New York: Kennikat Press, n. d.

Hanley, Wayne. *Natural History in America: From Mark Catesby to Rachel
Carson.* New York: Demeter Press, 1977.

Harrington, M. R. *Certain Caddo Sites in Arkansas.* New York: Museum of
the American Indian, Heye Foundation, 1920.

Harshberger, John W. *The Botanists of Philadelphia and Their Work.* Philadelphia: T.C. Davis & Sons, 1899.

Hollon, W. Eugene. *The Lost Pathfinder: Zebulon Montgomery Pike.* Norman: University of Oklahoma Press, 1949.

Jackson, B. Daydon, comp. *Index Kewensis: An Enumeration of the Genera
and Species of Flowering Plants.* 2 vols. Oxford: University Press, 1895.

Jackson, Donald. *Thomas Jefferson & the Stony Mountains: Exploring the
West from Monticello.* Urbana: University of Illinois Press, 1981.

———. *Valley Men: A Speculative Account of the Arkansas River Expedition
of 1807.* New York: Ticknor & Fields, 1984.

Jacobson, Daniel, Howard N. Martin, and Henry Marsh. *(Creek) Indians:
Alabama-Coushatta. American Indian Ethnohistory, Southern and South-
eastern Indians.* David Agee Horr, ed. New York and London: Garland
Publishing Inc., 1974.

John, Elizabeth A. H. *Storms Brewed in Other Men's Worlds: The Confrontation of Indians, Spanish, and French in the Southwest, 1540–1795.*
College Station: Texas A&M University Press, 1975.

Jordan, David Starr, and Barbara Warren Evermann. *American Food and
Game Fishes.* New York: Doubleday, Page & Co., 1904.

Le Conte, John L., ed. *The Complete Writings of Thomas Say on the Ento-
mology of North America.* 3 vols. Philadelphia: A. E. Foote, 1891.

Loomis, Noel M., and A. P. Nasatir. *Pedro Vial and the Roads to Santa Fe.*
Norman: University of Oklahoma Press, 1967.

Lowery, George H. *Louisiana Birds.* Baton Rouge: Louisiana State University Press, 1974 edition.

———. *The Mammals of Louisiana and Its Adjacent Waters.* Baton Rouge:
Louisiana State University Press, 1974.

Lundell, Cyrus Longsworth, comp. *Flora of Texas.* 3 vols. Menasha, Wis.:
George Banta Co. for the Texas Research Foundation, 1969–.

McCaleb, Walter F. *New Light on Aaron Burr*. Austin: Texas Quarterly Studies, 1963.

McClung, Mildred Mays. *Caddo Lake: Mysterious Swampland*. Texarkana: Southwest Printers and Publishers, 1974.

McCrocklin, Claude. "The Red River Coushatta Indian Villages of Northwest Louisiana, 1790–1835." Louisiana Archaeological Society Bulletin 12, *Louisiana Archaeology* (1985).

McKelvey, Susan Delano. *Botanical Exploration of the Trans-Mississippi West, 1790–1850*. Jamaica Plain, Mass.: The Arnold Arboretum of Harvard, 1955.

Malone, Dumas, ed. *Dictionary of American Biography*. 20 vols. New York: Charles Scribner's Sons, 1935.

———. *Jefferson and His Time*. 6 vols. Boston: Little, Brown & Co., 1952–1981.

Mathews, John Joseph. *The Osages: Children of the Middle Waters*. Norman: University of Oklahoma Press, 1961.

Mills, Gary. *The Forgotten People: Cane River's Creoles of Color*. Baton Rouge: Louisiana State University Press, 1977.

Oberholser, Harry C. *The Bird Life of Texas*, Edgar B. Kincaid, ed. 2 vols. Austin: University of Texas Press, 1974.

Owen, David D., et al. *Second Report of a Geological Reconnoissance of the Middle and Southern Counties of Arkansas*. Philadelphia: C. Sherman & Son, 1860.

Parsons, Mark, Jim Bruseth, Jacques Bagur, and Claude McCrocklin. "Finding Sha'chahdinnih (Timber Hill): The Last Village of the Caddo of the Kadohadacho in the Caddo Homeland." *Plains Anthropologist* (paper under review).

Peake, Ora Brooks. *A History of the United States Indian Factory System, 1795–1822*. Denver: Sage Books, 1954.

Powell, William H. *List of Officers of the Army of the United States from 1779 to 1900*. New York: L. R. Hamersly & Co., 1900.

Pratt, Henry Sherring. *A Manual of Land and Fresh Water Vertebrate Animals of the United States*. Philadelphia: P. Blakiston's Son & Co., 1935.

Pyne, Stephen J. *Fire in America: A Cultural History of Wildland and Rural Fire*. Princeton: Princeton University Press, 1982.

Rickett, Harold W. *Wild Flowers of the United States*. 6 vols. New York: McGraw-Hill, 1966.

Rowland, Dunbar, ed. *Mississippi: Comprising Sketches of Counties, Towns, Events, Institutions, and Persons, Arranged in Cyclopedic Form*. 3 vols. Atlanta: Southern Historical Publishing Association, 1907.

Schachner, Nathan. *Thomas Jefferson: A Biography*. New York: Thomas Yoseloff, 1957.

Shelford, Victor E. *The Ecology of North America*. Urbana: University of Illinois Press, 1963.

Shreve, Royal Ornan. *The Finished Scoundrel.* Indianapolis: Bobbs-Merrill, 1933.

Smallwood, William. *Natural History and the American Mind.* New York: Columbia University Press, 1941.

Streeter, Thomas W. *Bibliography of Texas, 1795–1845.* 5 vols., Cambridge: Harvard University Press, 1960.

Swann, Lester A., and Charles S. Papp. *The Common Insects of North America.* New York: Harper & Row, 1972.

The A. O. U. Check-List of North American Birds. Baltimore: Port City Press, 1957, fifth edition.

The National Cyclopedia of American Biography. 58 vols. New York: James T. White and Co., 1891–.

Tyson, Carl Newton. *The Red River in Southwestern History.* Norman: University of Oklahoma Press, 1981.

Uphof, J. C. *Dictionary of Economic Plants.* Lehre, West Germany: Verlag Von J. Cramer, 1968.

Usher, George. *A Dictionary of plants used by man.* London: Constable and Co., 1974.

Vines, Robert A. *Trees of East Texas.* Austin: University of Texas Press, 1977.

———. *Trees, Shrubs, and Woody Vines of the Southwest.* Austin: University of Texas Press, 1960.

Vogel, Virgil. *American Indian Medicine.* Norman: University of Oklahoma Press, 1970.

Warren, Harris Gaylord. *The Sword Was Their Passport: A History of American Filibustering in the Mexican Revolution.* Baton Rouge: Louisiana State University Press, 1943.

Waters, Frank. *Book of the Hopi.* New York: Penguin edition, 1977.

Webb, Clarence H. *The Belcher Mound: A Stratified Caddoan Site in Caddo Parish, Louisiana.* Salt Lake City: Memoirs of the Society for American Archeology, 1959.

Webb, Walter Prescott, H. Bailey Carroll, et al. *Handbook of Texas.* 2 vols. Austin: The Texas State Historical Association, 1952.

Weber, David. *The Taos Trappers: The Fur Trade in the Far Southwest, 1540–1846.* Norman: University of Oklahoma Press, 1971.

Weddle, Robert S. *Wilderness Manhunt: The Spanish Search for La Salle.* Austin and London: The University of Texas Press, 1973.

Wheat, Carl I., comp. *1540–1861: Mapping the Transmississippi West.* 2 vols. San Francisco: The Institute of Historical Cartography, 1957–1958.

Williams, Kenneth. *Systematics and Natural History of the American Milk Snake, Lampropeltis triangulum.* Milwaukee: Milwaukee Public Museum Press, 1978.

Willis, J. C. *A Dictionary of the Flowering Plants and Ferns,* revised by H. K. Airy Shaw. Cambridge: University Press, 1973.

Wright, Albert Hazen, and Anna Allen Wright. *Handbook of Snakes of the United States and Canada.* 2 vols. Ithaca: Comstock Publishing Assoc., 1957.

Zweifel, Richard G., ed. *Catalogue of American Amphibians and Reptiles.* New York: Society for the Study of Amphibians and Reptiles, 1971.

Articles:

Allen, John L. "Geographical Knowledge and American Images of the Louisiana Territory." *Western Historical Quarterly,* 1 (April 1971), 151–70.

Barnhart, John Hendley. "Brief Sketches of some Collectors of Specimens in the Barton Herbarium." *Proceedings of the Philadelphia Botanical Club* 9 (1926): 35–42.

Buscemi, Doreen. "The Last American Parakeet." *Natural History* 87 (April 1978): 10–12.

Calhoun, Robert Dabney. "The Taensa Indians: The French Explorers and Catholic Missionaries in the Taensa Country." *The Louisiana Historical Quarterly* 17 (October 1934), Pt. 3, 642–79.

Cox, Isaac J. "General James Wilkinson and His Later Intrigues with the Spaniards." *The American Historical Review* 19 (July 1914): 794–812.

——. "Hispanic-American Phases of the 'Burr Conspiracy.'" *The Hispanic American Historical Review* 12 (May 1932): 145–75.

——. "The Explorations of the Louisiana Frontier, 1803–1806." *American Historical Association Annual Report* (1904), 151–74.

——. "The Louisiana-Texas Frontier." *Southwestern Historical Quarterly* 10 (July 1906): 1–75; 17 (July 1913): 1–42; 17 (October 1913): 140–87.

——. "The Louisiana-Texas Frontier During the Burr Conspiracy." *Mississippi Valley Historical Review* 10 (December 1923): 274–84.

Cummins, W. F. "The Texas Meteorites." *Transactions of the Texas Academy of Science* 1 (1892): 14–18.

Curths, Karen. "The Routes of French and Spanish Penetration into Oklahoma." *Red River Valley Historical Review* 6 (Summer 1981): 18–30.

DeRosier, A. H., Jr. "William Dunbar, Explorer." *Journal of Mississippi History* 25 (July 1963): 165–85.

Ewan, Joseph. "Early History." In Joseph Ewan, ed., *A Short History of Botany in the United States.* New York and London: Hafner Publishing Co., 1969, 27–48.

Flores, Dan. "Peter Custis." In Keir B. Sterling, ed. *Biographical Dictionary of North American Environmentalists*. Westport, Conn.: Greenwood Press, 1984.

———. "Indian Occupation [on the Red River]." *The Shreveport Times Sunday Magazine,* September 16, 1979.

———. "The Red River Branch of the Alabama-Coushatta Indians: An Ethnohistory." *Southern Studies* 16 (Spring 1977): 55–72.

———. "The Saga of the Texas Iron." *Red River Valley Historical Review* 6 (Winter 1981): 58–70.

Geiser, Samuel. "Thomas Nuttall's Botanical Collecting Trip to the Red River, 1819." *Field and Laboratory* 24 (1956), 43–60.

Glover, William B. "A History of the Caddo Indians." *The Louisiana Historical Quarterly* 18 (October 1935): 875–946.

Gregory, Hiram, and Clarence Webb. "European Trade Beads from Six Sites in Natchitoches Parish, Louisiana." *Florida Anthropologist* 18 (1965), 24–40.

Guardia, J. E. "Some Results of Log Jams in the Red River." *The Bulletin of the Geographical Society of Philadelphia* 31 (July 1933): 103–14.

Hackett, Charles Wilson. "Policy of the Spanish Crown Regarding French Encroachment from Louisiana, 1721–1762." In *New Spain and the Anglo-American West*. Lancaster, Pa.: By George P. Hammond, 1932, 107–46.

Haggard, J. Villasana. "The House of Barr and Davenport." *Southwestern Historical Quarterly* 49 (July 1945): 66–88.

———. "The Neutral Ground Between Louisiana and Texas, 1806–1821." *The Louisiana Historical Quarterly* 28 (October 1945): 1001–1128.

Hardin, J. Fair. "An Outline of Shreveport and Caddo Parish History." *The Louisiana Historical Quarterly* 18 (October 1935): 759–871.

Holmes, Jack D. "The Marquis de Caso Calvo, Nicholas de Finiels, and the 1805 Spanish Expedition through East Texas and Louisiana." *Southwestern Historical Quarterly* 69 (January 1966): 324–39.

Hornbeck-Tanner, Helen. "Rebuttal Statement to Direct Evidence of Alabama-Coushatta Indians of Texas and Coushatta Indians of Louisiana." In Helen Hornbeck-Tanner, *Caddoan Indians IV*. New York and London: Garland Publishing Co., 1974, 149–54.

Hughes, Jack Thomas. "Prehistory of the Caddoan-Speaking Tribes." In Jack Thomas Hughes, *Caddoan Indians III*. New York and London: Garland Publishing Co., 1974.

[John], Elizabeth A. Harper. "The Taovayas Indians in Frontier Trade and Diplomacy, 1719–1835." 1, *The Chronicles of Oklahoma* 31 (1952); 2, *Southwestern Historical Quarterly* 47 (1952): 3, *Panhandle-Plains Historical Review* 26 (1953).

Bibliography

Jordan, Terry. "Between the Forest and the Prairie." *Agricultural History* 38 (October 1964), 205–16.

Lange, Charles H. "A Report on Data Pertaining to the Caddo Treaty of July 1, 1835." In Robert Neuman and Charles H. Lange, *Caddoan Indians II.* New York and London: Garland Publishing Co., 1974, 159–321.

Lawrence, George M. "Carmel: Rock Chapel in the wildwood." *The Shreveport Times*, March 11, 1979.

Loomis, Noel M. "Philip Nolan's Entry in Texas in 1800." In John F. McDermott, ed. *The Spanish in the Mississippi Valley, 1762–1804.* Urbana: University of Illinois Press, 1974, 120–33.

Miroir, M. P., R. King Harris, et al. "Benard de La Harpe and the Nassonite Post," *Bulletin of the Texas Archeological Society* 44 (1973): 113–67.

Mitchell, Jennie O'Kelly, and Robert Dabney Calhoun. "The Marquis de Maison Rouge, the Baron De Bastrop, and Colonel Abraham Morhouse. Three Ouachita Valley Soldiers of Fortune: The Maison Rouge and Bastrop Spanish Land 'Grants.'" *The Louisiana Historical Quarterly* 20 (April 1937): 289–462.

Moore, Clarence B. "Some Aboriginal Sites on Red River." *Journal of the Academy of Natural Sciences of Philadelphia* 14 (1912), 482–638.

Moore, R. Woods. "The Role of the Baron de Bastrop in the Anglo-American Settlement of the Spanish Southwest." *The Louisiana Historical Quarterly* 31 (July 1948): 606–81.

Morris, Wayne. "Auguste Pierre Chouteau, Merchant Prince at the Three Forks of the Arkansas." *The Chronicles of Oklahoma* 68 (Summer 1970): 155–63.

Morrison, Alfred J. "Two Students from Virginia at the University of Edinburgh; with a note regarding early botanical dissertations by Virginians at the University of Pennsylvania." *The Virginia Magazine of History and Biography* 21 (July 1913): 322–23.

Morton, Conrad V. "Freeman and Custis' Account of the Red River Expedition of 1806, An Overlooked Publication of Botanical Interest." *Journal of the Arnold Arboretum* 47 (1967): 431–59.

Nasatir, Abraham P. "More on Pedro Vial in Upper Louisiana." In McDermott, *The Spanish in the Mississippi Valley, 1762–1804*, Champaign, Ill.: University of Illinois Press, 1974, 100–19.

Norman, N. Philip. "The Red River of the South." *The Louisiana Historical Quarterly* 25 (April 1942): 397–535.

Pennell, Francis W. "Benjamin Smith Barton as Naturalist." *Proceedings of the American Philosophical Society* 86 (1943): 108–22.

Sauer, Carl. "Grassland Climax." In *Agricultural Origins and Dispersals.* Cambridge: Massachusetts Institute of Technology Press, 2nd edition, 1969, 3–20.

Sheldon, Sam. "Ethnobotany of *Agave lecheguilla* and *Yucca carnerosana* in Mexico's Zona Ixtlera. *Economic Botany* 34 (October 1980): 376–90.

Smith, G., and W. F. R. Weldon. "Crustacea." In volume 4 of S. F Harmar and A. E. Shipley, eds. *The Cambridge Natural History.* 10 vols. New York: The MacMillan Co. 1904, 152–54.

Smith, Ralph. "The Tawehash in French, Spanish, English and American Imperial Affairs." *The West Texas Historical Association Year Book* 28 (1952): 18–49.

Stahle, David, and Malcolm Cleaveland. "Texas Drought History Reconstructed and Analyzed from 1698 to 1980." *Journal of Climate* 1 (January 1988): 59–74.

Stannard, Jerry. "Medical Botany." In Ewan, *A Short History of Botany in the United States,* 146–52.

Strickland, Rex. "Moscoso's Journey through Texas." *Southwestern Historical Quarterly* 66 (1962): 109–37.

Upshur, Thomas T. "Hill and Custis." *The Virginia Magazine of History and Biography* 3 (June 1896): 319–21.

Warburton, Cecil. "Arachnida Embolobranchiata (Scorpions, Spiders, Mites, etc)." In S. F. Harmer and A. E. Shipley, eds., *The Cambridge Natural History.* 10 vols. New York: Macmillan Co., 1958.

Wedel, Mildred M. "J. B. Benard Sieur de La Harpe: Visitor to the Wichitas in 1719." *Great Plains Journal* 4 (Spring 1965): 37–70.

Wedel, Waldo. "The Central North American Grassland: Man-Made or Natural?" In *Studies in Human Ecology.* Washington: Pan-American Union, 1957, 36–69.

Whittaker, R. H. "Recent Evolution of Ecological Concepts in Relation to the Eastern Forests of North America." In Frank N. Egerton, comp. *History of American Ecology.* New York: Arno Press, 1977, 340–58.

Whittington, G. P. "Rapides Parish, Louisiana: A History." *The Louisana Historical Quarterly* 25–28 (October 1932 to January 1935).

"William Darlington." *Proceedings of the American Philosophical Society* 9 (1863–1864): 330–43.

Theses and Dissertations:

Cox, Isaac J. "The Early Exploration of Louisiana." Ph.D. diss., The University of Pennsylvania, Philadelphia, 1906.

Jones, Douglas Epps. "Geology of Bossier Parish." Ph.D. diss., Louisiana State University, Baton Rouge, 1959.

Scurlock, J. Dan. "The Kadohadacho Indians: A Correlation of Archeological and Documentary Data." Master's thesis, The University of Texas, Austin, 1965.

Bibliography

Wendels, Maria Anna. "French Interest in and Activities on the Spanish Border of Louisiana, 1717–1753." Master's thesis, The University of California, Berkeley, 1914.

Other Unpublished Material:

Britton, Morris L. "The Location of Le Poste des Cadodoquious." Manuscript in possession of the editor.

Flores, Dan L., ed. "Journal of an Indian Trader: Anthony Glass and the Southwestern Traders' Frontier, 1790–1810." Manuscript in possession of the editor.

Index

Accomplishments of Red R. expedition: 293, 317; in diplomacy, 302–307; in geography, 295–97; in natural history, 297–302
Acer rubrum var. *drummondii* (Hook. & Arn.) Sarg.: 108n29, 255 & n195. *A. barbatum; See A. rubrum. A. pennsylvanicum; See A. rubrum. A. saccharinum:* 114, 255 & n196
Achillea lanulosa Nutt.: 243 & n137. *A. santolina; See A. lanulosa. A. occidentalis* Raf.; *See A. lanulosa*
Adaes: *See* Caddos
Adaes, Los: *See* Los Adaes
Adams, John Quincy: 292
Adams-Onís Treaty of 1819: 308
Aesculus discolor var. *mollis* Sarg.: *See Esculus parviflora*
Agave virginica: See Polianthus virginica
Alabama-Coushattas: 140n25, 150n40, 303, 328; green corn dance of, 249–50 & n165; and Spaniards, 88, 132n16; village of, 148–50 & nn39–40, 157n49; warrior, il 155
Alcea rosea: See Althaea rosea
Alcedo alcyon: See Megaceryle alcyon
Alencaster, Real: 83, 125
Alexander, William C.: 131n14, 304–305
Alligator bonnet: *See Nymphaea alba*
Alligator fish: 237
Alligator gar: *See Atractosteus tristaechus*
Alligator mississippiens Cuvier: 140n26,

226 & n80, 236, 278
Allium canadense (L.): 220 & n47. *A. odorium; See A. canadense*
Aloe, false: *See Polianthes virginica*
Alston, John: 311
Althaea rosea (L.) Cav.: 218 & n26
Alum: 180, 267
Amangual, Francisco: 307
American Philosophical Society: 5, 6, 17, 40; Custis's specimens at, 213–14; *Transactions* of, 66
Ammospiza caudacuta: 236 & n102
Amorpha fruticosa: 215 & n8
Ampelopsis arborea (L.) Koehne: 215 & n10
Amphiuma tridactylum: il 226, 227 & n82, 301, 310 & n42
Anas: 195n32, 271. *A. carolinensis; See A. discors. A. discors* (L.): 234 & n95
Ancistrodon contortrix contortrix (L.): 236n103. *A. piscivorous leucostoma* Lacépède: 236n103
Androsace occidentalis Pursh: 240 & n121
Anhinga anhinga colubrina Bartram: 267 & n257
Annona Glabra: See Asimona triloba
Anolis caroliniensis Voigt: 227 & n81
Anonymous informants: 75–76, 83, 124
Antilocapridae: 275 & n277, il 275
Apaches: 13, 36n47
Apium leptophyllum Muell. & Benth.:

248 & n154
Apocynum cannibium (L.): 192 & n25, 262 & n234
Appalaches: 112–13 & n43
Apple-of-Peru: *See Nicandra physaloides*
Apricot-vine: *See Passiflora incarnata*
Aquilicia sambucina: See Ampelopsis arborea
Arbutus uva ursi: See Vaccinium arboreaum
Archilochus colubris (L.): 270 & n264
Arctostaphylos uva ursi (L.) Spreng.: 245 & n148
Ardea occidentalis Audubon: 222 & n60. *A. alba; See Ardea occidentalis. A. americana; See Grus americana. A. caerulea; See Florida caerulea. A. Ludoviciana; See Hydranassa tricolor*
Aretium Lappa: See Androsace occidentalis
Aricara: 38
Aricaras: 35
Aristolochia var. *hastata* (Nutt.) Ducharte: 248 & n156. *A. pistolochia:* 248 & n156; *A. serpentaria:* 219n33
Arkansas Post: 13
Arkansas R.: 23, 33; plan to ascend, 70, 311–13; plans to descend, 8, 68, 321; Spanish attitude to, 30, 72; Wilkinson on, 30n41. *See also* Three Forks trading post
Armenta R.: 27
Armesto, Andrés: 74
Armstrong, John: 89
Army Corps of Engineers: *See* U.S. Army Corps of Engineers
Arroyo Hondo: 12, 25, 285, 286
Arrowhead: *See Sagittaria*
Arum: *See Peltandra*
Arundinaria gigantea (Bartr.) Muhl.: 114 & n47, 133, 177 & n8, 191, 199
Arundo donax: See Arundinaria gigantea
Asclepias incarnata: 243 & n135. *A. filiformis; See A. lanceloata. A. lactifera:* 242 & n143. *A. lanceolata* Walt: 243 & n134. *A. verticillata* (L.); *See A. lanceolata*
Ascyrum hypericoides: 243 & n136
Ash: *See Fraxinus*
Ashley, Robert: 34, 35n46, 75n117
Asimina parviflora (Michx.) Dunal: 255 & n202. *A. triloba* (L.) Dunal: 114–15 & n48, 255 & n202
Astragalus canadensis (L.): 244 & n142. *A. carolinianus; See A. canadensis*

Astronomical observations: *See* Celestial readings; Longitudinal readings
Atchafalaya R.: 102n4
Atractosteus tristaechus Block & Schneid.: 225 & n77
Atropa physaloides: See Nicandra physaloides
Attoyac R.: 27
Audubon, John James: on Hunter, 45; il Mississippi kite, 235; il Natchez, 69; il parakeet, 209
Aureolaria grandiflora (Benth.) Penn.: 261 & n225. *A. flava* (L.) Farw.; *See A. grandiflora*
Avoyelles: 107 & n23
Awahakei: 31, 36n47, 305, 331

Baker's Landing: 107 & n23
Balsam apple: *See Momordica charantia*
Baltimore oriole: *See Icterus galbula*
Barr, William: 28n36, 31, 111n40
Barton, Benjamin Smith: 53, 172n16; and amphibiuma, 227n82, 310; curriculum of, 60n86, 227n82; and Custis, 58–59, 266 & n254, 278n285, 327; on geography of species, 214n7
Barton Herbarium: 213–14, 249n164, 300, 309
Bartonia bracteata: See Orobranche ludoviciana
Bartram, William: asked to accompany expedition, 57; *Travels,* 66
Bass, largemouth: *See Micropterus salmoides*
Bastrop, Baron de: 84–85, 173, 191n24; 207n41
Bautista, Gov.: 29–30
Bayou Badtka: *See* Bayou Bodcau
Bayou Bodcau: 142 & n31, 143n32, 238
Bayou Chanou: *See* Bayou Pasacagoula
Bayou d'Arro: 112n43
Bayou Datche: *See* Bayou Dorcheat
Bayou Dorcheat: 120n58, 134–36 & n21; 328
Bayou Gatte: 330n12
Bayou Jean de Jean: 112 n43
Bayou Pasacagoula: 135n21, 328 & n3
Bayou Pierre: 127n9
Bayou Pierre settlement: 68–70 & n107, 124n2, 132n16, 207n41; garrison at, 72–74, 88; trading post

at, 307
Bayou Rapide: 111n40
Bayous: 133, 134
Bear: *See Ursus*
Bear R.: *See* Sulphur R.
Beaver: *See Castor fiber*
Beech, Carolina: *See Fagus grandiflora*
Benton, Thomas Hart: 292
Berlandier, Jean Louis: 212
Bienville, Jean Baptiste Le Moyne,
    Sieur de: 11, 130n11, 198n33; on
    unicorn, 17n19
Big Broth Lake: *See* Lake Bisteneau
Bignonia capreolata (L.): 264 & n244.
    B. radicans: 238 & n108. *B. semper-
    virens; See Gelsemium rankinii. B.
    triloba; See Catalpa bignoiodes. B.
    unguis; See B. capreolata*
Big Track: 44
Biloxis: 113n44
Bindweed, field: *See Convolvulus
    arvensis*
Bindweed, hedge: *See Calystegia sepium*
Bison bison bison (L.): 168n11, 190 &
    n21, 208, 272 & n270, il 273
Bisteneau Chute: 135n21
Blackberry: *See Rubiaceae*
Black cherry: *See Prunus serotina*
Black-eyed Susan: *See Rudbeckia*
Black man on expedition: 62, 100, 203
Blackland Prairie: 168n11, 180n11,
    il 171
Black R.: 102 & n5, 103, 106
Blanc, Louis de: 37 n48
Blister beetle: *See Epicauta*
Blount, William: 77
Blue jay, southern: *See Cyanocitta
    cristata*
Blue R.: 330 & n16
Boats: for Arkansas R. trip, 312;
    "Chinese," il 43, 45; designed by
    Dunbar, 67; preparation of, 42, 100;
    speed of, 102n5, 120n56, 206n40;
    used on expedition, 67–68
Bobwhite, interior: *See Colinus vir-
    ginianus*
Bodcau Prairie: 190n21
Bodcau Swamp: 143n32
Boggy Creek: 330 & n15
Bois d'arc: *See Maclura pomifera*
Bois d'Arc Creek: 330 & n14
Books: *See* Library of expedition
Borassus flabelliformus: See Sabal minor
Bos americana: See Bison

Bordelin, Hypolte: 130n11
Botanical specimens collected by
    Custis: 142n30, 213–14, 244n144,
    il 246–47, 248n158, 249–51 & n164,
    300 & n27
Boundaries of Louisiana: *See* Louisiana
    boundaries
Bowdoin, James: 89
Bower, Captain: 281
Boyd Hill: *See* Medicine Mount
Bradbury, John: 212
Brevel, Jean: 19–23 & n23; 34; 115n49
Briggs, Isaac: 48
Britain: *See* Great Britain
Broom-rape: *See Orobranche ludoviciana*
Brown-eyed Susan: *See Rudbeckia*
Bucareli: 12
Buckeye, red: *See Esculus parviflora*
Buckthorn, Carolina: *See Bumelia
    lanuginosa*
Buckwheat, climbing false: *See Polygo-
    num scandens*
Buffalo: *See Bison*
Buffalo fosh: *See Ictiobus*
Bull-nettle: *See Cnidosculus texana*
Bumelia lanuginosa (Michx.) Pers.: 107
    & n22, 255 & n198
Burling, Walter: 287 & n13
Burr, Aaron: 62n92; and Ashley, 35;
    and Bastrop, 84–85; conspiracy of
    generally, 51n71, 54n77, 75, 77–83
    & n123; and Jefferson, 291–94;
    maps of, 19; and Minor, 42n54;
    and Miranda, 86n132; il 76; on war
    with Spain, 80n123; and Wilkinson,
    29n38, 51, 77–80 & n121; 284, 287–
    88n13
Bustard: 195n32
Buttercup: *See Ranunculus*
Buttonwood: *See Cephalanthus occiden-
    talis*
Buzzard Bluff: 189–90
Buzzard Creek: 330n12

Cabeza de Vaca, Alvar Nuñez: 10
Cactus opuntia: See Opuntia allairei
Cadelafita: 70n107
Caddo Gap: 164n7
Caddo L.: 169n12
Caddo Prairie: 145 & n34, il 148,
    176n6, 190n21
Caddos: Adaes: 12, 167n10; anthro-
    pological observations on, 168–72
    & nn14–17, 195n132; betwixt U.S.

and Spain, 163–68 & n6, 283–84, 287, 307n36; bow of, 169–70 & n14; Cahinnios, 164n7; declining population of, 112n43, 164n8, 167–68n10; and French, 11, 196n32; Hasinais, 11, 172n16; hunter, il 171; influence of, 302; Kadoha-dachos, 22n23, 124, 160n3, 167n10, 169 & n13; marriage among, 170 & n15; missions to, 12, 172n16; Nana-tsohos, 167n10, 168n11; Natchi-toches, 68n107, 167n10; Nassonites, 12, 167n10, 192n24, 195–96 & n32; and Taovaya-Wichitas, 165; Tawa-konis, 36n47, 38; villages, 9, 11, 132n15, 145, 159–60, 161–62n4, 168 & n11, 169 & n13, 184, 188 & n18, il 189, 192n24, 195 & n32, il 197; warrior, il 166; women, 192n24; Yatasis, 11, 68n107, 167n10. *See also:* Aricaras; Cadodoquia; Dehahuit; Flood legend; Great Caddo Confed-eracy; Pawnees; Taovaya-Wichitas
Caddo Cession of 1835: 150n40, 176n6, 308
Cadodoquia: 10; extent of, 124, 168 & n11; map of, 152–53
Cahinnios: *See* Caddos
Cajahdet: 140n24
Calcasieu R.: 27, 286
Callahan Divide: 306
Calystegia sepium var. *repens* (L.) Gray: 216 & n14
Cambarus: 237 & n106
Camp Miguel del Salto: See Neches R. camp
Campephilus principalis (L.): 222 & n64, il 224
Campté: 130n11, 328
Canadian R.: 13, 122, 297; course of, 22n23; discovery of, 23
Cancer crangon: See Cambarus
Cane, giant: *See Arundinaria gigantea*
Cane R.: 114, 115–18 & nn50–51
Canis latrans frustror Woodhouse: 271n267. *C. lupus nubilis* Say: 274 & n274. *C. lycaon; See Urocyon cinereo-argentus. C. niger gregoryi:* 274n274
Caprimulgus carolinensis: 222 & n63. *C. virginianus; See Chordeiles minor*
Cardicus virginicus: See Cirsium caro-linianum
Cardinal flower: *See Lobelia cardinalis*
Cardinal, Louisiana: *See Richmondena*

cardinalis
Cardinal spear: *See Erythrina herbacea*
Carmel, La: *See* Bayou Pierre
Carya illinoinensis (Wangh.) K. Koch: 104–106 & nn10–11, 108, 118, 126, 176, 190, 191, 252 & n172. *C. ovata* (Mill.) K. Koch: 255 & n17. *C. tomentosa* Nutt.; *See C. illinoinensis; C. ovata*
Casa d'Yrujo: 42
Casanas, Francisco: 172n16
Cashesegra: 44
Casmerodius albus egretta Gmelin: *See Ardea occidentalis*
Caso Calvo, Marqués de: 28, 29; on passport, 71–72, 74–75, 83
Cassia chamaecrista: 264 & n245. *C. fasciculata:* 240–41 & n125. *C. marylandica:* 245 & n149, 264. *C. occidentalis:* 264 & n246. *C. obtusifolia:* 264 & n248
Castanea alnifolia Nutt.: 256 & n204. *C. a.* var *floridana* Sarg.: 256 & n204. *C. ashei* Sudw.: 256 & n204. *C. pumila* Mill.: 112 n42, 256 & n204
Castor canadensis texensis Bailey: 274 & n275. *C. fiber:* 274 & n275, 330nn13–14. *See also* Fur trade
Catahoula R.: 102n5
Catalpa bignoniodes Walt: 259 & n217
Catfish. *See Ictalurus*
Cathartes aura teter Friedmann: 223 & n67
Catlin, George: 16, 171, 202, 205, 273
Cattail, narrow-leaved: *See Typha angustifolia*
Cattle: *See* Graziers
Caudadachos: *See* Caddos
Cedar: *See Juniperus*
Cedar Bluffs: 149n39
Cedar Creek: 330n12
Cedar, white: *See chamaecyparis thyoides*
The Cedars: 257n209, 329 & n6
Celestial readings: 62, 320–21. *See also* Longitudinal readings
Celtis laevigata Willd.: 254 & n188. *C. occidentalis; See C. laevigata*
Cephalanthus occidentalis: 154, 259 & n218
Cercis canadensis (L.): 255 & n199. *C. siliquastrum; See C. canadensis*
Cervus elaphas canadensis Erxleben: 276 & n278. *C. e. Merriami* Nelson: il

273, 276 & n278. *C. wapiti; See C. elaphas. C. virginianus; See Dama virginiana*
Cevallos, Pedro: 26
Cha'kani'na: *See* Medicine Mount
Chalk bluffs: 329n11
Chamaecyparis thyoides (L.): 254 & n187
Chameleon: *See Anolis caroliniensis*
Chenopodium ambrosioides var. *anthelminticum* (L.) Gray: 251 & n167. *C. anthelminticum:* 264 & n250
Chickasaws: 167n10
Chicken War: 12
China-rose: *See Smilax tamnoides*
Chinquapin: *see Castanea*
Chinquapin, water: *See Nelumbo lutea*
Choctaws: 167n10
Chokeberry, red: *See Pyrus arbutifolia*
Cholera: 167n10
Chordeiles minor chapmani Coues: 222 & n62
Chouteau, Pierre: 44n56
Chuck-will's-widow: *See Caprimulgus caroliniensis*
Cirsium carolinianum (Walt.) Fern & Schub: 249 & n163
Claiborne, William C. C.: 90; on Dehahuit, 160–61n3; on Glass, 305; on return of expedition, 281–84; seeking passport, 72, 75
Clark, Daniel: on Dunbar, 15; on Wilkinson, 29 & n38, 314–15
Clark, Daniel Jr.: on Nolan, 33n44; on Talapoon, 131–32n14
Clark, George Rogers: 6, 7, 35n46
Clark, William: 7, 35n46m 297. *See also* Lewis & Clark expedition
Clay: 192, 238, 267
Clear Lake I: 143n32. C. l. II: 188n17. C. l. III and IV: 195 & n31
Clematis glaucophylla Small.: 216 & n12; *C. cirrbosa; See C. glaucophylla*
Clitoria mariana (L.): 263 & n236. *C. ternatea; See C. mariana*
Clupea thrissa: 278. *See also Pomolobus chrysochloris*
Cnidoscolus texana (Muell. Arg.) Small: 248 & n160
Coal: 126n7, 180, 184, 266–67. *See also* Lignite
Colinus virginianus mexicanus (L.): 223n72
Collins, Joseph: 237

Colorado R.: 25, 26
Coluber versicolor: 278. *C. rhomboideus; See Lampropeltis triangulum*
Columbia R.: 8
Comanches: French trade with, 13; and Glass, 305–306; and Melgares, 174n1; Penateka, 131n14, 393, 304; and Spanish, 30, 38, 124, 307; and U.S., 32, 37, 289, 302–303. *See also* Medicine Rock
Comfrey: *See Symphitum officinale*
Commelina virginica (L.): 245 & n152. *C. vaginata; See C. virginica*
Compagnie des Indes: 12–13, 111n40. *See also* La Harpe, Bernard de
Compass plant: *See Silphium laciniatum*
Congress: *See* U.S. Congress
Continental divide: 22. *See also* Pyramidal Height
Conuropsis carolinensis ludovicianus Gmelin: 221–22 & n58, il 209
Convolvulus arvensis: 216 & n13. *C. repens; See Calystegia sepium*
Coragyps atratus Bechstein: 223n67
Coral bean: *See Eruthrina herbacea*
Cordero y Bustamante, Antonio: 37–38 & n49; and U.S. incursions, 86–87, 285, 286, 304; on U.S. intentions, 30n41, 76–77, 85; on Viana, 159, 173
Coreopsis lanceolata: 244 & n140
Corn cultivation: 154, 175
Cornus drummondii C. A. Meyer: 107 & n25, 255 & n201. *C. florida:* 108 & n31, 136, 255 & n200. *C. Sericea; See C. drummondii*
Coronado, Francisco Vásquez de. *See* Vásquez de Coronado, Francisco
Cortes, Juan: 124n2
Corvus brachyrhynchos paulus Brehm: 223n68. *C. corax; See C. cryptoleucus. C. corone; See C. branchyrhynchos. C. cristatus; See Cyanocitta cristata. C. Cryptoleucus* Couch: 268 & n259. *C. mexicanus; See C. ossifragus. C. ossifragus:* 223 & n69
Coshada Chute: 132n15, 135n21
Cost of Red R. expedition: 39, 63–64, 295 & n25. *See also* U.S. Congress appropriations
Cotinus obvatus Raf.: 220 & n44
Cotton cultivation: 111n40, 112, 150, 176
Cottonwood: *See Populus*

Cougar: *See Felis concolor*
Council for the Fortification and
 Defense of the Indies: 27
Coushatta Bluffs: 149n39, 175, il
 182–83
Coushattas: *See* Alabama-Coushattas
Coverup: *See* Publication
Coxe, Robert: 19n22
Coyotes: *See Canis latrans*
Crane, whooping: *See Grus americana*
Crataegus aria: See Pyrus arbutifolia
Crayfish, fresh-water: *See Cambarus*
Creek land cession of 1814: 315, 316
Creeks: 112–13n43, 150n40; lodge, il
 151; Pakana, 112–13n43; Taensa,
 112–13n43; villages of, 149n39;
 warrior, il 155. *See also* Alabama-
 Coushattas
Cross Timbers: 22n23, 36. *See also*
 Taovaya-Wichitas villages
Cross vine: *See Bignonia capreolata*
Crotalus atrox Baird & Girard: 278
 & n283. *C. horridus atricaudatus*
 Latreille: 278 & n283. *C.
 durissus*: 236-37 & n105.
Crotolaria sagittalis (L.): 244 & n141.
 C. latifolia; See C. sagittalis
Crow: *See Corvus*
Culver's root, eastern: *See Veronica-*
 strum virginicum
Cupressus disticha: See Tapodium disti-
 chum
Cushing, T. H.: 123, 173, 191n24,
 281, 285, 293
Custis, Peter: 59–61, 63–64, 100n3;
 after expedition, 309–10 & n42;
 scientific work of evaluated, 211–
 15, 241n125, 297–302. *See also*
 Barton, Benjamin Smith; Botanical
 specimens collected by Custis
Cut Finger: 174n3, 186n16
Cyanocitta cristata cristata (L.): 223
 & n70
Cylindrosteus platostomus platyrhincus
 DeKay: *See Esox*
Cypress, bald: *See Taxodium distichum*
Cypressus thyoides: See Chamaecuparis
 thyoides
Cyprinus americana: See Ictiobus
 cyprinella

Dama virginiana macroura (Raf.): 230
 & n90, il 233
Dams, natural: *See* Rafts

Dandelion: *See Taraxacum officinale*
d'Anville, Jean Baptiste Bourguignon:
 27
Darby, William: 161n4
Darlington, William: 58
Datisca hirta: See Apocynum cannibinum
Datura stramonium: 220 & n50
Daugherty, Thomas: 290–91
Dauni, Alexandro: 34
Davenport, Samuel: 28n36, 31, 111n40
Davis, George: 48
Davis, John: 34
Dayflower, common: *See Commelina*
 virginica
Dearborn, Henry: 90, 123; on Burr
 Conspiracy, 291; seeking leader, 47;
 and war threat, 174; and Wilkinson,
 80, 291
Deer: 195n32
Deer, whitetailed: *See Dama virginiana*
Dehahuit: and Claiborne, 284; death
 of, 308 & n39; on fur trade, 274n275;
 meeting with, 160–68 & nn3, 6, 7;
 messages to and from, 146, 148; on
 Spanish traders, 31; speech by, 163–
 65; and U.S., 302; on Viana, 193–94
Delaney Mountain: 175n4, il 182–83
Delays: 42, 44, 100, 120n56, 159,
 181n14. *See also* Difficulties; Speed
 of boats
Delphinium carolinianum Walt.: 248 &
 n159. *D. staphisagria; See D. caro-*
 linianum. D. tricorne Michx.; *See*
 D. carolinianum; D. virescens Nutt.;
 See D. carolinianum
Des Moines R.: 8
DeSoto, Hernan: 10, 164n7
Devil's-grandmother: *See Elephantobus*
 nudatus
Devil's shoestring: *See Indigofera hirsuta*
Dewberries: *See Rubiaceae*
Didelphis marsupialis virginiana Kerr:
 230 & n91. *D. opossum; See D.*
 marsupialis
Difficulties: anticipated, 54; of detour
 around Great Raft, 141–43, 154,
 318; of scientific work, 111–12n41,
 213, 300, 301–302n28
Digitalis flava: See Aureolaria grandi-
 flora
Diospyros virginiana (L.): 106, 108, 252
 & n175
Distances: measuring, 102n5; table of,
 328–32; total, 206n40

370

Dogwood: *See Cornus*
Dominguez-Escalante expedition: 19
d'Ortolan, Bernard: 204n39
Dowdy, Katie: 243
Drosera brevifolia Pursh: 244 & n144,
  *D. cuneifolia; See D. brevifolia. D.
  intermedia* Hayne; *See D. brevifolia*
Drummond's red maple: *See Acer
  rubrum*
Duck: *See Anas*
DuForest, John Joseph: 123, 125–
  26n6, 204n38
Dunbar and Hunter expedition: *See*
  Ouachita R. expedition
Dunbar, William: boats designed by,
  67; on botanist, 56; describing Red
  R. Valley, 15–17; and Freeman,
  50, 52; on guides and interpreters,
  131n14; and Jefferson, 15n18, 17,
  293, 313n49; on Louisiana boundary, 25; longitudinal method of,
  65n102; on military escort, 61–62;
  on morale, 90, 97; il 41; on prairies,
  210n46; on Spanish threat, 68–69,
  81; on Sparks, 203n37; and Wilkinson, 312; working on Arkansas R.
  expedition, 311–12; working on
  Red R. expedition, 39–42, 46–48,
  100, 324–25. *See also* The Forest
duPratz, Antoine Simon Le Page: 14,
  65, 213n6, 216n11
Durocher, Laurent: 35

Echean: 148–49 & n38, 157 & n49, 302
Echinops sphaerocephalus: 217 & n19
Eclipse of the sun: 141
Ecology: change in, 262n231, 264n245,
  272–73n271; nineteenth century
  theories of, 210n46; of pine barrens,
  108n35; of prairies, 208–10,
  272n270; of Red R. Valley, 133 &
  n18, 177–80n10. *See also* Under-
  growth
Ectopistes migratorius (L.): 271n266
Eglantine: *See Rosa eglanteria*
Egret, American: *See Ardea occidentalis*
Elanoides forficatus (L.): 222 & n61
Elder: *See Sambucus*
Eleagnaceae: See Forestiera acuminata
Elephantobus nudatus Gray: 263 &
  n242. *E. carolinianus* Raeusch; *See E.
  nudatus. E. scaber; See E. nudatus; E.
  tomentosus* (L.); *See E. nudatus*
Elephant's foot: *See Elephantobus*

  nudatus
Elk: *See Cervus elaphas*
Ellicott, Andrew: 40, 50; and Free-
  man, 50, 315; on Red R. mouth,
  101–102n4
Elm: *See Ulmus americana*
England: *See Great Britain*
Epicauta pennsylvanica DeGeer:
  279 & n286. *E. vittata* DeGeer:
  279 & n287
Erythrina herbacea: 119 & n54, 218 &
  n28, 242
*Erythrocephalus: See Melanerpes
  erythrocephalus*
Esculus parviflora Walter: 108n36
Esox: 237. *E. osseus:* 278. *E. reticulatus*
  LeSueur: 225 & n76
Essex Junto: 77
Eudocimus albus (L.): 234 & n97
Euonymous americanus: 244 & n143
Eustoma grandiflorum: il 246, 250n164
Exotic species: 214; *Althaea rosea* (L.)
  Cav., 218n26; *Apium leptophyllum*
  Muell. & Benth., 248 & n154;
  Convulvis arvensis, 216n13; *Echi-
  nops sphaerocephalus,* 217n19; Horse,
  13, 15, il 16, 31, 32, 38, 170n15,
  272n270; *Marrubium vulgare* (L.),
  220n51; *Mercurialis annua,* 239
  & n110; *Momordica charantia* L.,
  244n145; *Nicandra physaloides*
  Gaertn., 216n11; *Origanum vulgare,*
  262 & n233; *Periploca graeca* (L.),
  244n139; *Persicaria lapathifolia* (L.)
  Small: 242 & n127; *Portulaca oleracca,* 219 & n39; *Plantago major,*
  244 & n138; *Ranunculus bulbosa,*
  216n15; *Rosa eglanteria,* 219 & n34;
  Symphitum officinale, 218 & n31;
  Taraxacum officinale Weber, 220 &
  n48; *Verbascum thapsis,* 220n42;
  Vulpes fulva fulva (Demarest)
  271n268
Exploration of Louisiana before
  1806: 6
The Exploring Expedition of the Red
  River: *See* Red R. expedition

Fagus grandiflora var. *caroliniana* Fern
  & Rehd.: 257 & n213. *F. sylvatica;
  See F. grandiflora. F. pumila; See
  Castanea*
Flaco columbarius columbarius (L.): 234
  & n98. *F. communis; See F. colum-*

barius. F. furcatus; See Elanoides forficatus; F. peregrinus: 212, 268 & n262

False aloe: *See Agave virginica*

False foxglove: *See Aureolaria grandiflora*

False indigo: *See Amorpha fruticosa*

False Ouachita: *See* Missouri branch of the Red R.

Faux Anachitta: *See* Missouri branch of the Red R.

Felis concolor coryi Bangs: 271 & n268. *F. c. stanleyana* Goldman; *See F. c. coryi*

Ferrer, José Joaquin de: 101n4

Ferry across Red R.: 126 & n7

Filibusters: 86, 292; of Genêt, 6, 35; of Long, 51n71; of Magee, Menchaca, & Gutierrez, 28n36; of Wilkinson, 51 & n71, 80

Finiels, Nicholas de: 74

Firearms: of Indians, 13, 31, 38, 208 & n45, 306; on expedition, 66

Fires set by Indians: *See* Ecology

Flag of the U.S.: 123, 124, 146n36, 157 & n49, 193 & n27, 282, 283, 303, 304, 305

Fletcher, Nimrod: 207n42

Flint: 107n23

Flood legend: of Caddos, 170–72; of Indians, 172n16. *See also* Medicine Mount

Floods of Red R.: 103 & n6, 107, 110, 127, 133 & n18, 175–76

Flores, José: 204n39

Florida: 25–26, 50

Florida caerulea caerulea (L.): 267 & n256

Ford of Red R.: 193 & n26

The Forest: 15n18, 25, 90; il 71

Forestiera acuminata (Michx.) Poir: 109 & n37

Fort Adams: 51, 99

Fort Claiborne: 86

Fort Towson: 330n13

Fossils: *See* Petrefactions

Fowler, John: 181

Fox, gray: *See Urocyon cinereoargentus*

Fox, red: *See Vulpes fulva*

Fragaria virginiana Duch.: 242 & n129. *F. vesca; See F. virginiana*

France *vs.* Spain in Red R. Valley: 10–13, 23n24, 37, 111n40, 130n11, 175n4, 283. *See also* Louisiana

boundaries; Treaty of Paris; Treaty of San Ildefonso

Fraxinus: 126, 142, 145, 176, 190. *F. americana:* 114, 115, 254 & n189. *F. caroliniana* Mill.: 254 & n190; *F. excelsior; See F. caroliniana*

Freeman, Constant: 52

Freeman, Thomas: 49–54, 63; and boundary survey of 1797–98, 50; after expedition, 313–16; and Arkansas R., 311–13; and Barton, 58; building Ft. Adams, 99; choosing Custis, 58–59; on cypress, 254n186; and Ellicott, 50, 315; letter to McKee, 53, 54n76, il 73; obituary, 316; speech to the Caddos, 162 & n5

Fringilla caudacuta. See Ammospiza caudacuta

Frio Creek: 332n20

Fulton, Alexander: 113n43

Fungi: 249

Fur trade: 31, 38, 44n56, 230n90, 274nn275–76

Gaignard, J.: 192n24

Gaines, Edmund Pendleton: 62 & n92

Gallatin, Albert: 19, 314

Garcitas Creek: 10

Garfish: *See Esox*

Garlic: *See Allium*

Garrisons: 86; recommended by Wilkinson, 82; requested by Cordero, 85; assigned by Salcedo, 173

Gelsemium rankinii Small: 263 & n243

Genêt, Edmund: 6, 35

Gentian, prairie: *See Eustoma grandiflorum*

Geomys bursarius dutcheri Davis: 231 & n94

Gillespie, Mr.: 40 & n53

Glass, Anthony: 131n14, 157n49, 191n24, 208n43, 304–306 & n35

Glaucomys volans saturatus A. H. Howell: 274 & n273

Gleditsia: 126, 176. *G. monosperma:* 252 & n176. *G. aquatica* Marsh; *See G. monosperma; G. triacanthos:* 106, 252 & n176. ✕*G. triacanthos* var. *texana* Sarg.: 154 & n43, 256 & n208

Glycyrrhiza lepidota Pursh: 300n27

Goldenrod: *See Solidago altissima*

Gonzalez, José Maria: 86

Goose: 271

Goseascoechea, Jose: 306
Gran Montane: 12
Grand Council at Natchitoches: 303,
304
Grand Encore Bluffs: il v, 126n7, 328
Grand Excursion: *See* Red R. expe-
dition
Grand Ozages; 174n3, 186n16
Grand Prairie: 32–33
Grapes: 154–57 & n47
Grappe, Alexis: 134n20
Grappe, François Louis: 134 & n20,
136–40 & n25, 146–48, 162n5,
203n39, 327
Grappe's Bluff: 130 & n12
Grasshopper: *See* Locust (insect)
Gray, George: 307
Graziers: 136–40 & n24, 308
Great Britain: 89; settlers from, 111n40
Great Caddo Confederacy: 167n10
Great Plains; 210n46
Great Raft: 127–28n10, 131n13,
145n35, 169n12, 190n21; demoli-
tion of, 133n19, 135 & n22, 176n6,
177n7; detours around, 127n9, 134
& n21, 168–69n12, 207n41; il 128–
29, 307; map of, 137
Great Rapide: 110–11 & n39
Great Swamp: 127n9, 140n26, il 147,
207n41, 239n116; Dehahuit on, 161
Great Track: 44
Grecian silk vine: *See* Periploca graeca
Greenbrier: *See* Smilax bona-nox
Green L.: 143n32
Groundcherry: *See* Physalis
Grus americana (L.): 267 & n255
Guadiana, José Maria: 88, 132n16,
160
Guides and interpreters: 123, 131n14,
140, 142, 174 & n3. *See also* Grappe,
François Louis; Talapoon, Lucas
Gum, black: 176
Gum, sweet: *See* Liquidambar styraciflua
Gum, white: 126
Guns: *See* Firearms
Gutierrez-Magee filibuster: 51n71
Gypsum: 190 & n20, 267

Halesia diptera Ellis: 256 & n206. *H.
tetraptera; See H. diptera*
Hamamelis virginica: 256 & n205
Hamilton, Alexander: 6; and Burr, 77;
and Freeman, 50
Harris, Joseph: 107n21

Harrison, William Henry: 52
Hasinais: *See* Caddos
Haw: *See* Viburnum rufidulum
Hawk, eastern pigeon: *See* Falco
columbarius
Hawkins L.: 195n32
Hedera quinquefolia: *See Parthenocyssus
quinquefolia*
Helianthus multiflorus: 262. *H. stru-
mosus*: 248 & n155
Hemp: *See* Apocynum cannibinum
Hempshill L.: 196n33
Hendry, John: 277 & n280
Hercules club: *See* Zanthoxylon clava H.
Heron, great white: *See* Ardea occi-
dentalis
Heron, little blue: *See* Florida caerulea
Heron, Louisiana: *See* Hydranassa
tricolor
Herrera, Simon de: 159, 173 & n1,
207n41; marching, 191n24, 194n30,
207n41; negotiating, 282–85
Herring: *See* Clupea thrissa
Herring, blue: *See* Pomolobus chryso-
chloris
Hibiscus laevis Allioni: 262–63 & n235.
*H. fraternus; See H. moscheutos. H.
hirtus; See H. lasiocarpos. H. lasio-
carpos* Cav.: 262 & n229. *H. militaris*
(L.); *See H. laevis; H. moscheutos*
(L.): 238 & n109
Hickman's Prairie: 198n33
Hickory: 126, 136, 141, 145, 176, 177,
180, 189, 190, 191. *See also* Carya
ovata
Hidalgo y Costilla, Miguel: 207n42
Hietans: *See* Comanches
Hill, Basil: 121
Hirundo rivaria: *See Stelgidopteryx
ruficollis*
Holly: *See* Ilex
Hollyhock: *See* Althaea rosea
Honeysuckle, trumpet: *See* Lonerica
sempervirens
Horehound: *See* Marrubium vulgare
Horse: and Caddo marriage, 170n15;
feral, 15, 32; il 16; range of, 272n270;
trade in, 13, 31, 38, 306
Horse nettle: *See* Solanum carolinense
House, John: 34, 35
Huckleberry, tree: *See* Vaccinium
arboreum
Humboldt, Friedrich Heinrich
Alexander, Baron von, map by: 19,

il 20–21, 48, 65
Hummingbird, broad-tailed: *See*
　Platurornis platycercus
Hummingbird, ruby-throated: *See*
　Archilocus colubris
Hummingbird, rufous: *See Selasphorus*
　rufus
Humphreys, Enoch: 62, 64, 203
Hunter, George: 39, 42, 46–47 & n62,
　324; boats of il 43, 45. *See also*
　Ouachita R. expedition
Hydranassa tricolor Muller.: 222 & n59
Hydrocotyle umbellata Michx.: 218 &
　n24. *H. vulgaris; See H. umbellata*
Hylatomas pileatus (L.): 223 & n65, il
　224
Hypericum buckleyi Curtis: 217 & n21.
　H. densiflorum Pursh; *See H. buckleyi.*
　H. drummondii (Grev. & Hook) Torr
　& Gray: 217 & n20. *H. fasciculatum*
　Lam.: 240 & n123. *H. kalmianum;*
　See H. buckleyi. H. proliferum; See H.
　fasciculatum. H. quadrangulare; See
　H. drummondii

Ibis, white: *See Eudocimus albus*
Ibis, wood: *See Mycteria americana*
Ictalurus: 157, 225 & n75, 237, 277
Icterus galbula (L.): 236 & n101
Ictinia mississippiensis Wilson: 234 &
　n99, il 235, 301
Ictiobus cyprinella Cuvier & Valen.:
　278 & n281. *I. bubalus* Raf.; *See I.*
　cyprinella. I. urus Agassiz. See I.
　cyprinella
Ietans: *See* Comanches
Ilex cassine: 249 & n161. *I opaca* Ait.:
　108 & n34, 257 & n214. *I. verticil-*
　lata: 260n223. *I. vomitoria* Ait.:
　250n165, 257 & n214. *I. aquafolium;*
　See I. opaca
Illinois nut: *See Carya illinoiensis*
Imperialism of U.S.: 24, 26, 27–28, 51,
　54, 90n140; and Burr Conspiracy,
　77–80, 84–85, 291, 292. *See also*
　Filibusters; Louisiana boundaries;
　Texas
Indian pink: *See Spigelia marylandica*
Indian trade: *See* Trade with Indians
Indian trade goods: 63, 64, 123, 206,
　311
Indians: dwelling, il 121; French and,
　13; relocation of, 112, 307–308;
　Spanish and, 13, 30, 31, 35, 37–38,
83, 112n43, 124, 125, 150n40, 303,
　304, 307; squatters and, 308 & n37;
　U.S. diplomacy to, 23–24, 35, 37,
　55, 72, 302–303, 322–23. *See also*
　Alabama Coushattas; Apaches;
　Appalaches; Aricaras; Biloxis;
　Caddos; Chickasaws; Choctaws;
　Comanches; Creeks, Dehahuit;
　Firearms, Flood legend; Grand
　Council at Natchitoches; Iroquoian
　language; Medicine Rock, Missions,
　Mobilian language; Mound builders;
　Muskhogean language; Osages;
　Pasacagoulas; Pawnees; Shawnees;
　Sign language; Siouan language;
　Taboyases; Taovaya-Wichitas;
　Trade with Indians
Indigofera hirsuta: 218n30
Interpreters: *See* Guides and inter-
　preters
Ipomaea pandurata (L.) Mey.: 261 &
　n226; *I. solanifolia; See I. pandurata*
Iras Coques: 36n47
Iron ore: 120 & n58, 186 & n16
Iroquoian language: 188n18
Isle Brevel: 115 & n49

Jackrabbit, black-tailed: *See Lepus*
　californicus
Jackson, Andrew: 292, 315
James, Edwin: 100, 212, & n2, 295,
　332–33n21
Jasmine, yellow: *See Gelsemium rankinii*
Jatropha urens: See Cnidosculus texana
Jeems Bayou: 162n4, 169n12
Jefferson, Thomas: and Burr Con-
　spiracy, 291–92; and Dunbar,
　15n18, 17, 313n49; exploration
　plans of generally, 5–9, 311–13; and
　Freeman, 49, 52; instructions from,
　8, 39, 52, 53–56, 70, 162n4, 319–
　25; on Louisiana boundaries, 8, 24–
　26, 89, 295, 322; on mustangs, 32;
　and Nolan, 32–33 & n44; *Notes on*
　the State of Virginia, 66; il 4; on
　prairies, 210n46; on Red R., 8, 23,
　33–34; and Red R. expedition, 39–
　44, 46–49, 56–61, 70, 292–95;
　scientific interests of, 5, 172n16; and
　Sibley, 30; on Sparks, 203n37; and
　Wilkinson, 80–81, 285, 287n13,
　288, 291–92
Jerusalem oak: *See Chenopodium*
　ambrosiodes

374

Jimsonweed: *See Datura stramonicum*

Johnston, Joe E.: 135n22

Joutel, Henri: 192n24, 195n32

Juglans alba: 108, 157. *See also Carya illinoiensis; C. ovata. J. nigra*: 176, 256 & n203. *J. Petiolata* Custis; *See Carya illinoiensis*

Juniperus silicicola (Small) Bailey: 257n210. *J.virginiana* (L.): 145 & n33, 154, 176 & nn7, 10, 256 & n209

Jussiaea erecta: See Ludwiga leptocarpa. J. repens; See Ludwiga repens

Kadohadachos: *See* Caddos

Kalm, Peter: 216n11

Kansas R.: 8

Kelsey, Eliphalet: 98

Kiamichi R.: 206n40, 275n276, 328 & n13

King Nicholas: 91–94; omissions by, 100, 293, 301; on Ouachita R. expedition, 44; Red R. map by, 92–93

Kingfisher, eastern belted: *See Megaceryle alcyon*

Kingsbury, Jacob: 281

Kite, Mississippi: *See Ictinia mississippiensis*

Kite, swallow-tailed: *See Elanoides forficatus*

Kittsita Cammenuo: 36n47

Koasatis: *See* Alabama-Coushattas

Lacerta alligator: See Alligator mississippiensis. L. chameleon; See Anolis caroliensis

Lafitte, Pierre Bouet: *See* Cadelafita

La Harpe, Bernard de: 12–13, 175n4, 198n33; on Caddos, 195n32; around Great Raft, 127n9; with Taovayas, 36n47; on unicorns, 14,17n19

La Harpe's post: 13, 168n11, 198n33

Lake Bisteneau: 134–35n21, 136–40 & n23, il 138–39, il 147, 328

Lake Tso'to: *See* Soda L.

LaLande, Baptiste: 35

Lampropeltis triangulum amaura Cope: 236 & n104, il 237

Land grants to members of expedition: 64, 325

Langsdorff, Georg Heinrich von: 212

Larkspur: *See Delphinium carolinianum*

La Salle, René Robert Cavalier, Sieur de: 10, 26, 192n24

Las Piedras: *See* Bayou Pierre

Lathyrus venosis var. intonaesus Butt. & St. John: 217 & n22. *L. tuberosus* (L.); See *L. venosus*

Laurus Benzoin: See Lindera benzoin. L. sassafras; See Sassafras albidum

The Leander: 86n132

Leather flower: *See Clematis glaucophylla*

Ledyard, John: 6

Leon, Alonso de: 11

Leonard, Gilbert: 77

Leontodora taraxacum: See Taraxacum officinale

Lepisosteus osseus osseus (L.) *See Esox*

Lepus californicus melanotis: 195n32, il 270, 272 & n271. *L. timidus; See L. californicus*

Lewis & Clark expedition: 293; compared to Red R. expedition, 56, 61, 62, 64; cost of, 39, 63n95; firearms for, 66n104; purposes of, 7–8 & n6, 17, 82; scientific work of, 60–68n88, 65n102, 212, 213n6, 300

Lewis, John S.: 131n14, 304

Lewis, Meriwether: 7, 50, 53; compared to Custis, 301–302; death of, 314. *See also* Lewis & Clark expedition

Liberation of New Spain. *See* Imperialism of U.S.

Library of expedition: 65–66 & n103, 300

Licorice, southeastern: See *Glycyrrhiza lepidota*

Lignite: 120 & n57. *See also* Coal

Lily, celestial: *See Nemastylis nuttallii*

Lime: 120

Limestone: 267

Lindera benzoin (L.) Blume: 108 & n35, 109, 259 & n221. *L.b.* var. *pubescens* (Palmer & Steyermark) Rehder: 260n221. *L. melissafoila* (Walt.) Blume: 260 n221

Linnaeus, Carolus: 65, 66

Linnard, Thomas: 123, 124n2; on meteorite, 306n35

Liquidambar styraciflua: 253 & n 183

Lisa, Manuel: 44

Little Prairie: 181n15, 328

Little R.: 114, 115, 175 & n5, 190 & n 22, 329 & n7

Little Willow Pass: 168–69n12

Livingston, Robert: 89

Llano Estacado: 23, 33–34
Lobelia cardinalis: 263 & nn238–39. *L. siphilitica* L.: 249–50 & n165, 263 & n239
Lobelia, great blue: *See Lobelia siphilitica*
Locust (insect): 278 & n285
Locust (tree): *See Gleditsia*
Loftus Heights: 99
Loggy Bayou: 135n21, 328 & n3
Logjams: *See* Rafts
Loglines: 102n5
Lonerica sempervirens: 221 & n56, 251 & n170
Long, Col. Stephen H.: 135n22
Longitudinal readings: 48–49, 65 & n102
Long, James: 51n71
Long (Stephen) expedition: 23, 212, 313, 332-33n21
Lopes Arnesto, Andrés: 27n35
Los Adaes: 12, 27; U.S. attack on, 86, 124, 126n6
Louisiana: to France, 7; to Spain, 12; U.S. knowledge of, 14–17; U.S. purchase of, 3–7, 294
Louisiana boundaries: eighteenth century, 12; France and, 24, 26, 89; Great Britain and, 89; Jefferson on, 8, 24–26, 89, 295, 322; negotiations on, 24–28, 68, 89, 332n21; Red R. expedition and, 56, 83–84, 161n4; Spain on, 27, 72n111, 159–60; surveys of, 74 & n114, 82, 84–85, 161n4. *See also* Adams-Onís Treaty of 1819; France vs. Spain in Red R. Valley; Imperialism of U.S.; Neutral Ground Agreement of 1806
Louisiana Gazette: 54n77, 90n140; on Freeman, 313
Loxia cardinalis: See Richmondena cardinalis
Lucas el Talapuz: See Talapoon, Lucas
Lucas, Joseph: See Talapoon, Lucas
Ludwiga leptocarpa (Nutt.) Hara.: 261 & n227. *L. repens* Sw.: 240 & n120
Lutra canadensis texensis Goldman: 274 & n276
Lyrodendron tulipfera (L.): 118 & n52
Lytta vesicatoria: 279 & n287

Maclura pomifera (Raf.) Schneid.: 114n47, 170n14, il 243, 260 & n224
Madison, James: 292, 293n22

Magee-Menchaca-Gutierrez filibuster: 28n36
Magnolia grandiflora: 118 & n52. *M. tripetala:* 257 & n210
Magotty Bay bean: *See Cassia chamaecrista; C. fasciculata*
Mahon, Alexander: 107n21
Makes-Tracks-Going-Far-Away: 44
Maley, John: 118n51, 119n55, 132n15, 140nn24–25, 275n276
Mallet, Paul and Pierre: 23
Malva caroliniana: See Modiola caroliniana
Mandrake, American: *See Podophyllum peltatum*
Manifest Destiny: *See* Imperialism of U.S.
Maple: *See Acer*
Maps of Freeman & Custis: accuracy of, 65, 156, 213, 296, 297, 314; il 93–94; influence of, 295–97. *See also* Celestial readings; Longitudinal readings
Marcy, Randolph: 22n23, 317, 332n20
Mares, Jose: 18, 19
Marl: 104 & n7, 107 & n24, 238
Marrubium vulgare (L.): 221 & n51
Marshall, Humphrey: 65
Marshall, Moses: 6
Martin, John: 98
Massanet, Damian: 11
Mattan: 308
May-apple: *See Podophyllum peltatum*
Maypops: *See Passiflora incarnata*
Medical Repository: 66. *See also* Mitchell, Samuel L.
Medicine Mount: 172 & n17, 184–88 & n16, il 187
Medicine Rock: 17n19, il 18, 305–306 & n35
Megaceryle alcyon alcyon (L.): 236 & n100
Meleagris gallopavo Viellot: 195–96 & n32, 225 & n73, il 269, 270–71 & n265
Melgares, Fecundo: expedition of, 125 & n5, 173, 174n1, 297; and Walker, 42n53
Melanerpes erythrocephalus erythrocephalus (L.): 223 & n66, il 224
Melish, John: 295, 297
Meloe pennsylvanica: See Epicauta pennsylvanica
Mentha aquatica (L.): 221 & n52. *M.*

sativa; See M. aquatica
Mephitis mephitis mesomelas Licht.: 231
  & n92
Mercurialis annua: 239 & n110
Mermento R.: *See* Calcasieu R.
Meteorites: 17n19. *See also* Medicine
  Rock
Mexican Association: 29, 80, 99
Mexican tea: *See Chenopodium*
Mezières, Athanase ("Ánastacio") de:
  13; and Brevel, 22n23; on Medicine
  Rock, 17n19; on Taovayas villages,
  36 & n47
Michaux, François André: 6, 7,
  66n103
Micropterus salmoides Lacépède: 225
  & n79
Miera y Pacheco, Bernardo: 19
Milam, Ben: 193
Military escort for Arkansas R.
  expedition: 311–12
Military escort for Red R. expedition:
  61–62, 70, 123. *See also* Sparks,
  Richard
Milk snake: *See Lampropeltis triangulum*
Milkweed: 242–43 & nn133–35. *See
  also* Periploca graeca (L.)
Milkweed, swamp: *See asclepias
  incarnata*
Milkwort: *See Polygala incarnata*
Miller, William: 113n43
Miller's Bluff: 175n4, il 182–83
Mimosa strigillosa Torr. & Gray: 118–
  19 & n53, 217 & n17, 251 & n168.
  *M. puntata; See M. strigillosa. M.
  tenuifolia. See Schrankia hystricina*
Mimus polyglottas polyglottos (L.): 223
  & n71
Minnesota R.: 8
Minor, Stephen: 42 & n54, 74n114
Miranda, Francisco de: 86n132
Missions: to Adaes, 12; French, 99; to
  Hasinais, 11; at Rapids, 111n40; of
  San José to Caddos, 12; of San Sabá,
  13; by U.S., 323
Mississippi Co. *See* Compagnie des
  Indes
Mississippi R.: compared to Red R.,
  118; Ft. Adams on, 99; La Salle on,
  10–11
Missouri branch of the Red R.: il 205,
  331 & n17
Missouri R.: 25, 27; compared to Red
  R., 23; exploration of by Marshall,

6; U.S. knowledge of, 19n22. *See also*
  Lewis & Clark expedition
Mistletoe: *See Phoradendron flavescens*
Mitchill, Samuel L.: 14, 66, 294
Mobilian language: 113n44
Mobilization: *See* Spanish troops
  against Red R. expedition
Mockingbird, eastern: *See Mimus
  polyglottos*
Modiola caroliniana (L.): 218 & n25
Moingona R.: 8
Mole, eastern: *See Scalopus aquaticus*
Momordica charantia L.: 244, & n145
Monroe, James: 25, 89
Monsters: 15 & n19
Mooney, Edward: 98
Mooney, James: 166
Morale of expedition: 90, 120; deser-
  tion and disloyalty, 207n42
Morea vegeta: See Nemastylus nuttalli
Morhouse, Abraham: 85
Morning glory: *See Ipomaea*
Morus rubra (L.): 126 & n8, 255 &
  n197. *M. nigra; See M. rubra*
Moscoso, Luis de: 10
Mound builders: 167n10, 188n18
Mouse: *See Peromyscus*
Muhlenberg, Henry: 214n6, 216n11;
  cane of, 114n47; on Michaux,
  66n103
Mulberry: *See Morus*
Mullein: *See Verbascum thapsus*
Murphey, Edward: 111n40
Muscaninia rotundifolia (Michx.):
  157n47
Muskhogean language: 112n43,
  113n44
Mus ludovicianus Custis: *See Peromyscus
  leucopus*
Músquiz, Miguel: 32, 34
Mustang: See Horse
Mustela lutra: See Lutra canadensis
Mus tuza: See Geomys bursarius
Mycteria americana (L.): 268 & n258
Myrica cerifera: 108 & n28, 112, 242
  & n126, 260 & n222
Myrtle, southern wax: *See Myrica
  cerifera*

Nacogdoches: 12, 82
Nanatsoho Bluff: *See* Spanish Bluff
Nanatsohos: *See* Caddos
Napoleon I: 79, 89
Nassonites: *See* Caddos

Natchez: il 69
Natchitoches: 27, 119–20 & nn55–57, 123; foundation of, 11, 119n55; Grand Council at, 303, 304; name of, 112n42; on return of expedition, 281; as supply head, 101; trail to Santa Fe from, 13, 18. *See also* Ft. Claiborne
Natchitoches Caddos: *See* Caddos
Natchitoches Salt Works: 305
National Intelligencer and Washington Advertiser: 45, 294–95
Native Americans: *See* Indians
Nau, Anthony, map by: 23n24, 296–99
Navigability: of floodplain, 103n6; of Red R. branches, 114, 115
Navigability of Red R.: 154, 205, 206n40; reputed, 14–15; at Rapids, 110–11 & n39; at Taovaya-Wichita village, 132; above Sulphur R., 181 & n14; above Little R., 191. *See also* Great Raft; Rafts
Neches R. camp: 88, 132n16, 146 & n137
Negro. *See* Black man on expedition
Nelumbo lutea (Willd.) Pers.: 239–40 & n118
Nemastylis nuttallii Pick.: 248 & n153
Neri, Felipe Enrique: *See* Bastrop, Baron de
Neutral Ground Agreement of 1806: 286–87 & n12, 288, 294
New Madrid earthquake: 169n12
Newspapers: influencing Spain, 75; on Louisiana boundaries, 28 & n36; on Louisiana purchase, 3; on Ouachita R. expedition, 45; on Red R. expedition, 54 & n77, 203n37; on Red R. Valley, 15; Sibley on, 282; on war with Spain, 75, 90n140, 193n27, 281–82; on Wilkinson, 286
New species and varieties: 213, 214 & n7, 300–301; *Achillea lanulosa* Nutt., 243 & n137; *alligator mississippiens* Cuvier, 140n26, 226 & n80, 236, 278; *Amphibiuma triadactylum*, 227 & n82, 301; *Aristolochia* var. *hastata* (Nutt.) Ducharte, 248n156; *Arundinaria gigantea* (Bartr.) Muhl., 114n47; *Aureolaria grandiflora* (Benth.), 261n225; *Cambarus*, 237 & n106; *Carya illinoiensis* (Wangh.) K. Koch, 106n11; *Castor canadensis texensis* Bailey, 274n275; *Catalpa*

bignoniodes Walt., 259 & n217; Catfish, 225n75; *Cathartes aura teter* Friedmann, 223n67; *Chordeiles minor chapmani* Coues, 222 & n62; *Clematis glaucophylla* Small., 216n12; *Cnidosculus texana* (Muell. Arg.) Small, 248 & n160; *Commelina*, 245n152; *Cornus drummondii* C.A. Meyer, 107n25; *Corvus ossifragus*, 223n69; *Cotinus obvatus* Raf., 220n44; *Crotalus atrox* Baird & Girard, 278 & n283; *Dama virginiana macroura* (Raf.), 230n90; *Delphinium:* 248 & n159; *Drosera brevifolia* Pursh, 244 & n144; *Elephantobus nudatus* Gray, 263 & n242; *Forestiera acuminata* (Michx.) Poir, 109n37; *Gelsemium rankinii* Small, 264n243; *Geomys bursarius dutcheri* Davis, 231 & n94; ×*Gleditsia triacanthos* var. *texana* Sarg., 154n43; *Glycyrrhiza lepidota* Pursh, 300n27; *Hibiscus laevis* Allioni, 262–63 & n235; *Hypericum*, 217nn20–21; *Ictinia mississippiensis* Wilson, 234–36 & n99, il 235; *Ictiobus bubalus* Raf., 278 & n281; *Ictiobus urus* Agassiz, 278 & n281; *Juniperus silicicola* (Small) Bailey, 257n209; *Lampropeltis triangulum amaura* Cope, 236–37n104, il 237; *Lepus californicus melanotis*, il 270, 272 & n271; *Ludwiga leptocarpa* (Nutt.) Hara., 261 & n227; *Lutra canadensis texensis* Goldman, 274 & n276; *Maclura pomifera* (Raf.) Schneid., 114n47, 170n14, il 243, 260 & n224; *Mimosa strigillosa* Torr. & Gray, 119n53, 217n17, 251n168; *Nemastylis nuttallii* Pick., 248 & n153; *Oenothera heterophylla* Spach., 219n38; *Opuntia allairei* Griff., 221n53; *Orobranche ludoviciana* Nutt., 265–66 & n254; *Peltandra sagittaefolia* Raf., 217n18; *Pinus echinata* Mill., 180n10; *Pomolobus chrysochloris* Raf., 225 & n78; *Portulacca parvula* Gray, 261n228; *Portulacca umbraticola* H.B.K., 261n228; *Prenathes serpentaria* Pursh var. *barbata* (Torr. & Gray), 264 & n249; *Prunus mexicanus* Wats., 259 & n216; *Prunus munsoniana* Wight & Hedr., 259n216; *Quercus michauxii* Nutt.,

180n33, 253 & n181; *Ranunculus trisepaulus* Gill. ex Hook, 248 & n157; *Richmondena cardinalis magnirostris* Bangs, 225 & n74; *Rudbeckia bicolor* Nutt., 239n116; *Rudbeckia serotina* Nutt., 218n27; *Sabal minor* (Jacq.) Pers., 265n253; *Sassafras albidum* var. *molle* Raf., 255n193; *Satureja arkansana* (Nutt.) Briq., 242 & n132; *Scalopus aquaticus aerus* Bangs, 231n93; *Schrankia hystricina* Britt. & Rose, 218n23; *Sciuris niger bachmani* Lowery & Davis, 228n85; *Sciuris niger ludovicianus* Custis, 228–29 & n87; *Sciuris niger subauratus,* 228n86; Skunks, 231 & n92; *Solanum dimidiatum* Raf., 240n122; *Stegidopteryx ruficollis* Audubon, 268n260; *Sternula albifrons anthalassa* Burleigh & Lowery, 270 & n263; *Strix varia georgica* Latham, 234 n96; *Sylvilagus aquaticus aquaticus* (Bachman), 273n271; *Tradescantia ohioensis* Raf., 240n124; *Ursus americana luteolus* Griffith, 230n89; *Zanthoxylon hirsutum* Buckl., 114n46

Nicandra physaloides Gaertn.: 216 & n11
Nicholas, Wilson C.: 89
Nicholson, Doughty: 99
Nighthawk, Florida common: *See Chordeiles minor*
Noah: *See* Flood legend
Nolan, Philip: 32–33 & n44, 51n71, 75n117, 131n14, 303; and Freeman, 50; on water serpent, 15
North Fork of the Red R.: 23, 122, 331n20
Nuttall, Thomas: 212 & n2, 310
Nymphaea alba: 239–40 & n119; *N. odorata* Ait; *See N. alba; N. nelumbo; See Nelumbo lutea*
Nyssa sylvatica Marsh.: 254 & n191; *N. aquatica* (L.); *See N. sylvatica*

Oak. *See Quercus*
Oenothera grandiflora (Britt.) Smyth: 219n38; *O. heterophylla* Spach.; *See O. grandiflora; O. longiflora; See O. grandiflora*
Old R.: *See* Cane R.
Opladelus olivaris Raf.: *See Ictalurus*
Opossum: *See Didelphis marsupialis*
Opuntia allairei Griff.: 221 & n53. *O. memoralis* Griff.; *See O. allairei*

Oregon R.: 8
Origanum vulgare: 262 & n233
Oriolus Baltimorus: See Icterus galbula
Orobranche ludoviciana Nutt.: 265–66 & n254
Orobus tuberosus: See Lathyrus venosus
Ortoland: *See* d'Ortolan, Bernard
Osage apple: *See Maclura pomifera*
Osage R.: 33
Osages: 13, 22n23, 36, 44n56, 164 & n8, 168, 184, 192n24, 305, 312; Arkansas band, 44n56, 164n8; delegation, 44, 289
Osburn, Robert W.: 276 & n279
Otter: *See Lutra*
Ouachita R.: 33, 122n58; and Black R., 102n5
Ouachita R. expedition: 44, 114n47, 180n11; botanical collection of, 213n6, 300 & n27; maps of, 297; report of, 63
Owl, Florida barred: *See Strix varia*
Oxalis stricta (L.): 215 & n9. *O. violacea* (L.): 219 & n40. *O. acetosella; See O. stricta; O. purpurea; See O. violacea*
Oyster shells: 267

Paddle-fish: *See Plyodron spathula*
Padouca R.: 8
Palm, dwarf: *See Sabal minor*
Palmetto: *See Serrena repens*
Palo Duro Canyon: 10, 332n20
Palo Duro Creek: 332n20
Pani R.: 8
Panis: *See* Taovaya-Wichitas
Parakeet, western Carolina. *See Conuropis carolinensis*
Parilla, Diego Ortiz: 13, 36n47
Parsons, Joseph: 99
Parthenocissus quinquefolia (L.): 245 & n151
Pasacagoulas: 113n44
Passenger pigeons: *See Ectopistes migratorius*
Passiflora incarnata (L.): 220 & n41. *P. lutea* (L.); *See P. incarnata. P. minima:* 242
Passion flower, yellow: *See Passiflora incarnata*
Passport for expedition: 71–72 & n111
Patterson, Robert: 48, 49 & n66, 53
Paw-Hiu-Skah: 44
Pawnees: 35–36; Spain and, 83
Pawpaw: *See Asimina*

Paxton, Joseph: 176n7
Peach: *See Prunus persica*
Peale, Charles Wilson: 53
Peale, Rembrandt: 3
Pease Fork of the Red R.: 331n20
Pease, Seth: 47, 314
Pecan: *See Carya illinoiensis*
Pecan Point: 168n11, 329
Peltandra: 248 & n158. *P. sagittaefolia*
    Raf.: 217 & n18. *P. virginica* (L.)
    Kunth.: 217 & n18
Pendergast, Garrett: 50 & n85
Pennywort: *See Hydrocotyle vulgaris*
Perca ocullata: See Mocropterus salmoides
Perdido R.: 25
Periploca graeca (L.): 244 & n139. *P.
    secamone; See P. graeca*
Peromyscus leucopus leucopus (Raf.): 273
    & n272. *P. ludovicianus ludovicianus*
    (Custis) Raf.; *See P. leucopus*
Persicaria lapathifolia (L.) Small: 242 &
    n127
Persimmon: *See Diospyros virginiana*
Petrifactions: 190, 267
Philadelphia as scientific center: 52,
    58, 59
*Philadelphia Medical and Physical
    Journal:* 66. *See also* Barton, Benja-
    min Smith
Philebare, Mr.: 312
Philosophical Society: *See* American
    Philosophical Society
Phoradendron flavescens (Pursh) Nutt.:
    106 & n20. *P. seriotinum* (Raf.) M.C.
    Johnston; *See P. flavescens*
Physalis angulata: 220 & n49. *P.
    pubescens:* 220 & n45
Phytolacca americana (L.): 219n36. *P.
    decandra; See P. americana*
Pia Mingo: 150n40, 303
Pichardo, Antonio: 22n23, 24n26, 68–
    69n107, 193n27
*Picus principalis: See Campephilus
    principalis*
Pigeon wings: *See Clitoria mariana*
Pike, Zebulon Montgomery: on
    Cordero, 38n49; expedition of,
    51n71, 54n77, 58n83, 125n5, 174,
    287n13, 288–91; on Herrera, 173n1;
    pay of, 64; on Peak, 135n22; scien-
    tific work of, 64n101, 65n102, 289;
    on Viana, 87; and Walker, 40–42n53
Pinckney, Charles: 25
Pine: *See Pinus*

Pine barrens: 108nn30, 35, 175
Pinkweed: 262n231
Pinus: 145, 177; *P. echinata* Mill.,
    180n10, 253 & n185. *P. palustris*
    Mill., 108 & n30, 253 & n184. *P.
    sylvestris; See P. palustris. P. taeda:*
    253 & n185
Pioneers: *See* Settlers
Plane tree, American: *See Platanus
    occidentalis*
Plantago major: 244 & n138
Plantain: *See Plantago major*
Platanus occidentalis: 106, 107, 157, 252
    & n173, 176
Platte R.: 8
Platurornis platyrcercus Swainson: 270
    & n264
Plotus anhinga: See Anhinga
Plum: *See Prunus*
Po-a-cat-le-pi-le-carre: *See* Medicine
    Rock
Pocket gopher, plains: *See Geomys
    bursarius*
Podophyllum peltatum: 221 & n57, 239
Point Return: 142
Poison ivy: *See Toxicodendron radicans*
Poison oak: *See Toxicodendron quercifolia*
Pokeweed: *See Phytolacca americana*
Polianthus virginica (L.) Shinners: il
    241, 250 & n166, 263 & n240
Polygala incarnata (L.): 263 & n238. *P.
    vulgaris; See P. incarnata*
Polygonum pennsylvanicum: 262. *P.
    lapathifolium; See Persicaria lapathi-
    folia. P. scandens:* 245 & n146
Polyodon spathula Walb.: 278 & n282
Polypodium polypodiodes (L.) Watt. var.
    michauxianum Weath: 249 & n162,
    251 & n169
Pomolobus chrysochloris Raf.: 225 & n78
Poplar, yellow: *See Lyriodendron
    tulipfera*
Populus: 118, 126, 131n12, 145, 154,
    157, 176, 191, 252 & n171. *P.
    deltoides* Marsh.: 106 & n12, 107, il
    116–17. *P. heterophylla* (L.); *See P.
    deltoides*
Portulacca oleracea: 219 & n39, 261 &
    n228. *P. parvula* Gray: 261 & n228.
    P. umbraticola H.B.K.: 261 & n228
La Poste des Cadodoquois: *See* La
    Harpe's Post
Poste du Rapide: 111n40
Post oak savannah: 191n24, 208n43,

270
Postponement: *See* Delays
Power, Thomas: 72
Prairie Dog Town Fork of the Red R.:
    18n20, 23, 331–32n20
Prairie dogs: 272n271
Prairies: 208–10, 272n270
Prenathes serpentaria Pursh var. *barbata*
    (Torr. & Gray): 264 & n249; *P. alba;*
    See P. serpentaria. P. altissima (L.)
Prickly-mallow: *See Sida spinosa*
Prickly pear: *See Opuntia allairei*
Primrose, evening: *See Oenothera*
    grandiflora
Prinos verticillatus: See Ilex verticillata
Privet, swamp: *See Forestiera acuminata*
Procyon lotor fuscipes Mearns: 230n88. *P.*
    hirtus Nelson & Goldman: 230n88.
    P. varius Nelson & Goldman: 229
    & n88
Pronghorn: *See Antilocapridae*
Prunus: 154, 192. *P. angustifolia*
    Marsh.: 154n46, 259, & n216. *P.*
    gracilis Engelm. & Gray: 259 &
    n216. *P. mexicanus* Wats.: 154n46,
    259 & n216. *P. munsoniana* Wight &
    Hedr.: 154n46, 259 & n216. *P.*
    padus; See P. serotina. P. persica (L.):
    262n231. *P. serotina* Ehrh.: 106 &
    n16, 154 & n45, 252 & n174, 257
    & n215. *P. umbellata* Ell.: 259 &
    n216. *P. virginiana; See P. serotina*
Psittacus caroliniensis: See Conuropis
    caroliniensis
Public opinion: See Newspapers
Publication: of Ouachita R. expedition
    maps and reports, 45; of Red R. re-
    ports, 100, 273n272, 293–95, 301,
    310 & n42
Pumice: 238
Purcell, James: 35
Pursh, Frederick: 58, 300, 310
Purslane: *See Portulacca oleracca*
Purslane, marsh: *See Ludwiga repens*
Pyramidal Height: 19n22. *See also*
    Continental Divide
Pyrus arbutifolia (L.) L.F.: 259 & n220

Quechata Path: 207n41
Quercus: 136, 141, 142, 145, 176, 177,
    180, 189, 190, 191, 253. *Q. alba:* 253
    & n178. *Q. esculus; See Q. michauxi.*
    Q. falcata Michx.: 106 & nn13–15,
    157, 253n177. *Q. michauxii* Nutt.:

108 & n33, 253n181. *Q. nigra:* 108
    & n27, 157, 253 & n180. *Q. phellos:*
    253 & n179. *Q. rubra; See Q. falcata*

Rabbitt: *See Lepus californicus*
Rabbit, swamp: *See Sylvilagus aquaticus*
Racoon: *See Procyon lotor*
Rafinesque-Schmaltz, Constantine
    Samuel: 216n11, 310; applies for
    position on expedition, 57
Rafts: 127, 131. *See also* Great Raft
Ramón de Burga, Juan Ignacio: 88,
    194n30, 204; and Dehahuit, 163–
    64; marching, 124, 132n16, 146n37,
    159–60
Ramón, Domingo: 12
Ranchers: *See* Graziers
Ranunculus bulbosa: 216 & n15; *R.*
    hederaceus; See R. tricepaulus. R.
    trisepaulus Gill. ex Hook: 248 &
    n157
Rapide settlement: 111n40
Rattelsnake: *See* Crotalus
Rattlesnake root: *See Prenathes serpen-*
    taria
Rattle-vetch: *See Astragalus canadensis*
Raven: *See Corvus cryptoleucus*
Redbud: *See Cercis canadensis*
Red Chute Bayou: 141n28, il 144
Red R.: 9, 26–27, 70, il 116–17, 178–
    79; branches of, 114, 115, 122, 331
    & nn19–20; channels of, 133n19;
    depth, width, and current of, 102,
    103, 107, 126–27, 133, 145, 154,
    175–76, 181, 190, 199; froth on,
    136–40n23; great bend of, 190n22;
    headwaters of, 23, 26, 33–34, 297,
    317, 332n21; lengths of, 332 & n21;
    mouth of, 101 & n4; name of, 9, 19,
    104; U.S. knowledge of course of,
    17–23, 19n22, 332n21. *See also* Ferry
    across Red R.; Floods of Red R.;
    Ford of Red R.; Navigability of
    Red R.
"Red River": *See* Medicine Rock
Red R. expedition: leader sought, 39–
    42, 47–49, 52; members of, 99, 100,
    207n42, 286; naturalist sought, 56–
    60 & n88; objectives of, 26–27, 54–
    56, 71, 84–85, 100, 211, 320–21;
    route of, 46, 55, 67, 68–70, 81, 320–
    21. *See also* Accomplishments of
    expedition; Cost of Red R. expedi-
    tion; Delays; Difficulties; Indian

trade goods; Library of expedition; Military escort for Red R. expedition; Morale of expedition; Passport for expedition; Publication; Return of expedition; Rewards to members of expedition; Scientific supplies for expedition; Supplies for expedition
Red R. Valley: 102–104, 154, 175–81 & nn9–10, 207–208; ecosystems of, 133 & n18, 177–80n10; il 205; profile of, 184; reputed natural history of, 14–17, 208–10; soil of, 103, 106, 112, 136, 177n9
Red Shoes: 150n40
Reed, Samuel: 99
Reid, Corporal: 207n42
Resurrection fern: *See Polypodium polypodiodes*
Return of expedition: instructions on, 55–56, 123–24, 323–24; rationale for, 205, 206; U.S. reaction to, 281–87, 293–95
Rewards to members of expedition: 54, 64n99, 313, 325
Rhamnus caroliniana (Walt.): *See Bumelia langinosa*
Rhus coppallina (L.): 220 & n43. *R. coriaria; See R. glabra. R. glabra* (L.): 239 & n112. *R. radicans; See Toxicodendron radicans. R. toxicodendron; See Toxicodendron quercifolia*
Richmondia cardinalis magnirostris Bangs: 225n74
Río Bravo: *See* Río Grande
Río Grande: 25, 26, 34
Riparia riparia riparia (L.): *See Stelgedopteryx ruficollis*
Riverborne exploration, limitations of: 101
Rivière de L'Ours: *See* Sulphur R.
Rivière de Petit Bon Dieu: 114, 115, 126
Rivière la Mine: *See* Kiamichi R.
Rivière Noire: See Black R.
Robinia Pseud-acacia: See ×Gleditsia triacanthos var. *texana*
Robinson, John: 290
Rock jasmine: *See Androsace occidentalis*
Rock R.: *See* Bayou Pierre
Rodriguez, Mariano: 38
Rodriguez, Sebastian: 74, 87; on U.S. newspapers, 75n117
Rosa eglanteria: 219 & n34

Rose mallow: *See Hibiscus lasiocarpos*
Rough rust: *See Uredinales*
Round L.: 143n32
Round Prairie: 181n15
Royal Council for the Fortification and Defense of the Indies: 27
Rubiaceae: 219 & n35
Rudbeckia bicolor Nutt.: 239 & n116. *R. purpurea; See R. bicolor. R. serotina* Nutt.: 218 & n27. *R. hirta; See R. serotina*
Rusty blackhaw viburnum: *See Viburnum rufidulum*

Sabal louisiana (Darby) Bomhard: 265n253. *S. minor* (Jacq.) Pers.: 265 & n253
Sabine R.: 25, 286; fort urged by Wilkinson, 82; Indians on, 150n40. *See also* Spain east of Sabine R.
Sabine Uplift: 175n4
Sagittaria calycina Engelm.: 263 & n241. *S. lancifolia:* 254 & n150. *S. sagittifolia; See S. calycina*
St. Andrew's cross: *See Ascyrum hypericoides*
Saint Denis, Luis Juchereau de: 11, 23n24, 119n55, 130n11
St. Peters R.: 8
Salcedo, Manual: 29; on Sibley, 31
Salcedo, Nemecio: 42, 72, 83, 85–86, 125, 207n41, 286; and Rodriguez, 87
Salix: 104, 106, il 117–18, 133. *S. caroliniana* Michx.: 104n8. *S. interior* Rowlee: 104n8, 255n201. *S. nigra* Marsh.: 104n8
Salt: 15, 184, 208 & n44. *See also* Natchitoches Salt Works
Salt Fork of the Red R.: 331n20
Sambucus canadensis (L.): 219 & n37, 253 & n182. *S. nigra; See S. canadensis*
Sanders (hunter): 34
Sandpiper, lesser yellowlegs: *See Totanus flavipies*
Sandstone: 114, 238
Sand-weed: *See Hypericum fasciculatum*
Sandy Hills: 177n9
San José mission: 12
San Miguel del Salto camp: *See* Neches R. camp
San Sabá mission: 13
Santa Fe: Freeman and, 53; persons from U.S. at, 35, 307; Pike at, 289–91; route to, 13, 17–23, 18n20, 34,

36; trade with, 37
Sasparilla: *See Smilax bona-nox*
Sassafras albidum (Nutt.) Nees: 108 & n 32, 254 & n193
Satureja arkansana (Nutt.) Briq.: 242 & n 132, *S. capitata; See S. arkansana*
Say, Thomas: 212
Scalopus aquaticus aereus Bangs: 231 & n93
Schamp, George; 306
Schrankia Hystricina Britt. & Rose: 218 & n 23
Scientific supplies for expedition: 52–53, 64–65
Scientific work in Louisiana before 1806: 212–14, 268n262
Sciurus niger bachmani Lowery & David: 228 & n85. *S. n. ludovicianus* Custis: 228–29 & n87, il 229. *S. subauratus* Bachman: 228 & n86. *S. cinerius; See S. n. bachmani*
Scolopax flavipes: See Totanus flavipes
Scorpio Hottentotta: See Vejovidae
Scorpion: *See Vejovidae*
Seip, Frederick: 59 & n85
Selasphorus rufus Gmelin: 270 & n264
Senna, coffee: *See Cassia occidentalis*
Senna, wild: *See Cassia marylandica*
Serrena repens (Bartr.) Small: 245 & n147
Setochalcis vocifera vocifera Wilson: *See Chordeiles minor*
Settlers: 107n21, 130, 140n24, 176, 307–309 & n37, 314
Sha'chahdinnih: *See* Caddo villages
Shale: 175 & n4, 267
Shame vine: See *Schrankia hystricina*
Shawnees: 61
Shreve, Henry Miller: on Great Raft, 135n22; map by, 135n21, 137
Shreveport: 176n6
Sibley, John: 15n17, 22 & n23, 31 & n42, 47, 63, 65, 120, 123; and Glass, 304–305; on Grand Encore, 126n7; and Grappe, 134n20; on Great Rapide, 110–11n39; on Natchitoches, 119n55; and Red R. tribes, 35, 124, 302–303; on war with Spain, 282
Sicklepod: See Cassia tora
Sicyos angulata (L.): *See momordica charantia*
Sida spinosa (L.): 239 & n111. *S. Occidentalis; See S. Spinosa*

Sideroxylon mite: See Bumelia lanuginosa
Sign language: 131n14
Silphium laciniatum: 242 & n131
Silurus catus: See Ictalurus
Silver: 15, 17n19, 35, 305, 306n35, 330n13
Silverbell, two-wing: *See Halesia diptera*
Silver Lake Creek: 149n39
Siouan language: 164n8
Sison ammi: See Apium leptophyllum
Skunk: *See Mephitis mephitis*
Slave: *See* Black man on expedition
Smartweed: *See Persicaria lapathifolia*
Smilax bona-nox (L.): 239 & n115. *S. China; See S. tamnoides. S. rotundifolia; See S. tamnoides. S. tamnoides* (L.): 239 & n114
Smith, Thomas A.: 311
Smoke tree, American: *See Cotinus obvatus*
Snake: *See Coluber versicolor; Crotalus; Lampropeltis triangulum*; Vipers
Snake-bird: *See Anhinga*
Snakeroot, Virginia: *See Aristolochia serpentaria*
Soda L.: 145n35, 168n12
Solanum carolinense (L.): 218 & n32, 240n122; *S. dimidiatum* Raf.; *See S. carolinense, S. paniculatum; See S. carolinense. S. virginianum; See S. carolinense*
Solar eclipse: 141
Solidago altissima: 265 & n251
Sorrel, yellow wood: *See Oxalis stricta*
Sorrel, violet wood: *See Oxalis violacea*
Soto, Marcel: 307 & n36
Soule, William S.: 197
Spain: and Indians, 13, 30, 31, 35, 37–38, 83, 112n43, 124, 125, 150n40, 303; and U.S. incursions, 7, 27–30, 34–35, 38, 42, 47, 68, 75–76, 80, 82–86, 303–307, 308, 312; and Wilkinson, 81–83. *See also* France vs. Spain in Red R. Valley; Treaty of Paris, 1763; Treaty of San Ildefonso
Spain east of Sabine R.: 68–70, 281, 282
Spain, possibility of war with: 30, 38, 68–71, 78–80, 85, 89, 90, 174, 193n27, 203n37, 281–88; Burr on, 80n123; Herrera and, 173n1; Rodriguez on, 87
Spanish Bluff: 199 & n35, il 200–01, 329 & n9

Spanish moss: *See Tillandsia usenoides*
Spanish troops against Red R. expedition: 88, 124–25, 132 & n16, 145 & n37, 148, 159, 173, 191n24, 198–206, 294; in 1805, 72–74; number of, 191n23, 194 & n30, 203. *See also* Garrisons
Spanish–U.S. hostilities: at Grand Prairie, 32–33; Jefferson on, 56; at Los Adaes, 86; inspired by Wilkinson, 51 & n71
Sparks, John: 290
Sparks, Richard: 61–62, 64, 198–99, 203 & n37, 309
Sparrow, sharp-tailed: *See Ammospiza caudacuta*
Speed of boats: 102n5, 120n56, 206n40
Spice wood: *See Lindera benzoin*
Spigelia marylandica: 218n29, 221 & n55, 251 & n167. *S. anthelmia; See S. marylandica*
Spilogale putorius: See Mephitis mephitis
Spoonbill: *See Plyodon spathula*
Spring Bank: 180 & n12, 185
Squatters: *See* Settlers
Squirrel: *See Sciuris*
Squirrel, southern flying: *See Glaucomys volans*
Stelgidopteryx ruficollis Audubon: 268 & n260
Sterna minuta: See Sternula albifrons
Sternula albifrons anthalassa Burleigh & Lowery: 270 & n263
Stoddard, Amos: 103n6, 133n18
Stoney Creek: *See* Bayou Pierre
Stores: *See* Indian trade goods; Supplies for expedition
Strawberry bush: *See Euonymous americanus*
Strawberry, wild: *See Fragaria virginiana*
Strix varia georgica Latham: 234 & n96. *S. aluco; See S. varia*
Sugar maple: *See Acer saccharinum*
Sugarberry: *See Celtis laevigata*
Sulphur R.: 180 & n11, 308; La Harpe on, 13; mouth of, 181, 185, 328
Sulphur Wold: 177n9
Sumac: *See Rhus*
Sundew, insect-catching: *See Drosera brevifolia*
Sunflower: *See Helianthus*
Supplies for expedition: 64, 66n104, 90, 207n42; augmented at Natchi-

toches, 101, 123. *See also* Indian trade goods; Scientific supplies for expedition
Swallow, bank: *See Stelgidopteryx ruficollis*
Swamps: 133n18, 134, 143
Swan: 140n26, 195n32, 271
Swan L.: 140–41 & n26, 143n33
Sycamore: *See Platanus occidentalis*
Sylvilagus aquaticus aquaticus (Bachman): 272 & n271
Symphitum officinale: 218n31
Siren quadrupeda: See Amphiuma triadactylum

Taboayases (Taovaya-Wichitas): 124
Talapoon, Lucas: 33, 131–32 & n14, 146, 175n3, 304–305
Talfour, R. B.: 128–29
Talleyrand, Maurice de: 89
Talpa longicaudata: See Scalopus aquaticus
Tantalus albus: See Eudocimus albus
Tantalus loculator: See Mycteria americana
Taovaya-Wichitas: 22n23, 35–36 & n47, 208, 305; French trade with, 13, 36n47, 283; and Glass, 305; land of, 168n11; marriage among, 170n15; migration of, 13; Sanders with, 34; and Spanish, 30, 31, 37–38, 307n36; trade with, 131n14; and U.S., 32, 37, 302, 304; villages, 22n23, 36, il 202, 331 & n18. *See also* Medicine Rock
Taxodium distichum (L.) Richard: il 105, 106 & n19, 108, 136, 142, 176 & n10, 253 & n186
Taraxacum officinale Weber: 220 & n48
Tarshar: 308
Tawakonis: *See* Caddos; Medicine Rock
Tawayashos: *See* Taovaya-Wichitas
Tehowahimmo: 308
Tensas R.: 102n5
Tephrosia virginiana (L.) Pers.: *See Indigofera hirsuta*
Terán, Domingo de: 11
Tern, interior least: *See Sternula albifrons*
Testudo ferox: See Trionyx spiniferus
Tetrao virginianus: See Colinus virginianus
Texas: invades Louisiana, 162n4; U.S. claims to, 25, 26, 287, 292; U.S.

invasion feared, 77, 288; Wilkinson on, 80–81
Texas hercules-club: See *Zanthoxylon hirsutum*
Thistle: *See Cirsium carolinianum*
Thomas, Joseph: 107n21
Three Forks trading post: 44n56
Tickseed: *See Coreopsis lanceolata*
Tidball, J. C.: 151
Tierra Blanca Creek: 18n20, 332n20
Tilia caroliniana Mill.: 118 & n52, 154 & n42, 256. *T. americana* (L.); *See T. caroliniana. T. floricana* Small; *See T. caroliniana*
Tillandsia usneoides: 180n11, 221 & n54, 265 & n252
Timber Hill: *See* Caddo villages
Tinhioūen the Peacemaker: 36n47, 160n3
Tonty, Henri de: on Caddos, 195n32; on name of Red R., 9–10n11; post founded by, 13; in Red R. Valley, 11, 192n24
Tooeksoach: 308
Tortoise, Texas softshell: *See Trionyx spiniferus*
Totanus flavipes Gmelin: 268 & n261
Touline: *See* Grappe, François Louis
Toxicodendron quercifolia (Michx.) Greene: 217 & n16. *T. radicans* (L.) Kuntze.: 239 & n113
Trade route to Pacific: 17
Trade route to Santa Fe: *See* Santa Fe
Tradescantia ohioensis Raf.: 240 & n124. *T. virginica; See T. ohioensis*
Trade with Indians: 37; French, 11, 13, 198n33; Spanish, 28n36, 31, 124n2, 307; U.S., 31, 34–35, 111n40, 112–13n43, 131n14, 208n45, 304–307, 322. *See also* Firearms; Fur trade; Indian trade goods
Translators: *See* Guides and interpreters
Treaty of Paris, 1763: 13, 150n40
Treaty of San Ildefonso: 7, 24
Tricosanthes cucumerina: See Momordica charantia
Trionyx spiniferus emoryi Agassiz: 228 & n83, 236
Trochilus: 270 & n264
Trumball, John: 155
Trumpet creeper: *See Bignonia radicans*
Tuckahoe: *See Peltandra virginica*
Tucumcari Mesa: 18n20

Tulin: *See* Grappe, Françoi̥s Louis
Tulip-tree: *See Lyriodendron tulipfera*
Tupelo: *See Nyssa*
Turdus polyglottus: See Mimus polyglottos
Turkey, eastern wild: *See Meleagris gallopavo*
Turner, Edward D.: 86, 87, 123
Twelve-Mile Bayou: 168–69n12
Typha angustifolia: 262 & n236

Ulmus americana: 114, 115, 254 & n192
Undergrowth: on riverbanks, 133 & n18, 177, 190; in woods, 190, 253n184, 264n245
Unicorn: 14, 15, 17n19, 276–77 & nn279–80
U.S. Army Corps of Engineers: 135n22, 206n40
U.S. Congress appropriations: for boundary settlement, 89; to demolish Great Raft, 135–36n22; for Red R. expedition, 14, 63; for Arkansas R. expedition, 311, 312, 313. *See also* Cost of Red R. expedition
U.S. in Red R. Valley: 303–307
Upper Creek Confederacy: 150n40
Uredinales: 133
Urocyon cinereoargentus cinereoargentus (Schreber): 271 & n267
Ursus: 195n32. *U. americana americanus* Pallas: 230n89; il 232. *U. a. luteolus* Griffith: 230 & n89. *U. lotor; See Procyon lotor*
Usnea barbata (L.) Wigg: 265n252. *U. plicata* (L.) Wigg: 265n252

Vaccinium arboreum Marsh: 245 & n148
Valle, Dionisio: 72–74, 87n135
Vásquez de Coronado, Francisco: 10, 36n47
Vejovidae: 228 & n84
Verbascum thapsus: 220 & n42
Verdigris R.: 44n56
Veronicastrum virginicum: il 247, 249n164
Vial, Pierre ("Pedro"): 13, 83; map by, il 122; and Ramon, 132n16; Santa Fe route of, 18, 19
Viana, Francisco: 87–88; against expedition, 124, 159, 191n23, 193–94, 199–202n35, 204–206, 207n41; and Indians, 150n40
Viburnum rufidulum Raf.: 154 & n44,

259 & n219. *V. prunifolium; See V.
rufidulum*
Villarius catus (L.): *See Ictalurus*
Viola triloba: 220n46. *V. palmata; See
V. triloba*
Vipers: 236 & n103
Virginia creeper: *See Parthenocissus
quinquefolia*
*Viscum album: See Phoradendron
flavescens*
Vitus riparia Michx.: 157n47. *V.
lambrusca* (L.); *See V. riparia*
Viverra mephitis: See Mephitis mephitis
von Humboldt: *See* Humboldt,
Friedrich Heinrich Alexander,
Baron von
Vulpes fulva fulva (Demarest): 271 &
n268
Vultur aura: See Cathartes aura teter
Vulture, black: *See Coragypes atratus*
Vulture, western turkey: *See Cathartes
aura teter*

Wabash R.: 52
Walker, Juan Pedro: 40 & n53
Walker, Peter: 40 & n53
Walnut, eastern black: *See Juglans
nigra*
Walter, Thomas: 65
War: *See* Spain, possibility of war with
Washington, George: 6
Waterlily, fragrant: *See Nymphaea alba*
Water turkey: *See Anhinga*
Whitegrass Creek: 330n12
White Hair I: 44
White Oak Shoals: 193 & n26
Wichitas: 36n47. *See also* Taovaya-
Wichitas
Wilkinson, James: and Ashley, 35n46,
75n117; and Burr Conspiracy, 77–
83, 284, 285–87; and D. Clark, 29
& n38; and Dunbar, 312; and Free-
man, 50, 51; and Jefferson, 80–81,
285, 287 & n13, 288, 291–92; and

McKee, 54n76; ordered to border,
90, 284; and Pike, 288–91; il 79; on
Red R., 23n25, 33–34, 80–81, 291;
as spy, 81–83 & n126, 287 & n13,
292; trial of, 314–15; on war with
Spain, 30n41
Wilkinson, Lieutenant James B., Jr.:
289, 311 & n44
Willow: *See Salix*
Willow Chute: 143n32
Willow, primrose: *See Ludwiga
leptocarpa*
Wilson, Alexander: 57–58 & nn82–
83, 224, 234–35n99, 277n280, 310;
applies for position on expedition,
58; il 224; il by 269; and Seip, 59n85
Wily, Mr.: 47
Witch hazel: *See Hamamelis virginiana*
Wolf: *See Canis lupus*
Woodpecker, eastern redheaded: *See
Melanerpes erythrocephalus*
Woodpecker, Ivory-billed: *See Campe-
philus principalis*
Woodpecker, pileated: *See Hylatomas
pileatus*
Woodruff, E. A.: 136n22
Worm grass: *See Spigelia marylandica*

Yatasis: *See* Caddos
Ybarbo, Gil: 70n107
Ybarbo, José Ignacio: 34
Yturrigaray, José de: on garrison, 85;
on passport, 72; on Wilkinson,
287n13
Yrujo, Carlos Martinez: 83n126
Yucca louisianensis Trel: 241,
250 & n166.

Zanthoxylon clava Herculis: 113–14 &
n45, 257 & n211. *Z. hirsutum* Buckl.:
257 & n212. *Z. americanum* Mill.;
*See Z. hirsutum. Z. fraxinifolia; See
Z. hirsutum*